Revolutionary
Activism
in the 1950s & 60s

Ernest Tate, A Memoir

Volume 2, Britain 1965-1969

Preface by Phil Hearse

RESISTANCE BOOKS
London

Published by Resistance Books, PO Box 62732, London, SW2 9GQ.
Resistance Books is the publishing arm of Socialist Resistance, a revolutionary Marxist organisation that is the British section of the Fourth International. Resistance Books publishes books jointly with the International Institute for Research and Education in Amsterdam and independently. Further information about Resistance Books, including a full list of titles currently available and how to purchase them, can be obtained by writing to the address above.

Ernest Tate Vol 2: More revolutionary memories
ISBN 978-0-902869-60-8
EAN: 9780902869608

Editing & Final Proof Reading by Derrick O'Keefe
Book Design & Electronic Prepress by Lawrence Boxall
John Walmsley's photographs reproduced in this book can also be seen on his website: http://www.educationphotos.co.uk/

The text of this book is set in Minion Pro, a type designed in the U.S. in 1990 by Robert Slimbach.

Printed in Britain by Lightning Source.

Revolutionary Activism in the 1950s & 60s

Publisher's Foreword

RESISTANCE BOOKS IS PLEASED TO BE PUBLISHING THIS WORK. WE THINK it's an important contribution to the history of the left in Britain and Canada during a unique period, a political narrative of Ernest Tate's life as a socialist activist during the fifteen-year period from 1955 to 1970. In volume one he tells us about his arrival in Toronto in 1955 as a working-class immigrant from Northern Ireland and about how he quickly became engaged in radical politics. He provides us with interesting details of what political life was like in those years in a small revolutionary organization, the Socialist Educational League (SEL), which was affiliated to the Fourth International. We get to see how it was organized and we get a glimpse of some of its leading personalities as they sought to increase support for their ideas among working people. He underlines the importance of the American Socialist Workers Party (SWP) to its early years. One of the SEL's major activities was to organize cross-country tours to sell its monthly paper, the *Workers Vanguard*, across the vast expanse of Canada, tours that sometimes lasted up to six months. In a time when there was no Internet, it was often the only way to keep in touch with its supporters.

The ten-year period covered in volume one, from 1955 to 1965, was important for the left. The Canadian version of McCarthyism—although not as virulent as that in the United States, but equally as reactionary—had begun to recede, and a new radical consciousness had begun to emerge—almost surreptitiously, Ernest writes—that was influenced both by the victory of the Cuban Revolution in 1959, and the birth of the New Democratic Party in 1961. Regarding Cuba, a long chapter describes how, in order to defend that country's revolution and in response to the growing interest in it by Canadians, especially young people, the SEL initiated the setting up of the Fair Play for Cuba Committee. It became, as the author says, one of the most important campaigns to defend Cuba in the English-speaking world. This is the first time a comprehensive description of the Committee's work—and its difficulties—including the story of its remarkable leader, Verne Olson, have appeared. The birth of the New Democratic Party (NDP), a process that took a couple of years, posed new problems and opportunities for revolutionary socialists. There were many discussions about how they should relate to a party that had a social democratic programme and was further to the right than the old Cooperative Commonwealth Federation (CCF) which it had replaced. Those debates find their expression here.

Also described are the activities of revolutionary socialists in the trade unions, not easy in a period of low working-class consciousness. A couple of chapters provide us with important details about how the League for Socialist Action (LSA) organized its members in the unions, especially in the large transport companies in Ontario, those organized by the Teamsters' union. The LSA found itself at the head of a large rank-and-file opposition that had been deeply angered and frustrated by a trusteeship imposed upon it by Washington. Every contract renewal in those years saw widespread industrial action by the drivers, some that almost paralyzed the Ontario and Quebec economies for weeks at a time. This is the first time that story has been written giving the militants' side of that struggle.

Volume two covers Ernest Tate's political experiences in Britain when he was on assignment from the LSA to assist in the reorganization of the Fourth International's section. He describes his activities with the Bertrand Russell Peace Foundation, the birth of the International Marxist Group and the Vietnam Solidarity Campaign, including the tremendous effort to organize the famous Bertrand Russell International War Crimes Tribunal, the latter finally triumphing over both the opposition of American imperialism and the Soviet bureaucracy. In volume two, he also revisits the debates in the Fourth International about the guerrilla struggle in Latin America and provides a report, based upon recent information, about the tragic destruction in the seventies of a heroic guerrilla movement in Argentina led by Robert Santucho. The volume ends with Ernest Tate's return to Canada and his eventual parting of the ways with the LSA.

We are extremely lucky to have a preface to this volume written by Phil Hearse. A long-time Marxist and revolutionary leader, Phil was part of the student radicalization of the period the memoir covers and he was an active participant in some of the events described. One of the early founders of the Vietnam Solidarity Campaign (VSC) and International Marxist Group (IMG), he became one of the IMG's central leaders, including representing it on the leadership bodies of the Fourth International. His well-known website, *Marxsite*, and his writings circulate widely in the radical left in Britain and internationally. Readers, we are sure will find his assessment of those years insightful, as he provides an overview and draws a balance sheet of what was achieved by the revolutionary left in those tumultuous times. We are also fortunate to have a preface to volume one written by Derrick O'Keef, a writer and a leader in the Canadian anti-war movement. He is also the author of a Verso book, *Michael Ignatieff: The Lesser Evil?* and the co-writer of Afghan MP Malalai Joya's political memoir, *A Woman Among Warlords: The Extraordinary Story of an Afghan Who Dared to Raise Her Voice.*

Dedication

THE COMRADES LISTED BELOW, WHOSE NAMES APPEAR IN THIS BOOK, are no longer with us. They devoted their lives completely to the struggle for socialism. At various times they had a large influence on my life and are an important part of the story told here. I dedicate it to their memory:

Reg and Ruth Bullock (Canada)
Ross Dowson (Canada)
Pierre Frank (France)
Joe and Reba Hansen (U.S.A.)
Pat Jordan (Britain)
Tom and Karolyn Kerry (U.S.A.)
Ernest Mandel (Belgium)
Verne and Ann Olson (Canada)
Patricia (Pat) Schulz (Canada)
Ray Sparrow (Art Sharon) (U.S.A.)
Paddy Stanton (Canada)

A Word of Thanks

WRITING THIS BOOK WOULD HAVE BEEN ALMOST IMPOSSIBLE WITHOUT the help of my companion, Jess MacKenzie. Her patience and good humour were essential in helping me see it through to the end. Efficient at chasing down wayward facts and important information, she also photographed countless pages of archives for me on our many travels. Carefully reading each draft chapter after I had written it, she found my many errors and managed to curb my excesses. Aside from having an important part in the following story, she was also invaluable in finally getting it into print.

In the process of preparing this work, we consulted various archives in several countries, such as Library Archives Canada (LAC) the International Institute of Social History (IISH), Amsterdam, Warwick University Archives, Coventry, Britain and the Taminent Library in New York. Often working under the pressures of severe budget cuts, the staff of these important institutions was invariably helpful and cooperative. Of special importance were the folks at the Bertrand Russell Archives at McMaster University, Hamilton, Ontario. That's where we had the good fortune to meet Dr. Kenneth Blackwell, a key architect of the collection. He helped guide us through it, bringing to our attention important materials that we might have otherwise overlooked. We're grateful for his assistance. I also thank Richard Fidler for having read the chapters on Cuba and the birth of the New Democratic Party (NDP) in volume one and his comments about them.

Also valuable to us was the time we spent at the International Institute for Research and Education (IIRE) in Amsterdam, an independent research institution that is supported by the Fourth International. There we had the able assistance of Marijke Colle, its Director, and Hendrik Patroons, in finding our way through its archives.

Finally, I wish to thank the comrades of Resistance Books in London for taking the risk and having the courage to publish the final product.

Preface

IT'S A GREAT PLEASURE TO WRITE THE PREFACE FOR THE SECOND volume of Ernie Tate's memoirs of the 1950s and '60s. I first met Ernie and his partner Jess MacKenzie in 1967, when I was part of a small group of young socialists from the London Borough of Ealing recruited to the International Marxist Group (IMG). So it's the British part of the story that I know well. Ernie and Jess were, together with Pat Jordan, the IMG full timers in London, working out of a cramped office and bookshop in Toynbee Street in the East End of London. This book is a vivid account of what were fateful days in establishing the modern revolutionary left in Britain and is full of valuable lessons. What grabs the reader's attention is the creativity and sheer audacity of this tiny group of people, setting out to make a major political impact with almost no resources—and succeeding.

Until the middle 1960s the organised far left in Britain, such as it was, was dominated by Gerry Healy's Socialist Labour League—itself only a few hundred members. The SLL was ultra-sectarian with hardly any notion of the united front; in fact it was *the reflection of third period Stalinism inside the Trotskyist movement*. And its internal norms were highly authoritarian, even by the standards of today's 'democratic centralist' organisations. Against the SLL, the forerunners of the main organisations of the far left in Britain today were small and weak.

What started to change the situation was the new world and British context that developed in the mid-1960s. While the trade union movement was beginning to flex its muscles in the shop stewards movement, the militant socialist left had hardly any implantation among them. But the rise of a movement against the Vietnam war and the emergence of the student movement began to change things and lay the basis for a new kind of left. The role of the IMG in that was crucial.

At the beginning of 1967 the IMG was—through using united front tactics and through its Labour Party work—playing a role way out of proportion to its size, just a few dozen comrades. The weekly bulletin it sponsored—*The Week*—was widely read in the Labour and trade union left. It was the main organizing force in the emerging Vietnam Solidarity Campaign (VSC). And two of its members, Ken Coates and Tony Topham, were the leaders of the Institute for Workers Control (IWC), whose conferences and pamphlets began to popularise the idea of workers control that had received scant attention in the existing Communist Party and Labour left, or the SLL for that matter. As explained in this volume, the IMG and especially Ernie took on a crucial organising role in relation to the international Bertrand Russell Vietnam war crimes tribunal.

The decisive thing here in bringing a new left into existence was the VSC. The initiative to set it up in 1966 was taken by the IMG, but the International Socialists soon came in, without however taking much in the way of organisational responsibility. The decision to set it up was not so obvious: the Communist Party-led British Council for Peace in Vietnam, organised on the slogan of negotiations rather than American withdrawal, dominated the scene as far as this issue was concerned. The small group of comrades in the IMG leadership assessed that in the newly emerging student movement and beyond that the idea of *solidarity* with those in struggle, a clearly partisan campaign which stood with the oppressed and their fighting force, the National Liberation Front, could gain an echo.

It fact signs of that echo could be heard in the Oxford University 1965 teach in on Vietnam where Ralph Miliband, father of Ed and David, got a warm reception for a fighting intervention calling not for peace but for solidarity with "the heroic men and women of the National Liberation Front".

Widespread outrage at the genocidal brutality of American imperialism in Vietnam spurred teach-ins and protests throughout the student movement. In the fall of 1967 Jess and Ernie attended a conference in Brussels in which the German Socialist Students League (SDS) and French Revolutionary Young Communists (JCR) played a central role. When they reported back they were astonished at the political sophistication and militancy of this newly emerging European revolutionary left. The Brussels conference prepared the way for the February 1968 European Vietnam conference and a demonstration in Berlin, where thousands of young people astonished the local populace by marching behind banners of Lenin, Rosa Luxemburg and Che Guevara. A new left was emerging and the Fourth International played an important role in its birth.

The amazing range of political projects the IMG was at the centre of at the beginning of 1967 contained important contradictions that were soon to emerge, and Ernie and Jess were at the heart of the political debates they caused. The main public figure of the IMG, although he played little internal role, was Ken Coates. The story of his split with the IMG is told here so I won't anticipate, except to say that there were two main related questions involved. The first was what attitude to take to left wing trade union leaders like Jack Jones, Frank Cousins and Ernie Roberts with whom the IMG was working. When the I.M.G. felt that the Transport and General Workers Union (TGWU) had sold out the London dockers, Ken Coates wanted no criticism because, he argued, it would harm the working relationships inside the IWC.

Ken Coates began to see the IMG not as a revolutionary organisation but as a support network to his activities with the Labour Party and trade union left wings. As such he wasn't interested in building the IMG and was actively hostile to the west London teenagers just recruited who he regarded as ultra-left. IMG members were useful for doing to donkey work in producing *The Week* at Labour Party conferences, but not much regarded as comrades in a joint revolutionary enterprise.

The IMG was facing another basic problem linked to the conflict with Coates. The new left that the Vietnam war and the student movement were bringing into existence, was not much interested in work in the Labour Party. The IMG was recruiting students who wanted to build an open revolutionary organisation, while the official position of the organisation was still entrism. Between 1967-9 the tiny IMG leadership group, based really on Ernie Tate and Pat Jordan, was faced with very difficult organisational and political questions that would have important bearings on the future of the British revolutionary left.

Given the youth of the comrades involved they did an extraordinary job, but of course they made some mistakes. Necessarily the comrades led the turn away from entrism, although inevitably it led to some losses, including eventually some comrades who helped to set up Labour Briefing.

Through the VSC their working relationship with some of the members of the *New Left Review* editorial board, particularly Robin Blackburn, Quintin Hoare and Branka Magas became closer. Crucially the organisation recruited the comrade who was for much of the public the main face of the youth and student movements, Tariq Ali. Some very talented young comrades—for example Peter Gowan—were recruited from the universities. These people together with John Wheal were central in setting up *The Black Dwarf* a broad based revolutionary newspaper in 1969. The I.M.G. could be said to have had a 'strategic majority' on its editorial board and it helped to expand the audience of the IMG.

The emerging radicalisation went into hyper-drive in 1968, with the Tet offensive in Vietnam, the Prague Spring but of course mainly the May-June events in France involving the biggest general strike in history and the role of revolutionaries on a mass scale for the first time in Europe since the '20s and '30s. Another piece of good luck for the IMG was the role of the JCR, led by Fourth Internationalists like Alain Krivine and Daniel Bensaid, in the French events.

IMG women were closely involved in setting up the first conference in Oxford of the 'new' women's liberation movement and in establishing a journal of socialist feminism, *Socialist Woman*, at a time when the whole issue was disregarded by most of the left.

Ernie and Jess went back to Canada in 1969. When they left they had helped to lead the IMG into a totally new position, which in turn influenced the future of the whole far left. The SLL had been seen off as a significant force because its sectarianism repelled the new generation. The united front was established as crucial theme and mechanism for struggle. Solidarity with the colonial revolution, particularly Vietnam and Cuba, were themes pioneered by the Group. Links with the Fourth International—including its North American component—were crucial in the IMG's strongly internationalist profile, which in turn was a key part of its attraction to new recruits. The IMG was strongly identified with the new movements of the oppressed like the women's movement and black liberation and anti-racists movements. All these things were to echo loudly through the far left in Britain as it developed subsequently.

But there were clouds on the horizon. Entrism in the Labour Party had given the IMG an automatic link up with the labour movement. How to deepen that link as a public organisation was a constant source of debate and infighting in subsequent years.

Ernie here alludes to another problem. While the IMG's membership shot up from a few dozen to several hundred, the International Socialists' membership shot up from a few hundred to more than 1,000 by the end of 1969. In 1969 the Internationalist Socialist leader Tony Cliff approached the IMG with a fusion proposal that would have included the IMG comrades keeping their links with the Fourth International and with the right to publishing material internally and having access to the I.S. journals.

Ernie reveals here that he was in favour of accepting this proposal, but it was strongly opposed by Pat Jordan. Being on the verge of going back to Canada he felt in no position to put up a political fight when he would not be around to lead the organisation if he won his position. I think Ernie was absolutely right on the issue of a fusion with the I.S.; the whole history of the British far left over forty years could have been quite different if the IMG had taken another course.

For comrades in the militant left today, itself faced with how to take forward fundamental socialist principles through an incredibly complex social and political situation, Ernie's account is not just a fascinating look at the past, but full of insights and lessons for the future.

Phil Hearse
4th August 2013

Stephen Hawking (with cane), Tariq Ali and Vanessa Redgrave at the front of the March 17th , 1968 Vietnam protest.
Credit: Lewis Morley Archives

Table of Contents

Introduction

*T*HE GREATER PART OF THIS VOLUME IS TAKEN UP WITH MY EXPERIENCES in Britain. On assignment from the Fourth International, I worked with its supporters there to help establish a British Section of the organization. This is when the International Marxist Group was born. I describe how it came into being and some of its main personalities. In the course of this activity, I had the good fortune to meet the folks of the Bertrand Russell Peace Foundation (BRPF) and Bertrand Russell's formidable secretary, Ralph Schoenman. I provide details about the founding of the Vietnam Solidarity Campaign (VSC) and the role our group played in helping get it off the ground, including how we worked with others in united front activity to lead a series of large protest demonstrations, made up of tens of thousands of people—which many times led to violent confrontations with the police—against the war and which shook London in those years.

Also described in this volume is our activity in support of the Russell International War Crimes Tribunal that was called into existence by Russell to expose American war crimes in Vietnam. All of the Tribunal members were world-renowned public intellectuals. Our organization provided the activists for its Working Committee and carried out most of its day-to-day work. The Tribunal would come under tremendous pressure from the State and from day one faced an onslaught of opposition in the press, inspired mainly by the United States government, to prevent it from taking place, including having it banned in Paris and London and preventing its members from even getting to it.

In the midst of all this, we had the great misfortune to lose an important ally, when Isaac Deutscher, the first appointed member of the Tribunal, and one of its two British representatives, was felled by a heart attack and died in 1967. He had been critical in mediating the internal difficulties—and sometimes the misunderstandings—in the Tribunal members about how it should proceed. I discuss that here. Despite its problems, the Tribunal, through its proceedings and declarations, became a key vehicle for exposing America's criminal activities in Vietnam to the public.

A financial crisis in the Tribunal finally led to sharp differences in the BRPF, amongst its Directors, about how to deal with the problems caused by the Tribunal's failure to repay its loans to it. These were substantial. This led to Ken Coates, a leading member and a well known British Marxist intellectual, being expelled from the IMG. I describe how that came about.

In Latin America in those years, there were several guerrilla struggles underway. Directly inspired by the Cuban Revolution and many of them actively organized by Che Guevara, these struggles posed the immediate question of how the Fourth International, especially its sections in Latin America, should relate to them. This memoir deals with the central debate of the Ninth World Congress of the Fourth International in 1969, about this question. For history's sake, I have reconstructed that debate from my notes taken at the time. But as I wrote that chapter after a visit to Argentina, I give an account of the tragic fate of Robert Santucho and his comrades in the PRT, the official section of the Fourth International which took up arms against the State in the midst of that debate. The dispute about the guerrilla struggle in Latin America rocked the Fourth International to its core, and the resulting internal division set it back many years, I argue.

I have tried to stay away from an interrogation of the ideas that motivated us in those years. I have always been uneasy about retrospective judgments based upon hindsight and that always seem to be twenty-twenty. Of course, we could have done things better and it's easy to see now that some of our problems arose from our failure to grasp the nature of the period we were living through, including a lack of a good appreciation of the resiliency of capitalism and its ability to survive crises, including an underestimation of the ruling class' capacity to learn from such things. I think it was these kinds of errors that later led us into serious difficulties when it came to launching "a turn to industry" in the seventies in North America. But I have few regrets about all this. I was educated in the school that taught me to deal with mistakes as a normal part of trying to succeed, and that the worst mistake of all is to do nothing and allow oneself to retreat into a sectarian isolation. In the circumstances, I feel we did the best we could with the hands that we were dealt. If we are going to be judged, then it should be done in comparison to what all the other socialist groups were doing at the same time. Looked at in this way, I think the following pages will show that we acquitted ourselves fairly well. What I have tried to do is to give an account of our activities as they were lived during those incredible years, on the ground, especially by me.

© John Walmsley 1968

Tariq Ali and Vanessa Redgrave with Richard Branson (now of Virgin Airlines) immediately behind and between them, blocked by police from entering Grosvenor Square, March 17th, 1968. [To see more of John Walmsley's photographs go to www.educationphotos.co.uk/]

Chapter 1

The Fourth International in Britain

I ARRIVED IN LONDON ON MY NEW ASSIGNMENT TO HELP THE FOURTH International in the autumn of 1965. Alan Harris met me at the airport. It was something of an unpleasant surprise for me to walk out onto the parking lot in the cold drizzling rain. I had been away from Britain too long and had forgotten how truly miserable the weather can be. It was early morning. The traffic was very heavy and the large buses seemed to tower over Alan's small Austin as we headed to Connie's council flat in Tulse Hill, South London. The congestion made Vancouver's streets, by comparison, look deserted. Alan pointed out the high price of gasoline— "petrol" in Britain. Unlike Canada, where we commonly asked the attendants to "fill up the tank," in Britain, where the price of gasoline was about three times that of Canada, you only ordered by the gallon.

As I've mentioned previously, Alan had first met Connie on one of his trips to visit his folks in Lincoln in the late fifties, when we were all still on friendly terms with Gerry Healy and the Socialist Labour League. Connie had been Healy's secretary and office manager, a leading cadre in the SLL from its founding until she was forced out because of her opposition to Healy's organizational practices. Very knowledgeable about the left in Britain, she had been through the expulsion of the SLL from the Labour Party which she, incidentally, thought Healy had provoked. When I got there, she was working full-time as a teacher and she and Alan, at the suggestion of Joe Hansen, had set up a small mail-order book service, "Pioneer Books," which they operated out of their council flat. It had become the main public source for Fourth International literature in Britain and the main outlet for books from the American SWP's Merit Publishers. Essential to their operation was the production of a yearly mimeographed catalogue which they circulated widely by advertising it in most of Britain's left newspapers, a very early first step in establishing an open Fourth International presence in the country. Most of the profit coming in went towards accumulating more stock, Alan told me, so he was forced to find a full-time job so that he and Connie could make ends meet, which meant he was "practically paralyzed," as he said, when it came to doing political work. Their home was also a popular way station for leaders of the SWP and our group in Canada whenever they visited London.

After a few hours sleep, Connie and Alan brought me up to speed about the situation of our co-thinkers in Europe and how the international reunification process was proceeding. At the June 1963 Reunification Congress of the International, to which Alan and Ross Dowson were delegates, Alan had been a member of the Commission that had been set up to try and overcome the division in the British supporters of the International Secretariat. When he had arrived in England in the summer of 1963, Alan had been given the specific assignment of helping overcome that split. There had been no public, functioning pro-Fourth International group in Britain for many years, he told me, at least not since the division in 1953. At that time, the "official" section of the International Secretariat was the Revolutionary Socialist League, led by Ted Grant and Jimmy Deane, but it had suffered a split a few years earlier, when a small grouping led by Ken Coates and Pat Jordan had walked out and declared itself to be "a transitional group which is to 'fill the gap' while the necessary pre-conditions—organizational and political—are established for the construction of a functioning British section of the Fourth International."[1] It was known as the International Group (I.G.)

When he met up with the RSL in the summer of 1963, Alan said, it was in a sorry state and exhibited little internal or external life. Its paper, *Socialist Fight*, a monthly, rarely appeared. There been no annual conference for a while nor did it have anyone on staff. Its main leader, Ted Grant, was hardly ever around; he had a full time job and had to work fifty to sixty hours a week to make a living. Their headquarters was hardly ever open, with only a pamphlet on one topic for sale, a five year old one at that and about France. Its committees seldom met. It was in debt, and had not paid its dues to the International for many months.

But soon after he arrived, Alan agreed to go on staff and, probably as a result of the pressure from the International, he was elected the full-timer for the organization, at a modest salary of ten pounds a week. The agreement was that he would keep their offices open for regular hours every weekday and that any profit that came in from the sale of books—which he took personal responsibility to order from publishers—would go towards his salary. Unable to pay him his salary, they quickly reduced it to seven pounds a week, forcing him to get a part-time job. Despite this, Alan was able to help revitalize the group and one result was an increase in the number of people dropping into the headquarters to buy literature. That's when he met up with a small grouping of ex-SLL people who had been expressing an interest in a revitalized RSL, two of whom had been leaders of Healy's youth organization. After several discussions with Alan and Connie, they had been won over to the politics of the International, posing the possibility that any new united organization might be larger and more effective than what had existed before. Among them were two former editors of *Keep Left*, the SLL's youth publication in the Labour Party. They were to be included in the re-unification.[2]

In September 1964, a reunification conference eventually took place in Britain, but it was destined not to succeed because the RSL had clearly entered the process in bad faith. The RSL, by far the largest grouping at the conference, made sure it wouldn't go anywhere. Rejecting any notion of parity for the other two groupings with whom they had been in discussion about unity, and in an insanely factional manner, the RSL used its larger number of delegates to seize control with an overwhelming majority on the new organization's National Committee, allowing no representation whatsoever for the ex-SLL members who had been part of the discussions. They also vindictively punished Alan for his criticisms of them by keeping him off any of the "new" organization's leadership bodies. A few months after the conference, Alan reported to the Secretariat that although a few youth had been recruited and two issues of a new publication, *The Militant* had appeared, "Internally things have come to a standstill" in the organization. In an atmosphere of frustration and factionalism it had yet to even adopt a name or a constitution, and its Executive Committee, as in the pre-fusion times, meetings were poorly attended and infrequent. And it had yet to pay any dues to the International and gave every appearance of paralysis, a situation that was not helped any when its General Secretary headed off to India on a long trip.

Even though the RSL maintained a hostile attitude to the International because of its position on Cuba and the colonial revolution, absurdly, it still claimed to be the "official" section in Britain. By the end of the year it had lost the headquarters that Alan and Connie had put so much effort into cleaning and redecorating and had gotten into a dispute with Alan over the ownership of the small amount of literature they claimed he had "stolen"—and which he had purchased out of his own money—five pounds worth, it turned out. After that he set up Pioneer Book Service and ran it out of Connie's and his apartment. Three months after the "fusion" the RSL elected Peter Taaffe, who had been vociferously opposed to the re-unification, to the position of full-time National Secretary, the top position in the group.[3] Naturally, the Coates/Jordan grouping walked away, as did the SLL people. The whole thing had been a sham.

Alan and Connie told me that they had found the experience very frustrating. It was just after Wilson's first election, and politically the situation in the country had seemed very promising for the revolutionary left and it looked possible for the first time in a while that an alternative to the Healy organization could get going—that is, if the Fourth International's supporters could get over their factionalism and learn to cooperate with each other. And there had been a few promising signs of what the possibilities could be.

Just before I had gotten there, Connie and Alan, with the support of both groups, had helped to organize a defence committee for the imprisoned

Neville Alexander, a leader of the South African Unity Movement—supporter of the Fourth International and anti-apartheid leader—just as we had done in Canada. It was one of the main defense campaigns of the International at the time. The Alexander committee in England quickly won the support of a few prominent sponsors, including Sydney Silverman, a Labour Party MP, and held a large public meeting, attended by over one hundred people, to publicize the case. There was also some cooperation in another Fourth International campaign to support Hugo Blanco, the Peruvian revolutionary peasant leader who had been imprisoned in Peru and was in danger of being murdered. A "Defend Hugo Blanco Committee" had been organized in London, with Millie Van Gelderen, a long time Trotskyist and supporter of the Nottingham group, its secretary.

Alan and Connie told me that, despite the success of the Alexander and Blanco committees, they had attended many meetings with representatives of both groups—they both claimed to support the International—but it had been like pulling teeth getting them to cooperate with each other. When Alan would suggest joint meetings he got very little cooperation from the Grant people and even the Coates-Jordan group seemed to be only going through the motions. And the odd time when meetings would eventually take place they would often end up in spitting matches with one or the other side marching out. Grant's people, nevertheless, continued to attend the I.E.C. meetings that took place once or twice a year.

Alan and Connie told me they felt their work with the Grant group had been something of a waste of time, but that the Jordan and Coates people, on the other hand, were at least more cooperative and had a more positive attitude to the International. However, a major difficulty was that they were mainly located in Nottingham, and had very few supporters in London. To Alan and Connie, they seemed more politically "healthy" and seemed to be free of the sectarianism of the Grant people, especially in relation to the Labour Party. Grant's people were notorious for showing up at the LP annual conferences with their standard resolution, unchanged from previous conferences, calling for the "nationalization of Britain's thirty-two major companies," that seemed unrelated to time or place, without reference to what the rest of the left was doing and seemingly content to score "propaganda" points against the right wing and staying clear of any broad initiative that might defeat them.

The International Group, for their part gave every appearance of being free of this kind of sectarian pathology and was, primarily because of the intellect and personality of Ken Coates, at the centre of many broad political initiatives in the labour movement that made them look very appealing to the emerging "new left." The previous year they had been part of the discussion in the "new left" about setting up "Centres for Socialist Education (CSE)"—to carry out socialist education in the working class—of which Ken would become co-chair alongside Ralph Miliband, its main originator and who, alongside John Saville had recently brought out the *Socialist Register*. Isaac Deutscher was also an early supporter of this venture and had been involved in discussions about it at Miliband's home, along with Perry Anderson and people around *New Left Review*, most notably Robin Blackburn who was also a co-editor of *The Week*. The new project had a broad spectrum of support on the left, including the International Socialists (I.S.), whose Peter Sedgwick played a key role in setting it up. It had also won the endorsement of a few of the major unions, including some left Labour MPs. The high hopes with which it was launched in October 1965 were not quite realized. "(Forty) socialists met in Soho in response to an article by Ralph Miliband," *The Week* reported.[4]

My discussion with Alan and Connie about Britain was very easygoing and relaxed, especially between Alan and me, because we had been through so many common political struggles together and had even shared the same apartment at one time in Toronto. We spoke the same political language, so to speak, and shared the same political views. We were very conscious of how the North Americans were different from the Europeans in their approach to building their organizations and we had very defined ideas about how a revolutionary group should function if it was to be effective. Even though we did not consider ourselves part of a "faction" and were doing our best to overcome the past divisions, we still had our own unstated agenda to get the Fourth International to function on a more open, more professional, or, if you like, on a more business-like basis, more along the lines of the American SWP model, which we in Canada were trying to replicate and which we regarded as one of the most successful in the International.

A few weeks later I met up with Ray Sparrow. Not long before that Joe Hansen had fallen ill in Paris, causing a minor crisis in the midst of the preparations for the Eighth World Congress because he had played such an important role in driving the reunification forward. I remembered him from the time when he had been in Toronto to meet with Healy in the late fifties. He had suffered from gout and had difficulty walking to and from his hotel to our meetings. Gout is a debilitating form of arthritis characterized by intense pain in the joints and results from high levels of uric acid in the blood. Ray told me that Joe had also developed a serious case of phlebitis, where his veins, especially in his legs, became swollen and red and had developed blood clots. The Congress was scheduled to take place in a few months time, but Ray's immediate task was to provide as much help as possible to Reba, Joe's wife, in looking after Joe and in making sure he received the best possible medical treatment. Even though he was very weak and in hospital, Joe was still trying to figure a way to be able to attend the Congress, Ray told me, but the SWP would have no part of that and wanted him back to the New York as soon as possible.

I had remembered Ray from the fifties when I was in New York at the time of the split in Shachtman's Young People's Socialist League which led to the setting up of the SWP's YSA and had seen him several times at National Committee meetings at Mountain Spring Camp. While not a central leader of the party, he certainly had enormous prestige in the organization, going back to the thirties and he is featured in James P. Cannon's book, *Struggle for a Proletarian Party*, under the pseudonym "Art Sharon", as a correspondent with Cannon in the factional struggle against Max Shachtman and a name by which he was known to most party members.

In the CP youth in the 1930s, he had supported the Trotskyists in the split and had been a delegate to the SWP's founding conference.

A merchant seaman, a coxswain, Ray had been a leader of the Party fraction in the Seaman's Union until they were all purged in a combined action by the government and the union bureaucracy, whereby the fraction members had their sea-going documents cancelled, making it impossible for any of them to find work at sea. A skilled carpenter, he told me that after his papers were taken from him, he had some difficulty finding a job until he managed to land one with a construction company working on federal contracts repairing and constructing harbours on the East Coast. Through this, he became an expert in designing and building plywood forms for concrete structures, which led to him, in the late 1950s, playing an important part in the construction of New York's famous Solomon R. Guggenheim Museum, an iconic architectural masterpiece by the legendary American Frank Lloyd Wright.

Frank Lloyd Wright had won the commission for the new museum with an innovative design at the time, characterized by curved walls and exposed concrete surfaces. When the construction company working on the project had a look at Wright's drawings, they sought out Ray and he grabbed the opportunity to work on the new project. His experience in constructing curved plywood forms for concrete caissons in harbour construction, he told me, became invaluable in taking Wright's ideas off the drawing board and making them a reality. There were few people around in the construction trades who had this skill and it also helped that Ray could read and assimilate information quickly, something he had learned in the socialist movement while trying to hold down a full-time job and at the same time spending time reading to stay on top of what was going on politically. He also discovered that the largest source of the technical information about concrete technology was in the Library of Congress, which he consulted frequently.

Ray had been living in San Francisco before he came to Europe. His first wife, an invalid for many years, had passed away and he had recently re-married. Joe Hansen and Jack Barnes, who had become the SWP's new National Secretary as part of the change in generations leading the organization, had persuaded him to give up his construction superintendant job in the Bay Area and move with his new wife, Gloria, who was then pregnant with their son, David, to Brussels to continue with Joe's assignment working in Europe. When I met Ray in London, he was in the midst of arranging the re-mortgaging of his recently self-built home in Marin County to finance his stay in Brussels. Otherwise it would have been too difficult for his family, he said, to live on the meagre supplement that the party was providing him. Such were the sacrifices the cadres of the SWP were prepared to make for their organization. We saw a lot of each other over the next few years and we became very good friends.

The Eighth World Congress saw the consolidation of the unification that had occurred two years earlier. It lasted several days, with approximately sixty delegates present, representing more than twenty-five countries. It went very smoothly except for a minor hiccup when Michel Pablo's supporters tried to crash the event. Alan, Connie and I were delegates; the Grant people were there, but not Pat Jordan or Ken Coates. I don't remember if Jack Barnes or Mary-Alice was present, but I'm pretty sure Ray Sparrow was there as an observer, and Joe Hansen, despite all his planning and scheming to be there, had had a couple of setbacks with his health and was still in hospital in Paris.

I had been afraid that, without Joe's influence, the conference might be a bit ragged, but according to those I talked to, it was one of the best they had ever held, free from the factional and organizational manoeuvring that had characterized the Pablo years and with a higher representation of young people than at the previous conference. This was an early sign that the youth radicalization which had moved to the fore in North America might be making an appearance in Europe and could provide a base for opposition to the Vietnam War. Defense of the Vietnamese revolution and the need for all the sections to campaign actively around the issue was one of the main themes of the Congress. As was expected, the Grant people voted against everything. There was some discussion around a Secretariat's statement issued about the previous summer's

Algerian coup, and an amendment that said it had been a mistake to characterize the Ben Bella government as "a workers' and peasants' government," but it got a high vote in any case and everyone seemed to agree the United Secretariat had made a mistake in calling for armed struggle against the Houari Boumediene coup.

On the whole, from my perspective the unification seemed complete and there were very few traces of the old divisions and factional hostilities that had been very intense just a few years earlier. Personally, I felt completely at ease and had no inhibitions in moving around and talking to delegates who had been supporters of the International Secretariat during the old differences. I was on the Mandates Commission and everything was open and frank and the same was true of the British Commission, where I noticed that Alan Harris was listened to very carefully and respectfully, and where Grant's RSL was "decertified" and its designation changed to "sympathizing group," with the Coates-Jordan group given the same status.

The Grant people objected strongly to the change, as was to be expected, but they were told that because they had demonstrated a persistent unwillingness to participate in the International's campaigns and defend it against the attacks of its opponents, the International could no longer take any responsibility for them. Nevertheless, it was understood that I would continue with Alan's assignment of trying to get the two groups to cooperate with each other, and if possible, unify.

It was quickly apparent that Ernest, Livio and Pierre were the main leaders of the movement and they had the unquestioned respect of all the delegates. Alan told me that compared to 1963, the Congress was a model of efficiency and everything seemed to flow very smoothly but I thought to myself it could have been much better organized and guided more consciously. It was difficult to detect an overall objective for the Congress, other than the constitutional requirement that it take place, even though the International's Secretariat had agreed beforehand that it would be the building of the International through the maximizing of the new opportunities for growth presented by re-unification. In so far as this was the theme, it only revealed itself indirectly. The Congress had barely opened before Pablo showed us that he represented some unfinished business. Although he had walked out a year earlier, he wasn't entirely finished with us and still had a few manoeuvres up his sleeve to cause difficulties. Prior to our Congress, he had convened a meeting of his supporters in Paris, Pierre Frank told me, and now he seemed to be bent on preventing our Congress from taking place. He even went so far as to bring its security into jeopardy, so that he could claim his grouping was the "logical inheritor of the Fourth International."

During the first session, a few of his supporters, led by a person with the pseudonym "Anderson," tried to crash the event, even threatening its security. The Mandates Commission, which I was on, had refused to let any of them in unless they first affirmed their loyalty to the decisions of the Congress, a reasonable request it seemed to me, because hitherto they had been part of the Pablo grouping. They rejected this, and we were soon startled to hear their loud shouts ringing throughout the hall as they yelled their insults at the staff handling credentials. Fearful they might attract the attention of the cops, the Congress was compelled to adjourn for a while. I had visions of us having to reschedule it for some future date, but we got through that first day with no problems.

The only concession made was to seat two of Pablo's supporters from Denmark who said that while they agreed with him politically, they were opposed to his action in splitting. From the floor, they made a point of criticizing Ernest, Livio and Pierre for being "unfair" to Pablo, but I was struck by how little passion accompanied their complaints. They didn't seem to have their heart in it. I found what they said to be very interesting, however—they spoke several times—because it gave me better understanding of the kind of International Pablo was proposing, which was a movement of freewheeling tendencies, a kind of federal organization rather than the more politically focused one we were trying to build at that time.

But from what I could see Ernest, Livio and Pierre were not yet the coordinated team required for such a task. Their response to the unexpected small incidents—such as the Pablo's provocation—that can arise in any conference, no matter how well run, tended to be individual rather than collective. They seemed unprepared for what was happening, hesitant at times—as if there was no worked out policy for such eventualities. This could even be seen when Livio proposed a series of amendments to the resolution, "Progress and Problems of the African Revolution," that dealt with the question of Algeria. Most of the delegates felt the issue was too premature and that the matter would have been better begun as a literary discussion, several months before.

Earlier, in a United Secretariat meeting that had set the agenda, I hadn't understood this argument too well, but when the matter hit the floor, suddenly I could see its logic. I remember thinking some of the issues in the resolution (I don't remember their substance) were being used by the sectarians in our midst to distort the discussion and, even from Livio's point of view, it must have been far from satisfactory because his position wasn't really being discussed on its merits. Instead, we were continually being warned about "the dangers of opportunism," etc. I don't remember the content, but I do recall being very impressed with Ernest's and Pierre's interventions. In the end, it turned out that Livio did not have any supporters for his amendments, and even the Italian delegates disagreed with him. Good naturedly, he withdrew them when it was obvious to him he wasn't going to get anywhere. But again, it revealed a lack of cohesion in the leadership team and how easily the organization could become the victim of a clever factionalist. This is why it had been so difficult to come to grips with Pablo, even though the previous Congress, as Joe Hansen succinctly put it to me later, had "nailed his skin to the wall to dry."

Ever since the re-unification and after many visits to Paris, both the Canadians and the SWP had come to the conclusion that part of the difficulty in coming to grips with Pablo's factionalism was a result of the simple lack of coordination in the leadership team and the very weak "centre" in Paris, that, incidentally, had zero professional staff. To us, the leadership seemed to have a very loose structure, lacking a physical centre and was made up of a team of individuals who functioned mainly out of their homes. There was no single place to go to look at the correspondence from the different sections of the International, for example, or to see the previous decisions of World Congresses or records of previous meetings of the Secretariat and International Executive Committee. My impression was that these kinds of things were all scattered in and amongst the personal files of the leading cadres. The same was true of finances: there were no books available, only general reports. What there was of a "centre" was run by Pierre Frank on a part-time basis out of the tiny Paris office of the French section, and out of which he also helped produced and write *Quatriemme Internationale*, the International's quarterly journal. No one worked full-time for the organization. To live and support his family, Pierre was compelled to work at a part-time job. Ernest lived mainly from whatever he got from his writing and lecturing. The Belgian section did not even have a headquarters. In Italy, Livio Matain worked full-time as a teacher in Rome and Sirio Di Giuliomaria, the other leader of the Italian group, worked for a United Nations' food organization that had its headquarters there.

All the North Americans had been convinced, since the 1963 Congress, of the need to overcome this problem if we were going to be able to effectively lead the organization and take advantage of the opportunities opening up and at the same time counter our opponents on the left. Joe Hansen, before he had fallen ill, had been discussing this problem with Ernest, Pierre and Livio, and by the time we got to Germany we had finally reached an understanding the "centre" would soon be moved to Brussels. It was also agreed that Ernest and Luc Charlier, a very capable young Belgian comrade, would go on staff, full-time. Other decisions of the Congress, in addition to "decertifying" the RSL, included relocating from Paris to New York the International's weekly publication that covered international events, *World Outlook* (later changed to *Intercontinental Press*). Joe Hansen, along with the assistance of his wife Reba, had initiated this publication when they had located to Paris to help guide the re-unification.

With the RSL "decertified" and both of the British groups given "sympathizer" status, the problem was posed of what steps should be taken in London to try and get a proper F.I. group established there. It was generally understood, if not openly stated, that the "fusion" of the two

British groups had been a failure and that we couldn't expect much cooperation from the Grant group in the future—indeed they were hostile to us—but that the Nottingham group was much closer to us politically. Despite their shortcomings, they would be much easier to get along with because they seemed to be free of Grant's sectarianism. During the course of the Congress, Alan, Connie, Ernest, Livio, Pierre and I had several discussions to map out our next course of action in London—in other words, what I should do after Alan and Connie headed back to Canada in a few months.

While it was agreed that I should continue to try to get the two groups to cooperate, it was also understood that my first move would be to open a small office of some kind, out of which I would continue with Pioneer Book Service, which Alan and Connie had been running. The hope was that we would eventually convince the Nottingham people to send someone down to London to help out and establish a branch of their group there. The discussion was all still somewhat abstract to me because I had yet to personally meet many of the individuals being discussed. In addition, I was wondering how this would be financed. Everyone was of the opinion it would be impossible without some kind of subsidy. They suggested I put the suggestion to Canada that they subsidize me for at least a year, over and above what I was supposed to be getting for travel expenses. Frankly, however, I had no great hopes on that score because Ross never seemed to be able to get me the money he had initially promised me since I had gotten to London.

On my way back from the Congress, I stopped over in Paris, primarily to see Joe Hansen. He was in the American Hospital at Pte De Neuilly, at the time one of the best in Paris. It must have been top-notch; Pablo Picasso had recently been a patient, according to the *New York Herald Tribune*. Ray Sparrow was devoting a lot of his time to looking after Joe, ensuring he promptly received the treatment he needed. Ray remarked to me he that it was fortunate to have gotten Joe admitted there, a move facilitated by a doctor who was on friendly terms with our French section—who, I remember vaguely, may even have been a Lambertist. This was entirely possible, because of the high regard for Joe, even among his political critics on the left. Ray told me his medical bill, which would be paid by the SWP, had by then "reached astronomical proportions."

When I saw Joe he told me his health was gradually getting better but that he had suffered a couple of serious setbacks, "bumps on the road to getting better," he said, in one of his typical laconic understatements. He told me he had been given an anti-coagulant as a result of the phlebitis to prevent his blood clotting and a few days later had suffered a very severe allergic reaction and was almost a goner. Some "bump," I thought! He had discovered for the first time he was allergic to all kinds of drugs, including penicillin, and that was slowing down his recovery. No date had been set for his release, he told me, and he expected to be there for several more weeks. It was obvious he had been seriously ill—he had lost a lot of weight, his face was gaunt, his complexion pallid and he looked very weak. Yet he was alert and as sharp as ever as he quizzed me about the Congress, asking me my impressions of how it had gone. We also talked for a few minutes about the work in Britain.

I told him about the Congress decision recognizing two "sympathizing" groups in Britain and our moves to try and open an office in London within the next few weeks, before Alan and Connie headed over to Canada. I mentioned that a lot of the discussion about the personalities being talked about had been a little bit abstract for me because I had yet to meet any of them. For example, I had yet to meet the Nottingham people or any of their few London supporters. He advised I should proceed very cautiously and take my time to get to know the situation inside and out before making any organizational moves. I told him Alan and I were planning to go to Nottingham the following weekend, which would help give me a sense of who I would be working with. In any case, Ray was leaving for San Francisco for a month or so, to take care of some personal business—arranging for a mortgage and renting his house—before permanently relocating to Europe, so by the time he came back I felt we should have a good idea of the next steps ahead.

Once Alan, Connie and I got back from Germany, we began looking for an office to rent. Within a few days, we settled on one on the second floor of No. 8 Toynbee Street, near the famous market in Petticoat Lane, above a Polish delicatessen in an old three-storey building, which, by the way, is still there. Alan and Connie helped me move in. I bought an old second-hand oak desk and a couple of file cabinets for a few pounds and ordered a phone from British Telecom, which I remember took a long time to be installed. Our opening hours were posted on the door. Alan and Connie, even though they were anxious to be on their way to Canada, spent a few days going over with me the operation of the book service and its accounts. I had been helping Alan with the book service in their apartment for a few weeks so I knew a little of what was involved in meeting customers' requests.

One major problem we had was that it was still very difficult to place orders with some of the major publishers. They would not allow us to open an account and would always insist upon cash up-front for every order. The situation with suppliers was much more difficult than what I had experienced in Vancouver where I had helped establish a bookstore. A large number of our customers were students, and many times the orders for literature came from university socialist societies. Alan had warned me to be cautious with them; they sometimes were unreliable when it came to paying their bills. But, most importantly, we were in business. Before Alan and Connie headed back to Canada, Connie found me a temporary place to stay for a very reasonable rent, in the home of a colleague from her school. It was a Malaysian family with a house in South London, who also happened to be politically sympathetic to our views.

Soon I met up with Ray Sparrow again. He made no pretense that he could function like Joe, but with his years of experience in the working class and in the leadership of the SWP, and with his very sharp mind, he very soon won the respect of all the European leaders, especially Ernest, Pierre and Livio. It also helped that he was of their generation. But he also made a special effort to get to know the new youth leadership that was, happily, beginning to emerge in France. He applied constant pressure in Brussels to get the leadership to operate in a more professional manner, and I think it was him more than anyone else who talked Ernest Mandel into eventually devoting himself, at least for a while, to full-time work in the Bureau and in providing leadership to the organization on a day to day basis. Ernest was helped a lot in this work by Luc Charlier from the Belgian Section, who also worked on a full-time basis.

Jess and I came to know Ray quite well because he was in London frequently—about once a month—to visit us and he would very kindly let me stay with him and Gloria whenever I was in Brussels for Secretariat meetings. He turned out to be one of the most generous people I have ever known. I believe he would even buy a supply of books and periodicals from us just to help financially support the book service. It would have been impossible for him to have the time to read all the books he purchased. With his long experience in the SWP and American working class movement generally, he was a tremendous asset to us as we went through our many struggles in getting what would eventually become the IMG off the ground. He faithfully attended all our important events and meetings, sometimes even in the later stages when he was suffering from poor health.

Over the next few weeks, I met the scattering of people in London who had been generally sympathetic to the Fourth International in the past, some whose roots went back to the thirties and the Second World War period of British Trotskyism, the Revolutionary Communist Party founded in 1944, and a predecessor of the Healy organization.

I especially remember Charlie Van Gelderen, his wife Millie—both originally from South Africa—and their daughters, all of whom would later become active in the IMG. Millie headed up the British Defense Committee to help free Hugo Blanco, who was in a Peruvian prison because of his guerrilla activities. It was a central campaign of the Fourth International, and helped to get him out of prison and into exile in Europe[5]. I also got to know a small group of Iraqi students who lived in London and who were sympathetic to the Fourth International. They were in contact with Pat Jordan and the Nottingham group and would frequently use our office at 8 Toynbee St. as a meeting place. Most of them were from Mosel in Northern Iraq and they were trying to help build an underground socialist organization there.

Once a month I would help them in mimeographing their monthly journal, *Al Thawra (Revolution)*, a totally Arabic publication, which frequently carried the statements of the International in translation. We would sometimes pull all-nighters getting the 500 or so copies published. They told me it was the only socialist Arabic language periodical in Britain and that it circulated widely in the radical Arab community, and in Iraq to where a bundle of each issue was smuggled. Unsuccessfully, they tried to teach me Arabic. As we worked together, the room would often be filled with the music of popular Arab songs playing from a tape deck. All of them were in Britain on student visas and over the next couple of years many made their way back to Iraq. One of the ways we were of practical help to them was through Ernest Mandel who found a way to obtain the necessary documentation to allow them to get back to Iraq safely. I often wonder what their fate was under the terrible regime of Saddam Hussein and the subsequent imperialist occupation of their country, and whether they were ever able to escape that horror.

I also got to know Gerry Lawless very well around this time. He would often drop in to see me and to find out what was happening in the International. He was the leader of a small Irish group that was sympathetic to the International and located in Dublin. Gerry, like many Irish, was in London for work because unemployment was very high in Dublin. He had become well known in Ireland for having taken the British to court and winning—under the European Convention on Human Rights, adopted in the early 1950s—a case of discrimination against Catholics in the North. It wasn't very long before I got to meet the rest of his group in London, including Eamonn McCann who later would become a leader of the civil rights movement in Northern Ireland and a prominent Irish journalist and eventually a member of the British SWP.

That was also when I met Sean Morrissey, a very keen and energetic young man. Sean was a member of the Lawless group. He would later go on to help found a tiny armed-struggle grouping, Saor Eire, which became known more for its bank robberies than anything else. He ended up losing his life in a terribly misguided action that also would lead to many of his comrades being jailed. Sean Matgamna was also around the Lawless' group at that time and would later go on to give the International Socialists great difficulties when he "entered" their organization, before forming his own little grouping, Workers' Liberty. I found Lawless' Irish group a delight to be around and often after a meeting it was common for all of us to continue our discussions in a pub over a Guinness late into the evening where the topics ranged all over the place. Often they would discuss what was happening in the Dail (Irish parliament) and they seemed to know most of the major figures there as well.

Lawless' group was small and not even of sufficient size to be able to produce its own publication. Their connections with each other seemed to me to be more social than political at times, and there were a few strange characters hanging around them in those years. I remember once, after an evening at the pub, a young couple in the group offered me a ride home, which I gratefully accepted. When we got to their car, I was quite surprised to see a large power boat hitched to its rear. They must have seen the look of amazement on my face, because they quickly explained to me why it was there. They lived in an apartment, they told me, and couldn't afford the storage fees, so their solution was just to leave it permanently hitched to the car. Everywhere they went, back and forth to work, to meetings and demonstrations, they towed the thing behind them, without ever getting it into the water. It was a very unusual sight, to say the least, in traffic-congested central London.

After we established our office on Toynbee Street, it became a focal point for many supporters of the Fourth International who happened to visit London. I remember we had visits, for example, from some of the leaders of the Lanka Sama Samaja party, in Sri Lanka, which was then called Ceylon. They were affiliated to the Fourth International and had risen to be the Official Opposition in the parliament. The party was going through an internal crisis and they would make a point of visiting us when they were in London attending British Commonwealth meetings, in order to pass on their views about the internal disputes. I also remember that Daniel Camejo, brother of the late Peter Camejo who was a leader of the American SWP, also came to see us one year. He had made a documentary about Douglas Bravo's guerrilla operations in the mountains of Venezuela. Bravo, with the support of the Cubans, had split from the CP—after April 1965, when the party had taken the position of giving priority to legal forms of change— and launched an armed struggle; Camejo's documentary carried contemporary footage of Bravo's guerilla campaign.[6] He was trying hard to find a distributer or to have it shown on British television, because the Venezuelan military had successfully managed to erect a wall of silence around Bravo and had kept Venezuelans and the world from knowing what was going on. Daniel knocked on many doors and I tried to help him all I could by suggesting some people he should speak to, but, being new to London, I wasn't much help. I think he eventually left London empty handed.

I had come to Europe fully aware that, like our group in Canada, most of the International's sections in Europe were practicing some variant of the "entry tactic" and I was curious what this would look like in practice. Although faced with promising opportunities in several countries, in comparison to the mass based Communist and Social Democratic parties, the International's groups in Europe were similar in size to our groups in North America; that is, relatively small organizations made up of hundreds, not thousands, of members. This had also been Ross Dowson's observation when he had been in Europe in the late fifties. And while I think he may have underestimated the strength of the Belgian and French Sections, I found this generally to be the case for other countries. Certainly the Jordan-Coates group in Britain, which was also led by Alan Rooney, a local Labour Party leader, was very tiny, with only about twenty people at most. The Grant group was about three times as large, but still small. All were mainly active in the Labour Party. What distinguished the Coates-Jordan-Rooney group, however, was that it had an influence in the working class much greater than its small numbers would suggest.

Ken Coates had established himself as a major British left intellectual with important connections to the emerging "new left." One of the group's other prominent members was Tony Topham, close to Ken, and who had gained some prominence in the labour movement as a major propagandist for the ideas of workers' control. Ken, Pat and Tony had a common history in the left, having been members of the CP. They had broken from the Party after the Khrushchev revelations and the Soviet invasion of Hungary, when they began to look for another political alternative. Ken had joined Healy's SLL for a while, only to get kicked out along with Peter Fryer.

Ken, Tony and Pat then became active in the Nottingham Labour Party, joining in 1956, eventually getting in touch with Ted Grant's RSL which was the "official" F.I. section in the country, part of the Pablo bloc. For a while, Pat had edited their paper, *Socialist Fight*, but, he told me, right from the beginning he felt that Grant was an insecure sectarian who never really trusted him. The only reason he and Ken had tried working with the RSL, he said, was because of its formal connection to the Fourth International, since they were convinced its political line on many questions was a lot better than Grant's. He told me he had taken particular exception to Grant's notion that Syria was somehow a "workers' state" because it had brought some large capitalist establishments under state control. Ken and Pat's supporters were informally known as the "international group" after they had walked out of the Grant organization.

Before his expulsion from the Nottingham Labour Party—that had taken place earlier that October soon after I had arrived in London— Ken had been very successful in having several important resolutions passed at Party conferences, much to the chagrin of Harold Wilson. For example, there was a resolution condemning the Labour government for its policies in Yemen, where the British had used napalm in the British colony against the nationalist resistance. As far as I was aware, despite these kinds of successes none of the two F.I. groups in Britain carried out any political activities in their own name or in the name of the Fourth International—a big weakness, I thought.

None had "open," clearly identifiable Fourth International publications, nor were they identified in any public way with the Fourth International. Across the channel, the French comrades, around 100 members in Alan's estimate, were "entered" into the Communist and Socialist parties, and had begun to win a notable influence in the Union of Communist Students that was then under control of the French CP. The Belgian section, around fifty or sixty, led by Ernest Mandel, who wrote in Fourth International publications under the pseudonym of Ernest Germain, was "entered" in the Socialist Party and helped produce a popular left journal, *La Gauche*, which had evolved into the official journal of the Belgian LCR, the Fourth International section there. The Italian section was "entered" in the Italian Communist party and was beginning to carry out common activities with a promising oppositional grouping in the party that had recently formed in it and was organized around the journal, *La Sinistra*. I met some of these people when Livio brought them to a Secretariat meeting in Brussels.

Soon after we arrived back from Germany, Alan and Connie suggested we travel up north so I could get acquainted with the Nottingham group. Pubs were the usual place for the meetings for socialist groups in Britain, I soon found out. I recall that first meeting being an unstructured kind of gathering, about twenty-five people sitting around a table drinking pints of beer and surprisingly not in the least reflective of the many important initiatives in which it was involved. Sam Gordon, who had once been a leader of the American SWP and who was living permanently in London, had also travelled up for the meeting, but I don't remember him saying much.

In terms of organizational skill, the person there who seemed to me to be most experienced was Pat Jordan, a modest, soft spoken man who was mainly responsible for the production of *The Week*, a mimeographed socialist weekly co-edited by Robin Blackburn and Ken Coates that took its name from a radical weekly founded during the Spanish Civil War by the *Daily Worker* correspondent in Spain, Claude Cockburn. With no connections to Cockburn's except for the name, *The Week* was circulated widely in left trade union and left Labour Party circles, with a coverage of Third World struggles greater than any other British left journal.

Launched in July 1963, *The Week* had morphed out of a sequence of publications, beginning with the *International Bulletin*, a mimeographed monthly that was mainly a vehicle for carrying statements of the Fourth International. Then it became simply *The Bulletin*, then *The Weekly Bulletin*, finally ending up as *The Week*. It came on the scene with an impressive list of sponsors, many of them leading lights of the British "new left," including Perry Anderson, Michael Barrat Brown, Ralph Miliband, Tom Nairn, E.P. Thompson and Raymond Williams, all of whom today are recognized as major influences upon British Marxist thought.

The journal also had the support of a few significant trade union leaders, such as Ernie Roberts, a leader of the Amalgamated Engineering Union, along with several left Labour MPs. And it continued to expand its sponsorship list, with the famous novelist Alan Sillitoe declaring his support just as Ken was being expelled from the Labour Party. A few weeks later, shortly after I got to London, Bertrand Russell became a sponsor. Commonly known in left circles as "the Week group," the I.G. was faithfully applying its variant of the "entry tactic." Most of its political activity was confined to the Labour Party; they had no headquarters and were mainly centred in Nottingham. There was a much broader layer of socialist activists in the British Labour Party then, many of them loosely organized around *British Tribune*, a weekly that was the voice mainly of some of the party's more leftwing MPs. Many of these activists were also among the supporters of *The Week*.

Ken and Tony were lecturers at Nottingham and Hull Universities, respectively; Pat made his living—eight pounds a week—running a small shop in the St. Ann's area of Nottingham, the "International Book Shop" at #4 Dane Street, which mainly sold and rented out comics to neighbourhood children but which also carried some socialist literature for sale. *The Week* was produced there as well.

The group was on good terms with the people around *New Left Review*, who, under the leadership of Perry Anderson, had recently taken over the journal from E.P. Thompson and John Saville. I recall Robin Blackburn and Quintin Hoare's names being mentioned a lot in those early meetings, in a very positive way. Relations had become so close that by early 1965 *The Week* group had been in discussions with Perry Anderson, Robin

Blackburn, Tom Nairn and Quintin Hoare about a possible fusion of the two groupings but, even though relations remained warm, nothing ever came of this.[7] And along with Ralph Miliband and the *New Left Review* people, including Peter Sedgwick of the International Socialists, they had also launched the "Centre for Socialist Education" (CSE), whose purpose was to carry out socialist education in the trade unions, an idea that looked, at least on paper, to be a good idea at the time.

During this period, Ken Coates and Tony Topham had also begun to organize a series of conferences on the topic of workers' control. These very successful "unofficial" events occurred from time to time over several years and attracted large numbers of trade union militants to them. But the CSE went nowhere and disappeared within a few months. I attended a few of its small meetings with Miliband in attendance in London, where the discussion focused mainly around the problem of trying to get around the obstacle of the bureaucracy in the unions to reach the rank and file with socialist ideas—an intractable problem, Soon the CSE ceased meeting.

According to Alan and Connie, despite all this activity, the I.G. had only about twenty actual dues-paying members in Nottingham, a handful in Glasgow and Edinburgh and a loose association with a few political activists throughout the country. Most had been recruited by Ken and Pat, but Pat seemed to me to be the organizing backbone of the group. I don't recall the specific details of that first meeting in Nottingham, but I remember they spent quite a lot of time talking about *The Week* and future issues, and as can be seen from the foregoing, they seemed to have their fingers in a lot of pies, as the saying goes, but the top item on the agenda was their campaign to reverse Ken Coates' recent November 9th, 1965, expulsion from the Labour Party.

As Nottingham Labour Party chairperson, Ken had been able to reinvigorate the local party, getting at times over a hundred members out to its meetings, unusually large compared to when he took office. He had been in a battle with local supporters of Harold Wilson during the course of the previous year, when he had criticized local Labour Councilors for their inaction on housing. Stung by his criticism, they took organizational measures to rid themselves of him.[8] They soon kicked him out, using the pretext of his writings in "Briefing"[9] at the LP's Annual Conferences, where he had sharply criticized the Labour government's failures on the economy and immigration and Vietnam, and because of his having written for publications such as the *The Week* and the *International Socialist Journal,* the publication of the International Socialists, both of which the right-wing claimed were "Trotskyist."

At that first meeting of the I.G. which I attended, Ken was in the midst of appealing his expulsion to the National Executive Committee, but no one in the group, including Ken, thought they would be able to override the local party's decision.[10] Anticipating that his connection to *The Week* might be used against him, he had resigned as editor the previous June. The group's hopes lay in trying to get as much support from the rank and file of the Party, and indeed many constituencies sent him words of encouragement. The whole time I was in Britain, however, he remained excluded from the Party and he concentrated his efforts on developing a "workers control campaign" and working with the Bertrand Russell Peace Foundation, eventually becoming a Director.

While the bulk of the Labour Party was firmly under the control of the Wilson machine in those years, there still remained quite a few constituencies where the left retained significant influence and would often participate in municipal politics under a more radical programme than Labour and in such activities as the Campaign for Nuclear Disarmament's Easter "March to Aldermaston" or the South African Anti-Apartheid Campaign.

Because of the work of Ken Coates and Tony Topham, who had recently co-authored the book *Workers Control in Yugoslavia,* the group was out in front in Britain in developing a broad discussion in the trade unions about the issue of "workers' control" and workers' democracy. Compared to today, the trade union movement was much more powerful then, and many of the large factories had very active shop stewards' committees with radical conveners functioning on the shop floor, all of which is well documented by Alan Thornett who was active in the automobile industry in British Leyland and who describes in detail the campaign of the employers, the Labour government and the union bureaucracy to destroy their influence.[11] The discussion about workers' control was in its early stages then, but Ken and Tony were in the process of beginning a pedagogical campaign in the unions around the issue that would continue the whole time I was in Britain. They had already established very good contacts with a few of the national union leaders who seemed to be interested in moving beyond militancy to giving workers some idea of how democracy could be introduced into the workplace. A key instrument for this work was the *Voice* papers, politically centrist publications that Ken, Tony and sympathetic rank and file unionists helped to produce for this campaign.

Ray Sparrow

Chapter 2

At the Labour Party's Annual Conferences

A T THE LABOUR PARTY'S ANNUAL CONFERENCES IN 1966 AND 1967, I had the good fortune in getting a first-class, ringside seat to observe how the Nottingham group applied its version of the "entry tactic." I was amazed by it. It turned out that their courage and audacity in confronting the Wilson leadership was truly remarkable and was unlike anything we had ever attempted with the "tactic" in Canada. In Britain in those days, the trade union bureaucracy seemed more than ever to be politically integrated into the right-wing of the Party, and would, when required, exercise its muscle to support Wilson against the left which tended to have its base in the constituency parties.

It was a common phenomenon for the left to occasionally win a debate with a majority of the sitting delegates supporting them, but in the end, the unions would cast their infamous "block" vote—several million— and the party brass would simply crush them like a steamroller. But from what I could see, Ken, Pat, and the I.G. people were undaunted by this. They initiated the setting up of a broad caucus of oppositionists, comprised of supporters of *Voice of the Unions*, the monthly trade union paper published by shop-floor activists in the Midlands, the Labour Peace Fellowship, Labour C.N.D., the Bertrand Russell Peace Foundation and *New Left Review*. The objective was to try and situate the caucus so that it could optimize the left's influence by providing the delegates every day, no matter their political persuasion, with a steady and consistent stream of commentaries in a printed *"Briefing."* They published about 1,200 copies daily, of ten to sixteen pages each—really *The Week*, in a new guise—with information and commentary from a socialist perspective on the debates as they unfolded in real time on the convention floor. All of this was organized from a "campaign centre," typically a couple of rooms rented in the same hotel as the conference, equipped it with a mimeograph machine and typewriters.

I remember other leftists such as Quintin Hoare of *New Left Review* being very involved, but, if my memory serves me correctly, it was mostly the I.G. people who did the hard slogging of moving it along. It was an exhilarating experience participating in this struggle. There was little I could do in the conference since I wasn't a delegate, but I was able to pitch in to help in the production effort. Pat Jordan was pivotal to the whole operation. He seemed to be at the centre of everything and it was obvious to me he had done this many times before.

For me, it was particularly stimulating when at the end of each day's conference session, *Briefing* supporters gathered for a post-mortem of the day's activities and to discuss what the reply should be to some of the arguments advanced by the right-wing. Alan Rooney, Ken, Pat and Tony and others often worked late into the night typing their responses to the party leadership's arguments directly onto stencils and the rest of us would take turns proofing them and running them off on the Gestetner machine and stapling them together. Early in the morning we all stood outside the convention hall handing them out. I remember being especially surprised at the friendliness of most of the delegates to us as they entered the hall. Even some of the supporters of the Party leadership were eager to get their hands on what we were giving out.

It was totally unlike any experience I had ever had in Canada where the supporters of the NDP leadership would, for example, consciously avoid taking anything from us. I found the British experience totally enlightening and filed it away in my brain, in the hope I might be able to use it again when I returned to Canada. But I never had that chance. Now the Internet provides oppositionists anywhere similar opportunities, but lacking the physicality of what the I.G. was able to do. From my perspective, there was nothing much I could have added to make the

Nottingham group's intervention more effective, even though our group in Canada was also applying the "entry tactic" to the New Democratic Party and I had been around the party for a few years.

Compared to our group in Canada, Ken and Pat's group seemed more effective with their orientation, and had a lot more influence and a broader circle of contacts and friends. Usually in Canada when our group prepared for NDP conferences, in the preceding months we would try and prod some of the activists in the constituency organizations to submit resolutions, and through that we would attempt to push the party in a class struggle and socialist direction. At CCF and, later, NDP conferences, we would try to drum up support for those left resolutions which made it past the bureaucracy onto the agenda and make sure we had supporters who could speak to them. At the same time those of us who were not in the party, having been expelled for example, would sell our newspaper outside to the delegates as they were entering the hall, but we were in no way as inventive or experienced as the I.G. group.

The one major difference that we in Canada would have had with the British group was that we would have placed a higher priority on building our own organizations, the LSA and the YS, as independent organizations with their own range of political activities that placed us in a better position to appeal to radicals who were outside the NDP. In Britain, the activities of Ken and Pat's groups, before the campaign against the Vietnam war got underway, seemed to be mainly confined to the Labour Party, and despite all their success in winning support at annual conferences, they were still a very tiny organization, not commensurate with the mighty effort they were putting into their "entry" work.

The *Briefing* that was handed out every day at the Annual Labour Party Conferences was very well written, considering the hurried conditions under which it was produced. Many other left activists whom the I.G. people had been working with in the Labour party made a big effort in helping get it out. I don't remember all the issues the I.G. and its collaborators fought about, but I remember very well they had a big impact on the Party and punched considerably above their weight. I particularly recall a very memorable floor fight in support of a resolution that criticized the Wilson government's brutal attempts to break the back of the national liberation struggle in South Yemen which was then a British possession. The right-wing became almost apoplectic, their faces turning beet red when, in powerful and emotional speeches, *Briefing* supporters took the microphone to accuse them of being responsible for "burning babies with your napalm in Yemen."

What was even more remarkable about the *Briefing* effort was that it didn't cost the group a penny. In fact, to my surprise, it even made a surplus, something you don't see in the socialist movement very often. As we churned out the *Briefing* each day, I wondered to myself how we would be able to finally pay for all this. I was very surprised when on the last day of the conference, Pat handed a plastic bucket to each of us, with the word *Briefing*, clearly printed on the side in large letters and we stood outside collecting donations to help pay for the materials. Many delegates dug into their pockets and threw their loose change into the buckets while making supportive comments. We made more than enough money to cover our costs, Pat told me. That was the year the conference voted in its majority to support a resolution criticizing Wilson's Vietnam War policies, which it repeated the following year, the first time Labour Party annual conferences had come out in opposition to a sitting Labour Party government and a reflection of the mood of growing opposition throughout Britain against the war.

Portrait of Ralph Schoenman

Chapter 3

Ralph Schoenman and the Bertrand Russell Peace Foundation

C OMING FROM NORTH AMERICA WHERE THE ANTI-WAR MOVEMENT
was in its ascendancy, I personally was acutely aware of the
importance of Vietnam as a central political question for the left, and I
was anxious to know what the I.G. was doing about the issue. The F.I.
had declared that mobilizing opposition to the war should be a prime
activity for all of its sections, especially in the imperialist countries.

In my early meetings with the I.G. in Nottingham, it had been reported
that many small ad hoc anti-war committees had begun to spring up
around the country and the group itself had initiated such committees
in Nottingham and Hull. Most of its activity, however, was of a propaganda
character, focused primarily on exposing the Wilson government's
complicity in the war. IG members had worked hard to have resolutions
passed at annual Labour Party conferences on that issue and had organized
a campaign in the Party to raise medical help for Vietnam. They had,
however, yet to develop a unique position on the war that was different
from much of the "official" peace movement.

Earlier in 1965, before I had arrived, *The Week* had applauded a
protest by fifty Labour MP's calling on Wilson to take action to end the
war. It had also thrown its support behind a protest rally organized by
Fenner Brockway's Movement for Colonial Freedom that had broad
support in the Labour Party.[1] They also urged their supporters to
participate in a "Vietnam Week of Protest," organized by the CP-dominated

British Council for Peace in Vietnam—led by Lord Fenner Brockway. They were also trying to push what remained of the Campaign for Nuclear Disarmament (CND) to the left, beginning to develop a position that challenged the line of "negotiations" to settle the conflict. The group had also been active in the Labour Party backing up Bertrand Russell's campaign to force the Wilson government to grant visas to three representatives of the Vietnamese National Liberation Front (NLF) so that they could present their case to the British public, but Wilson remained totally unresponsive to these pressures.

Russell, in September, not long after a major article had appeared in the *Sunday Observer* about Ken Coates' struggle in the Labour Party, agreed in a very public way to become a sponsor of *The Week*. At the same time, a delegation from the Bertrand Russell Peace Foundation (BRPF) led by Russell's secretary, Ralph Schoenman, headed up to Nottingham to discuss cooperation in opposing the war.[2] He invited Ken to take a full-time staff position with the Foundation but Ken declined, on the advice of Ernest Mandel.[3] Ralph had been to Vietnam several times already to meet with representatives of the NLF and the North Vietnamese, and he was anxious to drum up support for a campaign of opposition to the war. Not long after this, however, Ken accepted Ralph's proposal to take a leadership position in the Foundation, becoming a Director, the beginning of a close relationship between it and the I.G.

Russell's idea, still in discussion at the time, was for some kind of high profile international body to publicize and publicly condemn American crimes in Vietnam. And over the next few months the I.G., partly because of the influence of the Foundation, began to evolve a "solidarity" position, critical of the line of "negotiations" that was then being promoted by the "official" peace movement. The I.G. was the main force on the left, alongside the Russell Foundation, calling for all those who opposed the American aggression to organize and march behind a single banner, and with distinct slogans, on the annual CND Easter March, calling for solidarity with the NLF and demanding that the Americans leave Vietnam unconditionally. Hundreds, mainly youth, marched behind the solidarity position in the 1966 Easter CND march. During the rest stops, we organized speak-outs promoting our position on the war.

Meanwhile, I had begun to experience serious personal financial difficulties. I was running out of money for day-to-day living, and I had just about exhausted my small cash reserve because of my necessary travels around the country and the travelling back and forth to Belgium for meetings. I was discovering that Ross Dowson would be less than prompt in sending the cheques promised me. Sometimes the cheque wouldn't arrive at all. I later learned from Ray Sparrow that, before I had left Toronto, the SWP and Brussels thought they had an understanding with Ross that the Canadians, in lieu of their dues to the International, would provide me with sufficient money to live and travel while I was there. All I knew was that I was supposed to receive a regular cheque from Toronto, an arrangement that I was sure I had made with Ross before I left. As far as I was concerned, there could not have been any doubts about the matter because I had committed myself to providing monthly financial support to Ruth for the raising of our son, Michael. There was no way I would have left Canada without something in place to take care of that, but by May 23rd of the following year, the matter was still being haggled over in Toronto with the Political Committee of the LSA finally agreeing to provide me "with $15.00 a week upon receipt of information concerning the role of this comrade in a full-time capacity."

One of the problems most of us faced in those years, as leaders of the organization, was that it was very difficult for those of us on staff to ask for money. It always seemed to be an issue with Ross. He set the example when it came to spending money, with his asceticism and monk-like existence. It made for a kind of moral pressure on us against asking the movement to live up to its financial commitments to us. There wasn't much money around in any case and usually the most committed gave the most, especially those of us who happened to be in leadership positions. This was the most important thing in our lives and was modeled, we believed, on Lenin's Bolshevik Party. It explains why a small organization such as ours was able to have so many people on staff. It was a common practice in the radical movement.

Many worked for nothing, living on unemployment insurance or with support from their companions. This led to people exhausting their personal resources, neglecting their health or even delaying seeing a dentist for many years at a time. In reality, it was a foolish economy, based on the notion that the revolution was not far away and would solve such mundane problems. What it really meant was that most ordinary workers who came into the movement, who had a family for example, would never be able to work full-time. It was as if, by these kind of sacrifices, we could make up for the fact that we were a small propaganda group. At one point, I was so desperate for money for Ruth and my son Michael, I was forced to make a personal appeal to Richard Fidler, a young leader of our Canadian group, for help. He kindly loaned me some of the money he had been saving for his education, close to a thousand dollars, a substantial sum at the time, to help take care of that problem.

Over the four-year period I was in London, I sent many letters to Ross asking about money. Even after Ray had raised the matter with New York and Ross would again promise to meet the Toronto commitment, he was consistently laggard in doing this. I knew that Ross, who frequently received personal financial help from his sister Lois, was very tight when it came to money. He lived on very little, and I began to believe he thought I should somehow be able to support myself from the "profits" of Pioneer Book Service. If this was true, it was an absurd notion. He should have known that the book service was a tiny operation with a very small stock of books; after the rent for office space and phone bills, there never was much surplus. The idea that it could be self-financing was only a fantasy.

Towards the end of 1965 I was running out of funds, and was steadily borrowing from the book service to get by, wondering whether or not to look for a paying job of some sort. I was reluctant to do this because, besides limiting my political activity, it would have meant officially changing my "visitor" status to permanent resident in Britain. This seemingly simple change would have placed my Canadian residency at risk, making it likely I would not be allowed back into Canada when the time came to return. Then, out of the blue, I had a stroke of luck that would eventually provide me with a way out of my financial woes.

Earlier I had been introduced to Ralph Schoenman, either through Ken Coates or Pat Jordan at a meeting about Vietnam. I remember having a brief conversation with him about the war, making clear to him that I was generally supportive of his and Russell's line. Recognizing that Russell and Schoenman's positions probably came from deep feelings of empathy for the most oppressed of the world, I found their line of building solidarity with the NLF, very appealing and consistent with what we had been doing in North America. He probably also recognized that, on the issue of Vietnam, my American comrades and I were different than many on the British left who were uniformly sectarian towards Russell and had taken very weak positions on the war and did not see any need to make special efforts to oppose it. It wasn't uncommon for Schoenman and Russell to be the object of their scorn and public criticisms. More so than the British far left or the Europeans, the Canadians, maybe because of our proximity to the centre of the American empire, could see up close the impressive role of the American SWP in fighting it. The party had been focused on the Vietnam issue since the early Sixties, and at its 1965 convention it had laid out a broad strategy of forming alliances with anyone who was prepared to resist it. An anti-war movement had already been formed in Canada when I had left for Britain. Even though it would never attain the scope or influence of the American movement, it would eventually carry out many successful rallies and marches in Toronto and Vancouver to raise opposition to the war.

In its early phase, the war was still very much below the radar screen for most of the left, with the American state maintaining the fiction that their involvement was limited to aid and advice to the South Vietnamese government, their puppet regime. Such was their stealth that many Americans did not even know the war was taking place, and the same was true in Canada. We were virtually alone in talking about the issue, and in the summer of 1963 I had led a *Workers Vanguard* tour across the country in an attempt to get the issue onto the left's agenda. One of our assignments was the organizing of meetings to talk about the war to get the message out to the broad left and the labour movement about the need for active opposition to it. Although not large—they were often organized on only a few days notice—those meetings were an example of our strong commitment to opposing the war. So when I arrived in London, I was more familiar than most with the issue and could talk about it with relative ease. At one of the meetings where Schoenman was speaking, I railed on at some length about the failure of the British left to mount an adequate response to its escalation. Not long after that, Schoenman had his secretary, Pamela Woods, phone me to come to the Russell Foundation's offices in Shavers Place in the Haymarket in London's West End for further discussion. I readily agreed.

We met fairly soon after that. I didn't know what to expect but I was anxious in any case get to know him a little bit better because by then he had become a controversial and larger than life figure on the British left. After the pleasantries were over—in Britain, that means asking the visitor if they would like a cup of tea—he immediately moved on to talking about what could be done to develop resistance to the war. He spent some time questioning me about the anti-war movement in Canada and I think he was a little surprised that I had been around the radical movement as long as I had. At age 31, I was only a year older than him. I remember he talked to me about the Foundation's plans at some length and we quickly had a meeting of the minds about the war—though it was mainly me listening to him. He was clearly contemptuous of the positions of the official peace movement, the CND, but it soon became clear to me he didn't hold the British left in very high regard either and was prepared to push ahead with the Foundation's projects, no matter what. He was literally bubbling over with ideas about how to oppose the war, some of them half-formed, but most of them well thought out.

It wasn't a very in-depth discussion, but I told him that as far as I was concerned, our group, the I.G., was prepared to give the Foundation all the help we could—something he was aware of already—but with the understanding we had only a few people in London. The same was true of the Foundation, which had only him and two other people—Chris Farley and Pamela

Woods—on staff, all of them working flat out helping Russell with his various campaigns. After that conversation, our group helped the Foundation organize many of his public meetings and press conferences, especially whenever he returned from his trips to Vietnam. We were the only group on the left in Britain giving the Foundation this kind of assistance and over the next few months we became politically close.

My immediate impression of Ralph Schoenman was that he was a very bright man who could have been successful in any field of endeavour he chose to enter, an appreciation that only increased over the two or three years I worked with him. I especially remember his well developed sense of humour—something he has never lost—with his ample supply of puns. He also made effective use of anecdotes from Russell—"Bertie", as he was known to those around him—to underline a point, interjecting them into conversation. He had a brilliant talent for mimicry, and people around the Foundation later told me he was not averse to cleverly imitating my then quite strong Belfast accent.

There were many who claimed Russell was but a figurehead for Ralph, but in my limited contact with the Foundation I saw no evidence of this. It's true that many of his letters and statements were prepared for Russell's signature by his London staff, but they always, from what I could see, went up to Wales first for Russell's signature before being sent out. And Russell's more substantial statements would be dictated in Wales and sent to London where Pamela Woods would usually type them.

Russell, because of his record of anti-colonialism, had won immense respect and appreciation in the Third World, much more than in Britain where the British establishment reviled him. Schoenman had travelled to Vietnam several times on Russell's behalf, to discuss ways of developing opposition to the war in Britain. Later, in 1966, he and Russell Stetler, a young anti-war American whom the Foundation had put on staff, had personally met with President Ho Chi Minh and Prime Minister Pham Van Dong to discuss the possibility of an international campaign to expose American crimes against Vietnam and to get their cooperation in the setting up of some kind of a war crimes tribunal.[5] He had also met with many other third world leaders to seek their support for such an endeavour. This included Kwame Nkrumah of Ghana—whom he spent a lot of time with—and Zukfliker Ali Bhutto, then Foreign Minister, and later president and prime minister of Pakistan, who would later be executed. The issue of the war seemed to just about consume very being in those years, and in opposing it, he gave every appearance of having unlimited energy. He was able to get by on very little sleep. Trying to keep up with him was a truly exhausting proposition.

The Foundation always seemed to be in a permanent state of fund-raising. Money was always scarce. To help it out one time, I found myself in the weird position of meeting with the personal secretary of Queen Elisabeth of the Belgians, the so-called "Red Queen." It was October 1965, when Ralph persuaded me that the next time I was in Brussels—I was there at least once a month for Secretariat meetings—to go and meet her.

The "Red Queen" had been assigned that characterization by the popular press because of her support for a variety of progressive causes and her travels at the height of the Cold War to the USSR, China and Poland, in open defiance to her own government and, of course, the Americans. Since day one, she had been a prominent sponsor of the Foundation and Ralph felt it important to get a report to her about what the Foundation was doing regarding Vietnam. The hope of course, was that maybe they could get some money from her.

His request to me had come out of the blue. It didn't bother me too much of course. In Canada, an important part of our political life was contacting people outside of our ranks for money to help the cause. I told him that while I was prepared to assist in any way I could, I was surprised he would give me such a task because I never had contact with such circles in my life before. His reply was very succinct: there's no one else to do it. These are words that I have often found have led me to do things I wouldn't normally think of doing. So, despite my hesitations, I accepted the assignment.

When I got to Brussels I called the number he had furnished me, and when I identified myself to someone at the other end of the line as coming from the Russell Foundation, I received a very warm greeting from a man who spoke with a cultured English accent. He obviously had been expecting me, and he suggested I should come over to dine with him right away. I was provided with the address. It was a very large home, I remember, a mansion, with the front of the house, like a lot of buildings in Brussels, rising from close to the edge of the street pavement. It was not a castle by any stretch of the imagination. No fence or gate, no moat. I rang the bell on the large imposing front door and was let in by a servant.

I was welcomed into the hallway by the person to whom I had spoken, the Queen's secretary, whose name, after all these years, I have forgotten. He was a tall thin man who appeared to be in his early sixties. He was very courteous and friendly and he soon put me at my ease. I was hopeful that we might get a financial contribution towards the Foundation's work, but I think he figured out very quickly that I was just a grunt carrying out an assignment. In any case he was very gracious towards me. We chatted for a while about the war. After a few minutes, it was like talking to another leftist.

It was a very odd feeling for me: sitting there in that large mansion talking about radical politics to a representative of the Belgian royal family—a monarchy which my comrades were demanding should be abolished on the way of setting up a workers' republic. I couldn't imagine such a meeting ever taking place in Canada, or London!

The secretary eventually invited me into the dining room. It was a long, large room, with a table running down the middle, similar to what one sees in movies of dining scenes in large mansions, and very cold. Can't they afford heating, I remember wondering. My feet were like lumps of ice as we sat at the table chatting, with him at the end of the table, and me to the side. The room was empty, except for the servant dressed in black with a white apron, who placed the dishes in front of us: a simple meal of salt cod with a glass of white wine.

As we ate, I got around to talking about our efforts to raise financial support, describing the many projects the Foundation was undertaking. That's when he gently brought the conversation to an end, saying the

Queen was "reviewing the moneys she was presently giving out to various causes" and that she would be in touch with Russell and that she was fully in support of the Foundation's activities. As I said good bye, I had the distinct feeling we wouldn't be getting much. Ralph never told me if anything ever came of it and, a few months later, I read the Queen's obituary in the papers.

Not long after that, Ralph asked me if I could help the Foundation out with another matter, again concerning fundraising. This time, he offered to pay me to do it. Despite the offer of pay, I was a little bit apprehensive this time because of the failure of my previous efforts in this regard. He mentioned that Russell had, a few months earlier, issued a public appeal for money, targeted mainly at the international artistic community, appealing to major artists who were sympathetic to Russell's activities to donate some of their work to the Foundation. This would then be sold to raise money. Many artists had responded and some of their work was now in the Foundation's offices, he said. Picasso and Miro had donated work, but these had been sold already. He was still in the middle of having a London gallery sell the remainder, but it was taking longer than he had expected to turn it into cash.

Regarding Picasso, David Horowitz once told me an apocryphal story about Ralph in connection to the famous artist—a precursor typical of the many stories Horowitz has told over the decades, usually concocted to serve his now right-wing political animus. Horowitz repeats the story he told me in his memoir, but now inserts Richard Burton and Elizabeth Taylor into the story for good measure. As Horowitz tells it, Picasso, for some reason or other, delayed meeting his commitment to Russell, and so Ralph journeyed to the famous artist's home in France where he "lay down in Picasso's driveway for three hours until the item was produced. Subsequently, he waylaid Richard Burton and Elizabeth Taylor, jumping out of an elevator in a hotel in Scotland to demand their performance on a similar promise."[6]

Caroline Moorehead, in her biography of Russell, repeats the same tale.[7] According to Ralph, none of it happened. "The Picasso story is invented," he recently told me from his home in San Francisco. "I never met Picasso and have never been to his house—let alone lie down in his driveway for three hours. As if Picasso's entourage wouldn't have the cops there in 2 minutes in such circumstances.

"I had a very good relationship with his gallery in Paris and Russell and I had corresponded with Picasso. I did visit Marc Chagall and Joan Miro. Miro later sent us a painting. Chagall promised but didn't follow through.

"As to Richard Burton and Elizabeth Taylor, I had a meeting with them in their penthouses in Dublin—not our first. The elevator to their apartment could only be entered with hotel authority from the floor below the penthouse.

"What was the similar promise? Had Burton and Taylor decided to change careers, take night classes in painting and donate a sketch?"[8]

Ralph's new proposal to me came around the time the Foundation was waiting for the works of art to come in for its fundraising efforts and he wanted to know if I could help him with another, different offer Russell had received. He told me that a West End theatrical producer had turned Alan Sillitoe's novel, *Saturday Night and Sunday Morning*, into a stage musical and it was scheduled to open on January 29th, a Saturday evening, in the Prince of Wales theatre in the Haymarket. The producer had offered to turn the opening performance into a benefit event with the proceeds going to the BRPF, an arrangement that may have been facilitated by Sillitoe, a socialist, who was friendly with Ken Coates and who had just become a very public sponsor of *The Week* at the time of Ken's expulsion from the Nottingham Labour Party.[9]

But there were a couple of strings attached to the theatre deal, Ralph informed me. The Foundation had to first produce the publicity materials for the musical—the poster—and help with the sale of its tickets. Ralph said he had committed Russell to the proposal and was now in the difficult position of not having anyone around to see the project through. He wanted to know if I could help him out and work with an artist who had volunteered her time to design the poster and to see it through to the printer. He said if I couldn't take on the project, he would be compelled to phone the producer and turn the proposal down, something he was extremely reluctant to do because it might alienate him as a future source of support. Again, I was very surprised at Ralph's request. I had only been in London a few months, and I was still trying to find my way around its streets. Even though I was badly in need of the money, I was nervous about taking on this new unexpected task, but he overcame my timidity with promises of help. "There'll always be someone around here to help you," he promised. Against my better judgment, I reluctantly agreed. I met the artist very soon thereafter. She was a professional freelance illustrator, a socially-conscious women, it turned out, typical of many young people at that time who had been inspired by Russell's work and who wanted to help the Foundation. Her studio was in Soho, a short distance from the Foundation's office. Within a few days she came up with a very good design for the poster that everyone at the Foundation approved, so we quickly had several hundred printed.

I ran around London trying to get the ticket agencies to take the tickets and worked hard to have the poster displayed in the windows of local shops, but it was hard going. I was an outsider and a total amateur trying to find my way around a strange city, and Ralph never seemed to be around when I needed his help. I felt totally out of my depth. I was also shocked at the open expressions of racism I saw everywhere in the small shops where we were trying to have our posters displayed. Compared to North America, where the civil rights movement had forced much public expression of racism underground, in London's West End it still seemed to be rampant and on full public display. In the windows of tobacconist shops, for example, it was common to see small, neatly hand-printed cards with notices for apartment rentals on them, stating: "No blacks or foreigners." It was all very legal, and defended at the time under British free speech laws.

The Foundation's people, Chris Farley and Pamela Woods, Ralph's secretary, seemed to think of promotion of the musical as "Ralph's project" and, tied up with their own work, were not of much use to me. It was cold and raining very heavily the night the musical opened on January 29th to a more than half empty Prince of Wales theatre; we had given away many free tickets and a few of us from the Foundation were present. I don't recollect much about it, but I do remember I didn't like it very much and found it boring, and I had the impression I was watching a dress rehearsal rather than a finished production. It was a poor reflection of Alan Sillitoe's great novel, I thought, and not very musical into the bargain. It closed within a few days, one of the shortest runs for a theatrical production in the West End that year and the Foundation got very little out of it. Even though it had put some money in my pocket, I was a little depressed by this experience and hated the sour taste of failure in my mouth.

All the running around the West End—often in the rain, badgering store owners to put up a poster and trying to get the tickets distributed—had been for nothing. But when I talked about it to Ralph a few days later I was surprised he didn't seem to mind too much. He said that was the nature of fundraising, sometimes there was a risk a project would not work out but he had a responsibility to take the offers of financial support from Russell's supporters seriously, especially if the Foundation was going to go back to them for more.

Another time I received a call from Ralph's secretary, Pam, to come over to the office to talk about another proposal he wished to put to me. After the lack of success of the previous two efforts, I wondered to myself what it could be this time and again it turned out to be one of those lucky coincidences that provided a partial solution to my need for income. Ralph wanted to know if I could help the Foundation out "of a bit of difficulty" that had been growing over the previous months. Specifically, because of the amount of publicity the Foundation had been receiving—and in response to its stand on Vietnam—there had been an upsurge in requests to send speakers all over the country to public meetings and to participate in the debates at university and college socialist societies, of which there were many in Britain.

The requests were piling high on his desk, Ralph complained. I think he may have been having difficulty getting his Directors to cover these meetings—he said as much to me—as sometimes there would be low attendance at them and they were often at the other end of the country, requiring the Directors to be away from London too long. In most cases, he told me, the Socialist Societies received some funding for this kind of activity, either from their administration's budget or from their college or their student unions, sufficient to allow them to pay the expenses and a modest honorarium—I can't remember how much—to cover a visiting speaker's travel, cost of food and accommodation. Ralph stated that if I took on the responsibility for handling these requests as they came in and to clear up the backlog, I could keep whatever monies came my way. They were usually paid to the speaker at the time of the meeting. He also assured me I could have the full-time use of one of the Foundation's automobiles, an Austin Mini that he was thinking of getting rid off in any case. I readily accepted and I don't know who was more grateful, him for now getting the problem off his desk or me for finding relief from my dire financial problem.

I didn't realize it at the time, but it would also become a godsend to me politically. It provided me with an incredible opportunity to work directly on building resistance to the Vietnam War while making contact with the budding anti-war movement throughout the country. As a result, wherever our Nottingham people had contacts with a student Socialist Society on a campus, they would encourage them to organize a meeting for the BRPF. It was a critical time. This wasn't that long before the radical upsurge in the universities when opposition to the war virtually exploded onto the scene. A few times a month, I was on the road meeting with anti-war groups and various leftists, and talking to many students—mostly young activists engaged in campaigning against the war—many of whom would later become prominent in the Vietnam Solidarity Campaign.

I was also at the same time receiving a fast education about the far left in Britain, meeting with the leaders of what seemed like a multitude of small groups all over the country who considered themselves Trotskyists and who had had, at some point in time, a relationship to the Fourth International. I also took the opportunity whenever I could to meet a few remnants of splinter groups that had come out of Gerry Healy's SLL. I managed to learn a lot about the SLL this way, but quite often I found that these grouplets would be loosely organized around some strong individual, very often a factory worker who more often than not was consistently and strongly dogmatic. At times, it felt like I was visiting a museum of "artifacts" from the recent history of the far left. None of these groups, it should be noted, played any role whatsoever in the subsequent anti-war movement which would quickly expand in the next couple of years. I hadn't planned it this way and it was by no means a lucrative living, but it dovetailed nicely with my main assignment of helping to build a viable Fourth International group and focusing our work in developing opposition to the war. It was a totally satisfying kind of activity for someone like me who considered himself a revolutionary. It was as if all my experiences in Canada since I had become a revolutionary socialist had prepared me for it.

I was not always alone at these university and college meetings representing the Foundation and I'm sure there were other meetings where Foundation people spoke in those early days. Sometimes Ralph or other Directors of the Foundation would come along with me, especially if there was a debate scheduled which required two from our side. That's how I first made my acquaintance with David Horowitz, today a prominent conservative ideologue in the U.S. In those days he considered himself to be a Marxist and a revolutionary socialist and sometimes he would write for *The Week* about foreign policy issues and about Vietnam.

On one occasion he and I represented the anti-war side of a debate before several hundred students at the Oxford Union. I especially remember how Horowitz was much better than me in competently explaining that the war was an act of imperialist aggression and a continuation of the American ruling class' history of hostility to the Russian Revolution of 1917, the major theme of a book he was working on and which the Russell Foundation was helping him get published.[10] He had few reservations in the debate, fully backing the NLF against the Americans and their puppets, with a mastery of the facts much superior to many in Britain at the time. A very able debater, he was extremely passionate about the issue and scathing in his criticism of Wilson's support for the Americans.

I remember that a few American students in the audience were outraged by his comments and took issue with his position, challenging his "patriotism," but he seemed unfazed by their criticism. Having witnessed those debates, I would never have predicted he would end up with the politics he has today, a spokesman for the hard right in America.

Horowitz had been part of the "new left" in Berkeley, California, in the early Sixties, a "red-diaper baby," as we called those who had mainly inherited their politics from their Communist Party parents. He had been an editor of one of the first "new left" journals in the United States, *Root and Branch*. Active in the early student protests against the Vietnam War and in the early opposition on the campuses against the anti-communist House Un-American Activities Committee, he had first come to prominence in radical circles with his book about student activism, a paperback about those demonstrations.[11] He moved with his family to Sweden to teach and to work on his history of the Cold War, the first to come from someone in the "new left" and who would rigorously challenge the anti-communist basis of American foreign policy. When he arrived in London in 1964 from Sweden where he had been working on his first major book,[12] Schoenman had appointed him to the Board of Directors of the Foundation and he had set up under the auspices of the Foundation, the Bertrand Russell Centre for Social Research to study imperialism. With the Foundation's help, he was able to devote most of his time to writing. He was extremely prolific.

I remember he let me see some of the early drafts of a few chapters of a new book he was trying to get finished, *Empire and Revolution*. To say the least, I was very impressed. He was also working on another book, a series of essays by Isaac Deutscher, William Appleman Williams and others that the Foundation was a helping to get published.[13] These books, although not based upon primary research, would help establish him in those years as a bright, new, young American "revisionist," foreign policy historian. To me, he was an example of the new generation of radicals who were finding their own way to Marxism, free of the morally corrupting influences of Stalinism, but also rejecting social democracy.

Horowitz had two small children and he told me his parents had helped him and his wife, Elissa, buy a flat in Highgate. Another baby, Benjamin, was on the way at the time. Jess and I visited them a several times in London. He and Elissa lived very modestly. They were so short of money they were barely able to afford a babysitter and seldom went out. To make ends meet, he was teaching at a military educational facility in London and was helping other writers get their manuscripts into shape, hopefully for publication. I'm pretty sure we were the first Trotskyists he had taken seriously and he was fully aware I was active in building the Fourth International in London. He visited me at Pioneer Books occasionally and bought many books and pamphlets about the early Soviet period. He borrowed a few books from me personally, which he would always return something I can't say for many others over the years to whom I have lent books.

I got along quite well with Horowitz and he always seemed pleased to chat whenever we bumped into each other at the Foundation's offices, but he gave me the impression that he was continually re-examining his commitment to Marxism and wondering if that was what he wanted to do with his life. I remember how he was thrown into intense emotional and political turmoil—like so many on the left, such as Jean-Paul Sartre and the grouping around his magazine, *Les Temps Modernes*—during the "eight day war" when Israel vastly expanded its territory at the expense of its Arab neighbours. As Horowitz pointed out to me then, Israel, had greatly increased its size as a result of the war, but he had reservations about publicly criticizing it.

He told me that even though he found Marxism very appealing, he was also interested in the philosophical writings of Martin Buber, who was not a Marxist. He was reading Marx's *Capital* and at one point dipped into economic theory, engaging Ernest Mandel in debate, until Isaac Deutscher, for whom David had enormous respect, told him that while he, Horowitz, had quickly learned a lot about Marxist politics, ". . . you still have to do a lot of homework before you can speak with any authority on Marxist economic theory."[14] He and I had many discussions about the policies of the Soviet state in the early twenties. I remember him arguing with me about "determinism" and Marxism and whether the belief that some Marxists had that socialism was inevitable obscured the relationship between subjectivity and revolutionary strategy, especially in relation to the outlook of Lenin and the Bolsheviks.

He had a great admiration for Sartre and was wrestling with trying to reconcile Marxism and Sartre's existentialism as expressed in Sartre's book, *Being and Nothingness*. After one heavy discussion, I remember loaning him George Novack's book, *Marxism and Existentialism*.[15] But I was truly out of my depth and I felt I wasn't very well equipped to argue with him, not having taken "existentialism" too seriously and having only read a few of Sartre's novels and de Beauvoir's, *The Mandarins*. It was a friendly back and forth over several weeks and I didn't make much headway. I don't think he was very impressed with Novack. He also loaned me a book he had brought out the previous year, a small volume on Shakespeare,[16] a quest to find existentialism in the great dramatist's work. Compared to Horowitz's work about American imperialism, the writing in that book is very convoluted, dense, and deeply abstract; I had a hard time getting through it. Others may have had the same problem: it didn't sell many copies, not his most successful work and a far cry from his later excellent studies of the Kennedy and Rockerfeller families. I have always thought it unfortunate that the American left was unable to hold on to him.

Chapter 4

Vietnam:

"an international war crime"

B Y 1966, OPPOSITION IN THE UNITED STATES TO THE VIETNAM WAR was rising in tandem with its escalation. The previous year, on May 2nd,1965, there had been larger than usual demonstrations against the war in New York and in San Francisco, and a mobilization in Washington in December brought out 25,000 people. On April 17, anti-war organizers had expected about 2,000 to turn out in Washington but were extremely surprised when over 25,000 showed up. In May, in New York City, over 200,000 students participated in strikes against the war and a hugely successful teach-in took place in Washington to debate government policy. A new movement involving tens of thousands of students swept the campuses, provoked mainly by the removal of draft deferments for college students, preparing the ground for what would become the most powerful anti-war movement in American history, with opposition to the war even penetrating the ranks of the army.

President Lyndon Johnson, ignoring the increasing opposition, cynically invented a pretext to expand the war, a blatant fabrication, much like a later George W. Bush and Tony Blair's false claims of "weapons of mass destruction" in Iraq to justify their invasion. Johnson claimed U.S. naval vessels had been the subject of an "unprovoked attack" by North Vietnamese torpedo boats in the Gulf of Tonkin. He asked for and received a blank cheque from Congress to widen the war and to launch a bombing campaign against North Vietnam, Laos and Cambodia, which would see an average of 800 tons of high explosives dropped daily on those countries over the following three years. The bombing was more intense than that of the Allies against Germany in the Second World War or of the United States against Korea in 1952. In October of the previous year, Johnson dramatically increased the number of troops in Vietnam from 120,000 to 400,000.

From the very beginning, the SWP was in the forefront of organizing to resist the war, around the demand, "Out Now!" In just about every major community, Vietnam protest committees were springing up like dandelions in the spring rain and the newly organized National Vietnam Day Committee, with representation on most campuses, issued a call for the first International Days of Protest for October 15 -16. While not on the same scale as in the U.S., in Canada we were doing the same, especially in Toronto and Vancouver.

The war was the central foreign policy issue in Britain then, even though—for the peace movement, especially the CND, the Labour Party left, the far left and many of the so-called "Trotskyist" groups—there was great confusion about it. Vietnam was very much on the back burner for many of the left groups and it was quite common for them to use the pejorative expression "Vietcong" to describe the NLF. The Fourth International's supporters in Britain held fast to the position of defending Vietnam's right to self-determination, which meant that all the American troops should leave immediately.

The Americans had no right to be there at all, we argued. We pointed out that when a mighty imperialist power such as the U.S. is engaged in the military occupation of a small third-world country the first duty is to declare solidarity with the victims and give support to their resistance. The main challenges to this position usually however, came from those forces in the peace movement whose views, in one form or other, reflected those of the CP. It was undoubtedly the dominant view on the left in those early days, and a possible carryover from the influence of the CND's "neutralism" from the early part of the decade. Even a passionate supporter of the Vietnamese such as Bertrand Russell, before he had swung to the left and adopted the "solidarity with the NLF" position, had welcomed the victory of the "peace candidate" Lyndon Johnson, when he won a landslide victory over Goldwater in the 1964 U.S. elections. In a letter to the President-elect, Russell claimed that the majority of the inhabitants of South Vietnam wished to be neutral in the Cold War.[1]

What the British CP and many left social democrats—and the broad milieu under their influence in the peace movement—were demanding as a solution to ending the war appeared at first glance to be deceptively simple: "we only want what the Vietnamese want." As a CP supporter put in a letter to *The Week*, "The NLF is quite willing to negotiate—provided the U.S. abides by the terms of the Geneva Agreements—and the CP fully endorses this demand."[2] We countered by asking, "that's the NLF position, but should it be ours?"

The 1954 Geneva Accords had been a compromise forced on the Vietnamese under pressure from their allies, China and the Soviet Union, at the same time as U.S. leading circles were discussing a nuclear attack against them, getting them to agree to a cessation of hostilities and with political representation to be decided by an "internationally supervised election" two years later. During those two years American imperialism managed to take the place of French colonialism and the elections were never held. Many in the "official" peace movement also backed the idea of "internationally supervised elections" to decide the fate of South Vietnam, but we challenged this position too, arguing that such a measure violated Vietnam's right to self-determination. By what right should the imperialist countries have this power, we asked? Would we put up with that in Britain in similar circumstances?

The willingness of the Labour government to provide diplomatic and rhetorical support to the Americans while hypocritically giving the appearance of being "neutral," saying that Britain would use its "good offices" to bring both sides together, enraged many, especially the youth. Opponents of the war began to step up their attacks on this hypocrisy, explaining that, when he was in opposition in 1954, Wilson had spoken out against American involvement in Vietnam in clear terms: "(Not) a man, not a gun, must be sent from this country to defend French colonization in Indo-China . . . we must not join or in any way encourage an anti-Communist crusade in Asia under the leadership of the Americans or anyone else." As was revealed later, Wilson's arrangement with the Americans when he formed the government was based upon a cynical cold cash deal: British international political support for the war, no matter what Wilson had said before, in return for American support—a three billion sterling rescue package—for the British pound, then under speculative pressure in the international currency markets, plus a loan of 400 million pounds.[3]

The best known peace movement in Britain in those days was the CND, and though in decline, its main activity every year was the organizing of the Aldermaston Marches at Easter. Even though CND called Wilson a hypocrite for supporting the Americans, its appeal for a "negotiated settlement" nevertheless essentially placed the Vietnamese and the occupying Americans on the same moral plane and at no time did CND call on its members to come out onto the streets about the issue. The International Group—and many others on the left, especially Bertrand Russell—argued that the CND position on Vietnam was in principle not much different from that of the Wilson government's call for "supervised elections" and a "negotiated" settlement to the conflict. And, especially now that Johnson had declared his support for "negotiations" as he was intensifying the war, it was no longer an effective position from which to resist it. The anti-war movement was slow in getting off the ground in Britain. This was somewhat understandable, because there was less at stake for the British people in the conflict. There had been an anti-Vietnam war demonstration in London as early as 1963. In May 1965, one of the first took place outside the U.S. Embassy, but these early protests were small and mainly made up of expatriate Americans, of whom there were many in London. The Communist Party also—through its various "front" groups such as the British Council for Peace in Vietnam (BCPV)—campaigned for a "diplomatic" solution along the lines of a "negotiated" settlement, but it had remained relatively ineffective even though it was the main left organization in the country addressing the issue. Soon the rising tide of opposition would sweep the BCPV aside.

A lot of those who opposed the war still placed their hopes on the Wilson government changing its policies, but the admission by the U.S. government in March 1965, that they were using napalm and CS gas in South and North Vietnam gave a big boost to those who were challenging Labour government policy. Sixty back-bench MPs, known as "The Tribune Group," named after their weekly left social democratic journal, *The Tribune*, had tabled an emergency motion in Parliament critical of the government. In the *London Times*, furthermore, numerous letters were published, signed by Labour MPs, demanding that Wilson do more to end the war and the Labour Party headquarters was flooded with resolutions from constituency parties criticizing the government.

In the summer of 1965, when Wilson denied visas to three NLF spokesmen who had been invited to visit Britain by Bertrand Russell, the BRPF launched a campaign to try and force him to change his position, organizing several hundred protestors to lobby Labour MPs at the House of Commons. And, in a sign of things to come, small Vietnam protest committees began springing up all over the country, usually led by socialist activists and often in communities where there were large concentrations of South Asians who were sometimes under Maoist influence. The international appeals coming from the American anti-war movement for "Days of Action" on Vietnam would eventually provide an inspiration for the left in Britain to organize solidarity actions on those dates. But it still took some time to build up the numbers involved in these protests. One of the first solidarity actions in London was held in October 1965, organized in response to an international appeal, drew only a couple of hundred people. Our group helped organize it and that was the best we could do at the time.

A factor reducing the turn out was the dreadful news we were getting from Indonesia. Over a million members and supporters of the Indonesian Communist Party and ethnic Chinese were being slaughtered in a systematic campaign that was revealed later to have been organized by the CIA in conjunction with the American diplomatic corps which provided many names of Communist Party members to the Indonesian military.

The Indonesian events led to some very large meetings in London, which tended to push the issue of Vietnam into the background. The early actions protesting the war were not very significant, with the most successful having around a thousand participants. Most of them were organized by London supporters of *The Week*, other socialists, and the Russell Foundation, along with a few South Asian groups. We usually pulled things off on short notice, and did not get much coverage in the papers. They were my first experience with protest actions in Britain and I remember I was quite shocked—maybe I was naïve—at the attitude of the cops to us compared to in Canada, especially when perchance only a few hundred protestors showed up.

Having heard a lot about the British cops being "different" from American or Canadian cops—"they didn't carry firearms" and were more "respectful" of protestor's rights—I was quickly disabused of any illusions on that score. One evening, on one of the first demonstrations we helped to organize, I was startled by the cops' stealth-like brutality once they were out of the public eye; it was worse than anything I had ever experienced in Canada. If a demonstrator stepped out of line for a moment or spoke back to a cop, they could easily receive a swift blow to the kidneys from a small truncheon, a sack-like tube filled with lead pellets which the cops kept concealed in their jacket pockets for this purpose. The memory of this viciousness against us by the police, I'm sure, played an important part in how protestors behaved when the police tried to push us around in later demonstrations in Grosvenor Square when they attempted to keep protestors away from the front of the U.S. Embassy.

In those years, Bertrand Russell, the 1950 Nobel Prize winner, was probably the most important and singular voice in the entire country challenging Wilson on the issue of Britain's complicity in the war. Politically heads and shoulders above much of the left, he stood out like a bright beacon telling the appalling truth about what the American aggression was doing to the Vietnamese people. Russell spread the anti-war message through speeches, and press release after press release issued by his Foundation, plus numerous letters to the editors of the national press. Early on, before the war had become a major foreign policy issue, in a letter to the editor of the *New York Times* in 1963, he had accused the American government of conducting a war of annihilation.

Not only was Russell scathing in his denunciations of American and British government policy, he also turned his fire on Moscow, accusing the Russians of providing insufficient aid to the Vietnamese, their so-called "comrades." Russell explained the Russians were giving better and more sophisticated military assistance to the government of Egypt—a third world country, but one still within the orbit of imperialism. When the Americans attacked North Vietnam in February 1965, Russell had appealed to the Russians, without any success, to provide North Vietnam with more up-to-date military equipment or even an air force capable of defending itself. Already in his nineties, Russell's prolific work was made possible with the assistance of his very able and energetic secretary, Ralph Schoenman, whom I've already mentioned.

An American, a graduate in philosophy from the Ivy League's Princeton University, Schoenman had fought hard against McCarthyism. After a two year legal battle, he was finally able to obtain a passport to leave for Britain in 1958 where he obtained an M.A. degree in economics at the London School of Economics. Very much inspired by the black civil rights movement and the lunch counter sit-ins in the American South, he sought to apply the same tactics to the anti-nuclear movement in Britain that had been launched in 1958 when the Campaign for Nuclear Disarmament (CND), headed up by Russell, organized thousands to march at Easter from London to the Atomic Weapons Research Establishment at Aldermaston, fifty miles away. Schoenman had been a key player in the setting up of the more militant Direct Action Committee against Nuclear War (DAC) to carry out civil disobedience in pursuit of banning nuclear weapons.[4] Increasingly annoyed at how tame and ritualized the annual Easter marches had become, and increasingly critical of CND's "multilateralist" positions, Russell parted company with the CND, teaming up with Schoenman to create a committee of "one hundred significant names" to carry out civil disobedience in public spaces.

In 1961 the "Committee of 100" caused a sensation in Britain and internationally by carrying out a series of non-violent sit-down protest actions, the largest ever seen in London. Thousands participated in sit-downs outside the Ministry of Defense and in Trafalgar Square, with many hundreds arrested. This was followed by a massive effort by the British state to suppress the movement under the Secrets Act. Six leaders of the movement received lengthy jail sentences. Lord and Lady Russell, along with Schoenman and thirty-three members of the Committee, were arrested for refusing to be bound over with regard to future actions. The Russells and Schoenman received two-month jail sentences. The Russells got out on probation, Schoenman went to jail. He became one of Russell's closest collaborators, eventually becoming his secretary and main spokesperson.

Since those years and especially with the rise of the colonial revolution, Russell had more and more turned his attention to the American aggression against Vietnam. He and Schoenman committed themselves to organizing as much political support as possible for the Vietnamese resistance, and in any way they could. Russell, with Schoenman's help, had set up the Bertrand Russell Peace Foundation in 1963. Its genesis was the Cuban Missile Crisis the previous October, at a time when the world appeared to be on the verge of nuclear annihilation. Russell thrust himself onto the international stage by publicly engaging Khrushchev in an exchange of letters, providing a means by which the USSR could explain to the world its position on the crisis without it being distorted by the Western media.[5] Even though Kennedy rejected the idea out of hand, it is generally recognized by many students of that crisis that the Russell-Khrushchev correspondence was a factor in helping to de-escalate it.

Russell had also attempted to mediate a settlement in the conflict between India and China, where there was a military buildup on their common border and India was challenging the McMahon line, the boundary line between the two countries that had been established by Britain when India was a colonial possession. Ralph and another Russell secretary had travelled to China on his behalf to convey Russell's thoughts on the issue to Chou En-Lai, and had travelled to India to speak to that government about the dispute. Russell's proposals for settling the conflict were rejected.

Russell also took up the issue of political prisoners who were suffering under repressive regimes around the world, putting resources, for example, into getting political prisoners released from prison in Romania. And, on January 4th, 1964, after East Germany jailed a political dissident, Heinz Brandt, and, despite worldwide protests, refused to release him, Russell returned the "Peace Medal" which the East German government had earlier awarded him.[6]

Because of Russell's great prestige—which had grown enormously as a result of his public interventions during the Cuban missile crisis—the Foundation had been set up with wide public fanfare. It was a logical extension of his campaign against the madness of nuclear weapons and his view that "neutralism provides one of the most promising means for resolving international tensions . . ." as a brochure the Foundation published at the time stated. The Foundation attracted sponsors mainly from the "small-l" liberal left, including a few heads of state from the Third World and such public figures as the Duke of Bedford in Britain, Lloyd Boyd Orr, Danilo Dolci, Indian Prime Minister Jawaharlal Nehru, Vanessa Redgrave, Dr. Albert Schweitzer, Queen Elisabeth of the Belgians, Dr. Max Born (the Nobel Prize winner for physics), Pablo Casals, President Kenneth Kaunda of Zambia, President Ayub Khan of Pakistan, President Julius Nyerere of Tanzania, Linus Pauling, Emperor Haile Selassi of Ethopia and Norodom Sihanouk of Cambodia.

Amazingly, even U. Thant, Secretary General of the United Nations, welcomed its birth with a public declaration. "While there may be differences of view about the wisdom of nuclear disarmament, and other similar ideas, I share the feeling of Lord Russell that the unrestricted manufacture, testing, perfecting, and stock-piling of nuclear armaments represent one of the greatest dangers to humanity, and one of the most serious threats to the survival of the human race."[7]

Russell was once recognized by *The Times* of London as the "most celebrated English intellectual of the 20th century," although, during all the time I was in London, this hardly seemed to be the case because much of the British press was extremely hostile to him due to his unrelenting criticism of the Americans in Vietnam. He was regularly denigrated by the yellow press. A few groups on the left, especially the far left, would often join in, holding him up to ridicule. A contemporary of Maynard Keynes, the famous British economist, Russell was well known for having had Ludwig Wittgenstein, the philosopher, as one of his students in the twenties. He was popularly known as "England's greatest living philosopher" and had publicly declared himself a pacifist in the First World War. Over the course of his life his positions on war and non-violence had taken on an odd trajectory. He supported the Americans' nuclear bombing of Nagasaki and Hiroshima in 1945, for example, and had called for war against the Soviet Union, but by 1965 he had discarded his position of "neutralism" and had become a resolute anti-imperialist, sitting on the editorial board of *The Week* and militantly backing the Vietnamese National Liberation Front.

It wouldn't be long before a few of the Foundation's prominent sponsors—such as Julius Nyerere, Kenneth Kuanda and Haile Selassie—would take their distance from it, with Kuanda making a public statement demanding that his name be removed from the Foundation's letterhead.[8] Russell was vehement in his opposition to national oppression, no matter where it was taking place. He would later support the resistance of the Czechoslovakians to the Russian occupation and initiate, along with Jean-Paul Sartre and other leading intellectuals, the setting up in Stockholm of a tribunal to investigate the Soviet Union's actions in that aggression.

Before I arrived in Britain, like most of the left I was very much aware of Russell's great reputation, and knew about the courageous activities of the Committee of 100 and the role he had played in the Cuban Missile Crisis, and I also was also very much aware that he was an important figure in philosophy. I had read his very popular work, *History of Western Philosophy.*[9] This tome was always stocked in our bookstore in Toronto and was highly recommended by Ross Dowson to those political neophytes such as myself who were just getting interested in radical ideas. I still have it on my bookshelf. It was my first introduction to the wide world of "bourgeois" philosophy outside of Marxism, and an important part of my early education. Russell's ability to make philosophical ideas accessible to the average reader in a straight-forward style, and to show the connections of the various schools of philosophical ideas over history to each other, from the Greeks to contemporary times, was an eye-opener for me. It was one of the few non-Marxist books that was popular in our ranks and which we would reference from time to time in those years.

Russell was held in high regard by the Vietnamese, naturally, and from early on the Foundation had been in active discussions with them about the best way to raise solidarity in Britain and get their cooperation in the possible setting up of a tribunal, comprised of prominent intellectuals, to investigate American military activities in Vietnam. Chris Farley, a Foundation Director, had been sent by Russell to Vietnam as early as 1964 and Schoenman had visited there several times to see the consequences of the war. He and Russell Stetler, another Director of the Foundation, would eventually meet a couple of times with Vietnamese President Ho Chi Minh and Prime Minister Pham Van Dong to discuss their cooperation in the event that Russell was able to establish such a 'tribunal."

Ken Coates was in the news a lot around that time. He had been featured in *The Sunday Observer* in an article about the British left and about his expulsion from the Nottingham Labour Party. Shortly after that, early in the Fall of 1965, Schoenman and a couple of the Foundation's people headed up to Nottingham to meet with him and to talk about the possibility of a broad-based campaign outside the Labour Party against the war, including Russell's idea of some kind of "war crimes tribunal" that would pass some moral judgment on the American actions. Russell had denounced Wilson because of his attitude to Vietnam and had publicly torn up his Labour Party membership card at a YCND rally in October of that year (an action that the I.G. disagreed with).[10] Nevertheless, Schoenman told them that the Foundation would help fund the organizing of such a campaign of solidarity and he was also pretty certain that the Vietnamese would back the Foundation's plans for a "tribunal."

The meeting in Nottingham was but an extension of the discussions he had been having with many on the left in those months, including supporters of *New Left Review*, but I think he had figured out pretty early that because of the I.G.'s earlier activity in the Labour Party on the issue of Vietnam, it might have the forces and know-how to help him make his ideas a reality. It was the beginning of the I.G.'s close alliance with the Foundation. Shortly after that, we in the I.G. agreed to send out a special appeal directed to all those who were growing alarmed at the increasing ferocity of the American aggression and British complicity in it. The first step proposed would be a large public meeting towards the end of December 1965 to launch such a campaign.

Although the I.G. had been very active in opposing from inside the Labour Party's policy on Vietnam, until the meetings with Schoenman it had not as yet contemplated an independent campaign on the issue. However, its attitude was beginning to shift on this. Primarily because of the influence of the F.I., which had declared opposition to the war a priority task for all its Sections, the I.G., in those months, had begun to look around for more effective ways to campaign against it. Until then, whenever it ventured outside the Labour Party, it had mainly supported the anti-war activities of other groupings, such as the Movement for Colonial Freedom (MCF), the BCPV, and the Labour Party-based, Labour Peace Fellowship (LPF). By the spring of 1965, the I.G. had yet to develop a "solidarity" position or even a consistent position on self-determination. On the Easter CND March that year, the I.G. had called for "recognition" of the NLF and the withdrawal of all American troops, but had also demanded ". . . immediate negotiations with the so-called Vietcong."[11]

While there was a quick meeting of minds between Schoenman and the I.G. about the idea of a "solidarity" campaign, Russell's proposal for a "tribunal" on Vietnam that would be comprised of leading international personalities who could pass moral judgment on the war was another matter entirely. When we first heard the idea we were a little bemused by the conceit of it. We questioned the idea, because of the suggested scale and large resources required for it and we wondered whether or not it would ever get off the ground. This is not to say that it wasn't an important issue for us. The F.I. leaders had discussed the idea in Brussels several times and I know for sure that Ralph had had several personal discussions with Ernest Mandel on the topic because Ernest had reported them to one of our Secretariat meetings. But as time passed and the idea matured in our thinking a little bit more, we began to think seriously about what might be some of its limitations and implications, even though we were a hundred percent certain that such an international body, if it managed to get established, could make a major contribution to the campaign against the war.

The inspiration for a "tribunal" that would be comprised of prominent intellectuals who would have no authority other than to pass moral judgment on the war had arisen out of the history and experience of such kinds of "commissions" that had existed prior to the Second World War, especially the one that had been headed up by John Dewey, the American philosopher, to deal with the infamous Moscow "show trials." That commission's purpose had been to try and save the lives of the Moscow defendants and to investigate the slanders of Stalin against Trotsky. It became known as the Dewey Commission, and despite its best efforts Stalin swiftly had the defendants executed.

Russell had been well aware of the Dewey project and had given his support to the British supporters of the Commission, but had not been active in it. What he was proposing regarding the American actions in Vietnam had obviously been informed by that experience. He was also reaching back to the Nuremberg trials, held at the end of the Second War by the Allied victors to try Nazi Germany's leaders. He hoped to throw some of the Americans' rationale for those trials back in their faces.

The idea of a citizens' "international tribunal" to right injustice was not new. The Comintern had utilized such a body to bring international pressure on the new Nazi regime in Germany in 1933, when it had used the pretext of a fire at the Reichstag to wipe out democratic rights and suppress the Communist Party, arresting its leaders and threatening them with execution. That international campaign was successful in getting most of the Communists released.

A history of these tribunals—including the Russell one—appears in the Klinghoffer book already cited, but unfortunately the authors seem so totally prejudiced against the American SWP, they can't even give recognition to its name when they write about the Dewey Commission. Their biases can also be seen in how they deal with the Russell Tribunal. Two of their sources turn out to be David Horowitz and Ken Coates, whose comments should have been treated more cautiously, if only for the sake of objectivity. Those two opponents of Ralph had their own axes to grind, so their versions of what went on should at least have been treated with a measure of caution.

For example, Horowitz told them by telephone that Schoenman was "enmeshed" in organizing "a Fifth International."[12] This morsel of gossip from Horowitz is taken at face value and repeated without checking it out. Such an idea coming from Schoenman would have been very surprising to anyone who knew him at the time. There's no doubt, of course, that like many of us he had hopes that an international anti-imperialist organization of some kind might have evolved out of the Organization of Latin American Solidarity (OLAS). Ken Coates had been the Foundation's delegate to the OLAS conference in 1967. But at the time Horowitz is speaking about, as far as I can recall, Ralph was sympathetic to the views of the Fourth International, in fact so much so that when he was in Cuba and met with Fidel Castro in connection with the Foundation's international work, one of his objectives was to arrange a visit by Ernest Mandel.[13]

Early on, Horowitz had taken his distance from the Tribunal. As he later wrote, "my political reservations caused me to take no part . . . I had removed myself psychologically and in every other way possible from the event . . ."[14] Those of us active in the work had been well aware of this, but whatever those "reservations" were, he never let on at the time, and I wouldn't trust the self-serving, retroactive ones he advances now, an attitude that has been no doubt heavily affected by his present-day conservative outlook. In the case of Coates, he was very active in the initial work of the Tribunal but ceased participating in it towards the end, also without any explanation, and he later got into a nasty dispute with Schoenman over money and control of the Russell legacy after Russell's death.

One would have thought that those differences alone would have cautioned the Klinghoffers to take what Coates and Horowitz said with a grain of salt, but unfortunately it didn't, and it is but one example of them allowing their own prejudices to contaminate their objectivity. Any negative comment made by anyone against Schoenman in the disputes among Tribunal members seems to get a lot of ink in their story. Obviously, his revolutionary outlook sticks in their craw, but even from their version it's clear that without Schoenman the Tribunal would have only remained a good idea.

When we were discussing the tribunal idea amongst ourselves in the Fourth International, we even considered that, to maintain its integrity and balance, such a "commission" should be prepared to dismiss some of the charges against the Americans if they were found not to be true. There couldn't be any guarantees, one way or the other, we felt. Otherwise, we feared, the whole thing might become discredited and end up as just another run of the mill gathering of "hacks," as someone said, coming together to announce a foregone conclusion, to make propaganda for the Vietnamese. No matter how worthy that may have been, such a "commission" would then have been easily dismissed as nothing more than a "front" for the CP, and would have had little effect upon public opinion. Little did we know, however, how close we would come to that reality, as will be shown later in this account.

There was considerable discussion amongst us about the thinking behind Russell's concept. I remember one discussion in a meeting with Isaac Deutscher, the famous biographer of Trotsky, Ralph, and David Horowitz. This was not long after Deutscher had agreed to become a member of such a "tribunal"– he was one of the first. He questioned the use of the word "tribunal" to define it, saying that implicit in the term was the notion that such a body would somehow have powers to implement its decisions and even bring the guilty to justice, which clearly couldn't be the case. He went on at some length to us about the inherent difficulties of the "tribunal" concept, saying he preferred the term "commission" because it much more accurately reflected the reality.

Deutscher also talked about the concept of "war crimes." Of course, we have to denounce the Americans for their crimes, he said, but the setting up of a committee to do this might just amount to nothing more than another protest organization of marginal value coming into existence. "For revolutionaries, for humanity," he said, "the question of war crimes pales against the greater crime of the actual war of aggression by imperialism—the war in itself is a war-crime!" It was a continuing issue in our discussions about the concept, almost right up to the day before the "tribunal" met in London on November 1966. That's when we finally came to an understanding that even though we would use the word "tribunal" in its title and to describe the new formation, it would in actual fact function only as a "commission."

Ray Sparrow, who was in Brussels at the time helping get the International's Bureau established there, told me he thought that even with some of the problems around its self-declared mandate and its self description, such a "tribunal" would be of immense benefit to the anti-war movement; that is, if we could pull it off, which was by no means certain. On one of Ray's trips to London—which were every few weeks—Ralph, who knew of the American SWP's role in helping organize the Dewey Commission, asked him if he would come over to the Foundation's offices to talk over the concept. I'm pretty certain this was the first time Ray and Ralph had met, and it turned out to be the first of several such get-togethers. I remember very well, after that meeting, how admiring Ray was of Ralph's boldness, his audacity, and the sheer scale of his ambition and imagination to get the idea of some kind of international tribunal/commission off the ground. Ray said he hadn't come across many individuals like Ralph. That meant something coming from Ray, who had a long experience in American radical politics and had been acquainted with some of the most important personalities in the American radical left.

The Russell idea of a "commission" or a "tribunal" on Vietnam was regarded very, very favourably by the American SWP, since in 1935 it had been the main political force in getting the Dewey Commission going. A few of its leaders such as Albert Goldman and George Novack had been involved almost full-time in its work. The famous novelist, James T. Farrell, author of *Studs Lonigan,* an SWP member at the time, had also been active in it. The leadership of the SWP understood the potential of such a "commission" concept in relation to Vietnam probably better than anyone else and was open to any idea that would help inspire the anti-war movement and further morally discredit the intellectual proponents of the war. As a result Russell's proposal was always given prominent coverage in *The Militant* and in *Intercontinental Press.* I didn't realize it at the time, but helping getting it going would consume a major part of our group's energy over the next couple of years.

© John Walmsley 1968

© John Walmsley 1968

TOP Pat Jordan (lower left) a leader of the IMG and VSC speaking from the plinth, Trafalgar Square, March 17th, 1968.

BOTTOM John Palmer, a leader of the International Socialists and the VSC speaking from the plinth.

Chapter 5

The Vietnam Solidarity Campaign

*T*HE VIETNAM SOLIDARITY CAMPAIGN (VSC) HAD ITS BEGINNING ON
December 20th, 1965, at a meeting convened by the BRPF to celebrate
the fifth anniversary of the formation of the NLF.[1] On the platform were
Ken Coates, Mark Lane, Ralph Miliband and Ralph Schoenman, who at
the conclusion of a long and detailed description of America's horrifying
brutality against the Vietnamese people, called for the British left to
organize a campaign against the war by mobilizing opposition on the
streets and setting up of an "international tribunal" to look into American
war crimes.[2] I had the good fortune to be included on the new campaign's
Preparatory Committee, along with Quintin Hoare of *New Left Review*,
Barbara Wilson, a recent recruit to our group, and Pat Jordan, who became
the Committee's secretary and coordinator.

The December 20th, meeting was a further deepening of the I.G.'s collaboration with the BRPF that had informally begun a couple of months
earlier. By December, our small I.G. group in London had become the main
force helping the Foundation organize most of its press conferences and
public meetings about Vietnam. Under the signature of Pat Jordan, the first
open letter to the broad left and all the anti-war activists we could find went
out urging them to come behind "a solidarity campaign" based on a
programme of fighting for an immediate end to the aggression, the withdrawal
of all American forces and an end of British collusion with the Americans.
We also called for "full support to the NLF." The purpose was to mobilize
on the streets all those who were becoming angry at the increasing ferocity
of the American aggression and British complicity in it.

With Pat Jordan's letter in the mail, our people in London moved right away to ensure the event would be as successful as possible. It became our number one priority and we immediately set about organizing a series of regional meetings that were tentatively projected to culminate in a founding conference by March 1966. Inspired by the example of the American anti-war movement, our aim was to build a similarly broad-based, mass, non-exclusionary movement in which anyone, regardless of political affiliation, could participate as long as they supported the aim of getting the American troops out of Vietnam unconditionally.[3]

It was during these early months that Pat, who had been travelling back and forth to London from Nottingham on the Foundation's payroll to help organize the conference, had begun to think about moving to London full-time. We had been talking about this for a while, and within a few weeks Pat made the move. It was part of our effort to get as many of our people as possible to relocate. We also asked a few other Nottingham people if they would do the same thing. This was a considerable sacrifice or incon-venience we were asking, but it was to be expected in the kind of cadre-type organization we were building, even if it was small. Geoff Coggan was one of the first to make the move. A recent recruit to the I.G. and a little older than Pat, I believe, he had been the Political Education Officer of the West Nottingham Labour Party. A very experienced local leader, he had managed our campaign against Ken Coates' expulsion. Coggan would later go on the staff of the Foundation and become the press officer for the Tribunal when it was eventually set up. Mike Martin, a young activist from Hull, also agreed to come down. These moves provided an important reinforcing of our small group in London, and it was only possible because of the high degree of commitment of those comrades to our group.

Political conditions were changing appreciably, making the building of a broad anti-war movement in Britain an increasingly feasible project. With news reports appearing just about every day in the media about American efforts to bomb North Vietnam into the Stone Age, many activists began to feel they could no longer wait until the annual Labour Party conferences to carry the fight against Wilson. It should be noted on that important front, within the Labour Party, that the I.G., as I've already mentioned, had accomplished some very positive work in this arena. Led mainly by Ken Coates, our Nottingham people had the previous year initiated a campaign in the Labour Party to raise money for medical aid for North Vietnam and had also led the campaign in the Labour Party to permit the entry of the NLF's official representatives into the country, part of a campaign by Bertrand Russell to allow their views to be heard directly by the British people.

In the run up to the VSC founding conference, the I.G. reached out to encourage a few Labour Party constituencies to send delegates, but we didn't really expect to get much from that area. A distraction was the approaching General Election. Even though the annual LP conference that year had adopted a resolution submitted by the Fire Brigades Union opposing Wilson's handling of the war—the first time an annual conference had ever opposed its own government, an action that would be repeated the following year—we fully understood that many of our potential supporters in the Labour Party would inevitably be swept up in the elections and would most likely put the Vietnam question on the back burner for a while.

The Vietnam issue had not matured sufficiently to overcome the fear on the part of many party activists that the Tories might come to power. As it was, Wilson was elected in March with a 100-seat majority after a campaign that saw very little discussion about the war. Before, when Labour only had a slim majority, Wilson had used that as an excuse not to do anything to challenge the ruling class, and when he finally achieved his large majority, he used that to steam-roller his internal critics into silence, successfully marginalizing them. The election of the Labour Party turned into a disaster for the working class and resulted in it suffering a severe defeat. In the spring, he broke the seamen's strike and implemented a wage freeze, and of course, he continued with his loyal support of the Americans in Vietnam.

Opposition to the war increased so much that by May 1966, when the American bombing of Hanoi and Haiphong began, Wilson was compelled—despite his seemingly new strength—to disassociate himself from the Americans. It turned out to be only a gesture, however, and as a result many Labour Party members began to leave the party in protest. The government's response was grossly inadequate and mealy-mouthed; Wilson's meekness in the face of the war's escalation only annoyed his critics even more.

An important factor in building the VSC's founding conference was the distribution of reliable information to broad left circles in Britain about what was happening in the war. Ralph Schoenman's visits to Vietnam were of tremendous value in this regard. In February 1966, he and Russell Stetler of the Foundation had a two and a half hour meeting with Vietnamese President Ho Chi Minh and Prime Minister Pham Van Dong to work out the arrangements for a possible war crimes tribunal.[4] That's when Schoenman broadcast his famous appeal to the American occupation forces, challenging their right to be there and explaining that the resistance of the Vietnamese was a war of national liberation against a foreign oppressor and similar to the struggle of the Americans when they were battling Britain to set up their own republic.[5]

Schoenman became a key speaker in our meetings in the build-up to the founding of the VSC, and we organized many press conferences for him so that he could report what he had seen on his travels. The media in London gave us very little coverage, if any, but I remember that those meetings were usually very well attended, with sometimes over 100 people showing up. This was evidence that we were beginning to attract a body of activists—many of them politically unaffiliated—to the new campaign. We were growing because we were providing information not available anywhere else. At one meeting, I remember the audience gasping audibly when, in a dramatic sweep of his hand, Schoenman pulled from his large brown briefcase, which was always by his side, a pineapple-sized cluster bomb—a dramatic way of showing the kind of anti-personnel weapons the Americans were raining down on the rural population of Vietnam. Shoenman's cluster bomb was unarmed, but it made the point.

By February 1966, after a lot of effort, we had managed to establish ad hoc committees in a few parts of the country outside London. In Hull, we had a meeting of eighty people, and in Nottingham we had another with over a hundred, where Ralph Schoenman, Chris Farley and Ken Coates were the featured speakers on the platform. These were the two cities where the I.G. had active groups. Our handful of members in Glasgow and Edinburgh also moved to establish a Scottish committee. At the same time, I was travelling the country several times a month, talking up the conference to university socialist societies and college student groups. Nevertheless, during the first few months of 1966, delegate registrations were only dribbling in. We were finding it increasingly difficult to get people to commit to attending. We even made a special effort to make sure the non-sectarian radical press in London understood what we were doing. I was given the assignment of meeting with the editor of *Peace News*, a pacifist journal published by the War Resisters International which had once been edited by Chris Farley. I also met with the editor of *The Tribune*. Both were weekly journals generally regarded as being part of the broad left, with *The Tribune* the voice of the Labour Party parliamentary left. Although both the editors of these journals were respectful about what we were trying to do, they gave me the distinct impression we couldn't expect much from them.

By the spring of that year, however things had begun to look up. Our spirits received a tremendous boost when the Berkeley Vietnam Day Committee in San Francisco issued an international appeal that the weekend of March 25-26th be set aside for days of protest. We were also encouraged when a Youth CND march in London, at which I spoke, attracted over 1000 people. Even though the action was not specifically on the issue of Vietnam, this was a significant number, especially considering also that we were in the midst of a General Election. This was a small but important sign, we felt, because anti-war activities in London had been at low ebb until then. Our response to the Berkeley appeal was to organize a large meeting at the London Welsh Association Hall that turned out to be a very successful affair, and which we reported in *The*

Week. Chaired by David Horowitz, the speakers were Robin Blackburn of *New Left Review*, our own Ken Coates, Raymond Williams—author of *Culture and Society* and *The Long Revolution*—and Ralph Schoenman, who read a message of warm support from Russell. Several hundred enthusiastic supporters made up the audience.[6]

We looked for possible supporters for our conference everywhere we could. On the CND's Easter March that year, we worked successfully to persuade potential pro-solidarity forces to form a single contingent behind our banner and, over the three days of the event, we succeeded in arranging many "speak-outs", open air meetings during the rest periods to promote the coming conference that by then had been pushed back until June. As a result of that kind of activity, we began to receive many letters from every part of the country asking for information about the conference. Requests for information also began to come in from a few trade union branches, including Manor Park AEU and West Ealing No.2, NUR. We also participated in the May Day March that year, with similar results. Even though we were in the midst of an election campaign, criticism of Wilson among party supporters had not totally subsided. The Scottish TUC annual conference condemned American actions in Vietnam. Of the 450 delegates, only eight voted against an anti-war resolution moved by Lawrence Daly, General Secretary of the Scottish National Union of Mineworkers and, incidentally, a prominent sponsor of *The Week,* who would soon become a mainstay of the Russell War Crimes Tribunal.[7]

Despite these successes, getting people to register for the upcoming VSC conference went painfully slow. By the middle of May, we still had no idea how many would show up. Part of our difficulty, we began to sense, lay with the Foundation's initial statement launching the campaign. It was a statement our group hadn't had much input into and that had been drawn up mainly by the Russell Foundation. (David Horowitz claims he wrote it, but most likely he prepared the initial draft, which is how these things were done in the Foundation.)[8] In our various activities— especially on the Easter March—we found that frequently that initial statement was being reduced by many of our supporters to the simplistic slogan, "Victory for the NLF!" a slogan that had more the quality of a wish rather than a political demand that would accomplish those ends. The problem reflected part of the difficulty of our unusual relations with the Russell Foundation.

Because of the informal nature of the I.G.'s alliance with the BRPF—and especially with Schoenman personally—we were more often than not called upon to be the enablers of their various projects, often without much prior discussion, especially concerning the nuances of its various statements. The Foundation—with its small Board of Directors, around half a dozen—was not a typical political grouping that one would normally find on the left, such as a membership organization that would have an elected leadership in place. Rather, it was organized primarily to promote Russell's views on the issue of the war. It was unique in this respect and I have never come across anything like it ever since. And it wasn't as if we in the I.G. were in a coalition of some kind where we could have collective discussions about objectives in regular meetings from time to time. It was often the case that our group would respond to Russell and Schoenman's positions—the great bulk of which we agreed with, of course.

My impression of Schoenman was that his revolutionary outlook had evolved from a sneaking sympathy with Maoism which—in those days with its criticism of the USSR—was sounding very radical. At the height of the Sino-Soviet dispute in 1965, Ralph had attended the Helsinki Peace Conference where he had represented Russell and had openly challenged the event's Moscow organizers on the issue of free speech and publicly confronted their attempts to curtail the voices of the Chinese delegation. In a mass meeting in Helsinki, Schoenman had provoked an uproar by criticizing Moscow for the low-level of its material support to the Vietnamese. As a result, the Soviet Stalinists loathed him, to the point, Chris Farley once told me, of physically threatening both of them, not an inconsequential matter coming from a state that had a history of murdering its left critics. Like many independent left intellectuals in the early Sixties, including quite a few in the ranks of the Fourth International, Ralph had been attracted to China's early criticisms of the Soviet Union and saw some hope for socialist renewal in the radical ferment that Mao had initiated.

As we struggled to build the June conference, we soon discovered that many of the British "Trotskyist" groups, such as Gerry Healy's SLL and Ted Grant's RSL were extremely critical of our focus on the Vietnam issue and were also adamantly opposed to any idea of an independent campaign about it. The I.S. were not as backward as those two, but did not participate much in helping us in the early stages—they were not part of the Preparatory Committee, for example—and stayed mainly aloof from our organizing, although a few of their members were active in local campaigns as the movement began to take off. Other than that, we had good support from the many "independent" left activists and especially from the milieu around *New Left Review* and the university student societies. Still, however, after nearly three months of organizing, we remained unsure how many people would show up. And when a series of our London meetings saw depressingly low turnouts, the Preparatory Committee moved quickly to recalibrate our earlier expectations. It seemed the "Victory for the NLF!" slogan was beginning to give us difficulties and was even threatening to play into the hands of our critics who were claiming that we wished to prolong the war.

We began to feel that the slogan—at least in the way it was being expressed—might stand in the way of attracting much broader forces to our campaign and prevent us from building a truly mass movement. So we began, slowly, to re-orient ourselves towards instead emphasizing a position of demanding that "the Americans withdraw from Vietnam." We were convinced that if this happened it would lead to the same result, the defeat of the Americans. The slogan was a British variant of the American anti-war movement's demand, "Bring the Troops Home." At the same time we saw the need to keep up our fire on the British government's "complicity" in the aggression. Most of these changes we brought about without much input from the Foundation's people, or specifically Ralph, who was pre-occupied fully with the effort to get a "tribunal" up and running, and was travelling the world trying to line up support for it.

There was also urgency surrounding our efforts to organize the VSC in those months, as we began to feel we might be running out of time. One of our concerns was that Wilson might bend to American pressure and send British troops to Vietnam, increasing British involvement in the war, something we wished to avoid at all costs because it would have meant an escalation of the war and an increase in the imperialist military offensive before we had even begun our campaign. Our aim was to keep the pressure on Wilson as much as possible, in order to keep this kind of option off the table. We also began to think of ways to ensure that this would be one of the major concerns at the upcoming conference.

Clearly we had been overly optimistic about how many would come to the conference. Perhaps "we should scale down the proposed attendance," wrote Pat Jordan, "balancing this by greater attention to delegates from organizations. If this is the case, we should go for a smaller hall (and cheaper) than the one I have booked. There is not only the consideration of price, etc., the political effect of having a half-empty hall is bad, but that of an over-crowded one is encouraging." So we booked a hall with a seating capacity for only 150 people.[9]

Up until then, we had only managed to attract the support of a few CND activists from the "official" peace movement in Britain. Most leading CND people managed to keep their distance from us, in large part a carryover from their resentment against Russell and Schoenman for having set up the Committee of 100, which most of them had opposed.

Vietnam was not at the top of CND's agenda. At their youth rally in Trafalgar Square where I had spoken, incredibly, out of four speakers on the platform, I was the only one there who addressed the issue of Vietnam. We all sensed CND was going through a crisis, and Vietnam must have been part of that. A few CND people, who had worked with Ralph and Russell in the "Committee of 100," had expressed some interest in what we were doing. But this kind of support was at best lukewarm, and I don't remember any of them playing a significant role in our work.

The notable exception was Malcolm Caldwell, a specialist on South East Asia issues who became one of our earliest supporters. He always seemed to be out of the country somewhere, but I had met him several times. He was a modest, self-effacing, gentle kind of man and I was surprised when I discovered that he had been the Vice Chairman of CND the previous two years.

Malcolm was a long time supporter of the Russell Foundation and a dedicated supporter of the colonial revolution. When the Cambodian revolution broke out, under the murderous bombing by the Americans, he became one of the revolution's most active supporters in Britain, travelling frequently to Phnom Penh. Later, in the seventies, he met a tragic end when he was murdered, allegedly, by dissidents in Pol Pot's regime.

We didn't despair entirely of persuading the so-called "Trotskyist" groups to change their views about Vietnam, however. Periodically, either Peter Taaffe or Keith Dickinson of the RSL would visit Pioneer Book Service to buy literature for their group. They were among our best customers. Because the relationship I had with them was a tiny bit warmer than cool, it was still possible for me to have a fairly friendly conversation with them from time to time. But I had just about given up any hope of them ever overcoming their hostility to the I.G. Frankly, after coming back from the World Congress, I had quickly come to the conclusion I couldn't expect much cooperation from them in any case, because they had every appearance of being on their way out of the International and it was only a matter of time before they cut their ties to us entirely. Nevertheless, the Secretariat was still trying to maintain a minimum of formal relations with them.

Pierre Frank and I had attended one of their functions in the early spring to see if we could get more cooperation from them. We were both very surprised that there were about sixty people in attendance at the meeting, including a good percentage of young faces in the crowd. Pierre remarked to me that, since the last time he had met with them, a few older members seemed to have dropped away, but their growth was notable. Another time, not long after that, they invited me to speak at one of their forums on the topic of Cuba. About twenty-five people turned out and while the discussion was very good from my point of view, I had the impression that most of them were new to radical politics and a couple of them told me they were glad it had taken place. But it seemed to me that, in those days, there was a mélange of positions in their group on this issue. A few of them agreed with the F.I., for example, that Cuba had carried through a fundamental transformation in its property relations and that it was now a "workers' state," but the leadership of the group was clearly hostile to the Cuban government and weren't hesitant in letting me know it. That's a position the Taaffe group, now known as the Socialist Party, maintains until this day.

Despite these differences, part of my international assignment in Britain was to try to get the RSL and the I.G. to cooperate with each other as much as possible. So during one of Keith Dickinson and Peter Taaffe's visits to our book service, I put to them the proposal for some kind of joint activity against the war, and raised the idea of their group's possible participation in the Vietnam campaign. They were extremely dismissive of Russell and generally pooh-poohed the whole notion of independent (by which I mean outside the Labour Party) activity against the war, saying that the I.G. was wasting its time, arguing that nothing meaningful could be done until the working class and the labour movement moved on the issue, pointing instead to their "good work" in the Labour Party. I wasn't about to let them get away with that line of argument. I made a point of telling them that at the previous year's Labour Party conference in Brighton—which I had attended—they hadn't had a single delegate there and that their so-called "strongholds," Hackney and Brighton, had submitted a mealy-mouthed, totally unprincipled resolution on Vietnam to the conference. What was clear to me from the discussion with Taaffe and Dickinson was that they didn't want to do anything that would interfere with their comfort level in the Labour Party; that was how their idea of "entrism" worked.

Above all, the RSL did not see any special need for socialists to campaign specifically on the Vietnam issue outside other general issues in the

British class struggle. I put it to them that defending a third world country's right to self-determination was the highest expression the class struggle in an imperialist country such as Britain could take. But it turned out to be a futile effort to get them to change their minds. Their attitude was only an extreme form of that held by many on the British far left, especially those who considered themselves Trotskyist. At another time, I raised the matter with Ellis Hillman, a Labour Councillor, who happened to be politically close to the RSL and whom I knew was friendly toward the Fourth International, to see if he could get them to budge, suggesting to him that their blinkered approach was not even in their own immediate self interest and was preventing them from making contact with new forces that were radicalizing outside the Labour Party. But I heard nothing back from him.

Around that time we had also met with the International Socialists. They were not as wrong-headed as the Grant people, but as an organization they seemed to take their own sweet time in making up their minds and it was hard to know from one day to the next where they stood on the issue. From what we could see, many of their people seemed to be acting as individuals and on their own initiative, rather than as a group. I don't remember their organization at that time making a clear statement on the issue. John Palmer seemed to be the most sympathetic to what we were doing. Others who seemed close to our politics on Vietnam were Chris Barker, Ian Birchall, and Peter Sedgwick, who had become very active in a couple of our local support committees. I remember a young Chris Harman, a student then who would become the main coordinator of their activities on Vietnam, having problems with the concept of a campaign that would seem to back the NLF—"a Stalinist organization," he told me. In fairness to him, I should mention that we ourselves were not uncritical of the Vietnamese Communists and were very well aware of their terrible history in this regard. At the conclusion of the Second World War, they had ordered the disarming and arrest of the Trotskyists in their stronghold of Saigon where they had been at the centre of the resistance to the French occupation forces. Many were executed without trial.[10] We countered this kind of criticism of the VCP, legitimate as it might be, by pointing out that what was underway in the resistance to the Americans was a social revolution that had a power greater than those who were leading it and we should not use our criticisms of Stalinism to stand aside from our duty to defend it.

The I.S. weren't wearing the same blinkers as the Grant people and had a much more pragmatic approach to the issue, first adopting a sort of wait and see attitude, and then becoming more actively involved at a later stage. Harman, after the VSC's founding conference, went on its National Council. When we issued our call for the setting up of an "Ad hoc Committee against the War," the I.S. became a very important part of it in building the mass mobilizations that would characterize the period.[11]

We even tried to get Gerry Healy's group, the SLL on board. We hadn't received any direct response from them to Pat's letter, but we were in touch with a few of their ex-members, such as Ted Knight, Secretary of the Lewisham Trades Council, and a few others who still considered themselves SLL sympathizers. Knight, who would eventually go on the VSC's National Council, wasn't particularly friendly towards me in the beginning. He was a bit factional when we first met, probably because of my association with the American SWP, but I ignored that in the interest of getting some cooperation from him. Pat and I met with him several times over a few weeks and eventually he told us that he had discussed the matter with Healy and Mike Banda and had gotten the impression from them that they "might be interested" in getting involved

Right from the beginning, however, our main problem turned out to be a few Maoist sects that had become attracted to the campaign mainly, I think, because of Ralph's support for the Chinese at the Helsinki Peace Conference. They had formed themselves into an "anti-imperialist front" of some kind. The main grouping, and with whom we had the closest contact, was comprised of supporters of a small magazine, the *West Indian Gazette and Afro-Asian News*, a monthly edited by Albert Machanda. He emerged as their main spokesman. I remember him as a large man who appeared to me to be in his fifties and who got about with some physical difficulty, a large walking stick in one hand. He was extremely voluble whenever we met and it was hard, as the saying goes, to get a word in edgewise with him. His connection to the Foundation had been due to him having met Chris Farley in Hanoi at an international conference for solidarity.[12] On his return to London, he had gotten in touch with Ralph, who then had referred him to Pat and me, we suspected mainly to get him out of his hair. As a result, Pat and I visited Machanda a few times in his bed-sit. Right from the beginning, we didn't have a very good impression of him. We were both put off by his very sectarian attitude towards building the campaign. It was our first engagement with the Maoists and we soon found out that they were as divided as the Trotskyists on many matters, if not more so. They fought each other savagely, but, when it came to their approach to us, they all seemed to have the same level of hostility. I never had much hope we would get anything positive from them.

In the weeks before the conference, tensions noticeably increased between Machanda and us. We were not surprised. He was not very pleased, he told us, with some of the discussion he had heard about China in relation to Vietnam and about some criticisms of the DRV that had been expressed from time to time at a few of our preparatory meetings. Political life must have been deeply disorienting for his little group, I remember thinking. It was impossible in those times to have a public meeting anywhere in London without a wide range of views being expressed from the floor, but I'm sure the fact that many of us were connected to the Fourth International was the main issue that stuck in his craw. Our Preparatory Committee tried to reassure him that the purpose of the new campaign was not to criticize those who were leading the struggle in Vietnam, but that nevertheless, we had to remain open, democratic and objective if we were to be credible to people who were opposing the war. We had to listen to all views, we told him, and above all, we couldn't control what was being said from the floor of our meetings. But he remained unhappy nevertheless. Strange as it may seem, his basic position was that the new campaign should adopt as its programme, the so-called, "Four Points" of the NLF" and the "Five Points of the DRV" for ending the war. It wasn't long after this, however, that we learned he had rented a hall nearby the conference site where his supporters could meet in the event of a walkout by his people.

The June 4-5th founding conference of the VSC in Mahatma Gandhi Hall turned out to be, despite our earlier fears of a low turnout, a fairly well attended affair. There were a few "solidarity" groups represented from Belgium, France, Italy and Switzerland—all of them Maoists, it turned out. There were also observers from the Chinese and Vietnamese Embassies. Russell personally opened the conference. I have no memory of it, but the *Sunday Observer* of June 5th reports he received an enthusiastic response from "200 representatives of trade unions, peace groups and left-wing organizations" and that he told them, "Britain has been made into a bully's lackey, and a brutal one at that."

There was a broad spectrum of the left on hand. Half a dozen constituency Labour Parties, and their respective Young Socialist clubs, had sent delegates, as had a few trade-union branches and Trades Councils.[13] I remember especially a good number of activists there, representing London's various anti-colonial organizations, a few of them South-Asian and many of them led by the Maoists. Several peace groups and university socialist societies had also sent delegates, but probably the largest number of delegates, the most energetic and enthusiastic, came from the various ad hoc VSC committees that in previous months had sprung up all over the country and seemed to be comprised mainly of young people in their early twenties or younger.

About a dozen of Healy's people were also present, led by Mike Banda, but none were delegates except for Ted Knight, who had managed to get elected as a delegate from the Lewisham Trades Council, "representing 60,000 workers," he would tell the conference. A few I. S. members and supporters were also delegates but I don't remember any of them speaking in the debates much, although John Palmer and Ian Scott—who had identified himself as an I.S. member—agreed to go on the National Council and not long after that Harman would be included on the VSC's

Executive Committee. He and Ian Birchall would go on to help us organize a conference of trade unionists about Vietnam later in the year. Those around *The Week* and their allies had just about mobilized everyone they knew in the country to come to the gathering and did most of the practical work in preparing it. They were the largest left grouping in attendance.

With Russell's opening speech (he left immediately after it), the conference got off to a good start. Despite the underlying tensions with the Maoists, things went fairly well. I remember a buoyant mood among the delegates and a general feeling of optimism that we might be able to organize something that would be effective in opposing the war. Ralph Schoenman, who chaired all the sessions, had written a "Draft Statement of Aims" that set out the broad outline of the new organization's direction. "We regard the struggle of the people of Vietnam as heroic and just," it stated. "We intend to work in all ways available to us in the support. We will campaign strenuously against British complicity. We declare complete solidarity with the National Liberation Front and the democratic Republic of Vietnam in their resistance to American imperialism. Only the defeat of the vicious aggression, only the withdrawal of American forces, weapons and bases and the triumph of the National Liberation Front and the Democratic Republic of Vietnam over their oppressors will serve justice and the principle of self-determination. The promotion of these aims is the purpose of our movement. The Vietnamese people alone have the right to determine the condition for ending the war . . ."

Several other policy papers were before the delegates and Schoenman was also scheduled to present a report of his recent trip to Vietnam and to elaborate on Russell's concept of an "international tribunal" about American war crimes. David Horowitz had prepared a draft paper for discussion; Chris Farley along with Pat Jordan had set out a few ideas about structure, but most of the material before the delegates had been prepared by members and supporters of the I.G. Pat Jordan had also prepared a paper, "Winning the Working Class Movement for Solidarity with Vietnam."[14] Richard Wilson submitted a proposal on financing, while Ken Coates and Alan Rooney put forward a resolution about the

British government's complicity in the war but which also sought to head off Machanda's concerns by including a sentence that stated: "Although co-chairman of the Geneva Conference in 1954, Britain has repeatedly failed to assist the implementation of the Agreements or to prevent the U.S. wrecking them." But Machanda would have none of it, and refused to accept it as a compromise.[15]

Most of what follows comes from a tape recording of the event that I have in my possession. It reveals that Pat introduced the "Draft Statement of Aims" that Ralph had drafted. By this time we knew where Machanda and his supporters stood and we were confronting the possibility of a major division before we had barely begun. They had prepared a counter-position.[16] Pat, in his usual patient and very calm manner, explained that what Machanda was putting forward was not really a programme based upon trying to achieve something in Britain, but about the politics of Vietnam. It would only succeed in committing us to a set of ideas that could change at any moment, depending upon the relationship of forces there. What would happen in the event that the Vietnamese entered into negotiations with the Americans, as they had done in the past, he asked? Our position should be to oppose the American presence in Vietnam even if the Vietnamese agreed to permit them to remain there. And repeating what we had been arguing all along against the BCP and their "front" groups, he demanded to know why an anti-war activist, from their comfortable position in Britain, would accept as a programme a horrible compromise that had been forced upon the Vietnamese at the time of Geneva and after a long and terrible war?

The Maoists, however, didn't seem to be listening to logic. Machanda's position, with its proforma gloss of "anti-imperialist" bombast—boiled down to nothing much more than ensuring that the new movement would be a political creature under the control of his sect. Aside from a few obligatory comments about the "nefarious collusion of British imperialism with American imperialism," he had virtually nothing to say about any specific anti-war activities in Britain that might help get American troops out of Vietnam, calling for us to "mobilize support . . . according to the programme of the NLF which corresponds with the 1954 Geneva Agreement." Then, in a true test of the delegates' patience, he proceeded to read out the full NLF and DRV programmes, probably the first time most of the audience had heard them in detail.

My tape recording of the event shows that the discussion from the floor on the two counter-posed positions took place in a fairly orderly way, with the participants listening carefully to the two speakers in a respectful fashion. We had done our best to avoid factionalism, primarily in the interest of having a clear discussion. There was very little heckling or interruptions. The debate lasted several hours but unfortunately there was very little changing of minds. As can be seen in the "Draft Statement of Aims," we were unambiguous about backing the NLF as the main liberation force fighting the Americans, but sensing Ralph's vulnerability about getting the Vietnamese government's support for a possible "war crimes tribunal" at some point in the future, I think the Machanda people had hoped they could perhaps neutralize him and make a bid to capture the new organization to turn it into a kind of "front" for themselves. To us it all seemed bizarre and something of a provocation.

There were many criticisms we could have made of the "Four and Five Points" if we had gotten around to an objective discussion of them—one of which would have been that they had been the result of the attempt by the Soviet Union to come to some kind of understanding with imperialism—but the least we could say, and to us it was obvious, they had been developed for Vietnam, for the struggle there. Indeed, one of the speakers from the floor pointed to a key weakness in what Machanda was proposing when he noted that one of the "points" Machanda had read out to the delegates had called for a "neutral and unaligned Vietnam." Why should we in Britain accept that, he asked? But the Maoists were impervious to such questions. They seemed to be solely bent on trying to take away the independence of the new movement before it was even born, attempting to tie it to the politics of another country, in effect making it a political appendage of that country's regime. We were having no part of it.

Machanda's main tactic in dealing with us, it had become obvious, was to confront the conference with an ultimatum: adopt his position or he and his people would walk out. In the end the lines had hardened so much it became impossible to even think of a compromise, and after many interruptions and shouts of "out of order!" Ralph finally put the "Draft Statement" to the vote. It carried with 82 for and 72 against. And as if that was not enough for the patient delegates, Machanda demanded that there be another vote on his defeated position. It was soundly defeated. And then, as if by a single command, he and his group leapt to their feet and as a body stormed out of the hall. Even though we were half expecting it, it was still a startling thing to experience and the delegates went quiet for a few minutes until several of the foreign delegations who had initially left alongside them—the Belgians, the Dutch, the Italians and the Swiss— rushed back in from the street, loudly demanding that they be allowed time give their reasons for leaving. It was sheer arrogance on their part, an affront to those who had remained in the hall. Having struck a blow at the conference's unity, most of us felt they had forfeited any right to be there, but Ralph, for some inexplicable reason, relented and with the work of conference badly behind in schedule, forced us to waste valuable time listening to each of them repeat—almost verbatim—Machanda's line.

A group of Vietnamese from their Embassy, about half a dozen, whom I recognized from my work around the Russell Foundation, had been sitting on the sidelines observing this whole show with a kind of fascination. We had no idea which side they would support in the dispute, but in the end they followed the Maoists out of the door. It was obvious that with Russell's proposal for an "international tribunal" in the offing, Machanda and his allies had been hoping for this. It was certainly a very uncomfortable position for Ralph to be in and I could see, as the debate progressed, his anxiety level beginning to increase as he sat on the platform watching with growing consternation what was playing out in front of him. I later learned that he was on familiar terms with many of the Vietnamese and knew a few of them personally, some of them even on a first name basis, having gotten acquainted with them because of his many trips to Vietnam and for having enlisted their support for the idea of a "tribunal." The question of their attitude to our work was no small matter, it should be stressed.

We very much needed Vietnamese cooperation for the investigating teams Russell was hoping to send send there to carry out the work of an "international tribunal." Pat and our people hurriedly tried to reassure Ralph that it would all work out in the end, and that the course the Maoists were proposing would go nowhere, but I don't think this was of much comfort to him. I'm sure that to him it was as if he was looking at all his hard work going down the drain. Then in a kind of act of desperation—after the foreign delegations, including the Vietnamese had left the hall to join Machanda—Ralph, presumably in the hope of trying to win them back, and without consulting any of us, proceeded to move a resolution from the chair asking that the conference declare its support for the "Four and Five Points." In a brief caucus of our I.G. people and their supporters, we decided to vote his resolution down and called for others to do likewise. His resolution was defeated. After the hard fight we had been through, our people objected to his somewhat arbitrary move, which we figured had resulted from his concern about his future relations with the Vietnamese.

Once Machanda's supporters had cleared out of the hall, we continued with the conference agenda the best we could. At that point, we were away behind schedule. A report from the Preparatory Committee that a meeting be organized as soon as possible to introduce the VSC to a wider public was quickly adopted as was a proposal that a local Hovercraft plant which was sending Hovercrafts to Vietnam, be targeted for leafleting and that educational materials about the war be prepared and directed at U.S. service-men in Britain. A report by Ken Coates—probably one of the best speeches that weekend—on the need to campaign in the Labour Party against the war was also agreed to. Two reports by Ralph Schoenman—one on his recent visit to Hanoi and another about Russell's proposal for an "international war crimes tribunal"—were referred to the incoming National Council. Fourteen people were acclaimed to this leadership body, with Bertrand Russell given the honorary position of

President, and Ralph Schoenman becoming Chairman. On the Council were Ken Coates, Quintin Hoare, Pat Jordan, Ted Knight, John Palmer and his comrade, Ian Scott, Tony Topham, Chris Farley, David Horowitz, Ted Knight, Barbara Wilson and me. As it so happened, this would prove be very much of a figurehead body that seldom ever met. The VSC, on a day to day basis was run by a much smaller grouping, made up mostly of I.G. people and a few of its supporters.

Within a month of so after the founding conference, the SLL began to give signs it was beginning to modify its approach to the new movement. We were hopeful that despite what had happened with the Maoists, the conference may have favourably impressed the SLL people who had attended and that they had reported back to Healy about Knight's election and were asking why they couldn't be part of it. Finally, and much to our surprise, Ralph got a call from Healy asking for a meeting, saying that the SLL was giving its support to a demonstration that we had in the works and that they would like to have a speaker on the platform of our next public meeting which was scheduled to feature Lawrence Daly and John Palmer.

Right away, Pat and Ralph met with Healy and Banda to welcome the SLL into the campaign. They readily agreed that the SLL should have a speaker on the platform of the upcoming meeting, but with a few conditions attached. We asked of them that there be no attacks on other political tendencies in the meeting or on speakers on the platform, such as a couple of left Labour M.P.s whom we were hoping to have as speakers alongside Daly and Palmer. Nor were there to be any attacks upon the North Vietnamese government for having signed the Geneva Accords in 1954, which from articles in the *Newsletter* we suspected they might be inclined to do, and finally we asked that they stop using the prejudicial, colonialist word, "Vietcong" to refer to the NLF in their paper, *The Newsletter*. Healy readily agreed to all of this and we accepted that Mike Banda, their most important leader next to him be on the platform of the forthcoming meeting.[17] And in the weeks after that meeting with Healy, we noticed that the word "Vietcong" had disappeared from their paper. There still was a lot of suspicion of course on our side because of their history, but most of us were convinced that at least it would provide an to engage them in common activity, even though many of us felt that this might increase a tendency towards a "workerist" kind of sectarianism in the campaign, always a problem on the left in Britain we had found out.

At the VSC meeting where Banda was scheduled to speak, I remember that it was an unusually large affair and with an audience of over two hundred, and what looked like about fifty supporters of the SLL there. A heightened sense of anticipation was in the air because news of SLL involvement had by then got around and many were curious about what Banda might say. When it came his turn to speak, he gave what I remember as a fairly straightforward and acceptable speech, keeping to the terms of Pat and Ralph's agreement with him and Healy. And after the speeches of Daly and Palmer—if applause was an indicator—there was a noticeable rise in the enthusiasm from their side and a positive mood of unity seemed to be spreading throughout the hall. That is, until Healy rose to take the microphone to put a halt to this new ecumenical mood, blatantly violating our agreement with him by launching a blistering attack upon the USSR, the British CP and all those sympathetic to it. It was as if he had given a signal to his people to break up the meeting. There was total bedlam for a few minutes with some of his people screaming at us, "We'll kill you!" and when Banda attempted to speak again, Ralph, who was chairing the event, refused to hand over the microphone to him, at which point Banda began to grapple with him to get it out of his hands. It required all of Ralph's strength to hold on to it.

Fortunately for us, even though it had only been a matter of weeks since we had gotten the campaign up and running, many of the young activists who had become involved had politically matured sufficiently to see through the SLL's tactics. Without much effort, we mobilized the majority of the floor against them—as we had with Machanda and his people at the founding conference—and when the SLL people couldn't get their way, they got up and stormed out of the meeting, just as the Maoists had done earlier.

I remember thinking at the time that Healy's behaviour in the whole affair had the distinct flavour of a charade about it. I'm convinced he was not that interested in unity under any circumstances. Probably, the only reason he had shown up was to convince his own people, who may have been asking questions about their strategy of keeping their distance from us, that we were nothing more than a bunch of "petit-bourgeois," as he would say, or something worse. His dead-end factionalism would very soon manifest itself in even more alarming ways.

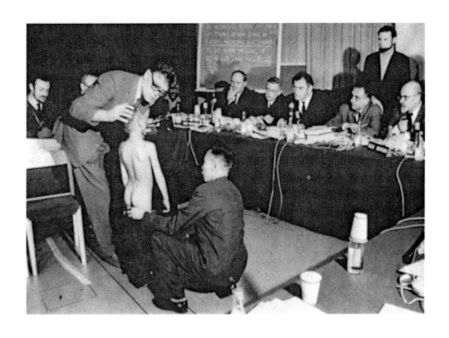

Stockholm, 1967: Nine year old boy, Do Van Ngoc exhibits terrible injuries from
napalm in Vietnam. Among the Russell Tribunal members seated at the table,
facing the camera left to right, are Dave Dellinger, Jean-Paul Sartre, and
Vladimir Dedijer behind the microphone. Sitting on the far right is Isaac
Deutscher and standing in the background is Ralph Schoenman.

Chapter 6

The Russell
International War Crimes Tribunal

*E*VENTS IN VIETNAM SOON PUSHED THE PROBLEMS WE HAD BEEN having with both the Maoists and the SLL into relative insignificance, as the growing anti-war movement simply passed them by. As the war intensified, the American bombing—including the use of napalm and the spraying of deadly herbicides—was widely reported in the media, with a consequent rise in anger among many about Wilson's underhanded and continuing support for the American war effort. More and more, the idea that their actions in Vietnam should be investigated by some kind of independent—but not impartial—public body seemed a reasonable proposition. Russell, for his part, used all his resources, financial and otherwise—as well as his immense stature as a public intellectual—to make it a reality.

Early in 1966, he issued a broad appeal to many of the world's leading intellectuals, "eminent notables and personalities," to support an "international war crimes tribunal" that would send teams of investigators, doctors, technical people and other trained observers to Vietnam and then report back on their findings. The tribunal, Russell wrote, should be comprised of "twenty-five notable personages," hopefully many of them Nobel Prize winners, to investigate and come to a moral verdict about the barbarous practices of the in that terrible war.

Among the "notables," twenty-four in all—most of whom were considered to be on the left and critics of American foreign policy—eventually agreed to be part of such a tribunal. They included Jean-Paul Sartre, the famous French existentialist philosopher; Simone de Beauvoir, the author of the critically acclaimed *The Second Sex*, which had helped inspire the international feminist movement; Gisele Halimi, a close collaborator of Sartre and de Beauvoir, and a lawyer and prominent defender in France of Algerians who had been imprisoned during that country's vicious war against the NLF; Laurent Schwartz, an ex-Trotskyist and one of France's great mathematical geniuses; as well as Gunther Anders, one of Germany's major literary personalities. From Brazil there was Josue de Castro, author of the important work *Geography of Hunger* and a UN delegate whose political rights had been revoked in 1964 by the Brazilian dictatorship. From Sweden there was Peter Weiss, playwright and author of the famous play *Marat Sade*. Joining the Tribunal from the U.S. were Stokeley Carmichael, the leader of the Student Non-Violent Coordinating movement in the American South; David Dellinger, a prominent leader of the American anti-war movement; and Carl Oglesby of the Students for a Democratic Society (SDS). Lelio Basso from Italy would also become a member. A socialist lawyer and legislator, he would go on to head up the Tribunal in the seventies after Russell's death.

The Tribunal had little representation from Britain. Aside from Russell, there was Lawrence Daly, leader of the Scottish Mineworkers, and Isaac Deutscher, the Marxist writer and biographer of Trotsky. One of the first to be invited, Deutscher became its co-chair. Russell hoped that the Tribunal would become a permanent body after it completed its Vietnam work: "I should wish to express the opinion," he wrote to Deutscher, "that the IWCT should remain in existence so that in the future, when war crimes may again be committed, we shall have the opportunity, if we wish, to reconvene even after our judgment with respect to Vietnam."[1] He later repeated this opinion in a message to the Tribunal.[2] Deutscher, who had his reservations about this perspective although he did not say much about it, nevertheless was critical to helping set the framework for the Tribunal's work and holding it together through some of its most difficult moments.

Also on the Tribunal was the Yugoslav, Vladimir Dedijer, a professor of international law and a teacher in the U.S. He was the only representative from Eastern Europe. Although he carried out valuable work in Eastern Europe promoting the Tribunal, he would later give us a big headache with his lack of discipline in relation to the press. Outside of Britain, it was the group around Sartre, de Beauvoir, Halimi, along with Laurent Schwartz and several French lawyers with connections to the French CP, who would play a major role.

As we prepared for its first session, the Tribunal's practical everyday work was carried out by a small Administrative Committee, which was appointed by the Foundation and met weekly. This committee consisted of Geoff Coggan, Chris Farley, Quintin Hoare, Pat Jordan, Setsure Tsurishima, Ralph Schoenman (when he was available) and me. The members of this body did all the "grunt work" of the Tribunal, renting halls for its meetings, reserving hotel rooms for those coming into London, booking the air travel for Tribunal members, preparing the press conferences, typing the statements and press releases and mimeographing them and sending them out.

Quintin Hoare, the business manager of *New Left Review*, stands out in my recollections for being very actively involved, almost on a daily basis, and taking time out from his commitments to the magazine to collaborate with us and to help us whenever it was required. His fluency in French and Italian had become a very valuable asset in the work. He knew Sartre and most of the Tribunal's French supporters personally, because of his work with *NLR*, and he would frequently pitch in to help us overcome the misunderstandings that would crop up from time to time and that were an inevitable part of a project involving so many diverse personalities and languages.[3]

The tribunal was a huge undertaking for a small group like ours. Fortunately, we had the help of people who were politically close to us at the time, such as New Zealander David Robinson, one of the leaders of the VSC. He would go on staff, along with Geoff Coggan who became the Tribunal's Press Officer. Amazingly, Pat Jordan also played a pivotal role in all this, churning out the Tribunal's many bulletins, all the while writing and producing the I.G.'s weekly publication, *The Week*.

It had all begun in August and September of 1965 when Schoenman met with representatives of the NLF in Helsinki to put before them Russell's proposals for a tribunal to pass moral judgment on the American actions in Vietnam. They were "warmly received," he reported, and so he later took the same proposals to representatives of the North Vietnamese government in Djakarta, who then invited him to Hanoi. It was on that visit to Hanoi with Russell Stetler that he made his dramatic anti-war appeal over Radio Hanoi to the American troops and where the Vietnamese stated their support for the Russell project.

By March 1966, the BRPF had forwarded a draft document to Vietnam proposing a structure for such a tribunal and a plan of work. The response to the proposals was slow in being returned from Vietnam to London, heralding the beginning of difficulties in moving the project forward.[4] After innumerable delays, it would not be until early November 1966 that we obtained the clear support of the Vietnamese government.

Just before the first session in London, Schoenman and Stetler met with President Ho Chi Minh and Premier Pham Van Dong, and received their formal cooperation. In an official communiqué, the Vietnamese agreed ". . . to receive six commissions, comprised of four members each to gather data in Vietnam between November and March."[5] The Cambodian government also declared its support for the project. It had been envisioned that the investigating teams would leave for North Vietnam and Cambodia immediately after the London session, but they would not be able to travel until the following year, a delay caused by a combination of pressure from Moscow, via the French CP, and the successful efforts of the Americans to persuade de Gaulle to ban the Tribunal in France.

An early task in selecting these teams was the "separating of the wheat from the chaff" amongst those "volunteers" who were pushing to have themselves included. Ralph, on behalf of the Tribunal, was very firm in excluding those—and there were many—whose motives were purely opportunistic or careerist with an eye to the possibility of a journalistic scoop.

All the team members had to be vetted and approved by the Tribunal. Dr. Gustavo Tolentino, a black Honduran medical doctor living in Toronto and a member of the LSA, who was part of a Tribunal Support Committee in Canada, was accepted, as was Tariq Ali and Setsure Tsurishima. Some applicants were rejected on security or competency grounds. The requirements were simple: they had to have the skills necessary for examining and making an assessment of the carnage the Americans were visiting upon the civilian population and "the unique weaponry," as Russell termed it, "employed by the United States as it tries to destroy a national revolution."

A few Tribunal members were also proposed for the teams, such as Gisele Halimi, Lawrence Daly and Carl Oglesby, a leader of the SDS in the U.S. The plan was that each team would be in Vietnam for periods of several weeks at a time. Once the process was underway, every time a team returned our group in London pitched in to help organize the press conferences and public meetings so that they could report their observations. Coverage of the Tribunal's work was very weak in the British press. In contrast, however, it was taken very seriously by the press of the Third World, especially by intellectuals in countries that had been former British colonies.

Already up to our necks in trying to organize the first conference of the VSC, scheduled for June 1966, our group was fully committed to ensuring that the Tribunal would also become a reality. Ralph and the Foundation made this as easy as possible by putting a few of our people on staff, all paid for by the Foundation. A big asset in helping organize our work was a young American, Russell Stetler, who had been with Ralph when he had met Ho Chi Minh. Ralph had brought him to London from the U.S. and had appointed him Director of the Foundation. In SDS while at Haverford College, he had been an early leader in the embryonic American anti-war movement and in coordinating the May 1964 demonstrations against the war in New York and San Francisco.[6] He was one of Ralph's closest collaborators within the Foundation.

Our first choice for the location of the first session had been Paris, where Sartre, President of the Tribunal, de Beauvoir, Schwartz and other prominent members resided, and where we had received good media coverage that seemed to indicate a rise in France of popular opposition to the war. It had been tentatively scheduled for March 1966, but even if we had been successful in locking in the Paris location, our troubles would have been far from over: we began to receive intimations that the tardiness of the replies from Vietnam to Russell's March proposal was but a symptom of deeper problems. Relations with the government people who Schoenman and Stetler had been dealing with in Hanoi apparently were not going well. Despite the enthusiasm and assurances that Schoenman had received eight months earlier, everyone now seemed to be dragging their feet, always a bad sign when one is dealing with a bureaucracy.[7] We suspected that there were probably differences within the Vietnamese leadership about the issue. Indeed, as the date got closer for the opening session in Paris, we had new fears about the possibility Moscow could be entering the picture and that the whole operation might fall into their hands through the agency of the French CP.

In our initial thinking about organizing the first session, we felt that before it took place we would have already sent a sufficient number of investigating teams to Vietnam in time for them to have their reports ready for it. Then, suddenly, we were thrown into a crisis when Ralph, Ken Coates and Russell Stetler reported back to us that the North Vietnamese and NLF representatives they had been meeting with in Paris had put forward an alarmingly different and narrow concept of the Tribunal. They were demanding the right to appoint the members of the next investigating team. As far as we were concerned, their terms meant they would no longer be independent investigative bodies, because they would only be receiving their evidence in the form of documents provided by North Vietnamese agencies. Only after these teams reported back to the International Commission of Jurists (ICJ), the Vietnamese in Paris argued, would a date be set for the first public launch. Moreover, they were even opposed to the Paris members of the Tribunal, including Sartre, its President, or de Beauvoir, or any others having any say in this arrangement. In addition, they were insisting that the entire process should be under the control of the ICJ, whose representative, Joe Nordman, a French CPer, Ralph had been negotiating with ever since the project got going.

Russell and Schoenman were extremely alarmed by this turn of events. It would have unquestionably undermined the political independence and credibility of the Tribunal, turning it into a kind of "front," something that would have gone against the very grain of everything we had been trying to achieve. And when Ralph proposed an alternative, such as an "independent" team to be sent to Vietnam by the end of October that would also include Mark Lane, the Vietnamese in no uncertain terms told him Lane would be "unable to obtain visas." On top of that, and almost by accident, we found out that the French CP was actively manoeuvring behind the scenes to promote an alternative to the Russell project by way of a British CP "front" organization that had been organized the previous year, the British Council for Peace in Vietnam, led by Lord Fenner Brockway who was hurriedly trying to put something together to compete with the Russell initiative and who had already publicly announced he would organize his own teams to go to Vietnam.

Luckily, we had learned all of this because Russell, it so happened, had been regularly receiving the BCPV's Executive Council minutes, and one day Pat Jordan, in connection with his work at the Foundation, had come across them and noticed that the CP lawyer, Joe Nordman, whom Ralph had thought he was dealing with on a good faith basis, had recently written the BCPV to endorse the Brockway initiative, even advancing to him several names of "notable" British individuals for its proposed teams.

When we learned of all of these manoeuvres, Geoff, Ken, Pat, Setsure and I began to feel overwhelmed. A kind of temporary paralysis set in, because without the cooperation of the NLF or the North Vietnamese government, we couldn't see a way forward. For years, I had been well educated in the CP's function as an instrument of Soviet Union's foreign policy and we had written about it extensively in our press ever since Trotsky, but I had never actually experienced it personally and up close and I was shocked by its crudeness. The difficulties this presented to us seemed intractable, and so we debated amongst ourselves for several days about the next steps.

We even thought of making an approach to the Cubans to see if they could help us out; Ken did in fact contact them, but nothing came of it. Then Ralph proposed something very simple, but risky. Although it might have meant we would never be able to get the cooperation of the Vietnamese, it nevertheless offered us a way forward. His idea was that we should simply try to leap over the roadblocks being erected by the CP by delaying the first public launch until a later date, which meant also a delay in dispatching the investigative teams to Vietnam.

Ralph proposed we use the delay to further consolidate the Tribunal idea by getting more "notables" to agree to serve on it and to concentrate our efforts on assembling our investigative teams and launching the first public session in November in London. He insisted that there was a division within those in Vietnam with whom he had been in contact, and that Ho Chi Minh and the Prime Minister were not receiving accurate information about Russell's idea for the Tribunal. A delay, he maintained, would allow the Viet- namese to reassess their position and give them time to act more independently from Moscow. He insisted that we could pull this off by carefully utilizing the immense international public prestige of Russell—whose commitment to the Vietnamese was unquestioned—in a kind of unspoken blackmail. Basically his proposal was to gamble on the probability of the Tribunal taking on its own momentum in international public opinion, which would make it easier for those in the Vietnamese government who we knew were behind the project to give it their support. This is the only way to checkmate the CP, he said, because they are at a severe disadvantage as they have yet to get their own initiative going and it will lack credibility in any case. It would be a highly risky move for us, but they will have no choice but to support the Russell project, he argued. We could see no other way forward and, after long discussion, we fell in behind Ralph, who said that Russell wished to continue inviting prominent individuals to become members. We doubled up our efforts to make sure the London event would be even more of a success than had been planned for Paris.

Our fears about the CP were very real. Their unhappiness with the Russell "tribunal" was clearly evident in their press. The British CP's

Morning Star barely mentioned it, and there was nothing in *Pravda*, their "bible", or in their East European papers. "The fact is," wrote Isaac Deutscher, "the Chinese and Soviet press ignore the Tribunal almost completely."[8] Then, on top of all that, Moscow began a "full court press", using their considerable resources and their many contacts to quietly undermine us. Potential Tribunal sponsors in several countries were visited by people in the CP, or those in its orbit, and the Foundation began receiving statements from some of its long-time supporters, endorsing the Brockway effort. It wasn't long before we realized that every Russian or Soviet sympathizer who happened to be visiting Britain in those days was going out of their way to see Russell in Wales, forcing the Foundation to station Chris Farley there full-time to fight them off.

I was astonished when Laurent Schwartz, who should have known better, stated his support for the Brockway initiative and said he wanted the Russell project to function in a similar way. Schwartz, a world-famous mathematician, was a Trotskyist from the thirties, who had in fact been with Trotsky in Turkey and Mexico. Although by the time I'm talking about he had parted ways with Trotskyism, he was still on good terms with Pierre Frank and Michel Pablo, and had been extremely passionate about the idea of the Tribunal. He had begun a campaign that year in France to raise a million francs—a very large sum of money at the time—for the North Vietnamese Red Cross and he and Sartre had set up a National Committee for Vietnam, with the support of many prominent intellectuals, a follow-up to their work in supporting the Algerian struggle for independence.

When I had first heard Schwartz's name mentioned in one of our meetings, I had no idea who he was, but when I asked Pierre Frank about him, Pierre was very pleased and very impressed that he was involved. He told me that Schwartz, aside from his world renown as a mathematician, was highly revered in France and had been very prominent in the opposition in France to the Algerian war. Knowing all this about him, I couldn't understand Schwartz's naiveté; it would have meant turning the Tribunal over to Moscow and it would not in any way have helped the Vietnamese struggle. He had been to North Vietnam several times and was on very good terms with the North Vietnamese, so we were suspicious that some elements in the North Vietnamese government might have put pressure on him to go along with them. I also suspect that, because of the internal difficulties we were experiencing and the scant forces supporting the Tribunal in London, he might have been fearful and doubtful about its future.

Isaac Deutscher may also have been influenced by a similar kind reasoning. Early in 1967, he had been devoting himself to "trying to break through the wall of hostility by which the Tribunal has been surrounded in this country, and to make a breach in the conspiracy of silence with which the British left has received it," as he wrote.[9] He had been speaking to prominent individuals such as Michael Foot, leader of the left in the Labour Party (who refused to have anything to with the Tribunal), to see if they would become involved. Brockway, his competing project having gone nowhere, arranged a meeting with Deutscher and Schoenman to discuss the Russell project. Sensing Deutscher's support for his involvement and after a subsequent house call to him, Brockway wrote to Russell directly expressing a wish to meet with him. Russell refused. "I write now to say that I have the firm impression that Brockway wishes to alter the Tribunal in such a way as, in my opinion, to reduce its political effectiveness," Russell informed Deutscher. "In addition he continues to receive the Whip from Wilson's Government and is subject to the sort of pressures which cannot assist us."[10] After that the matter was quietly dropped by Deutscher, who explained to Russell that there had been a misunderstanding and that he was not proposing Brockway for membership on the Tribunal.

As we busied ourselves preparing for the November session, I was uncertain that it would ever take place because of all the problems we were facing. They seemed insurmountable. That is until almost at the last minute when Ralph and Russell Stetler flew to Hanoi to meet with Ho Chi Minh and Pham Van Dong in early November to explain to them what was being proposed. After hearing them out, the two Vietnamese leaders threw their support behind Russell's proposal.[11]

Then there was the problem of money, or the lack of it, something that totally consumed Ralph's energy and constantly required our attention. In addition, we also had to fight the intrigues of the American and British security forces. A deluge of hostile articles in the American and British press began to rain down on us, compelling Russell to spend a lot of time countering them. British intelligence, MI5, the U.S. State Department and the Central Intelligence Agency had obviously orchestrated this, not that it required much effort. Some journalists were disposed to be against the Tribunal in any case, and obviously "planted" stories appeared in the establishment press. These were critical of the Tribunal and, without factual basis, reported "a schism" amongst its members, ridiculing Russell and Schoenman, often in very personal ways.

Ralph's marriage had broken down around then and he was going through a divorce. Details of his wife's allegations in the proceedings were mysteriously "leaked" and splattered all over the pages of London's newspapers. Around the same time, his much beloved dog, a German Shepherd, suddenly collapsed and mysteriously died while being kenneled when he was away on one of his trips. Considering the campaign against us by the various security agencies and their capacity for cruelty and vindictive pettiness, it was indeed a suspicious death. The U.S. was also putting pressure on some of the European governments to make life as difficult as possible for us by preventing any Tribunal sessions taking place on their soil. This was done in spite of the many assurances from Russell that what was being organized would not be a "trial" of the Americans, but a "commission of enquiry" similar to the Dewey Commission, carefully recognizing that no government would permit the organizing on its soil of a "trial" that might result in a judgment against a friendly government. Harold Wilson, further confirming his obsequious relationship to the Johnson administration, threatened to bar entry to Britain any of those who were on their way to attend the preparatory meeting. This prompted a swift public rebuke from Russell. What effect Wilson's threats had, we had no way of knowing.

The first session and preparatory meeting of what became known as the Russell International War Crimes Tribunal, took place in London on

November 13, 1966, at the Ambassador Hotel in Upper Woburn Place, in Bloomsbury. This was a major achievement in itself, considering the difficulties we had to overcome. Most of the members had arrived the previous day for a closed session, but Jean-Paul Sartre had reported he would miss that and would be there the following afternoon. This caused a small measure of consternation in the Foundation's offices because, incredibly it seemed to me, no one would be available to meet him at the airport. Afraid of a mix-up and wanting to make certain he would make an appearance for the first public session, Quintin Hoare finally turned to me to go and fetch him. "But I don't speak French," I protested. It doesn't matter, Quintin responded, it's no big deal, Sartre is very easy to get along with and is quite unassuming, all you have to do is just pick him up and bring him here. Somewhat apprehensively, I waited for Sartre at the airport and met him as he came through the arrival gates. He was alone, of small stature and carrying a small bag. He was easy to pick out because I had seen his photographs in the press many times. I approached him and introduced myself and told him I was there from the Russell Foundation and that they had asked me to pick him up and bring him to the meeting. It was all as casual as that. It appeared to me he spoke very little English, but I remember he thanked me for coming to get him and we drove to the hotel without saying much, if anything. I delivered him safely there, where everyone was anxiously awaiting him. That's how I came to meet the great French existentialist thinker; it wasn't very momentous.

I have a vivid memory of slopping through the London rain to get to the first session of private deliberations. The location wasn't intentional, but I remember thinking how appropriate to be so close to Russell Square, named in the sixteenth century for one of Russell's ancestors, the Duke of Bedford. It was late in the afternoon and Pat, David Robinson and Geoff Coggan were already at work on preparing the materials for the session. We had arranged for translators and brought along all the equipment we used to produce *The Week*: the mimeograph machine, the typewriters and everything else. Bob Pennington—who was on the fringes of the I.G.—also came along to help out. Bob had once been the London organizer of the SLL. He knew Connie Harris very well and he had broken with Healy a few years earlier, and was now interested in working with us. He had been involved in the so-called re-unification discussion with the RSL. He was a very experienced working-class organizer and he was amused to find himself working alongside us on that extraordinary project.

By the time I got there, the Tribunal was already at work and the members seemed to be having some difficulty obtaining agreement on a common statement about the purpose and aims of the Tribunal. Animated discussion was underway about a draft statement that Ralph, now confirmed as the Tribunal's Executive Secretary, had put before the members for consideration, but I can't remember what the specific sticking points were. A subcommittee had been struck to make a few changes and they were working on this before bringing it back to the full meeting that had recessed for lunch. Our committee—more like a secretariat than anything else—sat watching all this from the sidelines. The key players in the preparatory process seemed to be a couple of lawyers from Paris, Yves Jouffa and Leon Matarasso, who had come over to London to help out. Pat told me that Matarasso was a member or sympathizer of the French CP and a member of the ICJ, and may have been a friend of Sartre. Changes were proposed and agreed upon and finally, late into the evening, it was turned over to us to make further copies. The French lawyers literally rolled up their sleeves, pitching in to prepare the draft.

Vladimir Dedijer, who had been designated President, was a tall, physically imposing man, a professor of international law. He was showing some impatience with the progress of the proceedings, and he also rolled up his sleeves to help out. He was participating despite having suffered, just days before, the terrible tragedy of losing his remaining son in a climbing accident. A hero of the guerrilla war against the German occupation of Yugoslavia, Vladimir had recently brought out his famous biography of Tito. He was the only representative from Eastern Europe and he let me know in no uncertain terms he was "bored with this haggling over the text." Later, although he would work hard at promoting the

Tribunal in Eastern Europe, he would display a very volatile temper and would cause us numerous difficulties with his undisciplined and unofficial statements to the press.

The first public session opened the following day with Russell presenting a prepared statement. To get him to the hotel, and because he was so physically frail, we had arranged for two automobiles to bring him down from Wales—one to drive him to London and the other to follow closely behind as "insurance" in case the first car ran into trouble. It was the first time most of those of us at the gathering had ever seen him in person. He looked all of his ninety years. Very thin, his white longish hair glistening under the lights, slightly bent over at the lectern at the head of the large conference table, he spoke, formally opening the session which was chaired by Ralph. "We do not represent any state power," Russell told the Tribunal, his voice weak and slightly tremulous, reading from a prepared statement, "nor can we compel the policy-makers responsible for crimes against the people of Vietnam to stand accused before us. We lack *force majeure*. The procedures of a trial are impossible to implement.

"I believe that these apparent limitations are, in fact, virtues. We are free to conduct a solemn and historic investigation, uncompelled by reasons of state or other such obligations. Why is this war being fought in Vietnam? In whose interest is it being waged? We have, I am certain, an obligation to study these questions and to pronounce on them, after thorough investigation, for in doing so we can assist mankind in understanding why a small agrarian people have endured for more than twelve years the assault of the largest industrial power on earth, possessing the most developed and cruel military capacity."[12] Despite his measured tone, a powerful sense of moral anger seemed to envelope him as he spoke. It was as if he was summoning his last ounce of strength for the occasion.

Several other Tribunal members also addressed the gathering that day and thanked Russell for his courage, most notably Isaac Deutscher, co-chair of the Tribunal, who paid tribute to Russell for his perseverance in getting it off the ground. "May I, in the name of the authors," he said, "express to you, Lord Russell, our deep gratitude and tell you how very moved we have been to listen to your opening message, how very moved we have been by its profound emotion and wisdom. We shall try to conduct our work in such a way that it should at least in part come up to your very noble expectations."[13]

Then Deutscher, on a somewhat ad hoc basis, took it upon himself to co-ordinate the proceedings, making several suggestions about who should occupy which positions, such as who the three Vice-Presidents should be. He then turned the floor over to Ralph who reported on Russell's views—which were quite detailed—of how the work should unfold, what its terms of reference should be and how extensive should be the work of the investigating panels that would be travelling to Vietnam.

Regarding the financial arrangements for the project, Ralph stated, "that the financing of the Tribunal's work will be under the general jurisdiction of separate accounts and separate responsibility. So that there is no remote possibility of unworthy speculation on the part of those hostile to the purposes of the Tribunal as to the manner in which the work is financed . . ."[14] Schoenman's words are worth noting here because the question of money and a dispute over whether the Tribunal would re-pay BRPF the loans it had advanced to it, would eventually lead to many angry words from Russell and a virtual split in the Tribunal's functioning.

There was an inevitable slightly chaotic atmosphere surrounding the proceedings. It was the first time most of the members had met each other. There were a few notable absences from that opening session, in addition to Sartre, Simone de Beauvoir, Lazaro Cardenas from Mexico and Stokely Carmichael (who had been arrested in the U.S. due to his activity in the black struggle in the American South), had sent word they would be unable to attend. Peter Weiss—the Swedish representative—was also absent and had requested that he wished to serve on one of the commissions going to Vietnam, rather than on the Tribunal. Dave Dellinger, the American anti-war leader, was in Hanoi. Sartre was expected to attend the next day.

During the course of that day there appeared to me only slight dis-agreement among those present. The discussion was mainly around the question of the degree to which the Tribunal should remain objective in its investigations, but to me it was nothing substantial. There was unanimous agreement about its terms of reference and on the specific questions to be answered in the reports of the investigating teams. Had the U.S. committed aggression? Had it used experimental weapons? Had it bombed civilians? Had it subjected its Vietnamese prisoners to inhumane treatment? And was it guilty of genocide? It also agreed to set up a "working committee" in London, which would be the authoritative organ of the Tribunal between sessions to implement its decisions, and that the Tribunal would be responsible for funding its own activities.

I must not have been present for the discussion of this latter issue and have no memory of any concrete measures put in place to deal with it, but concern over significant amounts of money loaned by Russell to the Tribunal would soon loom large in our future relations with the Paris members. By the next session in Sweden, Russell would be bitterly reminding them that it had been "announced publicly to the press of the world, on behalf of our Tribunal last November in London, at the close of our private deliberations, that the Tribunal would repay to the Foundation what the Foundation had needed to spend on the Tribunal until the Tribunal was itself able to raise money and that the Tribunal would treat the expenses incurred by the Foundation as a loan. Our decisions on this is (sic) on record to the world . . ."[15]

When I look back, I'm still amazed at what the organizers and inspirers of the Tribunal achieved, even up to that point. It had been an enormous undertaking, something that only a state or a large organization with a mass membership and its consequent resources would have even dared to contemplate. Yet Russell and Schoenman, with their limited means and an indomitable passion for justice along with small bands of supporters scattered around the world, were able to get the Tribunal on to the world stage. And not only over the explicit opposition of the greatest imperialist power in the world, the United States and its agencies, but also against the manoeuvring of the Communist Parties who did everything they could to divert them from their course.

The failure of the CPs in these efforts, it's now obvious, was only symptomatic of the crises these parties were undergoing because of the problems they were having with their line on the war. For instance Leon Matarasso, a key member of the Tribunal, within a short time publicly condemned the CP for their policy on the war. It was also the reason why many intellectuals found it relatively easy to move independently of the CPs and give us their support.

And that support was growing. In Paris, towards the end of that month, we had one of the largest public meetings anywhere in support of the Tribunal, which opened with Sartre giving a rousing speech against the Americans. Those of us in the I.G. were exhilarated when he used his intervention at that meeting to declare his support for Hugo Blanco, the peasant leader and guerrilla fighter, a Trotskyist who at the time was in prison in Peru under threat of death and for whom the Fourth International had launched an international campaign to have released. Also speaking was our Japanese comrade, Setsure Tsurishima, and Lawrence Daly, the leader of the Scottish Miners' Union and a Tribunal member.

Ken Coates, who was also on the platform, told me that the hall was packed with over 6,000 in the audience, and on top of that several thousand had to be turned away for lack of space. We were also receiving good coverage in the French press; on November 24th, Laurent Schwartz gave a lengthy interview to *Le Monde*, detailing the work of the Tribunal and its importance in the international struggle against the war. Not long after, Sartre gave an extensive interview to *Nouvelle Observateur*.[16]

Unfortunately, soon after the November 17th London launch of the Tribunal, the Russell Foundation's relations with the French members began to suffer strain, however, most of it caused by the lack of clarity about where the money would come from to fund what we were undertaking along with a few simple failures in communication. Ralph—and sometimes Ken Coates, Pat, Geoff Coggan or I—had to travel often, sometimes more than once a week, between London and Paris to deal with the organizational problems that constantly cropped up as we were gearing up for the following session, the date for which still remained unresolved.

Furthermore, speculation was popping up everywhere, especially in the European press, that we were in trouble: "Needless to tell you that the papers here and in the Bundesrepublik (and apparently in Poland too) have already printed the news according to which the whole project has collapsed," wrote Gunther Anders from West Germany.[17] The "working committee" that was finally set up in London to run things had proved to be ineffective because for some strange reason—to this day, I can't still figure out—few of its members were resident in either Paris or in London. In reality, the direction of work was in the hands of Ralph who was frequently out of the country. He was travelling everywhere trying to set up national committees of support and putting in place secretariats in cities such as Copenhagen, New York, Paris and Stockholm. It soon became clear, to those of us in the I.G. who were working on the project, that he was not giving sufficient attention to the concerns of the Paris group, specifically de Beauvoir, Halimi, Sartre and Schwartz, who were crucial to its success.

Accusations began to be made, in private, by some of the Paris people that the structure (or lack thereof) that came out of the London meeting may have been intentional on Ralph's part, but this was clearly a gross exaggeration. It was more the simple and prosaic problem of a lack of reciprocity from the Paris people, in not wishing to fully step up to the plate and carry their end of the load, especially when it came to raising money. It would cause us a lot of grief.

Moreover, there were further complications. We soon learned that Ralph, Ken Coates and Russell Stetler, unbeknownst to Geoff Coggan, Pat or I, who were working virtually full-time on the project, in the setting up of "Amis de la Foundation Russell," a Paris support group for the BRPF, had allowed it to fall under the control of what I was told by Pierre Frank was a small group led by Claude Cadart, whom Pierre suspected were dissidents from the Pierre Lambert group, the Organization de Communist Internationaliste (OCI).

I'm convinced Ralph's motivation in allowing this to happen was to try to ensure that the Foundation, which he was above all responsible to and that was covering virtually all the very substantial expenses of the operation, would maintain some check on the Tribunal's Paris office about how the money was being spent. The funding issue had been left unresolved far too long, a mistake that would only get worse.[18] Finally, the Paris office just about stopped functioning and relations between Cadart and Ralph reached an impasse. Charges and counter charges were flowing back and forth between London and Paris about the "misuse of funds." The Foundation had spent money like crazy. It had purchased all the airline tickets for the teams going to Vietnam, each of them comprised of up to eight people, most times including the expense of food and hotels, plus much of the travel and hotel expenses of Tribunal members. In addition, there was the cost of wages and travel expenses of the London and Paris staff.

Large sums of money, it seemed, had been changing hands without proper records being kept. Gunther Anders complained that when he had been in London for the November session, he and his wife had been paid for their hotel and travel expenses, but no one from the Foundation had bothered to ask for a receipt. Chris Farley's reply was that at the time, "we considered it improper to ask any member of the Tribunal for such a formality."[19]

Unfortunately our group's alliance with Ralph and the Foundation also began to suffer some stress, but because of the implicit danger to the Tribunal, we felt compelled to defend Ralph against some of his critics, even though we figured there were occasions when things could have been handled better. From what we could see, important decisions were being made on the fly and were not thought through carefully enough or communicated clearly. This was probably a result of the enormous pressure Ralph was under and his anxiety over the simple fact that Russell and the Foundation would be forced to cover any financial shortfall once everything was behind us.

Money was a constant problem. A lot of it had flowed from the Foundation to Paris but at the same time there was not enough to pay staff in London on a consistent basis. It was always tight. If sufficient money came in, for example, Pat and Geoff would be paid; if it didn't, they had to do without. It was as simple as that. I wasn't affected so much because I wasn't on staff, but I worked on a project-by-project basis, with the Foundation covering the expenses of my trips. Money, while important to others working on the project, wasn't a critical factor for our group, the I.G., because we had made a political decision to do what had to be done to ensure the Tribunal came off as successfully as possible.

The same was true for Ralph. A constant complaint from him was that Paris was not doing enough to raise money and seemed to rely solely on the Foundation to carry that load. At one point, under Ralph's persistent pressure, Sartre finally agreed to put his name to a public financial appeal that the Foundation would circulate in Britain to support the work. Ralph asked me to write a draft, about two pages long. He forwarded it to Paris and Sartre put his name to it. We sent it out immediately. I don't think much money came in as a result of it, however; Pamela Woods, Ralph's secretary, told me only a few small donations were received.

Most of the money for the work had come out of Russell's personal assets, which were not as great as one would imagine for such an important and productive intellectual. Well into his old age, when most men would have retired from public activity, he had been compelled to write steadily and every day to make enough income to cover the needs of his family and his various political causes. Pamela, Ralph's secretary, once told me that because of Russell's relationships with the various women in his life— he had been married four times—and his financial responsibility in maintaining his offspring, a lot of his personal wealth had just about been exhausted. He soon sold his archives to McMaster University in Ontario, Canada, raising about $200,000—a very large sum in those days. Most of that went towards the work of the Tribunal in the form of a series of loans. I don't remember anything coming from the United States, but I clearly remember Chris Farley telling me they had received a contribution of 5,000 GBP from Zukfliker Ali Bhutto, then the Foreign Minister of Pakistan.

Russell, for his part, had turned over virtually everything he had to the Foundation, including the proceeds from the sale of his long-awaited three-volume autobiography. He had completed that manuscript in the years before the Tribunal idea had gotten off the ground, pledging to hold off releasing it during his lifetime, because many of the personalities who are featured in it were still alive. The financial demands of the Tribunal forced him to change these plans however; the publishing rights to the book brought in over 202,000 pounds.

I remember quite vividly the many hours we spent trying to untangle the mess we were in. At the close of one of our meetings in Paris one weekend, Gisele Halimi, a close confidant of both Sartre and de Beauvoir, engaged me in conversation. She and I had talked several times about the problems the Paris people were having in relation to London, so I wasn't entirely surprised when she button-holed me again. I think she figured I might have a sympathetic ear but I wouldn't have been at all surprised if she knew of my connection to the Fourth International. She was—and is—very respected in French radical circles and well known throughout the country, a very bright and politically sophisticated woman with a long history of involvement in the struggle to defend Algerian victims of French repression in France. I'm sure she knew her way around the French far left very well.

She quickly got to the point. Sartre and de Beauvoir were very unhappy, "all of us are unhappy," she told me, about the lack of information flowing from London. The "all of us are unhappy" phrase got my attention very quickly. I'm sure they had other differences about how things were being run, but I was in no position to evaluate them, nor was I in a position to do anything about them. I was not at the centre of what was going on, only helping Ralph out in any way I could, trying to prevent the task from totally consuming me. In such a project, anxious every day as we were about where the money would come from to pay for it, operating under severe pressure, including from the state, combined with the sheer size of the intellects and personalities involved, differences were inevitable and unavoidable. As I saw it, the problem lay in trying to manage the differences with Paris in such a way they would not get in the way of the project. First thing, I thought, was to try and get the petty things that were irritating them out of the way.

Sartre was the Executive President of the Tribunal, Halimi said to me, and he expected more from us. "He feels he is being ignored," she explained. Again, she had my full attention. "He says he feels he is being treated like a flower-pot," she went on, "some kind of decoration put there only for ornamental reasons." She emphasized that Sartre saw himself as an "activist" Tribunal member and definitely not a "figurehead." I took her comments with a grain of salt, however, because we never ever saw Sartre at our meetings and only dealt with his representative, Claude Lanzman, the editor of his journal, *Les Temps Modernes*. The same was true of de Beauvoir, I thought to myself, who was always represented by Halimi. I told her about the difficulties the Foundation was having in London carrying through with some of the Tribunal's work and the lack of financial resources, putting a plug in for some help there, but I don't think she was too persuaded. I had the distinct impression from her that the Paris people had an exaggerated sense of our organizational capacities. Nevertheless, to improve the flow of information, I pledged to see to it personally that she would receive, on a regular basis, all the press releases and reports the Foundation would be putting out in London. This was something that was easy for me to do and that I faithfully carried out until the final session. Not that there was much to send, just the occasional statement. But, at the same time, I would make a point of clipping the London papers if they had items about the Tribunal and enclosing them in the envelope that I would send regularly to her. She later thanked me for this, making a point to Ralph that if it hadn't been for me sending her stuff, the Paris people would not have known what was going on most of the time—a bit of an exaggeration to score a point, in my opinion.

I mentioned Halimi's complaints to Ralph, but, it seemed to me, he did not take them all that seriously. Sartre and the other Tribunal members in Paris are getting lots of information, he said. They had received every public statement from the Foundation as soon as it was issued and were receiving a regular bulletin, especially prepared for Tribunal members, which he would later say they were not bothering to read or respond to. I can't be expected to write to every individual member of the Tribunal, he said; they are putting all kinds of demands on us without holding up their end of the financial burden. And part of his difficulty, he said, was that he was unable to get direct access to Sartre, the Executive President, who up until the letter I had drafted, had been unwilling to sign letters for circulation to the public, requesting financial support for the Tribunal. Ralph's comments didn't reassure me. I became extremely alarmed and had visions of the whole thing falling apart. And that wasn't the end of it.

In another meeting, Halimi again privately raised concerns with me—this time it turned out to be a more serious matter. I couldn't quite get a handle on what the issues were that were bothering her, but I got the impression that there was some kind of conflict beginning to develop between de Beauvoir, Sartre and Schwartz and the people around them on the one side, and the newly organized "Amis de la Foundation Russell," led by Claude Cadart and his companion, Lily, the dissident Lambertists, on the other. I hadn't been entirely unaware that there were difficulties. Earlier, Ray Sparrow and I had wondered to ourselves why our French F.I. group was not more actively involved in helping out with the work. They certainly had many more members than our small group in London for that kind of thing. In different parts of the world, for example, under the influence of the F.I., we had begun to set up support committees.

Our Belgian comrades, whose organization was a lot smaller than that of the French, had taken a lead in organizing a large meeting and setting up a national support committee in their country.[20] Bala Tampoe, of the Lanka Sama Samaja party, had also set one up in Sri Lanka (then known as Ceylon) and the Canadians had set up a broadly based Tribunal support committee under the leadership of Ken Warren, a member of the LSA. At one of our regular United Secretariat meetings, during a discussion about building support for the Tribunal, I remember Pierre Frank reported to us that our French comrades were having difficulty getting involved because somehow a split-off group from the Lambertists had moved in to very quickly monopolize access and was blocking other left groups from participating. Pierre said the French F.I. group was hoping it could get Jean-Michel Krivine, a surgeon, on one of the investigative teams to

North Vietnam and couldn't seem to be able to make contact with anyone to talk about it. Jean-Michel was a brother of Alain Krivine, who would become a leader of the JCR, the predecessor of the LCR. Rather than getting into a conflict about this, and create a possible slanging match which would only damage the work of the Tribunal, Pierre said they had decided to back off, and support the Tribunal in other ways. Jean-Michel would eventually be proposed by French Tribunal member Claude Behar for one of the investigative teams, and he would travel to North Vietnam.

Finally the problems in Paris reached such a crisis point that we almost had a two-way split, not only between London and Paris, but also in Paris, between Cadart and Sartre's people. We couldn't seem to get anything done—not even things as simple as the issuing of press releases or making progress about assembling the investigative teams. At one point, our London Working Committee convened a series of meetings with the Paris people—not all of them seemed to be able to get to the meetings— that accomplished very little, but where a lot of wrangling took place with many charges going back and forth. Ralph was accused of acting arbitrarily and of making decisions without consulting anyone. At one meeting early in 1967, there was a minor revolt by the Paris people because of changes they alleged he had made. At another, complaints came fast and furious from Halimi about Cadart's actions or lack of them and he in turn was constantly phoning Ralph in London about their difficulties. Eventually, we hit a roadblock as the demoralization caused by the internal conflict continued to deepen.[21]

Out of sheer desperation, I'm sure, Ralph finally turned to me and Pat Jordan to discuss what could be done to improve the situation. "There have been certain tensions with Lily and Claude which I feel confident are unnecessary ones, and all of us here are very anxious to smooth over personal questions so that the work can prosper," he had assured Vladimir Dedijer. [22] All of us were under big pressure to move things along because a joint meeting of the Working Committee, made up of representatives from London and Paris, had by then proposed to convene three public sessions of the Tribunal, each of four to five days in length, with intervals in-between of several weeks. The first of these was scheduled to be at the Mutualité in Paris between April 10th and April 15th, the second in May and the third in June.[23]

We were becoming exceedingly anxious that the disagreements might leave us totally unprepared. After a long discussion, we finally agreed that it would be best for someone from London to go there full time to help guide the work of the Foundation's supporters. Ralph said he would talk about this to Quintin Hoare whom we all regarded as a very capable administrator and certainly up to the job. He was part of our London team and I knew for a fact he had kept himself very well informed about what was going on in Paris. To have him there would be a tremendous help, we all agreed. Because I was the only one available on short notice to make the trip to Paris, we decided I should leave immediately to meet with both sides in the dispute—to help pave the way for him. Such was his desperation, Ralph agreed, albeit somewhat reluctantly, that he would give his backing to any reasonable solution I came up with to deal with the crisis while I was there; that was the guarantee, I had told him, I needed before making the trip. He phoned Claude and told him I was on my way and I in turn phoned Halimi.

I wasn't looking forward to the trip to Paris very much, especially at the thought of catching the train to Dover and then the night ferry to Calais. The novelty of travelling back and forth to Paris had long worn off by then. I had made this exact trip very many times before, and I would never fail to get seasick on the ferry, a serious kind of seasickness that would almost incapacitate me and which would leave me hanging over the side vomiting during the whole voyage.

I arrived in Paris the next day very early in the morning and booked into a hotel. Later I met Claude and Lily at a restaurant they suggested for our get-together. The meeting lasted several hours. I must confess here, looking back on it, that I probably had started out with some feelings of factional animosity towards them but I know I was very determined to try and be objective. They turned out to be a charming and gracious couple, committed socialists and serious intellectuals in their own right.

I had no doubt about that, and as I listened to them, I had a great feeling of sadness about their situation. There was such an outpouring of bitterness and personal grievance against Sartre and de Beauvoir, and even against Ralph, I wondered how they could possibly keep going with the project. To a certain extent, they were victims of the difficult circumstances we found ourselves in.

The bottom line was that Sartre, de Beauvoir and the people around them were treating Cadart and Lily like minions. Organizational decisions about their tasks were often made without consulting them, they told me. And, even though they had committed themselves fully to the project, at considerable personal cost, they said their point of view was often ignored, making it increasingly difficult for them to function and carry out their responsibilities. They frequently felt humiliated and felt like quitting, they said, but they kept going because the project was of such importance to them. They also complained to me about Ralph, about the lack of finances coming from London and the minimum control their Paris people had over policy.

All of this was news to me, but as I sat listening to them, I knew it would be pointless for me to go and see Gisele Halimi before making some kind of decision. The fact that I, Ernest Tate, who was only helping out and was not an officer of the Tribunal, would be acting as a sort of mediator pointed out the ridiculousness of the whole business and the seriousness of the problem in Claude and Lily's relationship with the Paris Tribunal members. We were confronting a huge problem and there was no easy way out of the crisis. Even though it was all a little unfair, I felt there was far too much at stake and not enough time to look for a happy solution. I tried to be as gentle as possible, but, finally, I told them that while I fully understood their point of view and even agreed with some of it, if the decision came down to whom London should side with in the "dispute," it would have to be with Sartre. Sartre and his team were critical to the success of the Tribunal; Claude and Lily clearly were not. I told them I would be recommending to London that we withdraw support from them and that meant they would have to give up control of the Paris

BRPF office. They weren't very happy with what I told them. Their faces were glum. For the first time in my life, I felt somewhat guilty for acting like a heavy-handed bureaucrat, but I couldn't see any other option.

When I got back to London, I reported on what I had proposed. I had the sense Ralph was very relieved. After Cadart's resignation, I believe our relations with the Paris group around Sartre, de Beauvoir and Halimi improved a little in the following weeks. Cadart's name was removed from the Tribunal's letterhead, and Ralph, who was the General Secretary of the Tribunal, graciously offered him and his wife an apology for the way they had been treated. At the same time, he also apologized to the Tribunal members present for not keeping them sufficiently informed about his activities as General Secretary.

I remember wondering if Ralph was only going through this to get the crisis out of the way, more of a face-saving effort than anything else for all concerned, because he continued to go about his business as if nothing had changed. However, in the showdown with Cadart, we had managed to put the Paris BRPF and Tribunal offices on a more solid footing and formalized the composition of the Working Committee there, without a doubt facilitated by Quintin Hoare agreeing to temporarily relocate to Paris to help improve our relations with the Parisians. The Paris office, however, continued to be a financial drain on the Foundation.

As the Tribunal got underway, I thought its centre of power ideally should have been in Paris: that's where the core of those involved lived and it's where it had the most public support and had received the best media coverage. In Britain, on the other hand, where we had to fight for every little crumb of publicity that came our way, we were virtually ignored. The BRPF, despite its best efforts, was generally seen to be part of the "fringe" politics of the country. Consequently, some of that legacy had rubbed off on to the Tribunal causing it to function in a kind of political vacuum, with hardly any support from the broad left or from the peace organizations, especially where the CP had any influence. And our situation wasn't helped any by the insufferable attitude towards us from a few of the French intellectuals who were supporters of the Tribunal. It was like pulling teeth, for example, getting them to come to London for meetings or to work out some kind of parity arrangement between them and us.

Even in dealing with this problem, however, from what I could see Ralph seemed oblivious to the problems he was causing for himself and us. He was so focused on driving the mission forward he seemed impervious to any criticisms, not pausing to really consider if there might be any substance to them. For instance, at the meeting of the Working Committee in Paris where Cadart had resigned and where there had been a virtual revolt over some decisions London had taken, Ralph insisted that the next meeting of the committee should take place in London, two weeks hence. I knew and everyone else knew that the French members would be unable to attend and even when they gave various reasons why they would not be able to be there, Ralph still insisted on going ahead with the London meeting in any case. Of course, as the rest of us had expected, when the time rolled around for that next meeting, no one from France showed up. Yet at that meeting, despite our words of caution, he seemed to be unaware of the fact that of the five members of the committee in attendance, he was the only member of the Tribunal present and he proceeded to reverse all the decisions of the previous meeting where Cadart had resigned, including the decisions which had dealt with selection of the investigative teams and Tribunal dates, among other things.

He countered our words of caution, however, assuring us that Dedijer and Schwartz had given him personal authorization to make the changes. But when Schwartz heard about the changes, he categorically denied having done so. After that, relations with Paris just about went into a meltdown and the acrimony over finances surged to the surface again with so many charges and counter-charges flowing back and forth it became difficult for us to keep track of them. Even Deutscher, who was not involved in the day-to-day functioning of the working committee, wrote to Russell that he was ". . . worried about the state of the Tribunal's finances, which seem quite unsatisfactory."[24] There were many angry words expressed over this issue with the Paris people, especially at the meeting where Cadart resigned.

Despite the criticisms of Ralph, as far as I can recall, all our London people were of the conviction that the Paris Tribunal members had not done very much to raise money and seemed to have the attitude that the Foundation had unlimited resources. Moreover, most of us had the impression that the Tribunal members were a little surprised in the beginning when it was pointed out to them that they would have to raise money to finance its operation.

The main criticism that came from Paris was that they were unable to do anything because they did not know how the money was being spent. Earlier the financial committee chairman, Claude Jouffa, had resigned in protest. Money was being spent by the Foundation, they claimed, and there was no check on it. Who authorized the London office to spend the money, they wanted to know? What was its budget? Who determined the financial priorities? What happened when contributions came into the London office in the form of donations for the Tribunal? They demanded that the finances be handled by a certified accountant. Ralph and Chris Farley informed them that because of the way the Tribunal had got going, the expenses and income had been managed by the BRPF. And, to clear this up, all the financial records had been turned over to a notarized accountant, at a cost of 300 GBP, and that when his report was complete, it would be provided to the Tribunal.

But Paris was not happy with this arrangement either, and insisted that the books should be turned over to an accountant that *they* would choose. That, I'm sure, would have been unacceptable to Russell, because it would have meant a complete stranger poking through the Foundation's internal records. In any case, at the same meeting in Paris where Ralph had pushed for what turned out to be an abortive London get together, he assured everyone that the delay was due to the accountant and that he would present a detailed statement within weeks. There was little help from Paris on the financial issue and Russell made many appeals to the Tribunal for it to pay back its loans to the BRPF. Rather alarmingly, we even began to get indications that public support for the Tribunal was being discouraged by some of its members.

Schoenman learned this from Reimat Reich, the chairman of the SDS in Germany, who informed him that when his organization was in the midst of mobilizing support for the Tribunal, he was advised by Gunther Anders to hold off because the future of the Tribunal was so uncertain. "There is one matter which is somewhat disturbing to us. Several of our close German contacts . . . (were) advised to hold everything," Ralph wrote to Anders. When he received an immediate reply from Anders saying he was "speechless about your letter," Ralph answered that the leader of the SDS, Reimat Reich, had reported to him that when "He spoke with you last January in Vienna . . . you told him to hold back . . ."[25]

The financial issue was a major hurdle we couldn't seem to get over. It dragged on as an issue, with no solution in sight. On top of that, we spent many long hours trying to get our relations with Paris on a better footing: the first session would soon be upon us and it was scheduled for Paris in early April. Quintin Hoare, with his tact and multi-lingual abilities, played a critical role in helping us get through some of our difficulties. He had generously responded to Ralph's plea, going to Paris for a few weeks to help organize the Foundation's support group, with an agreement from Ralph it would initially be financed by London. Quintin also got better cooperation from the grouping that had been around Cadart. They also, apparently, had been unhappy with Cadart's leadership, because they seized the opportunity of his resignation to quietly take their distance from him.

Denis Berger, whom I later learned had once been a member of our French F.I. section, and who had been a supporter of Cadart, moved forward to assume a more prominent role in the leadership of the Paris group. He, and along with Jean-Pierre Vigier, an important French physicist and theorist in quantum mechanics, became much more active in the preparations for the Tribunal, as did Roger Pic, a journalist and maker of important documentary films about Cuba and China's Cultural Revolution.

I wasn't present at the subsequent meeting in Paris, the one following the fateful London meeting that had only five members of the Working

Committee present and which reversed the decisions of the previous meeting. I'm now relying on my memory and my own reports about it to North America and to Brussels. Ralph told us that the Paris Tribunal members, especially Sartre, were opposed to the idea of a series of three sessions of the Tribunal taking place over April, May and June, a proposal submitted from London with the support of Russell.[26] I had had my own reservations about this plan. I could well understand the Paris people not wishing to spend most of their summer in meetings and even Geoff, Pat and me were beginning to be skeptical about the practicalities of that idea, but Ralph suggested there might be political reasons behind Sartre's opposition and that he had detected divisions within the Vietnamese about the question of the Tribunal, and that the French CP, through Leon Matarasso, was intent on sabotaging it.

Our group knew enough to be aware that the CP was a big player in what was going on, but we had no independent means to assess the veracity of Ralph's version of it. It's possible that Ralph, we thought at the time, because so much was at stake financially for Russell and the Foundation, might have been losing some of his objectivity. Quintin, who was living in Paris, told me that while some of what Ralph was saying may have been a factor, he personally questioned how much it determined the final outcome. And later, appearing to underline Quintin's point, Leon Matarasso made a strong public criticism of the French CP's attitude towards the Tribunal that seemed to contradict Ralph's version of what had been taking place behind closed doors.

By the middle of April, Quintin let me know that two North Vietnamese who were connected to their Embassy in Paris, a Colonel Ha Van Lau and a Pham Van Bac, had also become active on the Paris Working Committee, something that had been arranged by Ralph when he was in Hanoi. This meant there was a staff of seven people in the office now working full-time on preparations, more than sufficient to carry out their tasks, it seemed, but soon the Committee began having difficulties finding a hall for the proposed Paris session and speculation began to appear in the French press that it would possibly be banned by de Gaulle.

The date was pushed back for sixteen days to April 26th, to take place in the Hotel Continental. We had initially been heartened by the choice of Paris, when de Gaulle seemed to give the appearance of bending to the rise in popular sentiment in France against the war by publicly condemning the Americans for their crude intervention in French affairs (the U.S. had publicly called on the French authorities to prevent the Tribunal meeting.) In light of this, we figured de Gaulle might have had difficulties reversing his position and moreover, we reasoned, his statement must have been made public only after he had first rebuffed the Americans in private, evidence of some kind of breach in U.S.-French diplomatic relations, we guessed. And to ascertain if there was any substance to the media stories about a possible ban, Laurent Schwartz had met with a government official whom he knew personally to feel him out—and he was assured there would be no ban.

Quintin Hoare and the Vietnamese made similar enquiries of the police and were also told there would be no problem. All this only served to give the Paris people—and us in London—a false sense of security that everything would go ahead as planned. Geoff Coggan, the official press officer of the Tribunal, issued a press release announcing a three-day delay in the opening, until April 29th, and a change in the venue to the Municipal Theatre, Issy les-Moulineaux.[27] This proved to be sadly mistaken. On April 19th, the Tribunal, with many members already on their way to attend it, was banned from meeting in France by the French government.

We had some hope it might be rescheduled in Havana, on an emergency basis. In the weeks prior to this, the Cubans had expressed some sympathy for the work of the Tribunal and we were hoping they might help fund it. Melba Hernandez from Cuba, one of their most important women leaders, and a veteran of the 26th of July attack on the Moncada fortress, had been a late addition to it. Jean-Pierre Vigier, one of the Tribunal's key supporters in Paris, had recently been in Havana working on this idea, as had Ken Coates who was followed there by Ralph and who happened to be in Havana as the crisis over the banning started to unfold.

When Ralph met with Castro around that time, Fidel suggested to him that instead of Havana, the facilities of the United Nations in New York might be used for a session that could be sponsored by the Cuban government.[28] Nothing ever came of Fidel's idea. In response to the French ban, an urgent meeting was quickly convened by Sartre's representative, Claude Lanzman, which included de Beauvoir, Schwartz and all the supporters in Paris, to deal with this crisis.

By then Deirdre Griswold had entered the picture. I had first met Deirdre in the fifties when I stayed at her home a few times when she was a young leader of the SWP's Buffalo branch when it was led by Sam Marcy. The group would later split from the SWP to form the Workers World Party. At Ralph's insistence she had taken the place of Quintin Hoare, who had returned to London, and she was acting as London's liaison with Paris—a move he had made without consulting us, I might add. When I learned of it, I was at first a little apprehensive about what her attitude would be towards our group because of our past political differences, but this proved to be a needless worry. She was soon joined in London by Maryann Weissman, another member of her group. Deirdre had become involved in the work of the Tribunal through her contacts with the Foundation made at the time of the Indonesian massacres when Ralph had been in Djakarta.

Indonesia was the scene of a brutal slaughter, which the Western press did not pay much attention to, when an estimated million or more members and supporters of the CP were hunted down by the military and killed. Because of the lack of news about the crisis in the media, the BRPF had begun a campaign to publicize and protest the slaughter. Russell had issued several press statements to protest the indifference to it in the media and expose what had happened. As a result, Deirdre's group, which after its walkout from the SWP had set up a new grouping, Youth Against War and Fascism (YAWF), and most likely inspired by Russell's statements, set about organizing a public campaign with the objective, as Deirdre wrote to Ralph, "to make people realize that such a decisive swing to the right in this day and age must of necessity have been made with the complicity of U.S. imperialism—we must ferret out the details of that complicity."[29] YAWF's hope was that something similar to the Russell Tribunal would "probe the responsibility for the Indonesian blood-bath."[30] They also published a pamphlet about the issue, *The Silent Slaughter: The role of the United States in Indonesia*, with an introduction by Russell. I had very little contact with Deirdre and Maryann, but Pat Jordan and Geoff Coggan soon assured me they had no difficulty getting along with them and their contribution to the work was greatly appreciated by everybody.

At Claude Lanzman's emergency meeting, decisions were quickly made to further postpone the Tribunal for another three days, from April 29th until May 2nd. What we found odd about this was that, aside from the delay, all the actions to deal with its consequences were simply forwarded to the Working Committee in London for execution. They asked us to make immediate enquiries to see if the Tribunal could be convened in either Stockholm, Algiers, Havana or Prague, in that order of importance. At the same time, they told us, we should communicate immediately with everyone involved—the Tribunal members, the teams of investigators and the witnesses who were to appear before it—to inform them about the delay. This request, when we learned about it, made us question what the Paris Working Committee had been up to in the previous months.

Why didn't they have the means to communicate this information themselves, we wondered? To make matters even more confusing, and for some unfathomable reason, all these requests to us for action did not reach us until very late. As a result, many of the Tribunal people began to arrive in Paris not knowing whom to contact or where to go. The Japanese delegation, according to our comrade Setsure Tsurishima, arrived on the originally scheduled date and wandered around Paris for five days, totally lost.

As all this was going on, the Tribunal's London group, now comprised of Deirdre Griswold, Russell Stetler, Geoff Coggan and Maryann Weissman, announced a series of press conferences in preparation for an "April 29th opening of the Tribunal." This, I could only figure, was a way of trying to force the French supporters to hold to the original date and to not delay it for the three more days that had been agreed to at the Lanzman meeting.

Later, Quintin told me that if the Tribunal had gone ahead on the 29th, as planned, it would have been a debacle because the Paris Working Committee was in a state of chaos due to the ban by de Gaulle, and many of the reports that were in preparation for that session had not been completed. Part of the difficulty, it seemed to me, was that instead of acting as a "liaison" between Paris and London, Deirdre was tending to act as Ralph's loyal "commissar" to push things along. That had the effect, it seems, of getting the backs up of everyone who was not part of Ralph's immediate circle.

A new location, Stockholm, was hurriedly found by Peter Weiss and the Tribunal's Swedish Support Committee there. The Tribunal—and the Foundation—had achieved widespread support in Sweden and we had every hope we would have a successful session at that new location. The Swedish CP supported it and the anti-war movement there was the largest in Europe.

Deutscher and Schoenman had recently toured Sweden and had spoken to several mass meetings of enthusiastic supporters, one in Uppsala on March 23rd. Peter Limqueco, a Director of the BRPF, had helped set up a branch there. In addition, there appeared to be no legal hurdles. The previous February, the Swedish Prime Minister had cabled Russell. While expressing opposition to the Tribunal, he stated he would not ban it because, constitutionally, he did not have those powers. It could go ahead as planned. However, publicly he had issued a statement saying he was opposed to it. Yet earlier, the Swedish government had granted visas to Tribunal participants.[31] Thus, as the Paris launch began to be called into question, queries were made to see if Stockholm could be an alternative. The answer came back, yes, and immediately Tribunal supporters there began to prepare the venue.

Because of the confusion caused by de Gaulle's ban, however, by the time the Tribunal members finally got to Stockholm on May 2nd, everyone was just about spitting mad—a lot of it focused on Ralph, who had arrived directly from Havana in time for the first private session. By then the American State Department had swooped down to lift his passport, using as a reason his trips to Havana and Hanoi. The French, at the same time, banned him from entering France. It wouldn't be long before he would also be barred from Britain.

At the first private session in Stockholm, Schoenman had come down very forcefully, I learned later, angry at the "chaos" in Paris and about the way Russell's money was being spent without any reciprocity from Paris. He demanded that the financial problem be put on the agenda for discussion right away. Most of those present wanted to avoid it, apparently, and Schwartz is said to have tried to have it postponed, but Ralph insisted upon going ahead with the matter anyway. Then Vladimir Dedijer took the floor, to launch a sharp verbal attack against Ralph, full of personal resentment about his "treatment at Ralph's hands." He was Chairman of the outfit, he reportedly said, yet decisions had been made without consulting him. Information had been sent out inferring he had been consulted when he in fact he hadn't been, and proposals that were attributed to him when in fact he knew nothing about them. There were no proper financial accounts, no records of expenditures, no minutes kept of decisions, he complained. It was a long list of grievances, like those we had been hearing from Paris over the previous months, oblivious to the fact that ever since the first session in London, we had received the minimum of help from them, and no money.

Every second week, under Ralph's editorship, we had produced a bulletin especially for the Tribunal members, letting them know who was being suggested for inclusion on the investigating teams, and asking for their recommendations. Only Tariq Ali and Gisele Halimi's names had been put forward as a result of this. It's "exasperating to be accused of failing to consult," wrote Ralph to Laurent Schwartz, "when it is the Tribunal members who have committed to respond to the bulletins which inform them of the proposals received by our Secretariat."[32]

Relations between Dedijer and London could not have been worse at that point. A tall, physically imposing man, we had quickly learned after the London session that he was always on a short fuse. Ralph, who is of average height and slender build, told us how once in Paris, the Yugoslav, in an outburst of uncontrollable rage, had jumped on him, grabbed him by the throat and at the same time bit him on his head. At other times he had physically assaulted Chris Farley and Quintin Hoare and had even, during an angry outburst, disgustingly, spat on Russell Stetler.[33]

Laurent Schwartz, at the same private meeting in Stockholm, did not go as far as Dedijer but took the opportunity to air a few of his own grievances, complaining about the proposed dates for investigative team departures, stressing and urging that there should only be a single Working Committee, but that it not be the London one and that it need not necessarily be in Paris. David Dellinger, the well-known American pacifist and anti-war activist from New York, a key member of the Tribunal in the U.S., said he was in agreement with Schwartz and then moved a resolution to that effect. It passed unanimously—nine votes for, with a few abstentions, with the actual location of the Working Committee to be discussed later in the session.

Other major differences that emerged in Stockholm were about how the Tribunal verdicts on the questions posed by Russell in the November session would be presented to the public. This was argued over the course of three private meetings. Would there be a legal background provided, or would it just be a straight yes or no. The lawyers were insisting that there be ample time allowed to present the reasoning behind the verdict— which would have meant an unavoidable delay—while Sartre, Schwartz, Melba Hernandez, and the Vietnamese wanted an immediate verdict.

Arriving several days late in the midst of all this, Lawrence Daly and Isaac Deutscher, both of them totally unacquainted with what had gone on before, insisted that the question of the "re-location" of the Working Committee again be placed on the agenda for reconsideration. Quintin Hoare told me he thought this was due more to a misunderstanding than anything else, but in any case Deutscher considered the proposal by the French to move the Working Committee to Paris to be a direct slight against Russell. Moreover, he was annoyed that the decision to move it had been made in Daly's and his absence, and by the behaviour of Dedijer in the chair, "a rude, chairman," he would write later, explaining why he had "tabled a motion of no confidence in him as our chairman." When his comments on the matter were ignored and his vote of protest rejected, Deutscher quickly got to his feet and left the meeting, thereafter only attending the public sessions.[34]

At another private meeting, nevertheless, the question of the Working Committee managed to find its way onto the agenda yet again. By this time, Ralph had modified his position, agreeing that perhaps it should be in Stockholm after all. Peter Weiss, however, a very active campaigner for the Tribunal and who lived in Stockholm, insisted it should be in Paris, probably not having the resources to see it through if it was relocated to Sweden. Deutscher later told me he had supported the idea of it being in London, but only because he did not wish to offend Russell. Now that the decision for Paris had been made, Deutscher thought this might possibly be the best arrangement for the future. He told me he had backed up Ralph in the early discussions, but seeing how he was approaching problems with a lack of diplomacy, he too became somewhat critical of him, considering him to be ". . . an erratic General Secretary."[35] What he didn't appreciate was that Ralph had just been banned from France, effectively preventing him from participating in the Tribunal's work if the Working Committee ended up there.

When the Tribunal finally got around to discussing finances, Chris Farley tabled a letter, dated May 4th, from Russell appealing to the Tribunal to meet its debt to the Foundation, an issue that still remained unresolved. Dave Dellinger, the American anti-war leader, upon seeing the letter, called it "an affront" to the Tribunal.[36] Earlier Ralph had shown the letter to Schwartz, who was in the chair at the time and who, because the meeting lacked a quorum, advised against tabling it. But Chris and Ralph proceeded to do so anyway.

". . . I have spent nearly all my time since our November session," Russell wrote the Tribunal, "in writing and broadcasting about the Tribunal and helping raise money through my writings. This money has been made available as it arrived, though on several occasions the Foundation was in severe financial difficulties. But by earning advances on future work, by spending money for future taxation and by the entire Board of Directors taking personal liability for the Tribunal, we have somehow managed. I have to admit quite frankly that I was never anxious to lend too much money to the Tribunal because I saw little evidence that it was raising money energetically and I feared that an easy income from the Foundation would only confirm the Tribunal in this pattern . . ." The Working Committee in Paris, he wrote, ". . . took a series of decisions without stating how these would be financed and left the Foundation in the position of having to find money for them or see the Tribunal collapse in public ridicule."

Earlier, when Russell had sent Chris Farley to the Working Committee in Paris to find out what concrete steps were being taken to raise money, Chris reported back to him that fundraising was not even mentioned in a meeting of several hours duration. He was told, when he spoke to one of the Members, "not to worry, as the Member hoped soon to send a substantial sum to the Tribunal." Nothing ever came of this, Russell noted, and at second meeting similar promises were repeated again with a similar lack of results. Russell proposed, "if the Tribunal feels on reflection that it is unable to keep this commitment, it should instead give the Foundation the world film, recording and publishing rights to the proceedings of the Tribunal, in the hope that the Foundation will be able to recover some of its losses . . ."[37]

A film by Jean-Luc Godard was being talked about around that time and it was hoped that this would bring in some money. But even this source of relief to the Russell Foundation seemed elusive when Schwartz, in an apparent rebuff to Russell, in a letter to the Tribunal—to which Deutscher objected—wrote, "The Tribunal reserves the copyright for all publications, photographs and films concerning its activity."[38]

At the private meeting in Stockholm, Ralph claimed that up until April 1st, the Tribunal owed the Foundation almost 25,000 GBP. This figure had been compiled, Geoff Coggan later told me, mainly from information Ralph had provided him during the course of the sessions and it would later be amended upward by Chris Farley to over 35,000 GBP—a huge sum for those times, equal to approximately half a million GBP today. It seems to have been a big shock to most of them.

Schwartz is reported to have replied that the Tribunal would recognize "a debt" to the Foundation, but not necessarily "the debt" Ralph was talking about and he proposed they establish a small commission that would include two London people, along with a chartered accountant to go over Ralph's figures. This is the normal way to deal with such things, he is reported to have said, especially since Paris had been asking for a financial statement for a considerable period, but with no results. Ralph's response was to tell Schwartz that, because of earlier demands from the Tribunal that the accounts be professionally audited, the Foundation's books had been forwarded to an accountant at a cost of 300 GBP and that his report was yet to be completed. This was treated with some skepticism and left the meeting at an impasse in dealing with the matter. Chris Farley had advanced a similar explanation four months earlier when he had answered Dedijer in a letter, with copies to Schwartz and Jouffa, that the financial records "are with our accountants and may not be available for several weeks, although we have requested them as a matter of urgency . . ."[39]

Schwartz would later repeat his complaints directly to Russell. He wrote that the figure of 35,000 GBP presented to the Tribunal was "unacceptable for several reasons. First of all, no detailed book-keeping has ever been furnished to us, despite all of our requests; on numerous occasions Jouffa, a member of the financial commission, asked Schoenman for a detailed account of this expenditure; this request was never complied with; the Japanese member, Mr. Morikawa has never received anything either; that is why these members of the financial commission resigned several weeks before the Stockholm session. The account presented to us by Schoenman has nothing in common with a true financial report; as such it is unverifiable, and therefore cannot be recognized."

"That is why," Schwartz continued, "the Tribunal decided that the new financial commission would examine in detail the accounts kept in the past, and check the accounts presented by Schoenman. It is quite obvious that no self-respecting organization can proceed otherwise; we can neither pay nor recognize as a debt the total which is indicated to us without possible verification."[40] Sartre is reported to have caustically observed, at this point, that the relationship of the Foundation to the Paris centre was similar to that of imperialism vis-a-vis the colonial countries—loans were imposed as was the manner of repayment, referring to the matter of the Tribunal's copyrights. Ralph would later characterize the analogy, in an angry letter to Schwartz, as insolent, reprehensible and insulting.[41]

Finally, it was agreed in Sweden that matters were far too complicated to be put into a letter and that a face-to-face meeting with Russell was necessary. They decided that in the near future they would send a delegation, comprised of Dedijer, Deutscher, Sartre and Schwartz to meet with him in Wales, an attempt to get around Ralph, of course, but which never ever got off the ground because before agreeing to it, Russell insisted that they should first acknowledge their obligations to the Foundation, a position that Deutscher fully supported. Schwartz said he would write to Russell and answer the questions about money posed in his May 4th letter and also arrange for the visit.[42]

According to Quintin Hoare, with whom I later spoke, the only person who seemed to be totally mystified by what was going on was Melba Hernandez, the Tribunal member from Cuba, who had to rely on an interpreter most of the time and missed a lot of what was taking place. Nominated by Russell, she had been a late but significant addition. She headed up Cuba's Committee for Solidarity with Vietnam. A lawyer and close associate of Fidel Castro's, she had been one of the main women leaders of the 26th of July Movement and a veteran of the assault on the Moncada barracks; she had been imprisoned alongside Fidel. Later she would become Cuban Ambassador to Vietnam and to Cambodia. Her membership on the Tribunal at that particular time was testimony to the importance with which the Cubans regarded the project and also was an indirect criticism of Moscow's hostility to it. According to Quintin, Ralph was the only one who took the time to talk to her in Stockholm; shortly after the session, he headed for Cuba to try and get help with the Tribunal's funding problems, I imagine, and at the same time discuss with the Cubans Russell's support for a solidarity campaign in Latin American.

Alongside the closed meetings in Stockholm, the Tribunal carried on with its scheduled public sessions. Various written reports were received from many specialists, such as one by Gabriel Kolko, the American radical historian, on the history of U.S. aggression in Vietnam.[43] Investigating teams who had been to Cambodia or North Vietnam reported their findings. Their reporters were interrogated by Gisele Halimi, who acted as a kind of "prosecutor" to deal with two of the questions posed by Russell at the initial November session: was the U.S. guilty of aggression in Vietnam and was it guilty of war crimes? The answer from the Tribunal was a unanimous yes, even though there were minor differences on other issues, such as, for example, between de Beauvoir and Deutscher that cropped up during the preparation of a public statement that was to be released at the end of the proceedings. Deutscher had condemned the Americans for fostering a "civil war" and de Beauvoir objected to the term, saying the Tribunal should not talk about "civil war" but only about American aggression and war crimes.[44]

Despite the internal difficulties and the unresolved financial problems, everyone involved considered Stockholm a great success, on the whole, and the Tribunal seemed to have broken through the barrier of silence that heretofore had surrounded most of its deliberations. Coverage by the international press was better than ever. In addition, many of the Tribunal's members were interviewed on radio and television, allowing them to highlight the important work of the preceding few days.

After the Stockholm sessions adjourned, Schwartz and company immediately placed everything under the control of the Paris Working Committee and re-organizing its structure, with little input from London. The Committee would now be comprised of Dedijer, Lanzman (acting for Sartre), Schwartz, Dr Bejar, Jouffa, Leon Matarasso, Vigier and Ralph, whose name must have been included solely for appearance's sake because he would be unable to attend any meetings in Paris, having been banned from France. Much to our anxiety in London, the solution to the financial crisis seemed to be as far away as ever, if not further, and while we did not talk about it publicly, the reality was that effectively a split had taken place between Paris and London—and we had been left out in the cold.

We had left the door ajar for the Parisians to escape their financial obligations, it seemed to us, and they had raced through it. I have to confess, the Foundation's people bore a lot of the responsibility for what ensued due to their sloppiness—for example, in failing to get receipts for expenditures, as can be seen in Farley's July 31st reply to Anders already cited. And as late as June 27th, Russell was telling Schwartz, ". . . our accountant continues his work and will, of course, be pleased to send a final statement of the accounts . . . to any other accountant designated by you."[45]

To this day I still do not understand why they were unable to present an acceptable financial balance sheet, at least up until the move to Paris. They had carried out all the practical work of setting up the Tribunal and Ralph, a central figure in the Foundation, was General Secretary of the Tribunal, after all, and bore a responsibility that the books should be in proper order and open to inspection. In the various archives I have consulted in preparation for this chapter, I could find no such records.

Schwartz's complaints had an air of legitimacy to them that was difficult to refute, although I have no explanation as to why the Paris centre could not at least have provided an even "partial" payment to cover some of the expenses that were easily verifiable, such as airline tickets and the like. Even they must have recognized that these were huge. The formalism and rigidity of the Paris people on this matter was seen by us as a clear attempt to avoid their obligations, and came on top of other problems. Ralph told us that often, despite his best efforts, he had been unable to meet the Tribunal people in Paris and complained, about Sartre specifically, that "he was unable to gain prompt and regular access to the Executive President and that this officer was unwilling to sign letters requesting financial support for the Tribunal."[46]

The 35,000 GBP figure that Ralph and Chris were talking about included all the outlays for the first London session. The Foundation had met those initial expenses out of its own funds. They included airfares from around the world, hotel expenses for many of the members, and, after the London event, it covered the costs of sending the investigating teams to Cambodia and Vietnam along with covering the travel and hotel expenses of our London people, who over many months, sometimes once a week, travelled back and forth to Paris, on top of salaries for clerical staff and the cost of the London office space.

The main reason for being unable to present acceptable financial reports, I'm convinced, was a lack of proper bookkeeping in the early phases of the project. The Foundation had only three people on staff for the longest time: Ralph, Chris Farley and Pamela Woods, in a small two-roomed office in Piccadilly, and it was only with the campaign to organize the Tribunal did it begin to increase its staff to meet the new demands being placed upon them. Up until then, Russell had raised money directly through public appeals to help finance his sundry campaigns, but the Foundation was not required to report to anyone outside its own ranks about how that money was spent.

The Tribunal was another thing entirely. An independent body requiring its own set of books, financial officer and a financial reporting system that had to be above reproach, something that didn't happen until later. I have no reason to believe there was any misappropriation of funds; in my experience we all worked very hard for virtually nothing. In the early days of getting the Tribunal established, it seems there was an unavoidable overlapping of expenses between it and the BRPF—there was no certainty it would be even a reality—and Ralph, who was travelling the world, probably had difficulties keeping track of the various monies being spent, which helped precipitate the crisis in Stockholm. I'm sure his hope was that, if only on a good faith basis, the Tribunal would take responsibility for the money Russell had loaned it. It was a major issue and, within a matter of months, the failure to resolve it would cripple the Foundation.

From what I knew about Ralph, I'm convinced that in Stockholm—unfazed by rank, intellectual or otherwise—he would have been like a bulldog, obstinate to the point of obnoxiousness in trying to get Russell's money back. I was told he was accused of being insensitive to the opinions of others, and, after Stockholm, Schwartz complained to Russell, "Although he is a very devoted and dynamic young man, who certainly possesses exceptional qualities, he also possesses very serious faults; he totally lacks tact and politeness, and all sense of organization and responsibility. It is scarcely tolerable for men like members of the Tribunal, who are internationally renowned for their intellectual and moral qualities and for their long struggle for truth and justice, to see themselves constantly treated airily or even contemptuously by someone who speaks on your behalf."[47] Everyone in Paris seemed to be lined up against him. Quintin Hoare told me that even the Vietnamese—who up until then, according to Quintin, had been on very good terms with Ralph—had become unhappy. They stated they had many grievances about his behaviour that they never specified. From what we know now, they were probably symptoms of the disagreements in Hanoi about the Tribunal project as a whole.

Not long after Stockholm, a copy of a letter from Russell to Dedijer, which had been discussed privately in Stockholm, began making the rounds. It had, by this time, gone to all Tribunal members, and was considered to be a sharp personal rebuke of Dedijer. It came very close to accusing the eminent Yugoslav jurist of being insane. When he returned from Stockholm, Deutscher, in conversation, let me know that he considered the letter to be an "act of revenge" by Ralph because of Dedijer's hostility. Deutscher told me he feared that, if it became public, there might be a lot of public squabbling and he might be compelled to resign because of the scandal. This never happened, of course, but it pointed to sharp underlying tensions in the Tribunal coming out of Stockholm.

Within a week the divisions became public. Relations—what little there were of them—between London and Paris just about evaporated entirely when an article based upon information obviously provided by Dedijer appeared in the London *Observer*, May 14th, 1967, under the headline, "Tribunal eases out Russell." The shift to Paris was seen as a "behind the scenes takeover by Paris, which has been going on for months..." and that "Earl Russell's name was gradually removed from the title and proceedings of the Tribunal. Jean-Paul Sartre, the 'executive president'; then dominates the Tribunal both publicly and in private, if only besides Russell, his was the sole name known to a wide public." Reporting a charge that Ralph had put the work of the Tribunal at risk because he had criticized Tage Erlander, the Swedish Prime Minister, about a possible banning in Sweden (something that Ralph would later vigourously refute in a letter to the British *Tribune*),[48] the article quoted an unnamed member of the Tribunal as saying the move from London to Paris was meant "to break the domination of Bertrand Russell."

Although there had been a split, this was a gross misrepresentation of what had transpired, because Ralph and the other two British members, Daly and Deutscher, had in fact supported the move. Moreover, the suggestion of significant political differences was news to all of us, because all the votes on the major issues had been unanimous. "Many members, particularly the Yugoslav chairman, Dr. Vladimir Dedijer," the *Observer* noted, "were disturbed by the clamorous anti-Americanism of Earl Russell, as conveyed by his American secretary Ralph Schoenman. Dr. Dedijer feels that this has discredited the Tribunal in the West and wants a less emotional approach."

The charge of "Anti-Americanism," a common accusation from ruling circles in Europe in those days against those who opposed the war, was of course scurrilous and a tipping of the hat to those liberals who were finding it uncomfortable sitting on the fence. Russell and Schoenman were radically opposed to the U.S. government's policies and their consequences in Vietnam, of course, but not to the American people whom they happened to believe were also victims of the war. Nothing was said in the article about money, it should be noted, the real source of the difficulties between London and Paris.

Russell's response to Dedijer was immediate and scathing. Dated the same day as the *Observer* article, his letter, which he circulated to all Tribunal members, stated: "I have refrained from writing you before now despite a long unpalatable history of private behaviour on your part for which I have great distaste. In view, however, of your recent public declarations I can no longer tolerate remaining silent . . . You have violated the restriction upon members to avoid speaking to the press about private discussions. You have also violated the proper procedure of the Tribunal by stating publicly, without authorization, that the Tribunal would hold its next session in the Vatican. These unauthorized statements have brought the Tribunal to ridicule and have called in question the association I have with a Tribunal which I inaugurated, supported in all ways and of which I am honorary President . . . I appreciate that you are an ill man;" Russell wrote, "this seems to me to make mandatory your withdrawal."[49]

And the financial problem seemed to be no closer to solution. Referring to Schwartz's promise, Russell wrote to Deutscher, ". . . I am exasperated to have heard nothing from him in the past two and a half weeks. In particular, I am anxious to receive in writing, confirmation that the very considerable loan which I made to the Tribunal will be honoured as previously agreed . . ."[50] On top of that, there were other financial obligations the Paris organizers refused to meet. They failed to pay Peter Weiss the $2000 they had promised him to help organize the Stockholm session and the American Courtland Cox, Stokely Carmichael's representative on the Tribunal, was stranded in Paris because the Paris Working Committee refused to pay his airfare back to the U.S. Hugh Manes, a former U.S. soldier, who had travelled to Stockholm to provide testimony to the Tribunal, was also stranded under similar circumstances.

Deutscher did everything he could to try and overcome the crisis that had erupted because of the *Observer* article, writing many letters to this end. "I have done my best to reduce, if possible, the Dedijer incident to insignificance. I do not think we should ask for Dedijer's resignation and I have communicated this view to Russell," he wrote to Daly.[51] He reassured Russell, "Our unanimous vote in Stockholm indicates that our differences are not of a fundamental character, but purely personal. We should ignore these differences . . ."[52] To Jean-Paul Sartre he wrote, "Russell feels deeply offended and incensed, especially by the press reports suggesting that the Tribunal had turned against him. I think we should do all we can to reestablish harmony. This makes it all the more urgent, in my view, that we should, with or without Dedijer, go and see him in Wales . . ."[53] To Schwartz, he complained about the famous mathematician's attitude towards Russell, writing in a frank manner and in a tone—perhaps a nod to their common political history—that one would expect from a comrade: "I must say that I am disturbed by the content and the tone of your letter to him." You should have first of all, Deutscher wrote, "confirmed in writing, that the Tribunal acknowledges its debt . . . but reserves its right and duty to verify the expenses incurred and establish the amount of the debt . . . This is really the minimum that he had every reason to expect from us. And, surely, the tone of our communication with him should have been less formalistic and frigid." He urged that the matter of the Tribunal's copyrights as a possible way to reimburse the Foundation should be left open, something that Schwartz and Sartre seemed to have closed off.

Money from the copyrights to the material from the Tribunal's sessions was seen by Daly, Deutscher, Russell and Schoenman as a way for the Tribunal to pay off its debt. Russell became very alarmed when there appeared to be no recognition of what he was seeking. ". . . I am shocked that the letter I received from M. Sartre and Professor Schwartz fails to acknowledge my letter of May 4th," wrote Russell to Günther Anders on June 16th, referring to his letter that Farley and Schoenman had read in Stockholm. "I suggested," Russell stated, "that if the Tribunal felt it was unable to pay its full debt to the Foundation, it should yield all publishing rights to the Foundation . . . Since the close of the Stockholm session, my proposal has been totally disregarded . . . an (sic) volume has been published in Paris, and a contract signed with a French publisher. (In a similar unauthorized move, Dr. Dedijer sold the Scandinavian rights of publication for a very small sum.) Thus the Foundation's right to this material has been rejected without even a courteous letter so informing me. By inference, our claim to any re-imbursement has been put aside."[54]

Deutscher fully backed Russell's position. "Generally speaking, I think that the manner in which we have been treating Lord Russell is absolutely inadmissible," he wrote to Schwatrz. "I would like to think that it is due to neglect rather than to intent. I strongly urge the Working Committee to make a sincere and determined effort to overcome the present intolerable situation and to put the whole relationship with Lord Russell on the basis of that warm admiration and respect for him which we express in public and which we showed him when he initiated the Tribunal. Whatever Ralph Schoenman may have said or done in the meantime, must not be allowed to affect our attitude towards Russell. As Sartre said to Schoenman in Stockholm: 'Vous, Schoenman, vous n'etes pas Lord Russell.'"[55] When Russell complained to Deutscher about the lateness of a reply from Schwartz, Deutscher came to his defense, explaining ". . . the reason why you had no further word from Paris was that Professor Schwartz had been away in Canada . . . He is a man of the highest integrity. The appearance of negligence on his part is due entirely to the fact that he has more commitments than he can cope with." Using the opportunity to stress Schwartz's importance to their work, he told Russell, "He is, as far as I can judge, the only member of the Tribunal in Paris who really works for the Tribunal. He is in addition the moving spirit and the organizer of the large scale and intensive campaign which is being conducted under the name *Un Milliard pour Vietnam*."[56]

It would be near the end of July before the hard feelings over money and the "Dedijer incident" would begin to abate somewhat. "I have recently exchanged a number of letters with Professor Schwartz," Russell wrote to Lawrence Daly, "and I feel some progress has been made towards resolving our differences."[57] But a new crisis struck the Tribunal around the issue of the 1967 Israeli-Arab War. It had broken out as the Tribunal was in the midst of preparations for its next session, scheduled to take place late in November in Copenhagen. The League of Arab Nations formally appealed to the Tribunal to get involved to investigate if Israel had committed war crimes. Sartre, supported by de Beauvoir and Schwartz—apparently without much thought for their positions as responsible leaders of the Tribunal and pre-empting any future position the Tribunal might have taken on the matter—declared in a press conference: ". . . that the State of Israel is at the present time proving its clear desire for peace and cool-headedness." [58]

Deutscher, Daly, Russell and Schoenman were opposed to getting involved—not that they were sympathetic to the Israelis—because, as Russell correctly observed, "it could easily lead to a public display of differences within the Tribunal."[59] These new difference certainly ended any possibility that the Tribunal would become "permanent" and showed what the difficulties could be if it moved in that direction, which is why the Tribunal chose not to investigate any international issue other than Vietnam. For example, when Portuguese exile organizations and national liberation movements in the Portuguese colonies appealed to it to hear evidence against the brutal methods of the Salazar regime, it was forced to turn them down.

Although, as Deutscher had assured Russell, that there were no serious political differences among Tribunal members—at least on the issue of Vietnam—there were certainly deep and smouldering tensions amongst those of us working in London about the shift to Paris—both about money and Paris' lack of consultation with London. These tensions just about burst into flames with Dedijer's damaging words in the *Observer*, and were by no means fully extinguished. They flared up again when Schwartz, alarmingly, refused to take his distance from Dedijer and instead, acting like his attorney, made excuses for his bad behaviour.

By June, without any of its British members in attendance—including anyone from the Foundation or the London Working Committee—they reorganized their operation in Paris, reaffirming Sartre, Schwartz and Dedijer as Presidents. Their statement announcing these decisions also reports that prominent positions were given to Yves Jouffa, Leon Matarasso and Abraham Bejar, and that Jean-Pierre Vigier was appointed "Secretary General." Ralph Schoenman, although still retaining that title nominally on paper, was pushed aside and relegated to the task of finding a country that would accept the next session.[60] Not a mention is made of Russell, the Honourary Chairman and inspirer of the project, and the person who happened to be its main financial supporter! It was as if he had ceased to exist.

The cleavage was just about complete. Because Ralph was barred from France, the "restructuring" meant that the London Working Committee was shut out from any meaningful participation. "One might justifiably complain . . ." wrote Russell Stetler, "decision making procedures were never so abused as they have in recent weeks when many important decisions, including dispatch of a new investigating team, have been taken without any meeting of the wider collective."[61]

The last public session of the Tribunal took place that November in Roskilde, a few miles outside Copenhagen, Denmark. Sadly by that time Isaac Deutscher was no longer with us, having died suddenly in Italy in August from a heart attack. One of the immediate consequences of this tragedy was that the London Working Committee had lost a powerful ally in keeping things on course.

Ralph Schoenman was prevented from attending the final session because he had also been barred by the Danish authorities from entering that country. In addition, problems that had resulted from having financed the Tribunal ushered in a deep internal crisis in the Foundation that led to three of its directors—including David Horowitz—resigning. It even led to a split in our Fourth International grouping over the manner in which all those who had been working on the various projects of the Foundation had lost their jobs.

Russell Stetler was the only one from London able to attend the session in Roskilde. The Foundation was very much on the sidelines there, with most of the preparations and organizing under the leadership of the Paris people. As Russell Stetler observed, in a letter to Ernest Mandel, "by the time it reached Copenhagen it was splitting apart at the seams, all the usual political differences having been brought into sharp focus and magnified by the public reaction of various members to the June war in the Middle East."[62] The press tended to confirm this appreciation, at least at an organizational level. Reporting three days after it opened about a "many sided crises" and "almost chaotic conditions made worse by the many weaknesses in the Danish organizational work," Gosta Julin wrote in the liberal Swedish daily *Dagens Nyheter*, "An increasing number of the Tribunal members express regret for their 'unavoidable absence.' Some of them seem to have got lost on the way. No one can give a precise statement about how many of the permanent judges are expected in Roskilde. A few of them have paid a very short visit to the Tribunal town but quickly returned back home. Others have arrived in Copenhagen but (have) not turned up in Roskilde. And so the Roskilde session has become a Tribunal of the deputies."[63] However, despite this grim picture, the final published record of the session shows that much good work was accomplished there.

Three U.S. ex-army personnel—a first—gave direct evidence about U.S. war crimes. Statements from Russell were read at the beginning and end of the session, but most of the time between was spent answering the remainder of the questions he had posed in London, about the use of napalm in Vietnam, the bombing of civilians, the inhumane treatment of Vietnamese prisoners and the issue of genocide. On the latter issue, according to the *Dagen Nyheter* reporter, there was some differences of opinion between Dedijer and Sartre, with both absenting themselves from the session to return to their hotels thirty kilometres away to clarify in writing their respective views, which Sartre would later elaborate in his book, *On Genocide.*

In conclusion, what I have described in the previous pages about the internal problems of the Tribunal—which were indeed severe—as it sought to carry out its work, should not be seen as uncommon phenomena in any similar campaign that lacks solid funding and which has no large institution behind it, since it challenges the given wisdom of the time. This is in their nature. In the Fourth International, this kind of activity falls under the broad category known as "united front activity," where extra efforts are made by radicals to involve larger disparate political forces for a specific end and has its origins in the early days of the Third International. In the case of the Tribunal, we were mainly dealing with individuals.

A great deal of effort is usually required to maintain the cohesion of such a mission. Often many of the internal difficulties are due to the fact that most of the individuals don't know each other very well, plus the ad hoc nature of what they are about. Often they only get by through begging, borrowing and encouraging everyone to financially contribute. This is the work of the many organizers and supporters behind the scenes who, unheralded, make the most sacrifices, juggle contingencies and scrape around for resources. More often than not, the question of financial support is dealt with without any fanfare; but it is the critical component of any political activity that is not "official" and which challenges the policies of the ruling elites. There are always tensions and, sooner or later after a particular campaign, despite the sometimes bitter feelings between some of the personalities, they often get back together again to work on the next pressing issue. In this case that can be seen in regards to Czechoslovakia.

When the Russians invaded that country in August 1968, a group of Czech intellectuals and writers appealed to the Russell Tribunal to hold an enquiry into the occupation.[64] Their appeal received widespread coverage in the press, and Ralph, with only Russell's moral authority behind him and his own powers of persuasion, over a period of six months, working out of suitcases and hotel rooms in many countries, including Yugoslavia and Czechoslovakia, often under a pseudonym because of his illegal status, took on the task of organizing a "conference of prominent figures in the anti-imperialist movement" to condemn the Russian actions.[65] Notwithstanding their previous criticisms of him, which I have outlined in preceding pages, by personally visiting them and engaging them in discussion, Ralph managed to persuade all the main players in the Tribunal to come together again for another big project. He was even able to persuade Vladimir Dedijer to work with him on a joint statement, to which Russell, Sartre and Schwartz, along with many other prominent intellectuals, attached their names, which stated: "We pledge our political resistance to this assault on the most conscious and devoted part of the Czechoslovak people and declare our solidarity with them. We demand the immediate withdrawal of all the occupying troops of the Soviet Union, including the secret police." The conference took place in Stockholm, February 1–2, 1969.

TOP *Vanessa Redgrave waiting to speak; Pat Jordan to her left, Richard Branson behind them, Trafalgar Square, March 17th, 1968.*

BOTTOM *Special guest, Alain Krivine, leader of the French Jeunesse Communiste Revolutionnaire (JCR), waiting to speak.*

Chapter Seven

Isaac Deutscher

*I*T WAS DURING THE FOURTH INTERNATIONAL'S WORK IN SUPPORT OF the Russell Tribunal that Jess MacKenzie and I had the good fortune to be in regular contact with Isaac Deutscher and his wife Tamara. We would see them at least every couple of weeks or so, up until his sudden death in Italy on August 6th, 1967. Naturally, it was a devastating shock to us when it happened. He had become an ally during our work with the Tribunal and we considered him a very good friend, if not a comrade. In his intellectual prime, at the age of sixty, he was felled by a heart attack while he and Tamara were on their way to a vacation in Padua, Italy. Like many men of his generation, he seldom exercised, if ever. A pipe smoker, he had suffered from high blood pressure for many years, and his recent round of public political activity had begun to wear on him. The previous summer, when he returned from his speaking tour of the United States, he was ordered by his doctor to take two weeks rest. "My heart worked up and jumped quite irregularly," he wrote the S.W.P.'s Paul Montauk.[1]

When Tamara called us after she got back from Italy, we immediately sped over to see her at their home in Kidderpore Gardens, near Hampstead Heath. She was distraught, red-eyed from crying, but grimly focused on making the necessary arrangements for his funeral. We assured her we were available to help her in any way we could, but I'm not sure if we were of much solace; we didn't know her very well personally. It was a strange feeling being there in their house with Isaac absent, seeing his pipe and tobacco sitting next to the phone in the living room, as if waiting for him to reappear and pick it up. In line with Tamara's wishes, our group took the lead in organizing a memorial meeting on September 22nd in Mahatma Gandhi Hall. Chaired by Ralph Miliband, over three hundred people came to honour and remember Deutscher, with many of the London left in attendance, including some who in the past had been critical of his work on Russia.

Deutscher had been part of that broad category of socialists known in Britain in those years as the "New Left." He had been especially friendly with the circle around NLR and had been a participant in early discussions at Ralph Miliband's home—along with Perry Anderson, Ken Coates and John Saville, among others—about a possible "fusion" of the British left. These sessions had led to Miliband launching the "Centres for Socialist Education," of which Deutscher, although critical of the project, had become a member. Miliband and Saville had launched the *Socialist Register* the previous year.[2] The memorial meeting, in many ways, turned out to be a large gathering of the "New Left," with a good number of the "old left" also in attendance. On the platform were people Deutscher had worked with over the recent past, including Perry Anderson, Lawrence Daly, David Horowitz, K.S. Karol, Marcel Liebman and Daniel Singer. The event was an impressive tribute to his memory.[3]

I had first met Deutscher in June 1966, when Ralph Schoenman invited me, along with David Horowitz, to meet him at his home, around about the time Deutscher was thinking of participating in the Tribunal. It was more of a social call than a meeting. The conversation that evening, as I recall, was very general, ranging over many topics, from Marx's *Eighteenth Brumaire of Louis Napoleon* to the then looming crises in Sino-Soviet relations, with him doing most of the talking, mostly in answer to questions from Horowitz and Schoenman.

Deutscher wasn't a tall man, I remember, about 5'8", slightly overweight and with a neatly trimmed Van Dyke beard. A regular contributor to the BBC's Third Programme, he had a well-practiced speaking style. In a slight Polish accent he talked with great confidence and authority, clearly dominating the conversation that evening. When Ralph introduced me to him, he asked me what I was doing in London. In reply, I mentioned that in addition to helping out with the Russell Foundation's work, I was also running a small mail-order book service, Pioneer Books; this information I recall, didn't seem to register much with him in any special way. I didn't mention anything about the Fourth International, thinking it would be better to leave that topic for another day. Ralph did most of the talking, mainly explaining what Russell was trying to achieve with the Tribunal and some of the internal difficulties Russell was having in getting it going. Ralph hadn't gotten very far in his report however, before Deutscher interrupted him. One of his concerns, he said, was the proposed Tribunal's "political narrowness" and the apparently low representation from Britain, which, he let us know in no uncertain terms, he considered to be "shortsighted". It should have a much broader political representation, he interjected. From what I can see it seems to be made up mainly of people from the "left," he said. "Who do you have from Britain?" he asked. Ralph replied, "We have been trying to get others, but for now it's only Deutscher," and a brief exchange ensued about ways in which to politically broaden the Tribunal, a discussion we had already been having amongst ourselves. I was quietly pleased with his observations about this problem, because it tended to reinforce my own feelings in this regard. I was painfully aware that in Britain, the Tribunal to a certain extent was a prisoner of Ralph and Russell's political history because they had already fought a hard fight against those under the influence of the Labourites and the CP on the Vietnam issue.

The political marginalization of the Tribunal in Britain was a problem all of us recognized—no one more so than Deutscher, who worked tirelessly to overcome it. He searched out many people he knew personally to get support. He even made a special effort to get Michael Foot, the leader of the Labour Party's left wing, to become a member, but without any success. Deutscher was very pleased when Fenner Brockway—at some point, with his own project for a tribunal going nowhere—paid him a visit, telling him he was supportive of the Russell idea.

Deutscher was not uncritical of the project which he would eventually co-chair and into which he would invest a lot of his time, having put aside for the moment what he hoped would be his next major work, a biography of Lenin. "This has been a time devouring job," he wrote Margaret Bonnet in Paris. "I am not very happy about this Tribunal; I do not like the legalistic pretence and would have preferred something like a Commission of Enquiry doing a good piece of propaganda and enlightenment and appealing to public opinion in a more modest and more serious form. However, I was outvoted over this by lawyers, who felt in their element dealing with legal concepts and fiction and by Sartre, whose dramatist's instinct is attracted by the stage effect of a Trial. Nor do I like this galaxy of intellectual stars. One strike of American dockers refusing to load munitions for American troops in Vietnam would be worth a hundred such Tribunals. Unfortunately, there is no hope of such a strike and the Tribunal is better than no action at all . . ."[4]

At that first meeting in his home, the conversation quickly moved to Deutscher's very successful tour of the U.S., which had been sponsored by the American anti-war movement. He was clearly elated by the experience. He had seen the anti-Vietnam war radicalization up close, and, moreover, had received a very warm reception on his lecture tour where he had given a Marxist perspective on the history of the Cold War to several mass meetings—an audience of around 15,000 in Berkeley, California, and one of several thousand in Washington, D.C. It was probably the first time many in those audiences had ever heard an alternative and radical critique of their government's foreign policy. It also gave him a chance to get a new appreciation of the work of the SWP, causing him to begin to warm to it a little. More than anything else, though, I believe it was this experience in America that persuaded him to modify his policy of public non-involvement in British left politics and eventually accept Russell's invitation to be on the Tribunal. It wasn't long after that visit with Deutscher that Ralph persuaded Lawrence Daly, the leader of the Scottish Mine Workers, to also respond positively to Russell's invitation to come on board.

Soon after that first meeting, and much to my surprise, I got a call from Tamara asking if it might be possible for me to come over to their house within the next day or so. They wanted to have a "chat about the Russell Foundation," she said. I was, of course, flattered. In my books, getting a call from Deutscher was akin to getting a call from Trotsky himself, but I suspected Deutscher had since been talking to Sam Gordon about the political lay of the land around the Foundation and Sam had suggested he get in touch with me to help fill him in about it. Sam's connection with Deutscher went back many years.

An American SWP leader from the thirties and the Second World War period, and a very capable writer, Sam had been forced into exile in London—along with his wife, Millie, a British citizen—by the McCarthy witch-hunt, and was prohibited by the State Department from entry into the United States. They now had a young son. Like most of the SWP's central leaders, his passport had been lifted by the State Department during the McCarthy period. Sam had been the SWP's informal representative in Europe for many years and he had gotten to know Gerry Healy exceedingly well, meeting with him frequently until Healy's split from the International Committee of which the SWP had been an important part. From what I could see, the break with Healy had been a heavy personal blow to Sam because it also meant a break with many of the people around the Healy group whom he had known over the years and whom he considered comrades.

When I came upon the scene, Sam had been loosely connected to the I.G. and working closely with Alan Harris. Jess and I did our best to continue that relationship. I remember him as being very sober-minded and very well informed about the British left. His knowledge became invaluable to us. From time to time, I would meet with him, usually at noon hour in a pub near Fleet Street where he worked as a proofreader for one of the national dailies, and occasionally Jess and I would visit him and Millie at their home. He had been an officer in the American army during the war, he would eventually tell me, and in that capacity he had been in a position to move around a chaotic wartorn Europe fairly freely as the German armies were collapsing. Covertly, he had used his position in the military to make contact with the various Trotskyist groups and individuals in the immediate post-war period, most of them in the anti-fascist underground, including in Germany, some of them in materially acute and dire circumstances, helping them to recover from the savage repression they had suffered and channeling material aid to them from the SWP. When I was in Germany, this was confirmed to me by Georg Junglass, an older man of the Second World War generation and a leader of the German F.I. section, when, without any prompting from me, he told me how Sam had searched him out at great risk to himself when George had been in some kind of Allied holding camp, and on the verge of death from starvation.

When I first met Sam, he was spending many of his evenings translating Rudolf Hilferding's major work on economics from German into English, with the hope of having it eventually published, but nothing ever came of this. Hilferding, Sam told me, was an economist during the period when the German and Austrian social democrats had been revolutionary before the outbreak of World War One and had greatly influenced Lenin's economic thinking. Many times Sam expressed his frustration to me about being "trapped" in London—a victim of McCarthyism—and having to spend so much of his time earning a living, rather than doing political work or his translation of Hilferding. Even I could see he was in a relatively pedestrian occupation then, obviously far below his intellectual capacities. He was hoping, he told me, that Deutscher, maybe through his connections in publishing, might help him find some escape from his situation. Later, Deutscher told me that, as much as he would have liked, he wasn't in any position to help solve that problem. Sam was disappointed that nothing ever came of this, but he was reinvigorated politically when we began organizing the VSC and I can recall him speaking from the floor at a few of our large meetings at Caxton Hall, electrifying the audience with his comments about American imperialism; many of our supporters at these meetings wondered where he came from and asked me who he was. Later, he was stricken with cancer and became very ill, but recovered after a long hospital stay. Much to his frustration, however, his ability to participate in political activity had become severely reduced.

I went to see Tamara and Isaac Deutscher the next evening following that first phone call. Even though Tamara had told me over the phone why they wished to see me, I still wasn't sure exactly what to expect. Deutscher was very well known to the radical left; his reputation had reached almost mythic proportions in the English speaking world because of his three volume biography of Trotsky[5], regarded by many scholars—including many non-Marxists—as "a masterpiece" which even the most begrudging of us around the Fourth International considered a truly incredible achievement. At the age of nineteen, he had joined the Polish Communist Party in 1926, becoming one of its main leaders. He was well known to many of the older generation in the Fourth International because of this early history. The Polish party, with its tradition of independence from Moscow—the party of Rosa Luxemburg—had initially resisted Stalin's increasing control of the Third International.

Deutscher, after a trip to Moscow, had become increasingly repelled by the ultra-leftism of "third period Stalinism" as it was being expressed in Germany, and became a supporter of the Polish Left Opposition. Expelled from the CP in 1932, "for urging united Socialist-Communist action against rising Nazism," he formally affiliated to the International Communist League, led by Trotsky, but voted against the formation of the Fourth International. In April 1939, a few months before the occupation of Poland by the German armies and the outbreak of the Second World War, he arrived in Britain as a correspondent for the Polish Jewish journal, *Nash Psheglond*. Offered a staff position in General Sikorski's Polish Army "in exile," he refused it and "from 1940 to 1942, I was an ordinary soldier in his army in Scotland, and I spent most of the time in a punitive camp to which I was sent after many strong protests against anti-Semitism in his army," he later told *The Jewish Chronicle*.[6] He finally settled in London. With limited English and very few financial resources, those days must have been very difficult for him. His first paying job was editing a Yiddish publication. In London he met Tamara and began to concentrate on making a living through journalism, eventually succeeding in developing an impressive career by becoming a top journalist for the London *Economist* and later for the London *Observer*. He also became a respected political analyst, crafting a clear and accessible style. Many saw his achievements comparable to that of his compatriot, Joseph Conrad, a literary giant who wrote in English even though it was not his first language.

Deutscher had come to international public attention not long after the Second World War with his reporting of the Nuremberg Trials, to which he was an accredited press representative. Eventually taking a position on the editorial board of the *Economist*, he overcame all obstacles to become one of the world's most authoritative commentators on the political economy of the Soviet Union and Eastern Europe.

I quickly sensed that Deutscher, because he and Tamara were unfamiliar with the Foundation or the people around it, felt that with their involvement in the Tribunal they were perhaps entering "uncharted territory" and that they possibly needed some "intelligence" on what problems might lie ahead. Because of the swirl of gossip and speculation in some left circles—and beyond—about whether the Tribunal would even take place, they were fearful, I think, of being associated with some kind of public fiasco and above all they were hoping for reassurance things were alright "on the inside", so to speak. Their feelings in this regard were perfectly understandable because there was always a cloud of malicious rumours floating around the project, often planted and circulated in a clever calculating manner by those hostile to the Russell Foundation and its purposes. It's possible that he and Tamara had gotten wind of some of this and had become slightly spooked.

When I saw him, after a few pleasantries, he began asking me about what I thought of this or that person around the Foundation. Then he mentioned a slight feeling of apprehension about Ralph, sensing that he was a somewhat impulsive and not necessarily giving him, Deutscher, the "straight goods" about what was going on. But I remember noting to myself how strongly he made the point that during a recent very successful speaking tour of Scandinavia where he and Ralph had spoken to several mass meetings, Ralph had been very respectful of him and had been "perfectly well behaved" in his presence.

It was clear that Deutscher may have been keeping an eye on Ralph to see if there was anything to the gossip he had heard about him. I tried to allay his fears, pointing out that Ralph over the years in CND, in the Committee of 100 and in the Russell Foundation, had probably developed a keen sense of how to leverage Russell's prestige to overcome possible political opposition and to get the broad support necessary to make the many projects of the Foundation a reality. Lacking the luxury of having an organization of any substance behind him, I told Deutscher, I suspected that Ralph would often use the force of his personality to get his way, and most likely had made a few enemies in the process. In addition, I mentioned, he didn't suffer fools too gladly and there were a few of those around who still carried their grudges against him from past battles. Tamara and Isaac seemed reassured with this conversation but I wouldn't have been too surprised to learn they were in touch with others about these matters.

Over the next few months, I became very comfortable in their presence. Not long after my partner Jess MacKenzie arrived in London, I brought her to one of our get togethers to meet them. We were greeted very warmly by Tamara at the door of their house, who called out, "Isaac, they're here!" He soon appeared behind her and I introduced him to Jess for the first time. She was wearing slacks. Right away he began kibitzing with her. "What do we have here? A young man, or a young women?" he asked. Jess, with her long black hair flowing down the length of her back, looked every inch the young women she was. Ah, hah, he said, I'm not too old to know the difference, and I can see she's a young woman. We all laughed. They made us feel completely at ease. It wasn't long after that they introduced us to their son, Martin, a young and sociable teenager. When Tamara heard that Jess was managing our Pioneer Book-service, she volunteered Martin to come over to help her out, which he subsequently did on a regular basis.

It's impossible to write about Deutscher without stressing the importance Tamara played in helping him with his work. She dealt with most of his correspondence and worked alongside him as a tireless researcher on all his books. They were truly a team. An intellectual in her own right, her book reviews had appeared, from time to time, in *The Economist.*[7] Tamara was his most important collaborator, his "helpmate" he would tell us, once explaining to us the exact meaning of that word as it appeared in the Oxford English Dictionary.

Often when Jess and I went to their home, we would find both of them in their living room working on the draft of some article or other, hurrying to meet a deadline, heads close together poring over it and discussing some reference or other to obtain the exact formulation of a particular phrase, and even arguing with each other in a good natured way. An important part of Deutscher's writing method, I could see, consisted of him dictating his words to her which she would then transcribe to produce a draft that would be further amended and worked on before producing a final text for publication. I figured it was this way of working which may have given his words on the page their lucid style and the appearance of an oral discourse. When I read his work, even today, it's as if I still hear his voice, with his slight Polish accent, in my ears.

During those few months when we were informally meeting with him, he was working on his 1967 George Macauley Trevelyan lectures, on the occasion of the fiftieth anniversary of the Russian Revolution, which would later become a book.[8] He did not say much about it at the time, but it was obvious to us that he was elated with having been chosen for this important series of lectures at Cambridge. He was the first non-academic to have been awarded that honour.

Finally, it seemed, in British academia there was significant formal recognition for his work. I soon got a good appreciation of how much this meant to him. One evening, as we were sitting around informally chatting, again in another meeting with Schoenman where Horowitz and I were present, in response to a casual query about his acceptance in academic circles he and Tamara talked at length, with barely suppressed anger about the many roadblocks that had been thrown in his way over the years to keep him from getting the recognition in academia they thought he deserved. Without the least hesitation or reservation, they stated they were fully aware their main opponent in this respect was the influential bourgeois academic, Sir Isaiah Berlin, a historian at All Souls College in Oxford, and a hanger-on of the wealthy Rothschilds, a very powerful pro-Zionist, Anglo-Jewish capitalist family, well-known for having been influential in the diplomatic negotiations in 1917 regarding the setting up of the state of Israel.[9] Both Berlin and the Rothschilds were particularly hostile to him, Deutscher felt, not only because of his Marxism but also because of his writings on Israel and about the Jewish question, dealt with in his book, *The Non Jewish Jew*, in which he originated the term "non-Jewish Jew" to describe himself and those, who in the Talmudic expression, "rode" outside the boundaries of Jewry—Spinoza, Marx, Heine, Freud, Rosa Luxemburg and Trotsky—who nevertheless represented something essentially Jewish.[10] He found the nationalism of the Zionists and Israel repulsive.

Deutscher had probably also stung Isaiah Berlin when he took a scalpel to one of Berlin's lectures on historical inevitability, in a sharply critical review in *The Observer*. Apparently, the spiteful Berlin used the full force of his considerable influence in the academic establishment to get back at him. As he was completing his work on the Trotsky biography, it seems, Deutscher had applied for a post of Senior Lecturer in Modern History and/or Economics that was being advertised for the newly created Sussex University. He had received a very warm response from Martin Wright, dean of its School of European Studies: "We are very interested indeed that you have been moved enough to apply . . . All my colleagues would be delighted if you could be associated with us . . ." This was followed up by a "very pleasant lunch" where an enthusiastic staff started discussing the possibility of Deutscher heading up a future Department of Soviet Studies, a suggestion that did not come from Deutscher. Two days later, Wright followed up with an encouraging note, saying, "developments at this level go through the University Council" (of which Berlin was a member) and that "the Vice-Chancellor asked me this morning to tell you how much he hopes that we shall come to a satisfactory arrangement." Then followed an inexplicable silence of a long three and a half months until the embarrassed Sussex Vice Chancellor, J.S. Fulton, finally wrote to Deutscher telling him he was not getting the position: ". . . if you feel disappointed at this decision I want to tell you we share it also."[11]

It was clear from the discussion that evening in their home with Horowitz, Schoenman and me, that they had been deeply humiliated by the experience with Berlin. It was only as I was writing these lines that I learned that one of the ironies in the situation was that a Bailie Knapheis was Berlin's personal secretary. She was the daughter of a close friend of theirs (or maybe even a relative), one Helen Klass, who lived in Winnipeg.[12]

After Deutscher's death, Tariq Ali's paper, *The Black Dwarf*, took up the matter again and blasted Berlin for his role in it. What had only been whispered in private until then became a huge public scandal—at least in academic circles. *The Black Dwarf* alleged that Berlin had blocked the appointment on the grounds that "a Marxist should not be a Professor of Russian History." As a result of the controversy, several weeks later Berlin wrote Tamara—"to clear my own record" and for self-exoneration—saying he had deliberately chosen not to reply to *The Black Dwarf* and that although what it said was "libelous," he had been advised that it would take "little notice of the fact that the statements ascribed to me were, in fact never made by me either in public or in private." But his explanation to Tamara of his role in the matter could not have altered her mind very much, and probably, reading between the lines, it would only have been further proof that he had indeed spitefully used his position to make sure Deutscher did not get the appointment.

". . . I was asked whether I thought it a good idea to create a Chair of Soviet Studies for Mr. Deutscher," Berlin wrote to Tamara. "My view, which I communicated verbally to Professor Martin Wright, was that Mr. Deutscher's remarkable gifts would benefit the University most if he were not called on (to) create a field of studies but to invigorate an existing discipline: that I should for example, be wholeheartedly in favour of the appointment, if, say, one other expert were in the Department to look after aspects of the field which Mr. Deutscher did not regard as central or relevant to what interested him most. I explained that as far as I was personally concerned, I should have been perfectly ready to support his candidature in any institution which possessed a department, or at least one or two teachers, in this field, e.g. at Oxford or Cambridge; or for a Research Fellowship anywhere at all; but that, although I did not think Mr. Deutscher ideally qualified for the Sussex job, I might well be mistaken: if the University's own people wished to appoint him, I should, if I were an elector, certainly not vote against him, or resist his election in any way, if only on the grounds that universities ought to be absolutely free to do what they thought it right to do, whether outsiders like myself thought it wise or not; that at any rate this is how I would act in this particular instance . . ."[13]

My reading of the letter suggests that Berlin under no circumstances wanted a Marxist, specifically Deutscher, to be in a position where there was no one else around to keep tabs on him. That's how I understand his words about "other experts" and "at least two other teachers." No matter what, for Tamara the facts were clear: the Sussex people were keen to have Deutscher, and a fair reading of Berlin's letter, at the minimum, shows he was less than enthusiastic. It would be preposterous to think that the new people at Sussex would have gone against the wishes of the eminent and influential Oxford don. The end result was that Isaac didn't get the job and Berlin had a lot to do with it. Only now, many years later, do we realize the full extent of Berlin's deceit in the affair. Michael Ignatieff's biography of Berlin reveals that his letter to Tamara was a piece of double talk because when he was asked for his opinion of Deutscher by the Sussex Vice Chancellor, B.S. Fulton, he replied "that Deutscher was 'the only man whose presence in the same academic community as myself I should find morally intolerable . . .'"[14]

Over the years Deutscher had developed important differences with the Fourth International. Aside from thinking Trotsky had made a mistake in setting it up, he also had important differences about the evolution of Stalinism, especially after Stalin's death in 1953, but he still considered himself an "independent Marxist" without formal links to any organized groups—a "heretic" from Trotskyism, but not a "renegade." From the discussions in his home, I had the strong impression, nonetheless, that he considered his thinking to be within the broad ideological orbit of

Trotskyism. I never ever heard him identify himself in this way but certainly that's how the social democrats and Stalinists saw him. One of the things that surprised me was how much he and Tamara were still directly connected to a broad international milieu comprised of Trotskyists and ex-Trotskyists.

Perhaps my initial attitude to him had been influenced by the SWP's faction fight with Pablo, but until I got to Britain I had been totally ignorant, for example, that Deutscher had travelled to Amsterdam in 1961 to act as witness for Michel Pablo and Sal Santen, two important leaders of the Fourth International, during their trial on charges they had engaged in counterfeiting for the Algerian National Liberation Front.[15] Indeed, his archives are abundant with proof that he maintained a warm and comradely correspondence over the years with such figures as Ernest Mandel of the F.I. and the SWP's Joe Hansen, George and Connie Weissman, and George Novack, especially about the latter's exclusion from the first New York "Socialist Scholars Conference," which Deutscher vigourosly protested. Often he would invite them to his home when they were in London and whenever he was in New York, he would visit Novack. He was especially close to Margaret Bonnet, an intimate of Trotsky's wife Natalya, and the European executor of Trotsky's literary estate; he would also go to great lengths to answer questions from Daniel Guerin, the French Trotskyist scholar, about his work. Even when it came to replying to someone enquiring about obtaining the services of a German translator, he unreservedly recommended Georg Junglass, the leader of the F.I.'s German section.

Even though the sectarianism of the various British groups that called themselves "Trotskyist" appalled him, I knew Deutscher happened to be in regular touch with the SLL. Unsolicited, he told me one day that he had a lot of personal admiration for Gerry Healy. He said he had an especially high regard for the SLL's work in the unions and the quality of many of their working class cadres. A few years earlier, Healy's group had developed a sizable force of militants on the building-site of the Barbican theatre and cultural complex when it was under construction, making headlines in the press about a series of job actions over workers' grievances, shutting the site down for many days at a time.

Deutscher let me know he considered the SLL to be one of the more serious groups that made up the British "far left" and it was rumoured in our circles that from time to time he wrote for the SLL's theoretical journal, *Labour Review*, under a pseudonym. Occasionally, Healy would meet with him, visiting him at his home to exchange views on current political events. In Healy's obituary of Deutscher, he claimed that at one time he had written for *Workers Fight*, a journal of the early British Trotskyists.[16]

Deutscher wasn't the only one on the British intellectual left who was impressed by the Healy group's "working class character," I should mention. I remember around then learning that Healy was making a special effort to court some of the people around *New Left Review* and one day he invited Perry Anderson and Robin Blackburn over to his premises to look at his print shop and meet some of his people. Perry mentioned to me, just like Deutscher, that he was impressed by Healy's seriousness about organization and the working class composition of his group. I replied—I think to his mild amusement—that the sociology of any small political group on the left should be far down the list of its attributes when assessing it. What's more important, as far as I was concerned, I told him, are the group's beliefs, how it relates to others and how it functions in the political world. Healy didn't get very far with the *New Left Review* people, as far as I remember, they were far too smart for that—but he had a special talent for pressing the "guilt buttons" of any intellectual he came across to enlist their support. Some of them—good academics—even became active in his organization. But not Deutscher; he was too politically experienced for that.

While I had a comfortable relationship with Deutscher, I don't wish to exaggerate this and I can honestly say that over the year and half or so I met with him, I never really got to know him very well as a person. The gulf between us was just too wide. I was always conscious in his presence that we were of two totally different personalities and from two different generations—he, with his powerful intellect, a product of the vanished era of pre-Second World War European Marxism and me, a working class activist without any formal education, politically formed mainly by my experiences in a small Trotskyist group in Canada. But I knew enough, in a friendly bantering manner, to challenge him, albeit carefully, a few times.

I remember once when he made a few disparaging comments in my company about the Fourth International, that I took to be a questioning of its very existence and which got my back up a little, I faced him directly on the issue, sort of poking fun at what he was saying. I posed a hypothetical situation to him, that of an imaginary apolitical young worker, who after reading a Deutscher book, for example, might become convinced of the need for socialism and shows up on Deutscher's doorstep to ask him for advice about what he, the young worker should do to help bring about this fundamental change. For me, I said, I wouldn't hesitate a moment because from what I knew from history, without their own organization, workers won't get anywhere and I would tell the young worker to join my group as the first step in trying to build such an organization which could help lead workers in transforming society. What would you tell the young worker? I asked him, and I knew I was appealing to his background as an active revolutionary leader, of which I knew he felt proud. Momentarily, he looked a little bit non-plussed, probably thinking that I had a bit of a nerve challenging him like that, but he came back, surprisingly, saying he would recommend the same thing. Better that than nothing, he said, in a sort of backhanded compliment.

Once I quizzed him about Cuba, wondering what he thought about it. He had yet to write anything substantial about its revolution. I'm sure he must have been pleased when Joe Hansen wrote to him, "We have heard that Castro is interested in your biography of Trotsky."[17] When I mentioned Joe's early analysis of the revolution that had concluded with him characterizing the first Cuban government as a "workers' and farmers' government" and his subsequent studies that concluded a "workers' state" now existed there, he was very dismissive of Joe's work and the discussion did not go anywhere. I'm not sure he had even read it. He gave me the overall impression that he didn't think the question of great importance, and, in that respect, he was not that far out of step with much of the British left. After that I tended to avoid that issue when we talked.

But I knew enough to realize that unmistakably, in his intellectual outlook, Deutscher, despite having lived in London for many years without membership in a revolutionary organization, saw himself as a world Marxist, part of the same pre-war generation of revolutionaries that included James P. Cannon, Pierre Frank, Joe Hansen, Michel Pablo, Ernest Mandel and George Novack, not that his relationship with those leaders did not have its difficulties, especially with those of the SWP. I had the strong impression he still rankled at the criticisms his earlier work had received from my comrades in the SWP, which I sensed anytime the topic of the American SWP cropped up in our conversations.

When Deutscher's first major work, his biography of Stalin, appeared in 1949,[18] it was strongly criticized by James P. Cannon who would also go on to condemn his new book on Russia, published in 1953.[19] "The originator and fountainhead of the new revisionism," wrote Cannon, "the modern successor to Bernstein and Stalin in this shady game, is the Polish former communist, named Isaac Deutscher, who passed through the outskirts of the Trotskyist movement on his way to citizenship in the British Empire."[20] Rejecting the traditional Trotskyist position of calling for a "political revolution" in the USSR to renew the revolution and to establish a workers' democracy, Deutscher had stated in his book "What the Malenkov government is carrying out now is precisely the 'limited revolution' envisaged by Trotsky"[21] and that through a process of self-reform, he said he believed the regime might be capable of meeting the needs of the Soviet working class in the fight to regain control of the economy. "A gradual evolution of the regime," he wrote, "towards socialist democracy," pointing out that a "balance of factors favours a democratic regeneration of the regime."[22]

From what I can see, Deutscher had in reality become a kind of surrogate for Pablo in the factional struggle that had divided the Fourth International in those years. "(H)is theory of self-reform of the Stalinist bureaucracy," wrote Cannon, "which he tries to pass off as a modified version of Trotsky's thinking, has made its way into the movement of the

Fourth International and found camouflaged supporters there in the faction headed by Pablo. Far from originating anything themselves, the Pablo faction has simply borrowed from Deutscher." But events in East Germany in the summer of 1953 opened up a chasm under many of Deutscher's assumptions—and Pablo's—when Malenkov's Soviet army crushed the East German workers' uprising. Both sides of the faction fight in the F.I. came out with statements in support of the uprising, an agreement that set the framework for subsequently overcoming in 1963 the division that had lasted for almost ten years.

In addition, aside from utilizing him as a convenient proxy in the debate with Pablo, there was an apprehension in our circles that Deutscher might possibly, somehow or other, begin to organize a counter grouping around his ideas to pose new organizational challenges to us. The announcement that he was working on a major biography of Trotsky, didn't help matters much either, causing some to question if this would also be used to push his "line." The first volume, when it appeared in 1954, received a further critical review by Cannon in the SWP's newspaper, *The Militant*. These fears however, turned out to be unwarranted. Deutscher remained an independent intellectual and his three volume biography of Trotsky turned out to be a masterpiece of the political biographical genre, excavating the great revolutionary's reputation from underneath a mountain of capitalist and Stalinist vilification. Just as the whole edifice of Stalinism was beginning to come apart, Deutscher's work became the vehicle through which many young radicals from various political backgrounds, including the Communist Parties, notably young intellectuals in the universities, found their way to an authentic Marxism, uncorrupted by Stalinism. And relations with the SWP warmed sufficiently for him in 1964 to seek George Novack's collaboration in producing a selection of Trotsky's writings and speeches, in a Dell paperback, which received wide circulation in student circles in those years.[23]

As Isaac got close to the date of the first of his Trevelyan Lectures, Tamara asked Jess and me if we would like to accompany them to Cambridge. We were very appreciative of the invitation, of course, because under normal circumstances we wouldn't have had the opportunity to be there, but I think there may have been some self-interest involved because their motivation probably was their wish to reduce the risk of not getting there at the appointed hour because of a possible breakdown of their vehicle. He didn't drive and he was dependent on Tamara in this respect, so I think they wanted us to be along just in case they had a problem with the car. As a result we heard all six talks at Cambridge with the audience increasing in size for each one, to the point that by the last session, there was hardly any room for all those who wished to attend. By the time of the last lecture, hundreds of students gathered outside the lecture hall, forming a long queue to get in. The turnout took Cambridge completely by surprise; attendance at the previous Trevelyan lectures had been very low, with only seven in the audience at the final lecture of the series.

It had been an amazing performance. He seemed to me to be at the height of his intellectual powers as he presented a historical materialist explanation for the Russian Revolution and a rigourous defence of it and its achievements over the previous fifty years, to a very attentive, mainly student audience. All of the Cambridge academic community seemed to have turned out to hear him. There was no patronizing, no dumbing down of his ideas as he explained the complexity of the Soviet Union's evolution, its enormous economic growth and the problems of bureaucracy that stood in the way of its future progress, and, as we know today, even its future existence.

As I sat there I was struck by how little daylight remained between his conclusions and those of the Fourth International's. For the life of me, I couldn't see any major differences. He had clearly pulled back from any earlier views he may have had about the "self-reform" of the bureaucracy. This could be seen in his comments on the Sino-Soviet conflict that had been raging for several years. Commenting on its possible effect upon "forward looking elements in the USSR," he stated that it might drive home one important lesson, "namely that arrogant, bureaucratic oligarchies, incorrigible in their narrow-mindedness and egoism, cannot be expected to work out any rational solution of this or any other conflict; still less can they lay stable foundations for a socialist commonwealth of peoples."[24] Of course in those days, neither Deutscher nor the Fourth International would have imagined that the Soviet Union would eventually collapse because of the criminal failure of the bureaucracy, and the workers' hostility to its corruption and inefficiencies, leading to counter-revolution and the victory of capitalism there.

It's interesting to note that our Pioneer Book-service in those years sold countless numbers of Deutscher's Trotsky biography throughout Britain and internationally. One day we were extremely surprised to receive an order from Cuba, the first of many. These orders accelerated after the visits to Cuba by Ernest Mandel. Significantly, Che Guevara was one of the first recipients. Ernest later reported to the United Secretariat that he learned Che had been very impressed with it. We later discovered that many of the books that we shipped to Cuba in those days eventually found their way into the hands of the top leadership of the Cuban Communist Party. This was confirmed recently, if indirectly, in an obituary of the late Celia Hart. She had emerged in Cuba in recent years as an independent Marxist and self-declared "Trotskyist," the daughter of the famous Cuban revolutionary leader Armando Hart. She lost her life in a tragic auto accident in Cuba in 2008. The obituary mentioned that she had found the Deutscher book in her father's library when she was a student and it had very much influenced her thinking and political formation, an example of the power of Deutscher's writing.

And even Fidel Castro was on familiar terms with his work. Simon Reid-Henry provides information to substantiate this, quoting an associate of Fidel's who reported that at a meeting with him Fidel announced to everyone present that "he had just read Isaac Deutscher's trilogy of Trotsky—that sort of work, it was typical of Fidel to turn to for general relaxation and it had got him wondering what might have happened had the Bolsheviks not signed the Treaty of Brest Litovsk, extricating them from World War One."[25] I would like to think that perhaps he had read one of the sets of the trilogy that Pioneer Book Service had mailed to Cuba. I'm sure Deutscher would have been immensely pleased.

Chapter 8

"We shall not hesitate to deal appropriately . . ."

ONLY A FEW DAYS AFTER THE FIRST SESSION OF THE RUSSELL Tribunal, I became a victim of Gerry Healy's violence. It happened as I was trying to sell a little pamphlet, entitled, *Healy 'Reconstructs' the Fourth International*,[1] outside Caxton Hall at an SLL meeting to celebrate the Tenth Anniversary of the Hungarian Revolution. It was the custom then—and still is—for the various left groups in London to sell their literature outside each other's meetings, a democratic tradition that the Trotskyists had stoutly defended over the years, especially in opposition to the CP, who, back when it was a more powerful force, would often try to prevent their critics from selling or distributing literature—sometimes through the use of violence. The tradition of promoting the free exchange of ideas is based upon the belief among socialists that workers should be free from any hindrance in the pursuit of those ideas that interest them. We don't have access to a mass media; one way we can publicize our views is by selling our literature at each other's meetings.

Our group had been actively promoting the pamphlet around London for several months. The SWP had forwarded us a copy as soon as it had come off the press and I must confess to a feeling of shameless schadenfreude as I read it, almost in disbelief at Healy's difficulties in trying to shoe-horn his "international allies," despite their significant differences with each other, into a common organization. I was especially delighted because the pamphlet showed clearly to all who wished to see that despite the success he was crowing about, Healy was a disaster as a political leader and would lead the SLL to ruin; I was hoping that maybe some people inside the SLL might eventually wake up to this danger. I knew the pamphlet would be a hot item on the left, so we ordered a thousand copies immediately, and got it out to our normal outlets in London's bookstores and began selling it on our literature tables around the city.

Before describing what happened outside Caxton Hall that evening, it is necessary to give some background about what had been happening with Healy's campaign against the Fourth International. By the end of the fifties, political events had forced a new question onto everyone's political agenda. As I've described earlier, the Cuban Revolution had confronted socialists with a problem: how to relate to these historic events—and how to fit them into their theories about social revolution. Both the majority of the International Committee, led by the SWP, and the International Secretariat led by Ernest Mandel had quickly come to the analysis that Cuba was "a workers' state" under the revolutionary leadership of Fidel Castro and the July 26th Movement, and that it was now an elementary duty of the Fourth International to defend it against hostility and attack by the U.S. government. This had formed an important part of the agreement between the Europeans and the North Americans as they worked to overcome past differences.

In North America, challenging this line of support for Cuba, a small opposition had developed inside the SWP led by Tim Wohlforth and Jim Robertson. The former claimed Cuba was still capitalist, while Robertson described it as a "deformed workers state." Bizarrely, as I've mentioned earlier, both called for the overthrow of the Castro leadership. Healy adopted a position similar to Wohlforth's, but he embraced both of these two groups who by this time had split from the SWP and incorporated them into his new international. He also lined up with Pierre Lambert of the *La Verite* group in France—who had originally been part of the International Committee—and the *Voix Ouvriere* group, named after their journal and which had split from the F.I. in 1943.

Healy's aim was to "reconstruct the Fourth International" at a special Congress in the first week of April 1966.

Within a couple of months, as luck would have it, copies of the correspondence and reports by some of the Congress' participants fell into the hands of the SWP, who promptly published them—hence the pamphlet that I was hawking that evening outside Caxton Hall. Joe Hansen's introduction was worth the price alone. A delicious mixture of humour, satire and irony, it's a biting commentary on Healy's despotism.

According to the correspondence which we exposed in our pamphlet, Robertson had shown up at the Congress feeling sick and under the weather, apparently, feeling the effect of a recent illness and a long flight from the U.S. So Robertson asked Healy "for permission" to be absent. Healy came down on him like the proverbial ton of bricks, demanding that the hapless Robertson apologize to the delegates and to also vote for a motion that contained his own condemnation. Healy termed Robertson's request a "petty-bourgeois reactionary act expressing the chauvinism of American imperialism, etc.", threatening him with expulsion if he did not go along with this procedure. It was like something invented by Kafka. Robertson, to his credit, of course refused this outrageous request, and was kicked out of the conference. As Joe Hansen wrote, that was the outcome Healy planned from the beginning, and the evidence of this, from one of Healy's letters, is reproduced in the pamphlet.

On top of his attack against Robertson—further demonstrating his strange idea of "reconstructing" his "International"—in the middle of the Congress Healy arbitrarily changed the political basis upon which the *Voix Ouvriere* group had been invited. This also forced them out. Healy's claim was that he had been unaware, until the moment of the Congress, that the group believed China to be a "capitalist state," a position with which Healy said he was in disagreement.

Despite these two splits, the Healyites touted the "Congress" as "the most impressive conference of the international Marxist movement" since the founding of the Fourth International in 1938. Joe, in his introduction, congratulates Healy on his "impressive ability to waive aside setbacks and defeats" and on his "success in organizing the conference in such a way as to make it a completely cut-and-dried affair before it even opened." As for Robertson and the *Voix Ouvriere* group, Joe notes somewhat sardonically, "they might seek consolation in the thought that they asked for it. After all they were well aware of the fraud built into the very foundation of this conference."

A key feature of Healy's modus operandi in building his group in those days was to create, from time to time, as large a spectacle as possible by pulling as many SLL members and supporters as he could into London for his rallies, busing them in from around the country. I had attended several of these affairs as an onlooker. While they always looked impressive—sometimes around 1500 in the audience—they were made up mainly of young teenagers, who, although solidly working class, seemed to be at a very low level of political sophistication. Despite its many problems, the SLL appeared to be having some success in directly recruiting working class youth to its ranks, even though the "churn" rate was high because of the difficulties in assimilating them.

Eileen Jennings would often open these meetings, with Healy, Cliff Slaughter or Mike Banda as the main speakers. It would have been impossible to imagine then that by 1985 they would be at each others' throats over Healy's abuse of women, including Jennings, leading to the destruction of their group. These impressive rallies were rah-rah-rah kind of events, pandering to the audience's low political level, designed more to raise morale rather than to educate, by creating a make-believe feeling of momentum in the class struggle.

Previously, when two members of our group had tried to sell the "Healy Reconstructs" pamphlet at one of these meetings, they reported back to us that as soon as they appeared on the pavement outside on a public thoroughfare, they were prevented from selling it, physically threatened by Healy's people and forced to leave. Healy had also prevented us selling *The Week* at that year's Labour Party conference, long before the pamphlet had arrived. We got an indication that the pamphlet had touched a nerve when we read in Healy's paper, *The Newsletter*, "We shall not hesitate to deal appropriately with the handful of United Secretariat agents who hawk it around the cynical fake-left in England." When we discussed this threat amongst ourselves, we were all of the feeling that if we let Healy get away with shutting us down so easily we would be giving him virtual veto power over what we could put out in the future. If socialists, we asked ourselves, are ready to fight the government tooth and nail if it acted in such an undemocratic way, why should we let a petty tyrant like Gerry Healy get away with such tactics? We decided to challenge him head on at the first opportunity.

Soon after that, I would find out firsthand what Healy meant by the words: "deal with appropriately." It was a rainy London night, November 17th, when I arrived outside Caxton Hall with the SWP's *International Socialist Review* and "Healy Reconstructs" in my hands. It was still well before the meeting time, and there were a few other literature sellers there, including a group of Irish communists selling their paper and someone from Peter Taaffe's group, selling the British *Militant*. I was initially greeted with some baiting by SLL supporters, who were selling *The Newsletter* in the doorway, but no one attempted to stop me selling my literature.

About ten minutes before the meeting was to begin, Mike Banda and Gerry Healy showed up and entered the hall. A few seconds later, Healy reappeared. His face reddened and his eyes bulged slightly when he spotted me. I thought for a moment he might burst a blood vessel— that's how angry he looked. He motioned to some of his people and pointed directly at me, indicating to them to get rid of me. Immediately, six or seven of them crowded around me, yelling at me to leave. I refused, of course, saying I had every right to be there. I tried to slide past them, in order to continue selling. The next thing I knew their hands were grabbing at me and my pamphlets went flying into the air. Some blows landed on me; I turned around and landed a few of my own. Having been raised on the Shankill Road, Belfast, a rough and tough area, I was no stranger to fistfights. But I was no match for Healy's goons. My glasses went flying and soon I was lying on the ground. They began kicking me repeatedly. At one point, I saw stars, and I lay there breathless for a few moments, dazed. Finally picking myself up, I retreated down the street, thinking only of revenge.

Ray Sparrow happened to be in town that weekend, so I called him to let him know what had taken place. He was shocked, and, in his own quiet and determined, tight-lipped manner, stated that this was a new low for Healy. "He'll pay for this," he assured me. His first advice was to get myself checked over medically to make sure I was OK. So right away he accompanied me to the nearest hospital emergency room where I was attended to by a doctor. I was shaken up and bruised, with a few black and blue marks on my body, my head was aching, but fortunately my injuries were not too serious.

Afterwards, Ray and I talked it over. We decided the best way to deal with the incident would be to alert the entire British left to what had happened. I then wrote the first of a series of "open letters" detailing what had happened to me, running off about six hundred copies of each. We sent these letters out all over the place, including to the various left journals for publication. David Horowitz looked them over and offered a few editing suggestions on how to make them more effective. *Peace News*, as it turned out, very courageously published one, as did the *Socialist Leader*, the paper of the Independent Labour Party. Healy immediately had his lawyers threaten legal action, and they were forced to print a retraction.

When I spoke to Dick Clements, editor of *The Tribune*, the journal of the Labour Party left, to see if he would also publish the letter, he refused point blank and told me they would not even comment on the issue, saying he was afraid Healy would take them to court for libel. I almost fell off my chair when he said he would not be surprised if this was not some sort of plot by Healy to get rid of *The Tribune*. This was a measure of the paranoia about Healy in the British left. And *The Week*, disappointingly, did not do much better either, printing what I thought at the time was a less than adequate editorial about the matter.

Pat told me there had been a big fight about it in Nottingham and some of the Labour Party "lefts," who had their names down as "owners" of the publication, threatened to take out an injunction if it printed anything stronger, because of their fear of Healy. But aside from this, I remember there was a general sympathy for me in the left about what happened. I got letters back in response to my Healy letters, expressing support, including a brief but much appreciated message of solidarity from Bertrand Russell. "I was very disturbed to read your letter to the press of November 20th," he wrote. "I had hoped that vicious physical assaults upon socialists in the streets of London had ceased with the collapse of the fascist movement in the late thirties . . . All that you say has my warmest approval. You deserve the widest support from all who care about basic freedoms . . ."[2]

Isaac Deutscher, of course, was extremely shocked about what had happened. I saw him not long after the incident, and he told me he had heard that I had been beaten, and asked me about it. I described briefly what had occurred. He became visibly angry and upset. If what I was saying was true, he said, he could not have such a person as Healy coming into his home any more. He felt it was necessary to confront Healy with my accusation. He then asked me to come to his home to face Healy directly while he personally questioned him about the incident. Of course, I agreed. This is not to say that Deutscher was unequivocally sympathetic to me in the affair; indeed, he told me that to sell such a denunciatory pamphlet outside an SLL meeting was far too provocative and I should have been aware that I was inviting trouble. I disagreed, but I felt that this implicitly was more of a condemnation of the SLL, because the material in the pamphlet stood on its own merits.

Deutscher's motivation in asking for the meeting was that he viewed himself as a friend of the left as a whole. He was alarmed at the apparent degeneration in political relations between two presumably Trotskyist organizations. He thought he could use his own personal and intellectual authority to intervene in the dispute and perhaps bring some resolution. Healy brought Michael Banda and Eileen Jennings with him to the meeting at Deutscher's home. I brought Geoff Coggan, who at that time was on the staff of the Bertrand Russell Peace Foundation.

Deutscher confronted Healy with the charge I had made against him. Although I was boiling underneath, I didn't say anything. Under Deutscher's questioning, Healy admitted that the people who had carried out the assault were members of the SLL. He admitted I had been booted while lying on the pavement. But he refused to take any responsibility himself for what had happened. He said that I had provoked the SLL members or supporters by saying things critical of the SLL. Then he had the gall to say that I *had attacked and beaten up his people!* Deutscher wanted to know how it was possible for someone lying on the ground and being kicked to carry out this feat. Indeed, Healy said, he had intervened personally and prevented me from having a worse hammering.

Well then, Deutscher asked, didn't you see to it that Tate received attention for his injuries? Healy had no answer. Deutscher turned again to the question of responsibility. "As a leader of the SLL, don't you accept responsibility for the action of your members," Deutscher asked? Healy refused to accept this and, in response, Deutscher quoted Lenin to him on the question of leadership responsibility. Yes in that sense I am responsible, Healy replied. Deutscher, clearly very angry, ordered Healy to get out. He rose to show him to the door and, as they headed out, Healy shouted at Deutscher; Banda, who had been silent until then, joined in. It was a bad blow to the SLL. Alone among intellectuals of stature in Britain, Deutscher until then could have probably been considered a friend of the SLL.[3] This incident marked an end to that.

What I found odd about the whole affair, however—maybe this was my Canadian naiveté at work—was that there was so little reaction, aside from Deutscher and Russell, on the part of many on the left. There was no sense of shock or scandal. It was as if everyone had become accustomed to his violence. This allowed Healy, I felt, to establish a terrible new norm for relations between socialists. I learned later that Healy was very adept and experienced at using lawyers to do his dirty work for him. When people complained about his violence, he would immediately have them threatened with legal action. He knew that most people do not wish upon themselves the bother of legal hassles, so they would just walk away from any legal fight rather than tangle with him. He had no hesitation about using the state to silence his opponents; but for our part, we simply ignored his threats.

I had consulted a lawyer who was sympathetic to our group, and he agreed the best way to deal with it was for me to act as my own counsel if there were any such charges emanating from him. I heard nothing more from Healy about this and at the next large meeting they organized in London, we made a special effort to sell the pamphlet outside. I was not there, but about six or seven of our group were outside, including Jess MacKenzie, to keep an eye on things, plus a few Irish comrades gathered there to provide moral support. We sold the pamphlet without incident. Although unknown to us at the time, our side was in fact well prepared for violence. Jess discovered later that the Irish comrades had prepared a hidden cache of rocks nearby. "Just in case," they said. We assumed that Healy, by then, had finally figured out he had too much to lose by continuing his goon-like behaviour. Many on the left were surprised I had made such a big fuss about Healy's violence. I remember Tony Cliff of the I.S. at one point telling me that he had been warning people for years about Healy, but no one seemed to take any notice. They thought that I was perhaps too naïve not to expect what had happened. The American SWP, however, took the matter very seriously and publicized the incident far and wide. In a statement in their weekly, *The Militant*, under the signature of Farrell Dobbs, their National Committee demanded that the SLL place Healy "on trial for sponsoring such methods" and to "expel all those involved for engaging in an act that dishonours the labour and socialist movement."[4] The SWP also demanded that Healy's international followers disassociate themselves from his violence. None of them ever did, including Tim Wohlforth, who shortly after declared his support for Healy's actions. In his writings long after he had soured on Healy, Wohlforth displays remarkable amnesia about that event.

Pierre Frank and Ernest Mandel outside a JCR rally at the Sorbonne, Paris, 1968

Chapter 9

The Russell Foundation Expands

THE INTERNATIONAL WAR CRIMES TRIBUNAL, WHILE A MAJOR ONE, was not the only project the Bertrand Russell Peace Foundation (BRPF) had on the go in those years. It was also backing Mark Lane's work challenging the official version of the circumstances surrounding the Kennedy assassination as reported by the Warren Commission. While I was working on the publicity campaign for the musical, "Saturday Night and Sunday Morning," it so happened there was no space for me at the Foundation's office in Shaver Place to work from—it was comprised of only two rooms—so I was provided with a room in one of Russell's London flats, as a temporary office. This also happened to be the accommodation the Foundation had provided Mark Lane, the New York attorney and Assembly man who had temporarily moved to Britain with his family to work on his book about the assassination.[1] The flat was also the office for his research staff.

Schoenman and Russell were generously supporting Lane by helping to finance his research. Lane had also become a Director of the Foundation and he was assisting it with some of its legal work. In March 1966, the Foundation had given its support to the case of a young American in New York, David Mitchell, who had been sentenced to five years in prison for refusing to go into the army. Lane had been his legal representative. And, after the Kennedy assassination, Russell had initiated the setting up of a British "Who Killed Kennedy Committee," among whose sponsors were the renowned British historian, Hugh Trevor Roper, novelist Kingsley Amis, Lloyd Boyd Orr, the Scottish doctor and biologist and winner of the Nobel Prize, and Michael Foot. Because so many individuals connected to the assassination had died in mysterious circumstances, Russell was fearful for Lane's personal safety, and the setting up of the Committee was a way to ensure he would get maximum publicity and perhaps provide him a measure of protection.

The Committee's other purpose was to try to pressure the U.S. government into revealing the truth to the American public about that fateful event. Lane's work was a continuation of that campaign. Occasionally and unfortunately, I had to disturb him in the mornings when I rang the bell to gain access to the large flat. I'm not too sure how happy he was at first that I was coming back and forth, but we chatted a few times and he was friendly enough. I would often see him and his assistant in discussion preparing the references as the book neared completion. Lane looked to me like he could use a good night's sleep; he always appeared so rumpled and distracted, hair uncombed, as he worked away trying to nail down the source of this or that fact for inclusion in his draft.

As I've mentioned, Ralph was often out of the country for long periods in those days. He had been many times to Vietnam and frequently we didn't see him for several weeks at a time. It was also around then that I was trying to extricate myself somewhat from the work of the Foundation, concentrating more and more on getting a Fourth International grouping established—the reason I was in Britain in the first place—and I wasn't spending as much time as in previous weeks on the Foundation's work. I also had begun to feel that we had too many members of our small group tied up in its projects and that we were on the verge of neglecting our own functioning.

Now and then I would still help out the Foundation with specific problems, whenever I could. One day, for example, Ralph called me to say that the Foundation's facilities were quickly becoming overcrowded and the Directors were looking for extra space to house their operations. They were thinking of buying a small building. Ever since I had first met him, he had been talking about the Foundation putting out some kind of monthly journal that would promote Russell's and the Foundation's views on major international issues.

This would be a major undertaking, a part of the reason the Foundation needed extra space. Ralph gave me the specifications for what he needed, and I told him I would check with local real estate offices to see what I could find.

It took me about a month of tramping around London's East End for me to find a place I thought would be suitable and of fair value, 41 Rivington Place. He and a few Directors looked it over and agreed that it met their criteria. The Foundation bought the freehold to the building, hired a contractor to renovate it and moved a lot of its work there. It was just north of Toynbee Street, close to the office I shared with Pat, but its fate would eventually figure prominently in an internal crisis the next year in the Foundation.

The Vietnam Solidarity Campaign grew rapidly that year and by November 26th it had established a wing in Scotland. *The Week*[2] reports that a successful conference in Edinburgh, much like the London one except for the dispute with the Maoists, was chaired by Willy Boyle of the "Scottish D.A.T.A. Council" and was attended by "over 110 delegates" from Constituency Labour Parties, several trade union Locals and various anti-war groups. It was addressed by Ralph Schoenman, Pat Jordan, Setsure Tsurishima, Malcolm Caldwell and Lawrence Daly. But the VSC, despite its growth and an impressive list of organizations supporting it, was still a very loose kind of organization, not much more in reality than a network made up of small ad hoc groups scattered throughout the country, with a few branches on some of the major universities. With the help of the Foundation to finance its staff and give it free office space at its new building at 41 Rivington Place, however, it was quickly evolving into a fairly effective campaigning force.

The VSC had about a dozen active branches in London by then and we were publishing a regular monthly *VSC Bulletin* and a series of pamphlets that allowed us to concentrate our fire on Wilson's complicity in the war. These we distributed throughout the country, giving activists lots of information and arguments with which they could confront their Member of Parliament, for example. One of these pamphlets, I remember—a particularly effective one, written by Ken Coates—became one of our most popular publications at Pioneer Books. With an ironic title, *The Dirty War in Mr. Wilson: Or How He Stopped Worrying and Learned to Love the Dollar*, it excoriated Wilson and the Foreign Office for their hypocrisy. We sold many hundreds to anti-war activists around the country.

We were also beginning to get an appreciation of the advantage of being a conscious part of an international anti-war movement. We increasingly coordinated our activities with anti-war protests in the United States, as the movement there effectively responded to the military escalation with successive mass mobilizations on the streets, issuing appeals for international days of action. It gave the new anti-war movement in Britain a feeling of confidence that we might be able to force Wilson to change his policy. Aside from the VSC, the space at Rivington Place quickly became the offices for many of the Foundation's projects, transferring over from the offices in Piccadilly. A lot of the activity of the Working Committee of the Tribunal, for example was organized from Rivington, including the publication of its bulletins and its promotional material. The new monthly journal of the BRPF on international issues had become a reality with the launch of *The Spokesman*. Most of its production, editorial work and distribution were organized from there. 41 Rivington Place had become a real hub, the centre of a growing anti-war movement.

The 1967 Youth Conference in Brussels.

Chapter 10

The Fourth International in London

*E*VER SINCE I HAD ARRIVED IN LONDON, ABOUT ONCE A MONTH I would provide the United Secretariat with an update of our efforts to get a branch of the International Group established there. The work had been proceeding slowly. The fact that the Coates/Jordan group did not have a branch in London as yet was seen by all of us as not only a problem in Britain—where we were attempting to pose an alternative to the SLL—but as a major gap in our work in Europe as a whole. The American SWP considered the resolving of this problem a top priority and it was always at the head of their agenda whenever any of their leaders visited London. For our part, we were steadily focused on trying to create the conditions whereby we could use the political strength of the International's centre in Brussels and its Sections around the world to help get a more formalized organization up and running. Now that we had a "united International," this task had become a little less difficult. This big job became a lot easier for me personally when, towards the end of 1966, Jess MacKenzie arrived in London from Canada. My life immediately changed for the better when she and I decided to live together.

It all began one December evening. I received a telephone call from her telling me she would be heading over to Brussels after visiting her family in Glasgow. The Fourth International's members and supporters in France had increased their activity and influence in the CP youth wing, so much so that they were in the process of being expelled because of their defiance of the CP's line on Vietnam, which was all about getting the Geneva Accords implemented. Together with the Belgian Jeunes Gardes Socialistes and our French comrades, they had issued an international appeal for radical youth to come to a conference in Brussels, March 11th–12th, 1967, to develop a European-wide campaign against NATO In advance, they had issued a call to the International's few youth organizations to send people to Europe to help with its organization.

In response, the Young Socialists in Canada had sent Jess, who spoke French, to help out and Ross Dowson had given her my telephone number in London to get in touch with me. Her first question was whether we had an organization in London. Not yet, I said, but we're in the process of getting something going, and I suggested she come over to Toynbee Street so we could talk. We went out for dinner; she paid, because I was broke as usual.

After our initial re-acquaintance in London just before Christmas in 1966, Jess returned to London soon after the New Year celebrations, and we picked up where we had left off. I suggested going out again, and we went to a theatre the next evening. She very generously bought the tickets for a play at the Haymarket Theatre. Right from the beginning we were very comfortable in each other's company, and a romance developed that has lasted ever since. She became a crucial partner in my work in London and everything I have been involved in since. The story I am writing here about those years in England is just as much hers as it is mine.

Soon after London, she headed to Brussels where she took up her assignment to help the conference, and was on staff for a couple of months, helping get the printed materials ready, organizing registration of delegates and arranging their billeting. I attended the conference as an observer but I don't have any memory of the debates there. Such was the small size of our youth forces in Europe that, with just over 150 voting delegates, we considered it a huge success and an important breakthrough. It adopted a statement, "A Programme for European Young Socialists," that focused on the war and which laid the basis for the Fourth International to take advantage of the impending youth radicalization. It was primarily a big boost to the morale of our French youth, the main inspirers of the conference and who would soon constitute themselves as the Jeunesse Communiste Revolutionnaire (JCR).

After the Brussels conference, Jess quickly came to the conclusion that Europe would be a much more interesting place to be than Canada, and decided to remain in London. She took over the running of Pioneer Books and, to my eternal gratitude, put its finances in order so that at last we were able to get a handle on its profitability. At the same time, with her experience in the YS in Canada, she became a big asset in the task of getting a F.I. group going. We were together every day, working full time on that project and poured everything we could into the effort. We succeeded, for example, in spending all of the several thousand dollars in savings she had managed to accumulate while working in Canada.

Although political life was more stimulating in comparison to Canada, we found the living conditions in London left a lot to be desired. I remember it was always difficult and expensive to find a decent place to live, for example. There was a severe housing crisis in those years, especially for people who were not from there, because most working class Londoners lived in low rent public supported housing.

One of our first places was a particularly memorable and musty smelling cold-water walk-up flat above a grocery store in North London, from whose owner we rented the space. There was no bath—only a bathroom and toilet on the ground floor which was shared with other tenants, and you had to have a good supply of shillings on hand to feed the meter before you could run the bath. The landlord also expected us to buy all our groceries from his store, and would get visibly upset if he saw us carrying bags that did not come from him. From there, we participated in the Hackney Labour Party, attending many of its monthly meetings, but we never had much time to be involved in any of its other activities. Our situation improved considerably, however, when Connie Harris, who still had her council flat in Tulse Hill, asked us to move into it while her daughter Sue was off studying overseas. We were overjoyed with Connie's help. It was a tremendous boost to our quality of life and we stayed there until our return to Canada.

In the process of getting a formal Fourth International group up and running, we had the help of many of the International's sections in different parts of the world. One of those was our section in Japan who helped us out in a very practical way. Setsure Tsurishima, otherwise known as "Okatami," one of its leaders, was a professor at Kyoto University on sabbatical to study English. As soon as he arrived in London, he immediately got in touch with us and began to participate in our activities. Jess and I got to know him very well, and he often dined with us. Sometimes he would cook us a Japanese meal, although cooking was not his strongest skill, I remember. Soon after Setsure arrived in London, I put him in touch with Ralph Schoenman and he threw himself into helping with the work of the Tribunal on its Administrative Committee, while also becoming an important speaker at our VSC meetings. He was included on a Tribunal investigative team that went to North Vietnam. On his return, I vividly remember his report, delivered in halting English, to a packed meeting in London. He spoke about how he had witnessed the massive destruction caused by the American bombing that was attempting to send the country back to the Stone Age. He also acted, from time to time, as a guide and translator for delegates of the various Japanese labour groups who came to London in connection with the work of the Tribunal.

Another important resource was Sirio Di Giuliomaria, a leader of the Italian section and a member of the Secretariat. Jess and I also got to know him very well, and we spent many hours together, socially and politically. He was extremely supportive, always in good humour—often with a joke on the edge of his tongue. Sirio came to London frequently, even spending his annual vacation there and staying for weeks at a time working with us and showing great enthusiasm for what we were attempting. Because many of the people around us were new to revolutionary politics, he was of tremendous assistance in helping us bring them up to speed on our conception of revolutionary organization. Early on he led a very successful day-school for us on the topic "Building the Revolutionary Party," part of which was a discussion about the "entry tactic." Sirio had been on the staff of the United Nations in Rome, he told me, working on its international food programmes, but had been purged from that job because of his radical background. We also had regular visits from American and Canadian comrades, especially when there were meetings of the International leadership. And, during the International Days of Action against the war, many activists from the International's various sections in Europe showed up in London to participate in our activities.

Our aim in establishing a group in London was to be in a position to make it possible, for the first time in decades, to at least have an open Fourth International venue, where its leaders would have a public platform to present the International's analysis of world events. Early on, Pierre Frank explained to me that, because many of the groups that claimed to be supporters of the F.I. had been either "dissident" or "buried" in the Labour Party, or both, this hadn't existed in Britain in a long time.

Pierre was very pleased when we were finally able to organize our first public meeting in the name of the International, which featured him, Livio Maitan and Ernest Mandel. It was a kind of watershed moment for us—and for many of our sectarian opponents. With Pat Jordan in the chair, the meeting was billed as "An International Symposium on Imperialism." That evening the hall was packed, with over a couple of hundred people in attendance. It turned out to be a rather tumultuous affair, especially towards the end, running well past the time we had to be out of the hall. Many representatives of the London left were there, including most of our critics, among them the I.S., Ted Knight of the SLL and Peter Taaffe of the Grant group, all of whom took the floor to voice their criticism of the F.I. and especially of our group in London.

A tape recording of that event in my possession reveals—at least at that moment—the abysmally poor attitude of these self-proclaimed Trotskyists towards the colonial revolution, an old problem in Britain and an issue we would continue to debate with them throughout the course of our activity in organizing opposition to the war then raging in Vietnam. Some of them, virtually ignoring Livio and Pierre, jumped to their feet once the speeches were over to attack Ernest, zeroing in on the F.I.'s position, which he had passionately emphasized in his speech, of calling for the left to give top priority to defending the Vietnamese revolution.

Pat, in the chair, calmly and patiently let all the critics have their say, even the most hostile. And Ernest, in his usual manner, answered all of them vigourously and in detail, at length, no matter how ridiculous the question. Almost to a man—and they were all men—the critics argued that the first duty of revolutionary Marxists in Britain was to "raise the consciousness of the workers' movement" in Britain. That's "escapism," Ernest retorted to a somewhat discomfited Ted Knight. "The Mensheviks were the first to use that argument," in opposition to Lenin, he said.

The forum on imperialism was but one of many we held in those days. Another that I remember very well was on the Chinese Cultural Revolution. Sponsored by *The Week* and with Ernest Mandel as the speaker, it turned out to be very popular. Over one hundred people were in the hall for what became a very lively three-sided debate between us, the International Socialists and the Maoists. I also remember several successful forums we organized for David Horowitz, including one where he introduced a new Penguin book he had recently edited.

We could usually anticipate an audience of about fifty or sixty for these kinds of events. This kind of activity was unusual, because forums where there would be open discussion were few and far between in London, and those that did happen were often poorly attended. We saw an example of this in March 1967, when a few of us attended a *Tribune* meeting about Vietnam that only attracted a small audience of less than fifty people—in a five hundred seat hall—even though they had an impressive lineup of eight Labour MPs on the platform, including Michael Foot, the leader at the Labour Party's left-wing. Our group's forum programme was very important in helping to get us established and it became one of our most important means of recruiting to our small forces.

Every time I was in Nottingham, I kept pressing the I.G. people, without entirely making a pest of myself, of the need to move quickly to get something going in London; Ray Sparrow would do the same. My first breakthrough in accomplishing this task came in early 1966, when Pat began to think about relocating. Up to that point, I had been functioning more or less as the I.G's London proxy, working out of Eight Toynbee Street—though I was beginning to have some success in reactivating a few of the group's London supporters and even recruiting some new people. At the same time, our group's work with the BRPF was intensifying—leading up to the Tribunal, in due course—and we were working closely with it to get the VSC off the ground. In those early months, Pat travelled back and forth from Nottingham to help with this work. By August of that year, he told me he was seriously considering moving permanently to London. I was so pleased I could have hugged him. He said he was fed up with commuting back and forth, and that he had discussed the matter with the Nottingham people and had received their full support. The move was made easier because he would be receiving a regular stipend from the Russell Foundation for his work there. Later he would become a member of its Board of Directors.

Part of the deal with his comrades in relocating to London, at least for the transition period, was his agreement to travel to Nottingham each week to help get *The Week* out. The publication was critical to our work in the Labour Party, and we weren't about to give that up. I was fully aware that Pat put the most work into getting it into the mail every week. I've never met anyone—before or since—who could type stencils faster than him. Without him it couldn't have continued. But I did wonder, because of the pressure on Pat, how long this arrangement could last.

Pat knew better than anyone that, if we were ever to build a group nationally, it was essential to have a branch in London. As I've mentioned, it had been at the top of my agenda since I had arrived in Britain, and I was fearful that if we delayed much longer in getting something going, we would miss capitalizing on all of our good work on Vietnam. London was the undisputed political centre of the country, and a major world city to boot. That's where all the other socialist groups had their headquarters, that's where the action was. If a group did not have an office in London, it did not seem to carry much weight with the radical left nationally.

Due to our activity in the VSC, we had begun to attract a layer of new people around us. Most of them had little previous experience of belonging to a political group, but they were interested in our ideas. We noticed that they had come to identify with us in the public debates we seemed to be constantly engaged in. It was not uncommon, for example, when we were at a meeting selling our literature, for a few people to come up to us and enquire about the F.I., wanting to know whether we had a group in London, and how they could be in touch. Of course, the other left groups were quick to identify us as an "United Secretariat" grouping in their polemical criticisms. But I was convinced, more than ever, that if we had an open, functioning organization in London, we would be better able to define ourselves in our own terms. As we moved toward solving this problem, however the Nottingham group began to undergo a differentiation over the matter.

Ken Coates, a major leader of the group, began to express some hesitation about making the move. As a consequence, he was the object of a few critical comments from some of his comrades, more grumbles than anything else, it seemed to me. Although Ken had just about recruited all of its members, organizationally Pat was the backbone of the group, keeping it functioning and holding it together on a day to day basis. I couldn't help but observe that Ken, more often than not, was quite content to sit back and let Pat carry that load.

Ken did not take much part in the practical functioning of the group, it seemed to me, but was always coming up with ideas about how to move the group forward. He was recognized in Britain as an important intellectual in his own right and had won a high standing in the radical left for his opposition to Wilson in the Labour Party. Most of the group's major initiatives seemed to have been thought up by him, such as its activity in the Labour Party to get medical supplies for Vietnam and its efforts to force the government to allow NLF representatives into the country. He was also prominent in the Campaign for Socialist Education (CSE), which had been launched by Ralph Miliband and others with a big splash the previous year.

Ken had a new idea just about every month, it seemed, about what the group should be doing. Sometimes it was difficult for us to keep up with him. It was enough to make one's head spin. And, despite the huge amount of energy it had been putting into these activities, the group was not growing much. There was an increasing dissatisfaction about this state of affairs, which I began to notice when I attended the group's meetings in Nottingham. I could see it in the side comments and jabs, and I began to detect a tone of cynicism about some of Ken's proposals. Then Pat informed me that a kind of "palace revolution" had started in the group, as a bunch of the younger members began to assert their leadership. When I heard of this, I was immediately concerned about what Ernest Mandel's response might be to this development—afraid he might interfere to come to Ken's rescue.

Ken, in the past, had organized many of Ernest's speaking tours on campuses around Britain. I knew they were very close. I had heard Ernest, at different times, express high regard for Ken's political acumen. I'm sure he had high hopes Ken would evolve into an effective leader of the International, although I don't remember, despite Ernest's pleading, Ken ever attending a Secretariat meeting, even though earlier in the decade he had been a regular participant.

While I too had great respect for Ken's capacities and imagination, I had my own reservations about his willingness to do what had to be done to make the breakthrough in London. The Secretariat, including Ernest, agreed with me that it should keep its hands off matters. This came on top of an existing understanding I had from the Secretariat that, personal considerations aside, as an organization we had to have a policy such that when any of its members made visits to Britain, they would go with one specific purpose in mind—to help build the group. As far as I was concerned, visiting "personalities" and "names" or speaking to others was considered to be secondary. I was determined the International leadership should concentrate maximum effort on getting us established in London and I was making sure everyone was on board with that task. At the core of the differences in the British group, however, especially between Ken and Pat, was an evolving and differing conception of how the "entry tactic" should be applied, and a recognition that the way it was practiced in Britain was a form of "deep entrism," implicitly pushing the task of building a public organization off to some, undetermined time in the future.

It's not that there were any serious political differences amongst any of us about our primary analysis of the British Labour party, from which the "entry tactic" was derived. No one questioned this. Historically, we saw the trade union's affiliation to the party as an important step in the political development of the British working class on the way, we hoped, to breaking with the capitalist parties and creating their own class political formation. Rightly or wrongly, we categorically rejected any notion that a rising class struggle and a rising political consciousness in the working class would bypass the Labour Party.

In the General Election we called for "Labour to Power." We understood the Labour Party to be a "workers' party" in composition, a "bourgeois" workers' party, if you like. This could easily be seen in the party's programme and in its loyalty to British imperialism's foreign policy and in the trade-union bureaucracy's striving to see social changes take place within the framework of capitalism. We believed these policies would make it impossible for the Labour Party to meet the needs of the working class and that conflict would ensue when the workers demanded that a Labour Government provide solutions to the social crisis, which included the desperate lack of housing in the urban centres, the high rent increases and unemployment, for example. By providing leadership in such a conflict, we were convinced, revolutionaries would eventually be able to win the workers to their programme and lay the basis of a truly mass revolutionary party.

One of our notions at the time—a kind of schema, really—was that the working class would seek revolutionary solutions to its problems via a series of approximations, moving to revolutionary politics from one leader to the next, casting each aside before finding a leadership adequate to the task of seizing power. It was a rather formalistic way of looking at this possibility, I now believe, but it was very similar to our position in Canada in relation to the CCF and, later, of the LSA's orientation to the New Democratic Party, which can be seen in the policy positions the LSA adopted at that time. Other major sections of the International in Western Europe had maintained similar orientations to their respective working class mass political movements.

In France, F.I. supporters were "entered" in the CP and also in the SP; in Belgium, they had been entered in the SP and were now involved in setting up a new "centrist" party; in Germany they were "entered" in the Social Democratic party; and, in Italy, in the Communist Party. In South America, our Argentine group was "entered" in the Peronist movement, and in Bolivia we were working with the Juan Lechin wing of the Movimiento Nacionalista Revolutionario (MNR).

Differences about the "orientation" and the "entry tactic" would usually erupt around what I liked to call "technical" issues rather than about the substantive political questions involved. In Britain, it was around the issue of setting up a group outside the Labour Party in London and the carrying out of "independent" work on the issue of Vietnam; in Vancouver, when I was there, it was about establishing a "public face" for the group and setting up a headquarters and a bookstore.

I remember this was brought to the fore for me when I got to Europe in 1965 around the time of the 8th World Congress, in the seemingly technical discussions within the International's leadership body about moving the International's centre to Brussels and the renting of an office space to accommodate it there. Many of the Belgian comrades at the time raised the objection that such an action would endanger their "entry" work. This was despite the fact that at the time of the "reunification" in 1963, and under firm pressure from Joe Hansen, they had agreed to set up an "open sector" of their organization. This decision had remained on the books without any action being taken to implement it.

According to them, we couldn't have anyone publicly associated with the Fourth International around them, and opening an office would complicate their "entry" work. I remember quite vividly, seeing the problem posed in a report to the Secretariat by Ernest Mandel on Belgium. He said most of the group there was totally absorbed in the setting up of "a new party," a split from the Socialist Party, which, he added, was recruiting to itself about 1,000 members a month. While I was very pleased about the promise of a "new party," what bothered me most about his report, I remember, was that there was very little mention of what was happening to the Fourth International group. I got the distinct impression it was low down on Ernest's list of priorities. It was only after the probing by the Italians, Livio and Sirio, that we began to get a more realistic assessment about what was happening on that front. In fact we learned, contrary to what one would expect from that promising report, that membership in the F.I. group in Belgium had been actually stagnating.

They had only sixty or seventy members, if that, and I got a distinct feeling, from the discussion, that there was some demoralization in its ranks. One of the Belgians reported that many of the "cells" did not meet because of "lack of time" and that their openly F.I. journal, *La Lutte de Classe*, had not appeared for many months and that they had no one on staff. This despite the fact they had a few members working as full-time functionaries—"full-timers" for the "new party." Effectively, they had become the apparatus of the new centrist formation. To me, what seemed to be happening was that they were transferring their "entrism" to the new party—in reality a "centrist" formation—without thinking through its implication. They argued that the "new party" had "the transitional programme of the Fourth International" and that this created special difficulties in that if they allowed a situation to develop where they could be charged with having a "dual" membership, their "centrist" allies and the Communist Party would use this against them.

When Ray Sparrow and I gently suggested the idea of opening a bookshop or some kind of public face that would allow them a measure of independence behind which we could function as a Fourth International grouping, they said there were too many difficulties involved in going down that road. As a result of that discussion, Ray later told me, he began to have doubts about the move of the International's headquarters from

Paris. Moreover, he was beginning to get exasperated by the methods of work and lack of consultation and what he perceived as the lack of control over leading people's activities and their lack of accountability. He was effectively isolated in Brussels, he told me. Very few people from the group seemed to be willing to talk to him because of the perceived dangers to the "entry tactic." This occasionally took bizarre forms.

Once, when I attended an IEC meeting in Brussels, a body many times larger than the Secretariat and to which the latter was responsible, that met at least twice a year between Congresses, we were told to adopt clandestine-like methods to get to the location of the meeting. Participants were instructed in advance to arrive at the train station and wait there in the waiting room with a copy of a particular journal prominently displayed under their arm and that someone would come and collect them. This was not to escape detection by the police, as one would imagine, but by local social democrats. It was not always a foolproof method, however. One time a few of our Arab supporters, who for some reason had not received their instructions about waiting at the station, simply followed others whom they had observed carrying the journal to get there.

But we were beginning to make small strides forward in Britain. When Pat Jordan went on staff for the Foundation and became one of its Directors, it was the first time in his life he had been paid for his political work and it allowed us to consider renting an office for *The Week* in London. The commute to Nottingham every week had become too much of a burden. Eight Toynbee Street, by this time, had become a political centre for us and we used it often as a meeting place for our discussions. Although it was a large room, it was not large enough to also accommodate the production of *The Week*. In a happy coincidence, there was an empty office above us, so I asked the landlord if we could rent it and he was quite happy to oblige.

Pat moved in right away, along with all his files and the all-important mimeograph machine. We shopped around the second-hand stores and found an old desk, some filing cabinets and a few chairs for him. He got to work right away. Until then, I hadn't fully appreciated the amount of energy required to meet the punishing schedule of putting out the journal. With a title like *The Week*, we didn't have much flexibility and we had no choice but to get it into the mail every week. I don't remember if any of the stencils were cut in Nottingham, but the people there—mainly Ken Coates, Alan Rooney, and Tony Topham—wrote many of its articles, and some would come in from Labour Party activists throughout the country, but it was Pat who put most of the effort into getting it produced, sometimes directly typing his articles on to stencils as the rest of us waited to run the mimeograph machine and collate and staple the pages together. In the midst of all this, he would also be heading back and forth from the Whitechapel tube station to the Foundation's offices in Piccadilly to help with the work there.

Jess and I helped out whenever we could, and it sometimes required all of us to put in all-nighters to meet the deadline. Occasionally, when Pat was on vacation, Jess and I and a few of our people in London would find ourselves with the task of putting out *The Week*. Usually Pat prepared for this by leaving us most of the copy at hand ready to type onto stencils that we would look over and sometimes modify because political events required it. And from time to time we would be forced, like him, to write articles directly onto the stencils to fill space. It was a skill I had brought with me from Vancouver, when I had helped produce the monthly *Young Socialist Forum*. It came in handy in London.

Pat had been an active socialist all his adult life. Jess and I saw him a lot in those years. We usually had lunch together every day—our staples were good old artery-clogger bacon-and-egg sandwiches with cups of strong tea from a café across the street. In my mind's eye, I can still see him now, a large, bulging brown leather briefcase hanging at his side as he came into the office in the mornings, slightly out of breath after climbing the stairs. He was of short stature, about 5'5", not yet forty but looking much older, with a round, roly-poly body shape and an apple-cheeked cherubic kind of face, slightly graying hair and beginning to go bald. I don't ever remember him getting out-loud angry and it's strange to think that not long after that, a British national paper would see him as being "the most dangerous man in Britain." He gave a general overall first impression of meekness, but in reality he was as tough as nails and one of the most committed people I have known. He had virtually no personal life, with a prodigious capacity for work and a very sharp mind. Side by side, we went through many debates and struggles together over the course of the next few short years. Pat was always like a rock.

Extremely patient in discussion, I remember he would try to avoid making harsh judgments and would usually allow people time to make up their minds about an issue, although he was not always consistent in this. Pat was very good at mathematics, apparently self-taught, and had done his conscription service for the British Army stationed in Germany during the Berlin blockade in 1953, working as a cipher clerk decoding Russian transmissions, a circumstance he found very amusing because he had been a member of the British Communist Party for many years. Jess and I learned a lot from him about the British labour movement generally, and the far left in particular, as we chatted over lunch. He was a great teacher as we worked alongside each other, Jess and I developed a liking and admiration for him as a good human being.

With Pat's permanent relocation to London, Jess, he and I set about the task of organizing a formal branch of the I.G. in London, a process that would lead to the setting up of a new national organization with a new name and a major shift in the group's orientation to the Labour Party as expressed in the "entry tactic." Not long after Pat, as I have already mentioned, Mike Martin, a member of the I.G. from Hull, joined us; he became one of our key people in the VSC. Geoff Coggan also arrived in London. On the staff of the Nottingham Labour Party as Press Secretary, he had been fired when Ken Coates had been expelled, and was looking for work. He was appointed alongside Ken and Pat to the Board of Directors of the Foundation, becoming its company secretary. Ken Tarbuck, a long time member of group who had been studying economics and living in London, also got involved.

Also helping us in that early period were a few people from Toronto—most of them originally from Britain who had immigrated to Canada and had been active in the LSA in Toronto—who had now returned to London. They became very important in helping us get established, demonstrating once again the power of a united international organization that could focus its efforts on a common project. Pat Brain, my old comrade from English Electric in Toronto, was one of the first. Originally from Birmingham, he had moved to London from Toronto. Then there was Jim Clough, who had been active in the Toronto YS, and who recently married and found a job in London. Working in the printing trades, he had acquired skills that would later become extremely valuable to us. He had developed into a competent graphic artist and would eventually design all the posters for the VSC that it used to publicize its demonstrations. He helped us silk-screen and print thousands of them at very low cost. Also returning to London from Toronto was Frank Gorton, an engineering draftsman, originally an immigrant to Canada, and his wife Toni, a Canadian. She was trained in graphic design. Both had been active in our group in Toronto and Toni had been one of the founding members and a leader of the Young Socialists and had been active in the founding of the NDP.

I later heard it suggested that these people from Canada had been purposefully sent to London by the Americans and Canadians to act as a kind of secret faction to influence the new organization, in some irregular kind of way. This is simply untrue. They were attracted to London because a lot of exciting political activity was taking place there and they thought it would be a stimulating place to be. The Canadians did not operate as a secret caucus of any kind nor did we have a common social life. Because of their experience in Toronto of working in a disciplined group and having been educated in Trotskyist ideas, however, they were invaluable in helping us build the organization and integrate new members.

By this time, we were gathering a lot of new people around us. Recruitment seemed to be fairly easy. I'm sure I'm leaving a few names out, but I especially remember, in this regard, a very bright young couple, Richard and Barbara Wilson, who were working on completing their degrees in organic chemistry at London University, playing a very active role in that formative period. Barbara turned out to be a very good speaker and became important in helping us popularize our views about feminism and women's liberation, chairing one of the first forums organized by the British left on the issue, sponsored by *The Week* at which a very youthful Sheila Rowbotham and Robin Blackburn of NLR spoke.

That's also when we met up with Bob Purdie. From Glasgow, a steam-fitter in those days, he had been active in the Amalgamated Engineering Union in Scotland and had come to London to look for work. His skills as a trade unionist were very important in helping ground the group in the working class. He later became one of its main leaders. We also had a few people at Ruskin College in Oxford, organized around a very capable young activist, Bernard Reaney, and a Canadian from Montreal, Stan Gray, who was on a Rhodes scholarship, whom I had known in Canada when he had been in contact with the YS.

We also picked up a few people from Healy's organization, among them a young working class couple, Keith and Valerie Veness, who considered themselves revolutionaries. Keith told us that he had been kicked out of Healy's YS after an argument with Healy. He told us he had been forcefully pushed down the stairs from Healy's office in Clapham Common onto the street after voicing disagreement with the SLL's position on the war. They had been attending our public forums and told Pat they were interested in working with us. We had also begun to meet up with people in the Communist Party youth who were disgruntled with their line on Vietnam.

Paul Franklin, Frank Hanson and Phil Hearse, three teenagers who had been active in the Outer London YCL, also joined us. And, soon after that, Peter Gowan, then a student in his very early twenties, signed up as well. Peter would become a leader of the group and the International in the seventies and develop into one of the country's major Marxist intellectuals. Phil Hearse also became a full-time leader of the group in the early seventies and was elected to the International's leading body, the International Secretariat. He is currently a supporter of the International Socialist Group organized around the monthly publication *Resistance*, which he writes for, and also runs the excellent website, *Marxsite*.

Jess and I renewed our acquaintance with him in recent years, as we had done with Peter Gowan who had become a well-known political scientist and writer in Britain and internationally. A professor at North London University, an editor of *New Left Review*, and a brilliant analyst of Eastern Europe and Russia, Peter was the author of a profoundly insightful work about imperialism and the American empire.[1] Tragically, Peter died, at the age of 63, of mesothelioma, a cancer caused mainly from asbestos, something he had been exposed to while teaching in the London school system in the 1970s. Jess and I were very fortunate to have renewed our acquaintance with him in his final years.

All those I have mentioned here—and I'm sure I've forgotten a few and I apologize if I have—were some of the first members we recruited in London. The marvelous thing was that they were genuine youth, still in their teens or early twenties and with lots of energy to spare.

Jess MacKenzie at the 1967 Youth Conference in Brussels.

Chapter 11

The International Marxist Group

*T*OWARDS THE END OF 1966, OUR PEOPLE IN LONDON HAD EVOLVED into functioning, if somewhat loosely, as a London extension of the Nottingham I.G., and from time to time, meeting in our Pioneer Book Service office, where we planned our work in the VSC and in the Labour Party. By my estimation, we had about twenty-five people around us by then, some of them activists we considered to be "supporters" and whom we hoped to recruit soon. With Pat Jordan living permanently in London, we began to make the move, with the agreement of Nottingham, towards a more formally structured group. Day-to-day decision-making was concentrated in London and we began to set up a "tighter" organization, modeled, with a few modifications, along the lines of—I must admit—the LSA back in Canada. This "Canadian" influence was only natural considering my political experience and the fact that some of the more active members of the group came from Toronto. Pat was very happy with the direction we were heading. For the first time we would have an effective national organization, albeit small, with its headquarters in London.

We scheduled the first National Conference for January 1967. About forty-five people were there, with around half of them in their early twenties. There was representation from Nottingham, London, Oxford, Glasgow, Brighton and Edinburgh. In the pre-conference discussion, differences of opinion that had been under the radar for some time now began to show themselves, naturally enough. Debate centred on how the new group should view itself. One view, expressed by Ken Coates and his supporters in Nottingham, tended to see the new organization as primarily a focal point for the "broad" left, around which some kind of "regroupment" might eventually take place. This view, as I interpreted it, assigned a lower priority to the task of building what we had at hand, more or less like how the I.G. had been functioning since its founding. I don't remember if Ken ever submitted a resolution asking for a vote on his views, however. Another resolution, submitted by Ken Tarbuck, the content of which I don't remember, managed to get nine votes.

The "perspectives" document put forward by Pat, laying out our tactics and political orientation, received overwhelming majority support. I remember thinking that one very positive feature of the conference, aside from structuring ourselves on a more formal basis, was to at least allow some of the differences that had been percolating amongst us to come to the surface so they could be discussed in an organized way. The conference also adopted a slim constitution, containing only a few simple clauses that set out rules by which to run the organization. Unfortunately this included—over my objections—a ridiculous clause stating that any member of the organization had the right, at any time, to have their written contributions published and circulated throughout the organization, whether it was a pre-convention period or not. It didn't happen while I was there, but it could have easily caused the group to become a permanent discussion group and not an organization focused on carrying out political tasks.

It was an attempt, I think, of trying to seek some kind of timeless guarantees that would guard against the un-democratic practices seen in organizations such as Gerry Healy's. For me, however, it was another terrible example of how the break in revolutionary continuity represented in Britain by the Healy split, and the sectarian evolution of the Grant group, led to a situation where even some of the positive features of those organizations were readily dismissed and thrown out, like the proverbial baby with the bath water, forcing us to start our work all over again. It was a terrible price we had to pay for the unprincipled splits we had witnessed in the past in Britain.

The conference also elected a "National Committee" (NC) to be the governing body of the organization between conventions. It included Ken

Coates and Ken Tarbuck, and had representation from around the country. It was decided, unanimously, that the resident NC members in London would constitute themselves as the "Political Committee," in order to give leadership to the organization between NC meetings. Pat was elected National Secretary, the most important position in the new organization. Not long after that we formally reconstituted the I.G. in London as a branch of the IMG. Unlike union branches or Labour Party constituencies, which usually met monthly, we agreed to meet weekly. Political life in London had a weekly cycle, therefore, we were convinced, this was a necessity if the branch membership—which was sovereign in our view— was to have maximum control and input into the group's functioning.

I can't remember if we adopted any new tasks at that first meeting, but we did elect a small executive committee to plan our activities and finances. When Jess MacKenzie returned from Brussels, she was elected the group's first branch organizer, the most responsible position on the committee. Aside from managing our book service, she was at the same time able to devote a lot of her time to that position. Our office had become a virtual office for the group.

As far as I can recall there wasn't much, if any, debate or discussion about the name, IMG. It expressed exactly what we were, with no illusions about our real limitations: "International," because of our belief in world revolution, international solidarity and our affiliation with the Fourth International; "Marxist" to distinguish ourselves from social democracy and because that was where the methodology of our politics was derived; and "Group", because we did not see ourselves as a political party as we believed such parties of the working class had to be mass parties, or parties with a history of mass links to the working class. Of course, like most of the national sections that made up the Fourth International in those days, we aspired to become a mass organization, or part of a mass organization of the working class, but we were very aware of where the sectarian traps and mistakes on this issue could lead. It was not a matter of programme or declarations but of an actual relation to the working class. Ultimately, this meant having the capacity to have an influence on the politics of the country at the level of the state. We were acutely conscious of our limitations on that score. It wasn't a matter of having a list of programmatic positions and asking people to subscribe to them and on that basis become members. For us, membership in the IMG required a deeper commitment. We saw ourselves as a "vanguard" organization within the framework of the "entry tactic" in relation to the Labour Party. We saw the group as a cadre-building kind of organization, as yet unable to appeal directly to the working class in its own name. We were unanimous in thinking our political relationship to the working class had of necessity to be mediated through the Labour Party. In a nutshell, our aim was to appeal primarily to those already politically mature militants—who considered themselves socialists or Marxists to one degree or another—to join us, offering them a whole basket of ideas derived from a Marxist analysis in order to build a politically coherent force capable of intervening in the day-to-day class struggle.

Our immediate priority was the building of our own public organization with the hope of winning to our ranks the small cadre of political activists who were close to us politically and who had expressed some agreement with our views on the need to give a high priority to defending the colonial revolution, specifically Vietnam and Cuba. Related to this, we also took time and made special efforts to defend those revolutions where private property relations had already been overthrown. To be considered for membership, prospective recruits had to have shown a commitment to the struggle for socialism on a day-to-day basis; this was easier to do in Britain than Canada, for example, because Marxism had much broader support among working people. All of us were very sensitive to avoid becoming what is commonly referred to on the left as a "talking shop," an "all inclusive" kind of organization that would be thrown into a crisis and paralysis every time we wished to issue a public statement about political events or take some kind of common action.

Defining ourselves as the "International Marxist Group,"—an "open", public organization of the F.I.—at that time wasn't simply a name change for the I.G., continuing "business as usual" activities tied mainly to the political cycle of life in the Labour Party. It was much more than that. It was a recognition that the political landscape was changing quickly, becoming much more favourable for us. A youth radicalization was sweeping the country, with new forces appearing on the scene almost overnight who might be won directly and rapidly to our ideas. Similar changes were occurring in other countries. We were modifying the "entry tactic" similar to how the youth of the French section of the F.I. had changed theirs within the French Communist Party, as they adopted more "independent" activities such as campaigning against the Vietnam war, right up to their break from the CP in 1967. The same was true of our Canadian group, I might add. With the founding of the NDP, the LSA had also modified its orientation to the point where it not only regularly ran in municipal elections, but it also ran federally in by-elections, for example, in order to put forward a clear socialist programme to let working people know where we stood.

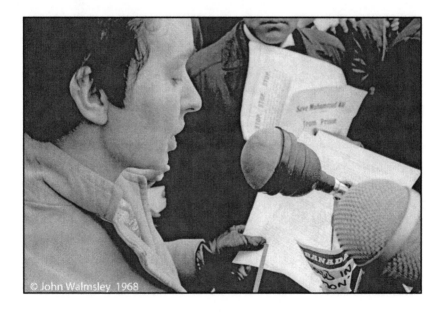

Barbara Wilson of the IMG and VSC, speaking from the plinth, Trafalgar Square, March 17th, 1968.

TOP Jess, Sirio Di Giuliomaria and Ernie in Rome, 1969

BOTTOM LEFT Phil Hearse (left) outside LSE, with Frank Hanson in a light
sweater facing the camera, 1968

BOTTOM RIGHT Bob Purdie and Pat Jordan

Chapter 12

The Death of Che Guevara

O NE MORNING, IN OCTOBER 1967, JESS AND I AWOKE TO THE STUNNING
news that Che Guevara had been captured in Bolivia and executed.
We were horrified at his brutal murder, but his defeat wasn't a total
surprise to our group. With his overall tactical approach to the question
of social revolution, we had doubted he would ever succeed there. Nevertheless, because of his selfless struggle on behalf of the oppressed, he
had become a hero of new radicalizing youth everywhere. It was a
momentous occasion for our small group in London. The American
SWP immediately rushed out a special edition of The Militant, with Che's
picture covering the entire front page. We ordered several thousand to
come by air to London and the IMG organized a special memorial meeting
for him that seven or eight hundred attended. It was our largest public
forum ever and it turned out to be one of the most popular issues of The
Militant we had ever sold.

Latin America was very much at the centre of our discussions in those
years, especially after the Havana Tri-continental Conference of 1966 and
the conference of the Organization of Latin American Solidarity (OLAS)
in Havana a couple of months prior to Che's death. All the signs indicated
that the Cubans were heading towards setting up some kind of a new
international formation that would promote guerrilla war in Latin America
where most of the people lived under various kinds of military regimes.
Even though the United Secretariat at that time disagreed with the Cubans
about their rural armed struggle views (it would later move closer to the
Cuban position), it took the OLAS conference very seriously, enough to

send three leaders there: Joe Hansen of the American SWP, Ken Coates from London, representing the Bertrand Russell Peace Foundation, and Ross Dowson of the LSA, along with delegations from virtually all of our Latin American sections, with especially large ones from Argentina and Bolivia. In a major speech at the OLAS gathering, Castro strongly criticized the Venezuelan CP for its betrayal of its left wing. When our people returned they told us that rumours were rampant that the Cubans were on the verge of initiating a new revolutionary international, an armed struggle formation that would begin rural guerrilla warfare.[1]

Immediately a discussion ensued amongst us about how we would relate to the Cuban initiative. This put on the table the question of the role of rural guerrilla warfare as a strategy in the struggle for socialism in continental Latin America, not as an abstract notion about what might happen in the far future, but in the present. This discussion had been bubbling along since we first received the news that Che, who for over a year had dropped out of sight in Cuba, was in Bolivia. After a brief, aborted campaign in the Congo, he had returned to Cuba in December 1965 and had begun to train a group of volunteers to accompany him to Bolivia in an effort to open a guerrilla front with the aim of replicating the success of the Cuban Revolution—first in Bolivia, then Argentina, but eventually in all of Latin America. Before leaving Cuba, he had issued his historic call for working people everywhere to come to the defense of the Vietnamese against American imperialism by the creating of ". . . two three, many Vietnams." Arriving in Bolivia in October 1966, he launched a guerrilla operation in March 1967.

Not long after that, at Secretariat meetings, we exchanged information and discussed what this new development might mean for the left. I recall that Ray Sparrow and I were the only ones of those present who were skeptical about whether Guevara would succeed. Both of us thought, especially me, that it was something of an adventure and might even lead to disaster. I was surprised in the discussion, however, when it turned out that Ernest Mandel was much less critical than either of us.

Mandel had been a central leader of the International virtually since its founding—and would remain so until his death in 1995. He played a key role in overcoming the 1953 division. Well known as one of international Trotskyism's leading theoreticians, respect for his work amongst academics had increased greatly with the release of his master work in political economy, *Late Capitalism.*[2] His writings on "Euro-Communism" and on the potential for rivalry between Europe and the U.S. were accepted in the broad left as a signal contribution to the debate about those issues. Before coming to London and long before I had ever met him, I had some reservations about him, most likely having been influenced perhaps by the factionalism arising from the polemics between him and the SWP during the "Pablo dispute" that was raging when I first joined our Toronto group in 1955. In these debates, Mandel went by "Ernest Germain," his pseudonym. Notwithstanding these differences, I remember that the SWP leadership held him in unusually high regard. I specifically recall in 1956, Tom Kerry—the SWP's Organizational Secretary, a gruff sort of character, not known for readily handing out compliments—telling a group of us a story at the cadre school at Mountain Spring Camp. Kerry recounted how when James P. Cannon had returned from one of his trips to Europe immediately after the Second World War, he had reported back to their Political Committee on the state of the Fourth International, telling them, "we have a genius in Brussels, a young Ernest Mandel." Cannon saw very early that Ernest would become a major leader.

Ernest had become a revolutionary socialist while still a teenager. His father, a member of the German Communist Party, had been among the first to rally to Trotsky's side during the fight with Stalin. When I attended Secretariat meetings in Brussels, sometimes he would invite me to stay overnight at his home where he lived with his mother. I remember her being invariably charming and gracious, always making me feel welcome, although she would usually retreat to a back room somewhere almost as soon as I showed up. When I mentioned this to Ray Sparrow, he told me he had noticed the same thing and that he thought it might be a simple case of her simply feeling uncomfortable having strangers around. She didn't speak English, but I wasn't aware until the recent biography of Mandel by Jan Willem Stutje [3] that she had a remarkable history in her own right, having been an active communist militant alongside Ernest's father during their resistance to the German occupation of Belgium.

At the time of our early exchanges in the United Secretariat about the significance of Guevara's guerrilla campaign in Bolivia, Ernest had just returned from Cuba, where he had met with high-level officials of the Cuban government. In conversation over supper with Ray and me one evening, he told us that from what he had heard from his contacts, the Cuban state was fully behind Che's Bolivian operation. Ernest may have had some reservations of course, but I remember him insisting with some forcefulness, that with the resources of the Cuban state and the modern communications technology they had surreptitiously placed at Che's disposal, the guerrilla forces led by him could be successful. Thinking he should have known better, I was slightly discomfited with Ernest's view as I felt we were beginning to cast aside some long held positions about how social revolution would take place.. But I shouldn't have been surprised. My experiences with him over the previous couple of years that I was in Europe had taught me that, while he was a marvelous human being, and that he would put a lot of energy into dealing with organizational questions, because of his enthusiasm, and generosity with his time, he would often be capable of making mistakes and we—I'm talking about all the North Americans here—especially Joe Hansen—would often wish he would leave those matters to others and devote more time to his intellectual work.

Ernest's primary evaluation of the Guevara experience seemed to me not to have been worked out too well and was strongly influenced by the zeitgeist of the time, the thinking of the new radicalizing youth who seemed to be enchanted with the ideas of guerrilla warfare—those the majority of the Secretariat would later call "the new youth vanguard"— many of whom had recently come into the organization, especially in France. We faced a possibility of losing them, I remember him telling me in a personal conversation one day, if we did not support the new radical line. Livio Maitan, the leader of the Italian section, who had been to Latin America many times, was in agreement with Ernest, but probably with fewer reservations. I don't remember Pierre Frank's position at that stage of the discussion or him saying much, but I recall that he had been very critical of the OLAS conference, where the Cubans had projected a continental guerrilla strategy but he would later become an advocate of that position.

The question of guerrilla warfare was by no means new to our movement. No one in the Fourth International, that I remember, had ever opposed it in principle. It was seen essentially as a tactical question and was part of the agreement proposed by the SWP in a resolution that had been adopted at its 1963 Congress to set the basis for the re-unification of the movement, that stated: "13. Along the road to revolution beginning with simple democratic demands and ending in the rupture of capitalist property relations, guerrilla warfare conducted by landless peasants and semi-proletarian forces, under a leadership that becomes committed to carrying the revolution through to a conclusion, can play a decisive role in undermining and precipitating the downfall of a colonial and semi-colonial power. This is one of the main lessons to be drawn from experience since the Second World War. It must be consciously incorporated into a strategy of building revolutionary Marxist parties in colonial countries."[4]

BRIEFING

to all demonstrators:

'Street Power'

WE STICK TOGETHER—WE GO THE WHOLE ROUTE—WE TAKE THE STREET—WE WANT NO ARRESTS—WE LINK ARMS—WE KEEP ARMS LINKED—AND THEN WE LINK ARMS AGAIN!

WE STICK TOGETHER—Our physical solidarity demonstrates our political solidarity with each other and with our Vietnamese comrades. We link arms; we stay in the street; we draw stragglers back into the demonstration. This is the only way to defend ourselves from any possible interference.

WE WORK IN GROUPS—The unit of any demonstration can only be the self-disciplined group. Groups of fifty to a hundred people in earshot of each other take action to achieve the goals of the demonstration. Within these larger groups, small groups of friends stay side by side throughout the march to carry out the policy of No Arrests, and to restrain each other from any unnecessary heroics. People alone should try to make up such small groups, and small groups should come together into larger ones, right here and now.

WE GO THE WHOLE ROUTE (see map)—If anyone at all should try to divert us, we simply move forward along the route, sweeping aside obstacles, giving obstructors no time for violence.

WE TAKE THE STREET—For maximum solidarity and effect, we expect to fill the streets. To do this, we will have to extend our lines of linked arms as necessary. Coherent groups of marchers should try to move up alongside the march where the road broadens, and fall back where it narrows, rather than lose their internal solidarity by moving as individuals to make up the varying width of the march.

WE WANT NO ARRESTS—Whatever happens, the situation can never be met by individual, adventurist actions. Responsible, collective action can only be that taken by the mass of demonstrators as a physical whole. We minimise the chance of arrests when we make it impossible for any individual to single himself out for the police, and impossible for the police to single out any individual. Self-destined martyrs please note that the Committee has no lawyers and no money to get some with!

WE HOLD OUR GROUND—It is just possible we may be obliged by external interference to halt somewhere between here and Hyde Park. If a stationary front is formed, with the demonstrators facing some obstruction, people in the front line should turn to the side, so that they present only hips and shoulders to the outside of the march. The outer arm should go round the waist of the demonstrator in front, the inside arm should link on to a second such line of demonstrators behind the first, and facing to the opposite flank. We must keep the perimeter of the march unbroken! Even when standing still, we set the terms of our presence in the streets.

WE DON'T SPLIT—In solidarity with each other and with our Vietnamese comrades, we co-operate to achieve the goals of the demonstration. To fill the route. To occupy Whitehall. To demonstrate our power. To set aside all interference. To rally in Hyde Park, where we will state our case, explain and discuss the demonstration, and begin the autumn campaign.

> **Most of us are not willing to support acts of passive civil disobedience, or of terrorism. Individuals who may have such minority actions in mind are warned not to rely on the mass of demonstrators for protection.**

WE EXPLAIN IT ALL—From the Rally in Hyde Park, we take the message

P.T.O.

"Street Power"
  Instructions for how to avoid confrontation with the police

Chapter 13

Crises in the Russell Foundation

WITHIN A FEW WEEKS, CHE GUEVARA'S DEATH HAD AN UNFORESEEN and unfortunate effect on our group's work in London. Ralph, our closest ally in the Bertrand Russell Peace Foundation was banned from entering Britain after having been to Bolivia, as I've mentioned previously in the chapter on the International War Crimes Tribunal. He was in Bolivia trying to help those facing danger as a result of the defeat of Che's forces, a group that included the prominent French intellectual Regis Debray. Che, before his capture and murder, had invited Debray to Bolivia to spend some time with him and travel in the mountains with his guerrilla group. A Professor of Philosophy at Havana University, originally from France, he had come to prominence in left circles as a polemicist for Che's views, through a recent short book of essays, a so-called handbook for guerrilla warfare.[1] Debray had been in Bolivia the previous year, helping to recruit fighters for Che's campaign and scouting possible locations to begin operations.

According to Lee Anderson, Che's biographer, Debray had earlier, while in Cuba, been recruited into Cuba's intelligence network and become one of its underground couriers.[2] His public cover while in Bolivia was that he was a journalist, working for the French publishing house, Maspero. Debray had arrived at Che's guerrilla camp just as a unit of the Bolivian army had detected its location. He wanted to stay and fight but wasn't unhappy when Che recommended that he try and make his escape. He seized the opportunity to get out at the same time as an Anglo-Chilean reporter, who had been at the camp interviewing Che, was leaving. Debray was unable to outsmart the military with his journalist's credentials and was imprisoned. Anderson writes that Che sent Debray "out with news for Cuba," and told him, that he (Che) "would write a letter for Bertrand Russell asking for help in organizing an international fund in support of the Bolivian Liberation Movement."[3]

Debray's arrest sparked an international outcry and many on the left, including our group, mobilized to defend him. For us, it was a key component of developing solidarity with the resistance to the Latin American dictatorships. Earlier, before Debray's arrest, the Russell Foundation had already been in touch with the Cubans and had begun to initiate a campaign of support for the struggle in Bolivia, asking Lawrence Daly if he would be part of a team that would visit Bolivia to report on the conditions of the miners (a proposal Daly had to turn down because of his union commitments).[4] With Ralph and Ken Coates travelling frequently back and forth to Cuba during the course of the Tribunal's work—Ralph would eventually meet Fidel Castro—the Cubans were most likely very well informed of Russell's readiness to come to Che's aid, a fact that Che seemed to have been well aware of too.

There was widespread speculation in many circles that Debray would be quickly murdered because of the hysterical public campaign against him in Bolivia—posters were plastered everywhere in the area where he was imprisoned, labeling him an assassin. Fortunately this didn't happen, but within six months he was placed on trial. To try and ensure the proceedings in Bolivia would be fair and would receive maximum international exposure, the Russell Foundation quickly organized a delegation to accompany Ralph there, comprised mainly of *New Left Review* people—Tariq Ali, Robin Blackburn and Perry Anderson—along with a leader of the Fourth International's German section, Lothar Menne, to act as observers. They hoped to provide credibility to Debray's claim that he was simply a journalist who had been in contact with Che for an interview. They wanted to gain time for international pressure to grow sufficiently to cause the Bolivian military to hesitate in pushing for Debray's physical elimination, something they felt they had already helped achieve with their agitation around his case. In the end, Debray received a thirty-year sentence, but that was commuted in 1970.

With Debray's trial delayed, the Foundation's team returned to Britain Ralph, however, remained behind until November, working on a report that would form the basis of a legal brief in defense of Debray for presentation to the military tribunal. When he appealed to the trial judge to be allowed to submit his evidence of irregularities and the military's criminality in the case, he was immediately thrown in prison and then deported.[5] Over the several months Ralph was in Bolivia, our group in London had little contact with him. He seemed to be functioning very much on his own, but my suspicion is that he was liaising in some way with the Cubans—possibly through Melba Hernandez—who were doing everything they could to save Debray.

When I had initially learned that Schoenman was organizing a team to go to Bolivia, I had fully expected that at the most he would be only there for a couple of weeks—considering his responsibilities—and that he would be back in London to guide our work in support of the Tribunal, which since the split with the Paris committee had become increasingly difficult. Communications between the London and Paris Secretariat had almost ceased to exist by then and whenever I enquired of Chris Farley about when Ralph would be back, he would always be vague in his answers. It was as if Ralph was out of touch with him too. And this separation would become permanent.

Upon his arrest, Schoenman's passport was nullified by the U.S. State Department. From Bolivia he was deported to Peru, and from there to Panama. When he attempted to return to Britain, he was refused entry.[6] It was a major catastrophe for him—and for us in London. For weeks he travelled around Europe's airports, looking for a country that would allow him admittance—"on the planet without a visa," as Trotsky once said. At one point he was arrested in Germany, deported and ended up in Ireland where he was promptly jailed, causing the issue to be raised for debate in the Dail, the Irish parliament. He was prevented from attending the Danish session of the Tribunal—which would end up being its final session—in Roskilde, the follow up to Stockholm. Ralph had become, in his words, the "Flying Dutchman" of the anti-war movement. He had by this time been provided with travel documents by the North Vietnamese government but was arrested in Amsterdam before getting to Stockholm, where he was again arrested and savagely beaten by the police. From there he was sent to Hamburg and, finally, against his will, flown back to New York.

After Schoenman was banned from Britain, it wasn't long before the BRPF entered a paralyzing internal crisis. Factional struggle broke out amongst its Directors about how to deal with the financial difficulties that had been precipitated by the non-payment of Russell's substantial loans to the Tribunal. By then, I had stepped back from the affairs of the Foundation and was devoting more of my time to helping guide the VSC and the building of our F.I. group. Geoff Coggan and Pat Jordan alerted me to what seemed to be a conflict among the Foundation's Directors about how to deal with its financial problem. Then one day David Horowitz took me aside to tell me that now that Ralph was out of the picture, a power struggle seemed to be underway over the Foundation's future and the situation was starting to look very bad.

Whilst its prestige had reached new heights due to the Tribunal, the reality was that the Foundation had borne the bulk of that cost, and by the fall of 1967, as we were in the midst of preparing for the October 22, VSC first mass mobilization and looking forward to the next session of the Tribunal in Copenhagen, it began to run out of money. It wasn't the first time this had happened, and it seemed the crows were finally coming home to roost. During the previous summer, the staff had worked six weeks without pay. With an average budget of around 2,500 GBP a month, it now was facing another shortfall, and would be unable to pay its staff for the next two months; it seemed impossible to find a bridging loan to cover operations until more money—an expected seven thousand GBP, which was due on January 2nd along with a further 7,000 GBP due in February—came in. The loans advanced to the Tribunal had never been repaid and it looked like they never would be.

With Isaac Deutscher's death, we had lost a major ally in exerting moral pressure upon Dedijer, Sartre, Schwartz and de Beauvoir to live up to their financial obligations to Russell, and nothing was happening on that front. Expectations that substantial money would be raised from international film, recording and publishing rights, assigned to the Foundation by the Tribunal after an acrimonious tussle, proved to be illusory. "Talk of the sale of sole rights to television companies at a figure of 100,000 pounds," wrote Geoff Coggan, turned out to be empty words: "there was no return whatsoever."[7]

The personal implications of this situation were enormous for the Directors. Horowitz—who had been on the Board for several years and who in the midst of the crisis had announced he would be returning to the U.S.—noted, "In the event of Lord Russell's death . . . income obtained by the Foundation in the form of gifts over the last year will be accessible for death duties. This income—from his autobiography— has been estimated at 100,000 pounds. Possibly a tax rate as high as 80% (estimates of income next year, 250,000 to 660,000 pounds) would be subject to death duties . . . The accountant's had suggested that 80% of all income should be invested in local government stock as it was received. This was not done because of the needs of the Tribunal. The Directors were of the opinion that this took the place of an investment because the Tribunal had agreed it would repay the money lent it by the Foundation."

A sense of panic ensued, Horowitz observed, when it dawned on those responsible for the Foundation's affairs the extent of their liabilities "to meet the consequences should the amount in hand be insufficient to meet death duties," and that they would "not be able to declare bankruptcy."[8] The Board, with Peter Limqueco (from Sweden, and of whom I have only a vague memory), Ralph Schoenman and Tony Topham out of the country, had six functioning Directors: Geoff Coggan, Ken Coates, Chris Farley, David Horowitz, Pat Jordan and Russell Stetler. Until then, they had mistakenly assumed that with the elapse of one year from the date of a Russell gift, there would be no tax in the event of his death. To their collective horror, after consulting a tax consultant, they discovered otherwise.

"It's ludicrous," remarked Geoff Coggan, "that we should have found out on October 9th, that the period of full liability for death duties on gifts extended for two years after the date of the gifts, and not for one year as we had been led to believe all year." [9]

The difficulty in large measure was also due to the Board's haphazard way of functioning, for which, it's now clear, both Farley and Schoenman, being the longest serving members of the Board, bore the major responsibility. For example, it was only when Geoff and Pat were appointed to the Board the previous April that regular meetings became the norm and, "It was only then that any form of accounting was undertaken." [10] Coggan noted that the financial situation was no better or no worse than it has been for the whole of the past year. Many of the Foundation's initiatives, such as the Latin American solidarity campaign when Ralph led the Foundation-sponsored team to Bolivia or the sending of a team of investigators to the Middle East at the time of the Arab-Israeli war to look into charges the Israelis had committed war crimes, were launched outside of any Board deliberation and had never been brought before it. The Middle East team—which was never permitted by the Israelis to visit the occupied territories—never even issued a report of its findings.

Another case, although it did not involve a large sum of money, was symptomatic of the confusion in the Foundation's affairs. Twelve hundred GBP was handed over, despite the organization not having much money, to someone who said he was sailing to Vietnam—presumably with medical supplies. The yacht apparently never even left the harbour. Coggan argued that these kinds of things fitted into a "consistent pattern over the months, of a totally complacent belief that our projects will attract sufficient support to cover a substantial proportion of their costs . . . everybody appears to have been mesmerized by the prospect of manna from Pourhyn-deudrath (where Russell lived in Wales—E.T.) in the form of the archives." [11] The difficulties had arisen, Coggan would later add, "because of the diversity of activities—not a single one of which has been seen through to a conclusion, and all of which have left a trail of unresolved problems on practically every director's desk . . ." [12]

When Pat Jordan phoned him to discuss the developing financial crisis, Ken Coates was in the midst of preparations to set up a print shop and offices in Nottingham, all to be financed with 50,000 GBP from the Foundation. He did indeed panic. "Pat rang me and told me if I had any assets, to get rid of them," he claimed. He resented being told that his phone bills—paid for by the Foundation—would have to be reined in, saying that he had not been informed about new rules governing this expense. Large enough to cover the cost of a secretary's wages, Pat would claim. Ken's immediate reaction was to launch a power struggle within the Board against Geoff and Pat, virtually paralyzing the Foundation and making it impossible to raise funds to deal with its difficulties. He wrote to the Directors, blaming Geoff and Pat for the crisis: "The latest example of the heroic incompetence of our Rivington St., apparatus reached me this morning . . . I have still seen no minutes for the period between July and 21st of September . . . All Rivington Street is an elaborate waste of money," he wrote.[13]

It's noteworthy that this letter tends to back-up Geoff and Pat's complaint about the difficulty of getting Ken to meetings, since he himself indicates that he had not attended any for about twelve weeks. "Since being a member of the board," Pat would later explain to the IMG, "he attended just three meetings. They have been held weekly for seven months."[14] In what appears to be an attempt to distance him personally from the financial mess, with an eye, I think, to possibly establish the grounds for a diminished responsibility for it, Ken wrote to the Directors, "I have never seen a balance sheet. The only accounts I have ever been shown concerned airfares for the Tribunal . . . The Middle East trip was supposed to be non-financing. I asked Chris (Farley) to postpone it . . . I have been assured that there is plenty of money, to finance, for instance, the Nottingham office."[15] Chris Farley, the longest serving Director amongst them, who sided with Ken, proposed "the emptying of the Rivington Street office promptly," but recommended that the staff be given "14 or 28 days' notice as appropriate" and that Geoff and Pat be given 28 days and that he would voluntarily go off staff.[16]

Forty-one Rivington Street—"an elaborate waste of money," according to Ken Coates—was the small office building, a freehold owned by the BRPF that, as I've already noted, I had helped them find. After it was purchased, it had quickly become a very busy place. Most of the BRPF's external campaigns were run from there. It's where the periodicals and Bulletins of the IWCT, and the BRPF were produced and mailed, including its new supposedly mass circulation monthly magazine, *The Spokesman*. (On paper, this had seemed like a good idea at the time, but with little advance preparation—and very limited channels of distribution, I should add—the first mailing of 8,000 brought in only 125 subscriptions and many thousands of copies had to be dumped. It was an inauspicious beginning for a publication that continues to this day.)

Geoff, Pat and David Robinson worked full-time out of the building and it was from there that most of the Foundation's public forums and public relations work were organized. It was also the National office of the VSC that had two of the Foundation's full-timers dedicated to it, but who at the same time when required, according to Pat, also worked on the Foundation's many projects. Aside from that subsidy, which included rent, the VSC raised its own finances and paid for its own meetings and publications. In total, about seven people worked in the building, some of them clerical and most of them sympathetic to the politics of the IMG.

Ken's behaviour in the Foundation crisis shouldn't have been a surprise to any of us. Since the founding of the IMG, we had been aware of his increasing unhappiness with its evolution. Relations between him, and Pat Jordan and Geoff Coggan, and indeed most of the IMG, had been strained for many months. According to Pat and Geoff, Ken had become increasingly difficult to talk to about the Foundation's business. "He refused to be part of our counsels," Geoff would later write.[17] Ken had withdrawn from the activities around the IWCT and no longer attended our Working Committee meetings in London, partly as a result of the cleavage between the Paris office and us, but also because of his huge commitment of time to the Workers' Control Institute, which was becoming very important in his and Tony Topham's lives. Moreover, some of his special projects seemed to be going nowhere. The CSE, which he had initially hoped would help "regroup the British left," had by this time almost ceased to exist, only serving as a convenient banner under which he and Tony organized their "workers' control" conferences, and as a label for their publications.[18]

I had experienced the CSE failure first hand shortly after I had arrived in London from Canada when I had participated in a few of their first meetings. It had been based on the illusion that the left could work with the unions somehow, without confronting their bureaucracies, to allow Marxists to gain access to their memberships for "educational" purposes. It proved to be an impossible dream. Each meeting—of most of them that I remember with Ralph Miliband in the chair—turned out to be smaller than the previous one, until the London CSE, without any explanation to those who had rallied to its cause, stopped meeting altogether. A similar fate had also befallen the May Day Manifesto group in which Ken and Tony had also been prominent. This was another initiative endorsed by a long list of academics and assorted intellectuals—supposedly to fill the ever perennial vacuum on the left and to intervene in the working class—that had quickly evaporated into irrelevance after its launch on May Day, 1967. The only trace it left of its existence was a well written Penguin book of essays, mainly by academics, about the Wilson government.

Tactical differences between Ken and the rest of the IMG leadership about work in the Labour Party had also become sharper by this time. Earlier, when I was in Brussels, Ernest Mandel had mentioned to me that Ken was beginning to express some uneasiness about the setting up of the IMG, and that Ken was wondering whether it had been a correct move for the group, becoming even more critical than he had been at the founding conference. Looking back on it, I now suspect that Pat had proceeded along that path without consulting Ken much or perhaps Ken, because of his leadership position in the group—he was one of its founders, after all—felt he had some kind of veto rights over the direction we were supposed to be taking. I had always assumed that Pat and Ken, despite their tactical differences in relation to the Labour Party, were close to each other and in regular communication, but obviously their relations had become strained when Pat transferred to London. I had also noted that, when we carried out the group's reorganization, Ken had drawn back from participation in its activities. It is possible that the setting up of the IMG had come as a bit of a surprise to him. I never ever saw Ken at any of the National Committee meetings since the IMG's founding, an obvious symptom it turned out, of his increasing alienation. The situation had begun to have every appearance of being a "cold" split between him and the rest of the IMG.

That year Ken and Tony, like most of us in the IMG, had placed a lot of our hope on the emergence of a possible "broad left" in the Labour Party that would be led by Frank Cousins, Jack Jones, and Ernie Roberts, prominent left trade union leaders—the latter two recently elected heads of their union—who were voicing opposition to Wilson. Ken and Tony, without discussing it much with the rest of the IMG, had put all their efforts into involving these leaders in what would be a new, " broad left" opposition. Pat accused Ken of wishing to dissolve the IMG into it—around the slogan, "Decisions Matter"—to try to force Wilson and the Parliamentary Labour Party to, for once, respect Annual Conference resolutions. That campaign went nowhere, however. When push came to shove, the new union leaders caved in under the pressure of the party bureaucracy, leaving Ken and Tony on their own.

That they had clearly misestimated the willingness of the union leadership to resist Wilson; the extent of this failure could be seen in the teach-in that year they organized in Scarborough, in a large conference hall with a capacity to hold over a thousand delegates. It turned out to be a major flop, with only a handful of delegates showing up; there were more people in the bar upstairs than in the hall. The IMG and its supporters, on the other hand, had kept their distance from this failure and had concentrated instead on getting resolutions through on Vietnam.[19]

In dealing with the Foundation's financial crisis, Pat and Geoff tried hard to persuade the rest of the Directors to hold off from taking any drastic retrenchment measures until Ralph Schoenman—who in previous times always seemed to be able to raise money for the Foundation's "formation and functioning, and provided the political drive and initiative that had given it its international status"—had the opportunity at least to participate in the decision making.[20] But Coates, Farley and Stetler wanted no part of this and pushed ahead with their plans, regardless of the consequences. Horowitz later told me he had opposed the campaign against Geoff and Pat, but by the time of the Directors' meeting to discuss the matter, six people no longer had jobs, including Pat and Geoff, and all the Directors had seen their salaries reduced. According to Horowitz, the discussion had polarized around two basic positions on the Board, with Ken Coates, Chris Farley and Russell Stetler demanding everything be cut to the bone. Geoff Coggan and Pat Jordan, in opposition, proposed instead the setting up of "an investment fund" and the immediate launching of fundraising effort among Foundation supporters. They argued, "we are not in a financial crisis," saying it was a "chronic situation" that had been made worse because after the sale of Russell's archives there had been a "relaxing of restraint in expenditures", but now there had been a "drastic pruning of staff and commitments" to help remedy the situation. They took a swipe at Ken, saying, "at least one member of our board seems to (have) panicked to such an extent that his judgment is severely affected."

Geoff and Pat avoided addressing the matter of the 80,000 GBP liability that all of them would be subject to if Russell for some reason was to immediately expire, saying that the Directors had to take a "calculated risk" in the matter for the next couple of months.[21] That argument, coming from two Directors who didn't have a penny to their names, couldn't have inspired much confidence in their fellow Board members, most of whom did not have much money either. Ken, however, was a full-time university lecturer who did have a few personal assets, and so he would have been at risk of losing everything if the tax man had come calling. Under the tax laws, furthermore, declaring bankruptcy was not an option for any of them in that situation.

Horowitz pointed out that Ken and company had failed to show how their proposal would meet the immediate need to have 80,000 GBP in hand. Their reaction was inspired by panic, he wrote—agreeing with Geoff and Pat—and if the problem became public, he said, it would only serve to make matters that much worse and cause the creditors to panic. This would make it that much more difficult to raise from supporters even the minimum amount of money required for the Foundation's daily expenses. Horowitz proposed a blending of the two proposals: make some cuts and mobilize the supporters to create an "investor fund."[22] But Ken, now taking advantage of the crisis to drive his own agenda forward, would have none of it. He carried the day, forcing Pat and Geoff off the Board; within a few weeks, he fired them. Everyone was unceremoniously dismissed from Rivington Street to get it ready for a quick sale.

As the financial crisis was unfolding, the VSC was also told to pack its bags. I was on its Executive, so we hurried to find another office, not far from Toynbee Street, at 100 Commercial Road, for which I personally signed the lease—with some hesitation I might add, because of fears that some day it might not be able to pay rent. Fortunately, this proved to be a needless worry. This kind of move had been in the works for some time, prior to the Foundation's financial crisis, so we were partially prepared for the change, feeling it was probably better that the VSC have its own space in any case. We wanted to get out from under the wing of the Foundation, even though the Foundation had been critical in getting it off the ground. The VSC was by then, in our estimation, capable of raising its own funds, having become a reasonably stable political formation. There was no reason, we felt, it should not be able to stand on its own feet.

Relations between Ken and Pat broke down completely not long after Ken's October 10th letter and October 11th memorandum, resulting in Ken refusing to talk to Pat anymore, or to recognize any of his communications, written or otherwise.

The reason for the break was what I consider to have been an ill-advised "open letter," marked "personal"—in reality a "declaration of war" against Ken—written by Pat and sent to Tony Topham, one of Ken's closest collaborators and a personal friend, and clearly intended for as many eyes as possible. For me, it wasn't one of Pat's proudest moments. "This letter is quite open," Pat wrote, "and in no way secret from other people in our movement." Pat complained to Tony about Ken's October 11th memorandum and accused him of reacting "in a purely capitalist manner. In fact, his *sack everyone immediately* policy is worse than that of the average capitalist. The average capitalist would not be so capricious and light-minded."[23]

This latter allegation drove Ken into a fury. He pointed to the contradiction in Pat's behaviour, since in a recent Directors' meeting Pat had made a sudden volte-face without consulting those who were about to get the axe, and had voted for their firing. "You had to, as I said, no choice but to agree to sacking the staff, because we can't pay them," Ken wrote.[24] Tony fully backed Ken, as was to be expected, arguing, "Ken's proposal . . . was a disinterested attempt to grapple with an extremely serious situation . . . the whole of his memorandum was a matter of collective discussion." [25]

It remains to be seen how much Ken's proposal was "disinterested," but to me one of the main problems with Pat's letter to Topham was that it had all the earmarks of a personal statement and was obviously factional in intent. Pat nowhere indicates in his letter that he is writing as the General Secretary of the IMG or on behalf of the organization. But it's clear that Pat wanted to get something quickly into print around which he could mobilize everyone in the IMG for a showdown with Ken, a kind of fait accompli on his part. It was all very crude. Within a very short time he had laid charges against Ken, stating that with Ken's letter and his Memorandum of October 10th and October 11th to the Foundation's Directors, Ken "had violated the discipline of the organization and the principles of democratic centralism . . . by proposing measures which would have a drastic effect on our most successful field of work and on our most important journal, outside the movement, without having raised these proposals within our movement and within the committee of which comrade Kork (Ken's pseudonym) is a member." The IMG's National Committee supported Pat and set up a Control Commission to look into the charges. Ken was the first person to be expelled from the organization since its formation. It was a swift affair.

My memory of my own attitude at the time to those events is that I was just as annoyed at Ken's action as was Pat, and even though I had not been too happy with the way Pat had dealt with Ken, I must confess it truly did not cause me that much concern. Over the years, however, my feelings about Ken had softened a little, to the point that I began to think we might have made a mistake and the differences between him and Pat could have somehow been overcome. But after reviewing the correspondence in the archives, in retrospect I don't see how Pat had much choice, even if he dealt with Ken so brutally. Geoff and Pat's main problem in the Foundation was that they behaved like "employees" of the BRPF, and not as Directors or as leaders equal to Ken. As the money problems deepened, it's clear they dithered and kept hoping the money from the Russell archives would soon be coming in—they admitted as much—or that somehow, Ralph Schoenman would turn up to help them out. In the past, he always had, but it wasn't to happen this time.

Whether one agrees with him or not, Ken, who had not been all that involved in the day to day running of the Foundation, made the decisive moves to remedy the problems and rescue the situation from disaster, even if it was out of a sense of personal survival. Geoff and Pat, on the other hand, although they resented very much how they were—and had been—treated by Ken, could not make the change from being followers to being leaders. Not that it would have mattered much anyway if they had. Compared to them, Farley and Stetler had much closer relations with Russell and his wife Edith, having been to Wales many times and having stayed at their home over the years; Geoff and Pat had seen them only a few times, and mostly on social occasions.

Ken's expulsion from the IMG, it so happened, took place while I was in Canada dealing with a few personal matters. Jess and I were planning to return there after the forthcoming Ninth World Congress and visiting Canada periodically was a way for me to maintain my status. I usually went back at least once a year, because I was afraid that if I stayed in Britain for an extended period, the Canadian authorities might use my absence as a pretext to force me to re-apply for residency status, with the possibility they would keep me out of Canada permanently. The rules about that kind of thing were much more relaxed then than now and one could stay away from Canada for long periods without losing one's status. Still, I always felt apprehensive about the situation because every few months during the whole time I was in Britain, the British authorities, on some pretext or other, would drop by Pioneer Book-service to check my British passport.

Jess called me long distance in Toronto to tell me the group had expelled Ken. When I got back to London, she told me that when Geoff and Pat lost their jobs, Pat had called a special meeting of the Political Committee, in *The Week*'s office, and placed a motion proposing Ken be expelled. By virtue of being branch organizer in London, Jess was also a member of that body. She fought valiantly against the motion, upset mainly by the speed by which it had been introduced and with very little discussion. The politics behind the dispute were not made clear, she said. The matter was being dealt with in a purely organizational way, she argued, with the IMG not learning anything from it. Moreover, she felt Ken had not been given adequate time or opportunity to be present. She tried hard to persuade Pat to withdraw his motion and delay things, but everyone at the meeting was opposed and fully backed Pat. A large majority of the PC, including the other Canadians on the committee, voted with him. Pat later told me that the speed of his action in moving to expel Ken had been carried out with the intention of shocking Ken into stepping back from pushing people out of the Foundation. This didn't make much sense to me at the time—and it still doesn't—because in any case, by that time, most of the IMG people had already lost their jobs in the Foundation. It was a little like closing the barn door after the horses had bolted.

Looking back on it now, it's possible I had contributed a little bit to what had taken place because before I had left for North America, I had told Pat I was as bothered as he was with Ken's actions and I advised him he should resist any effort by Ernest Mandel to use his prestige with IMG members to interfere in the group and begin acting as Ken's "lawyer." In the Secretariat meeting before I had departed for Canada, when I reported on the crisis that was developing, Ernest Mandel raised the alarm that Ken might walk away from the IMG Ken had been in touch with him to let him know about the crisis, he said.

Ernest was afraid that we would lose Ken and wanted to know what we could do to save him. Later, when I discussed the matter with Ray Sparrow, I told Ray I was fearful that Ernest, because of his high regard for Ken and Tony, might, over his best judgment, allow himself to be drawn into the dispute. I said I was opposed to any moves that would override the IMG's leadership in the matter and that we should be prepared to live with any mistakes it made in this regard. Ray agreed with me, understandably because this was consistent with the SWP's view of how the International's leadership should function: they should refrain from interfering in the affairs of the sections against established leaderships. When I reported the Secretariat's discussion to Pat, its effect may have been to remove any inhibitions he may have had about taking the action he took.

Within a year, Geoff and Pat would be followed out of the BRPF by Ralph Schoenman. No longer Russell's secretary, in the middle of June 1968, in an attempt to have the ban on entering the U.K. lifted, Ralph managed to briefly sneak in using false documents. "The Government's attempt to keep me out of this country where I have lived for ten years," he told *The Sun*'s Victor Chapple, "is nothing more than harassment inspired by prejudice against my views. Unless I am detected by the authorities—and I don't intend to make myself easily available—I shall stay here until justice is done."[26] Wearing a disguise—much to Russell's annoyance—he had travelled up to Wales to see him. "Again, after his ostracism by the British government," Russell would later say, "he appeared here—his last visit—done up in a preposterous 'disguise' late one evening. It did not occur to him that in doing so, he was exposing me to the charge and penalties of harbouring someone forbidden entry into Britain. He simply could not resist flamboyant showing off."[27]

During that summer of 1968, we were all very busy in the VSC and with the Vietnam Ad hoc Committee's preparation for a forthcoming demonstration on October 27nd and I didn't see him then. He stayed away from us, probably out of security concerns, but he couldn't resist tweaking the noses of the British authorities, publicly holding them up to ridicule, by making a special point of having his photograph taken by a professional photographer standing outside #10 Downing Street, the British prime minister's residence. In the photo, Ralph has a large grin on his face, as large as life, alongside two policemen who were always stationed there.

The photograph received big play in the British press. And, while we all laughed at the joke, we believed it had been a serious mistake on his part to flaunt his illegal presence in Britain, especially in that way. It's sufficient to make the authorities look incompetent, we thought, but to rub their noses in it, as he had done with the press caper, was a bit of a provocation and would only inspire them to redouble their efforts to grab him. Not long after that, as he was travelling by taxi in London, he was arrested and kicked out of the country. Knowing what we know now from those days, I'm now not too sure whether or not it had made that much of a difference that he had made the authorities look incompetent: the police had their spies everywhere and I'm sure they were well aware of where he was at all times. He was barred from entry to Britain and it would be several years before he would be allowed back into the country.

From the time of his expulsion from Britain, Ralph worked on Russell's various projects out of the Foundation's New York office—which had previously been staffed by Russell Stetler—under a written agreement with the London office that he would be provided an administrative budget for the work there. Ken and company defaulted on this commitment, he claimed, and he was compelled to change the name of the New York office to the American Foundation for Social Justice, (AFSJ) "to prevent our work in the United States from being undermined by public statements and acts made in London over the name of Bertrand Russell when it is no longer reasonable to do so. We received a letter from Lord Russell in February 1969, saying that he had retired from public activity because of the weight of years." The AFSJ attempted to carry on in the tradition of the Russell Foundation, with Arthur Felberbaum, my old comrade from the New York YSA, its Executive Secretary.[28]

Schoenman's fight against his expulsion from the Foundation had been a bitter one, and deeply hurtful to him. It's easy to understand why. He had been its main leader and public face since its beginnings, in charge of all its activities and with the sole authority, for example, to sign and issue cheques. Having poured his life into it, he was now watching it all go down the drain. At a severe disadvantage because of his forced removal from the scene of battle, he was not about to let himself be pushed out so readily. But by then his relationship with Russell was beginning to fray at the edges, the warning signs of which must have been already apparent to him. Russell, in the first draft of his autobiography, which he was preparing, had made a few negative personal comments about him. Russell wrote that Ralph was "surprising unlicked," and that he was "aggressive and entirely undisciplined and I realized that these characteristics might well make him seem 'a dangerous young man' to anyone of whom he did not approve . . . the essential intolerance of opposition and the ruthlessness of his rush towards whatever happened to be his immediate objective . . . the ascendancy of the ego over intelligence." In his final draft, however, Russell softened these words. In any case, Ralph took strong exception to the first draft and in an angry letter to "two co-directors" of the Foundation, called it "a betrayal of all the years I have devoted to the Foundation and to Bertie, years in which I have worked flat out at the risk of my life for twenty hours a day." And then in what can only be described as a case of careless braggadocio, he characterized Russell, in a deeply wounding comment, as not having been much more than a figurehead in their collaboration over the years. "The truth is that every major political initiative that has borne the name of Bertrand Russell since 1960," he wrote, "has been my work in thought and deed."

In those months, being by then not involved in the Foundation's activities in any way, I had not been aware of Russell's criticisms nor was I aware of Ralph's unfortunate angry reaction to them—he had been away since the summer of 1967. From what I know today, however, this was an obvious exaggeration that seriously diminished Russell's legacy and had provided confirmation to all those who had dismissed him over the years as being "senile" and nothing more than Ralph's instrument. Although physically frail and weakening in his last years, and obviously having good days and bad ones, from what I had observed over the time of my contact with the Foundation, and contrary to Ralph's assertion, Russell always seemed to be carefully watching its work with considerable interest and a sharp eye, not letting much get past him. In this respect, it's interesting to see his notes to Pat Jordan—who was carrying out the function of editing the Tribunal's *Bulletin*—where Russell makes a few critical remarks about the *Bulletin's* contents and at the same time makes a few sharp comments about the failures of the Paris Secretariat.[29] While it's true that the first drafts of many of Russell's statements, his letters to the press for example, may have been prepared by others, but anything that required his signature he would always read first—as he says in his autobiography. I was reminded of the intellectual acuteness he carried late into his life when I recently re-read the third volume of his autobiography.[30] This was reinforced for me, more recently, when I looked at Nicholas Griffin's work. It shows that Russell's mind, although not what it was a few years earlier, was sharp almost to the very end.[31]

Schoenman's intemperate letter turned out to be sweet music to his detractors in their struggle to oust him from the Foundation. Russell writes that he was not shown it for over a year and a half, not until late November 1969, whilst he was in the process of writing his "memorandum." He was, understandably, outraged by it. If he had seen it at the time, he said, he would have broken immediately with Ralph. And this he did, in a 7,000 word "memorandum." While paying Ralph his due—he was essential to their work and without him the War Crimes Tribunal would not have taken place—his critique was nevertheless devastating. "Were I to list his kindnesses to me," Russell stated, "the list would be very long and would include many generous deeds that must have cost him dear in worry and work. I found the quickness of his mind, although it made for considerable superficiality and glibness, immensely refreshing as I did his sense of fun and absurdity and irony, although this often created difficulty, unrestrained as it was by any sense of decorum. In fact, in a world made up largely of people who act, if at all, only upon second or more thoughts and guard themselves well with subsidiary clauses, his companionship was as welcome as a delicious breeze on a muggy day."

Russell, in considerable detail, relates Ralph's personal failings as he saw them, from the Committee of 100 up through the Sino-Indian conflict, the Helsinki Peace Congress, the Cuban Missile Crisis, to the War Crimes Tribunal, including accusing him of financial irresponsibility in the affairs of the Foundation and absenting himself from his duties by remaining abroad for unnecessarily long periods of time—a criticism that I had heard earlier about Ralph from Pamela Woods and Chris Farley. Russell also appeared to be changing his attitude in a more positive direction towards those critics of Ralph who, despite their severe political differences with him, had complained to Russell in private about his "behaviour" without apparently mentioning those differences.

A puzzling aspect of the statement is that Russell says he dismissed Ralph as his secretary in 1966.[32] This is indeed curious because this change in their relationship was unknown to most of us around the Foundation at the time and Ralph had always represented himself as Russell's secretary, including in public meetings alongside Russell where Russell had ample opportunity to correct such a wrong impression.

"As late as 1967," Ralph would later point out to *The Daily Telegraph*, "I appeared at Press conferences with Lord Russell. He had plenty of opportunities to disassociate himself from me then if he had wished."[33] News of Russell's "Memorandum" did not break in the press until many months later, the following September, after Russell's death the previous February. It appeared that either the Foundation, or Russell's wife, Edith, had sent it to Reverend Michael Scott, one of Russell's collaborators in the Committee of 100, who had unsuccessfully, been trying to get it published in the London dailies. The "Memorandum" had been rejected because of a fear of legal problems—until the *Black Dwarf*—with Tariq Ali no longer at the helm—got hold of it and published it, along with their own introduction showing how far that publication had drifted to the right. The *Black Dwarf* displayed their full hostility to Ralph's politics, saying that his "pugnacity had isolated Russell from the British Peace Movement" and that "Russell's political work was vilified because of his secretary . . ." going on to suggest that a reason for the silence of the capitalist press regarding the work of Tribunal was that it "was the work of Schoenman and not Russell." With that, the floodgates were wide open. Several major publications—including *New Statesman* and the *Observer*—rushed to get it into print and many who had been in the past on the losing side of political battles with Ralph, jumped to put the boot in. And there wasn't much he could do about it.

In a letter to Tamara Deutscher, around the time Russell's Memorandum was completed, Schoenman—almost anticipating its contents—bitterly accused Coates and Farley of having engineered against him "a series of despicable statements . . . forged over the name of a senile old man, Bertrand Russell." Ironically enough, it was a charge often made in earlier times against Ralph by his enemies, and it had deeply annoyed Russell when that piece of gossip about what Ralph had said was passed on to him.

"From the time the British government banned me from England," Ralph continued to Tamara, "Ken Coates and Chris Farley have set about to seize control of the Foundation. Their primary objective was to gain complete control over the $750,000 which were raised through the sale of Russell's autobiography and the sale of his archives . . . They further sought to get hold of money raised in the U.S. for use in the U.S. They set up a print shop in Nottingham as a separate corporation, appointing Directors who included themselves and excluded me. Apart from the fact that their behaviour includes the criminal misappropriation of corporate assets, the basic element is the wholly unprincipled political practice it reveals. The consequence has been to totally discredit Ken, not to mention Russell, among the American left." [34] I have never seen a rebuttal to Ralph's allegations, but the Klinghoffer's say that when Ralph was expelled from the Foundation, Ken Coates and Chris Farley issued a statement against him, charging, "it was Schoenman who had pocketed the U.S. advance on the third of Russell's autobiography." [35] The BRPF, which retained the copyright to much of Russell's work—the revenue from which continues to grow to this day—went on to organize numerous international tribunals on various issues and, in terms of travels abroad, Ken Coates took the place of Ralph as Russell's representative until his death. It is still located in Nottingham and continues to publish *The Spokesman*, as well as running a publishing company that has produced many books of interest to the labour movement. In later years Ken would again become prominent in the Labour Party, working with Tony Benn in leading the resistance to Tony Blair's embrace of neo-liberalism. Ken, at 79, died on June 27th, 2010, of a suspected heart attack. He remained active on behalf of the working class until the very end.

TOP *Vanessa Redgrave arguing with police to allow the demonstrators through, Richard Branson behind her, Grosvenor Square, March 17th, 1968.*

BOTTOM *Police attacking protestors, Grosvenor Square, March 17th, 1968.*

Chapter 14

Tariq Ali and
"The Battle of Grosvenor Square"

*A*N IMPORTANT FACTOR IN OUR SUCCESS IN BUILDING OPPOSITION to the Vietnam War was the special advantage we enjoyed because of our group's relationship with the American SWP. In that period, organizing opposition to the war was at the top of the agenda of all of the Fourth International's sections, but our American co-thinkers led the way on the issue. They were among the main organizers of the protests across the United States. A simple piece of intelligence, such as knowing in advance the date of the next proposed action in the United States made life that much easier for us because, in consultations with our allies, it helped us overcome what can always prove to be a major difficulty in planning a protest: setting the date, and we would always give a quiet prayer of thanks to our co-thinkers in the SWP for their help in this regard.

Reliable information about the American anti-war movement could always be found in *The Militant*, the SWP's weekly journal, which we received each week by airmail. Along with reports at United Secretariat meetings, we were always on top of what was going on in other countries. What was happening in the war itself, of course, was critically important and we followed the newspapers closely, sometimes organizing, even in the evenings during the week, emergency type actions to protest each new escalation.

When an international call was issued by the U.S. anti-war movement for a day of protest for October 22, 1967, the newly organized Vietnam

Solidarity Campaign (VSC) immediately set that as the date for our next major event to take place outside the American Embassy in Grosvenor Square. We quickly produced a poster—designed by Jim Clough of the International Marxist Group—and sent it out to all our VSC groups, who pasted it on walls all over London. We also printed a small adhesive-sided version that became very popular with many young anti-war activists, who plastered it everywhere. This caused us to be threatened with legal action by the London Underground when it became ubiquitous throughout their system.

Our optimism that October 22nd would be a larger than usual action went through the roof when we saw that the publicity material was flying out the door as fast as we could print it, and everywhere we went we would see our posters glued to walls all over London. The mood of opposition, especially in the universities and colleges, rose dramatically and almost over-night our meetings around the country were packed full, even in the smaller colleges, and many times we would have over two hundred people turn out when we were only expecting fifty. VSC groups were springing up all over the place, organized by young people we had never heard of until then.

One of our closest collaborators in helping build these actions turned out to be Tariq Ali. Today known internationally as a writer and essayist and long-time member of the editorial board of *New Left Review*, during the course of those protests he emerged as their main public voice. He is now internationally recognized as a dedicated and articulate campaigner against imperialism, especially in relation to the occupation of Iraq and Afghanistan, the American intervention in Pakistan, and the NATO bombing of Libya. Before the rise of the anti-war movement in Britain, Tariq had been President of the prestigious Oxford Union, and in the summer of 1965 was one of the organizers of the first teach-in against the war. That year he had been a delegate on behalf of the British Peace Committee to the CP-dominated Helsinki peace conference, the one where Ralph Schoenman had created a sensation that had upset the Russians so much when he demanded that the Chinese be allowed to address the gathering.

Tariq had also been a member of the first of the Russell Tribunal's investigative teams sent to Vietnam. "A red diaper baby," he comes from a middle class Pakistani family. His father was the editor of one of the largest mass-circulation dailies in the country. Tariq, over those next few years, would emerge in Britain as a revolutionary socialist and champion of the oppressed.

A nasty by-product of Tariq's prominence in the protests was that voices began to be raised in ruling circles calling for his explusion from Britain. In response, Bertrand Russell, Ralph Miliband and the editorial board of *New Left Review* issued a joint statement of protest.

Frequently he was the object of racist insults and physical threats, often made publicly by spokespersons for the right-wing. Jess and I experienced this right-wing hostility to him first-hand one day. It was after a May Day demonstration outside Transport House, the Labour Party Headquarters in London, and we were walking along a street near the Houses of Parliament idly chatting to Tariq and not paying much attention to what was going on around us. All of a sudden, we were startled by the sudden eruption of loud shouts and catcalls from a large crowd across the street. Inspired by the racist rhetoric of hard-right Tory MP Enoch Powell, the dock-workers and meat porters had been demonstrating and protesting for several months in the spring of 1967, including going on strike against the government's policy of allowing black and third world immigrants into Britain. That day the dockers had been to the Commons to give support to Powell, who headed up that despicable campaign. Some of them had spotted Tariq, who, because of press and television coverage, was instantly recognizable to anyone. The three of us immediately backed up and tried to retrace our steps to get away from them and suddenly they started chasing us. One of them quickly caught up with us and grabbed Tariq from behind, and it was only after I whacked the assailant with my rolled-up umbrella—which happened to be quite large and a necessary piece of equipment in London—swinging it as hard as I could with both hands like a baseball bat to give him a good crack to the side of his head, did he let Tariq go. Unfortunately I hadn't hit him hard enough because as he stumbled he grabbed my umbrella and reached out to pull me towards him. For a brief moment I had visions of him grabbing me. I let him keep the umbrella and Jess, Tariq and I made off down the street, running as fast as we could. Such was the response Tariq was getting in some circles because of his outspokenness and activities against the war.

Tariq had no reservations in supporting our efforts to build the VSC and was always the first to respond to our requests for help, whether it was helping us raise money or speaking at our rallies or in the debates within the left about the way forward. He could always be counted upon to be a solid ally. This was in contrast, I remember, to a few other public personalities and intellectuals on the left who would often quietly tell us they supported our campaign but they always seemed to keep their distance when they were needed to help out. It's true that after a very successful action, many of them would be supportive of what we had done, but frequently their support was not much more than words and often we could hardly get a penny out of them. This is not unusual. Anyone who has been involved in activist politics must have experienced this phenomenon first hand. Activists are always grateful for the support from wherever they can get it, even if it's only words. Most campaigns—sometimes even the largest—are led by a relatively small number of people, usually the most dedicated who see a firm connection between the ideas in their head and what they must do to make them more than abstractions and who do most of the work and give the financial support to keep things going.

I remember once when the VSC was especially in need of money, we launched a fund drive amongst our supporters to try and get help. Tariq suggested we contact Vanessa Redgrave, a very public supporter of many progressive causes who was also a sponsor of the Russell Foundation. He was on very good terms with her and she had spoken at a few of our events, usually at his invitation. He thought she might help us financially. This was before Vanessa had been won over to Healy's organization by her brother Corin, who was then rumoured to be a member of the SLL I remember it well because I was assigned to go and see her.

Tariq arranged the appointment for me to meet Vanessa at her home. She was friendly and gracious, and she made me quite welcome in her home. Not yet contaminated by Healy's sectarianism, she even invited me to stay for lunch. Unfortunately there was another person present who was competing with me for her attention, a young black man from the U.S. who was looking for money for some kind of children's educational project he was involved in back home. I imagine many were asking for financial help. I was there for an hour or so talking to her about our plans, with him listening in, and sometimes he would take the occasional verbal jab at me to try and get me out of the way. I got nowhere when I asked her for money.

The fact that she was prepared to stick her neck out in a very public way to protest the war—putting her career at risk when so many others in the entertainment industry were either silent or supporting the war— was a big contribution all on its own. Not very long after that, unfortunately, she became enamoured with the politics of the SLL and the cult of Gerry Healy; no doubt he got more money out of her than I did for the VSC. When I visited her, she quite firmly told me she was only interested in putting her money into a Montessori school up the street from where she lived and which she thought was doing good work in her community. Recently, I felt a special sadness for Vanessa when I read in the press that Amanda Richardson, her daughter and also a talented actress, had been killed in a terrible skiing accident in Quebec. Amanda may have been one of the children running around Vanessa's living room that day, interrupting our talk as her mother attended to her needs.

Tariq, then in his early twenties, was just out of Oxford. Although prominent in student politics and still growing as a serious intellectual, I had the impression that he was relatively inexperienced in the factional politics that characterized much of the British far left in those years. He made no pretences otherwise, and obviously he came to gain a measure of confidence that we in the newly minted IMG knew what we were doing when we were engaged in those political battles. I also think he was appreciative of the fact that by then we had developed a reasonable capacity for organizing. He may even have been aware of our relations with the Fourth International, but I'm not sure how much he was aware of the significance of this or even what the International was, though I am sure that, like many of his generation, he knew of Ernest Mandel's work and had a measure of respect for him. (Sadly, many years later, Tariq, his views now changed, would write a very bad novel in which he cruelly caricaturized Ernest and which revealed more about Tariq than the great Marxist thinker.[1])

Above all, I think, Tariq recognized that of all the British left groups, we were the least insular regarding the struggle for liberation by the colonial peoples, and he came to rely on us as allies in defending their cause. In 1968, no one in Britain spoke on this issue as often as Tariq. His speeches against the war to our large meetings served to energize thousands. Prior to the various demonstrations and meetings, our team would often discuss among ourselves—including Tariq when he was available—what we wished to see happen and we would work out a common line together. This would inform his statements to the media, which was absolutely critical for us, as we will later see. Sometimes we wouldn't see him for months at a time because he would be out of the county, but when he returned he always made a point of getting in touch with us again to get brought up to speed about what was going on. At the same time, he was trying to launch a career as a writer and journalist, all of which ate up a large amount of his time and consumed a lot of his energy.

Contrary to how it appeared in the press, he was not involved in the actual day-to-day functioning of the VSC. He was not on its executive body nor had he played any noticeable role in its formation or its conferences. I don't remember him attending any of the coordinating meetings of the Ad Hoc committee we had set up to organize the demonstrations, and yet he became the Vietnam protest movement's most effective public voice. Very early we had developed a practical understanding with him, a kind of division of labour, whereby he pursued his own special projects—he and Clive Goodwin were in the process of launching a radical new journal, the *Black Dwarf*—and we would take care of the VSC.

At a certain point, we had grown so politically close that we began to consider recruiting Tariq to our ranks. Eventually I raised the matter in the London IMG. His name, as was the usual procedure, was placed on a list of possible recruits who should be talked to about membership. Several weeks elapsed and still no one, to my chagrin, had been in touch with Tariq to talk to him about membership. So, at one of our meetings, I asked how things were progressing with Tariq, and Pat Jordan mentioned that he had learned through the grapevine that the I.S. was in discussion with Tariq and that he was thinking of joining them. On that news we immediately assigned a couple of people to meet with Tariq to pose the question to him. And, after just a few days, Tariq became a member of the IMG. He was a very important addition to our ranks and he would eventually become one of our most well known leaders.

The demonstration on Sunday, October 22th, 1967, was the largest action we had organized up to that point. As it happened it was the first in a series of mobilizations, each much larger than the last. It was effectively the beginning of a mass Vietnam protest movement that would sweep Britain and eventually involve hundreds of thousands. From early on, we lead it based on a policy of non-exclusion. Our activities were open to all, and we permitted anyone to carry any slogan they wished on the protests— as long as it opposed the war. Our estimate was that approximately 20,000 people turned out that Sunday; the press said 10,000, as usual cutting the real number in half. It turned out to be one of the most militant demonstrations seen in London in a long time, according to the press, and it was certainly one of the most violent, an expression of the deep anger many people felt about the war.

When we got to Grosvenor Square, the location of the American Embassy, the police were already amassed there, many on horseback blocking our way. In previous demonstrations we had encouraged participants not to put up with police brutality and to resist police violence, because we were convinced that the police, as they had done in the past when fewer protestors showed up, would attempt to intimidate and try to demoralize the protestors in this way. After a momentary hesitation, the crowd pressed hard against the phalanx of cops and broke through.

The police immediately attacked us, kicking and shoving, including trying to run us down with their horses. Many of their navy-blue uniforms became covered with white blotches, as they were peppered with small muslin bags of flour. Many helmets went flying as the police met with stiff resistance; they tried to force the protestors into a corner of the square where they could be encircled—an early form of "kettling"— unable to move forward or back. More police than protesters were injured that day, and there were numerous arrests. The next day, the press, aside from condemning the protesters, shed a few crocodile tears for the several horses which the police claimed had been injured.

There was a slight lull in the anti-war mood after the October 22nd action, but towards the end of the year, and early in 1968, opposition to the war reached new heights. The evidence was everywhere. The previous autumn, student unrest roiled many campuses, with students at the London School of Economics leading the way in demanding representation in the decision-making processes of the university administrations. Many educational institutions were occupied by their students.

Our VSC speakers travelled the country speaking to very large gatherings of supporters. At one point Ralph Schoenman and Tariq returned to London in a state of high excitement to tell us about an exceptionally large rally they had spoken at in Glasgow. Unexpectedly, they said, several thousand had turned out to hear them. Tony Southall, the leader of our Glasgow group and the Scottish VSC, and one of the organizers of the rally, told us that they had been caught totally by surprise by the numbers—they had only been expecting a couple of hundred, if that. And the VSC's finances improved immeasurably. Just before Christmas, mainly due to Tariq's efforts, we organized a very successful evening of entertainment with many folk-singers on hand for a concert at the Roundhouse in North London to help finance our next major action, which was expected in the spring.

Early in 1968 we received another call from the American anti-war movement, appealing for international mobilizations against the war in March. In response, the VSC began to plan for another action on March 19th, the anniversary of the first protest in Saigon against the Americans in 1950. Again, it would be in Grosvenor Square, in front of the U.S. Embassy organized under the aegis of the Ad Hoc Committee. We moved the date forward a couple of days so as not to conflict with a planned Youth CND activity that day. The March 17th action turned out to be almost identical to the previous October's, only larger, much more turbulent and just as militant. Trafalgar Square was packed with demonstrators and the fountains flowed a bright red, the water looking like blood as protestors threw in packets of dye. Over 30,000 turned out, more than we had expected. In the midst of it all, the IMG and the VSC calmly set up its literature tables close to the plinth and sold literature like mad.

Unlike today with the Internet where anyone can instantly have information available and socialist analysis about events half way around the world, in those days it wasn't so easy to get good information free from capitalist bias. It was one of the few times in my life I've experienced large crowds gathered around me waiting to buy literature, as if afraid everything would be sold out and they would be unable to get anything. Copies of *The Week* literally flew out of our hands and the VSC table was soon emptied of its pamphlets. We sold all our literature and I remember Jess MacKenzie, who was organizing the sales, telling me that she and our comrades helping her could hardly carry all the cash in her big Mexican leather bag because it was so heavy.

There were a few speeches from the plinth that day. Vanessa Redgrave spoke, as did Tariq, Pat Jordan, Barbara Wilson and John Palmer who represented the VSC. Alain Krivine, a leader of the newly minted Jeunesse Communiste Revolutionnaire (JCR) in France, whom we had brought especially over for the occasion, also spoke that day, but my overwhelming impression of the event was that the audience was not that interested in what they had to say and was most anxious to head towards the American Embassy—as if afraid they would miss an important appointment. I'm sure if we had waited very much longer, the massed gathering would have taken off for Grosvenor Square without us. Tariq, Vanessa, and the platform speakers, along with Pat Jordan were in the lead as we headed out of Trafalgar Square, arms linked across the front, taking up the whole street, the crowds behind us chanting slogans against the war. When we arrived at Grosvenor Square, we were again met by a wall of thousands of police, many on horseback determined to keep us from entering. A virtual tidal wave of humanity surged behind us, packing the street so that we could neither move forward nor back.

The yelling was so loud you could hardly hear yourself speak; it was bedlam. A few us at the head of the march paused for what seemed like an eternity, arguing with the police to let us through. But it quickly became impossible to provide any leadership about what to do. Where I was standing, the police formed themselves into a kind of battering ram and violently pushed the crowd back, something that was being repeated on all the streets leading into the square. When the demonstrators refused to move, the police quickly became more brutal and, as if on a single command, they began to punch people in the face. This, however, was not a CND peace march nor a Committee of 100 affair, where protestors would sit down passively in the middle of street and wait to be arrested. This was a new generation.

The protestors under our leadership began to fight back. Fists began to fly as they tried to defend themselves. The police had provoked a riot. Again, they were pelted with bags of flour and, from many eager hands, marbles and ball-bearings were thrown onto the pavement to help immobilize the horses and a few of the police were pulled from their mounts and many police helmets went flying in a high arc above the crowd on their way to finding new owners. Young people could be seen wearing them everywhere. The riot lasted several hours as the police cleared the surrounding streets. Because of the action of the police, the leadership of the VSC lost contact with each other and we were unable to exercise any control over what was taking place. If the police were to be believed—they claimed in the media that over 300 of their people had ended up in hospital—they again suffered more casualties than the protestors.

The press reported that over one hundred and fifty demonstrators had been injured and four hundred arrested. It became known as "The Battle of Grosvenor Square." A few of our people were arrested in the melee, among them Mike Martin, who was on the executive of the VSC, and we spent the next couple of days getting him and others out of jail;

the BRPF generously came to our rescue by helping pay some of the fines. Surprisingly, there was very little damage to property with only a few windows smashed. What had become very obvious to us, and that could also be seen in the previous October's action, was that we were beginning to attract to our activities individuals and groups who couldn't care less about Vietnam but whose main interest lay in fighting the police. But there was another and more positive development around the March 17th action.

During the IMG's post-mortem of what had transpired, we noted that although its most active component was mainly students and youth, many of them working-class, there was a solid core of CP and YCL activists who seemed to be there in an unofficial capacity and who tended to be more disciplined and generally, we had observed, had tried to avoid physical conflict with the police. Although the CP had established a "front" led by Lord Fenner Brockway, the National Committee Against the Vietnam War (NCAVC), and generally had maintained a sectarian aloofness towards the VSC and had stayed out of the Ad Hoc Committee, March 17th had revealed that many of their supporters were becoming more and more drawn into our activities. We never found out what impact this had on the internal life of the CP.

As a result of that demonstration, Tariq Ali became firmly established as a major public personality in the British media and a spokesperson for the new mass movement.

I don't know what effect the demonstration had on Wilson and his Labour Government, but there must have been some consternation in ruling circles. Unlike "peace" demonstrations of the past that had been usually led by clergymen with a few Labour MPs on the platform—decorously trying to persuade Wilson to moderate his support for the Americans, and generally not challenging the imperialist nature of British foreign policy—these demonstrations were militant, hostile to Wilson and in solidarity with the Vietnamese, and led by a whole variety of revolutionary socialists very much outside the tradition of British reformist politics. Tariq Ali was in his element.

© John Walmsley 1968

Barbara Wilson, a leader of the IMG and VSC getting ready to speak; Ernest Tate
to her right, Trafalgar Square, March 17th, 1968.

Chapter 15

An "autumn offensive"

A S I'VE ALREADY MENTIONED, THE AMERICAN ANTI-WAR MOVEMENT was an important example for us in how we organized. Like the Americans, we felt that if we were to have successful demonstrations, it was imperative to build a broad and effective "united front." We managed to achieve this mainly through the aegis of a loose, unstructured "ad hoc committee," called together for the occasion, rather than the VSC itself going it alone. That's how the protests in October 1967, and in March 1968, had been organized. From its very beginning the VSC had declared that it wished to work with anyone on the central objective of mobilizing as many people as possible on the streets around the "anti-negotiations" position to show, to all those who wished to see, the extent of popular opposition to Wilson's Vietnam policy.[1] Early on, from when we in the VSC had sensed a public momentum building against the war, we had been acutely sensitive to the fact that the various groups who had mobilized alongside us in the past were not willing to continue putting aside their specific criticisms of the VSC—or even the IMG in some cases—to fully engage in getting people out onto the streets. To overcome such barriers and to get around any mistrust, before each major action we initiated an "Ad Hoc Committee" around a few minimum demands, but that had at its core the demand that the Americans should get out of Vietnam immediately.

In many cases this kind of cooperation occurred spontaneously at a local level, with ad hoc committees popping up all over the place, giving the lead to how the VSC should proceed nationally. Four or five of these broad formations arose in London, for example, allowing activists of different political persuasions to work together at a local level. This phenomenon rapidly spread across the country, often in communities unknown to us at the centre. It was a means by which many members of the CP and the Young Communist League became involved.

The exception, of course, was most of the Trotskyist groups such as Gerry Healy's SLL and Ted Grant's RSL, who all but ignored us. This was not true of the International Socialists, however, who while involved in the VSC, but mainly at a local level and on the universities, were much more comfortable being part of the Ad Hoc Committee. Although they considered themselves Marxists, or even Trotskyists, and one would have expected them to see things the way we saw them in regards to the war, they had their own specific criticisms of our group and the new arrangement of the Ad Hoc Committee allowed them to participate more fully in the campaign and with a greater measure of enthusiasm, despite, for example, their misgivings regarding the VSC's position of calling for the victory of the NLF. John Palmer, a well known radical journalist with the *Guardian* who was in the leadership of the I.S. in those days, had been on the executive of the VSC and was very supportive of the idea of the Ad Hoc Committee, as was the young Paul Foot, who had a weekly column in the *Sunday Observer* in those days and would regularly write pieces critical of Wilson's policy on Vietnam.

In the loose Ad Hoc Committee that began to prepare for the next mobilization, Chris Harman—then a student at the London School of Economics—was the leader of the I.S. caucus in the Committee. Ian Birchall was active at a local level, as was Peter Sedgwick, but I don't remember them playing any significant leadership role at the time. We also had the support of a few Young Communist League clubs, plus a few Labour Party activists and some of Albert Machandra's Maoists who had by then constituted themselves as the British Vietnam Solidarity Front. Although there may have been a few peace activists involved, there was no representation from the "official" peace movement, the CND. Indeed the unstructured Ad Hoc Committee tended to be overwhelmingly made up of representatives of the various left groups that populated the political landscape in Britain in those days, which is not to say we didn't have support from sections of the broad labour movement. Many trade union locals and CLPs also supported our actions.

The radicalization of youth in Britain that year was part of a general trend sweeping the world. This was also seen in Mexico City during the preparation of the Olympics in 1968, when student protesters challenged the government's educational and social policies—especially the failure to deal with the issue of high unemployment. The Mexican protests ended in a bloody repression when, during a mass assembly in the Plaza de Las Tres Culturas, the police from hidden locations in the surrounding apartment buildings fired upon the students, killing hundreds and injuring many more. Thousands were arrested and many disappeared. Closer to home In Northern Ireland, the civil rights movement, many of whose leaders had been inspired by the London Vietnam protests and many of whom we knew personally, took to the streets to protest years of religious discrimination and repression of the Catholic minority. They would eventually involve tens of thousands in demands for change. In France, from the early part of the year, our F.I. people there found themselves in the forefront of an unprecedented radical upsurge around demands to end high unemployment among youth and educational reform in the universities. Our comrades had been part of a split from the Union of Communist Students over the issue of Vietnam and the CP's attitude towards the French government. This led to the formation of the Jeunesse Communiste Revolutionnaire (JCR), which would later become the Ligue Communiste Revolutionnaire (LCR) and the official French section of the F.I.

The LCR played a key leadership role in the street battles, when demonstration followed upon demonstration, from January 1968 on. As the protests grew larger, the state mobilized violent responses by their security forces to suppress them. At one point, I remember Ralph Schoenman became so inspired by the LCR's activities that he generously responded to our appeals for financial support by scraping together 5,000 GBP out of his own pocket to send to them. I know this for a fact because I personally delivered it to Paris, on his behalf. The political situation in

France at that time was like having a knitted garment in one's hands; if you pulled on a loose piece of wool hanging from it, the whole thing would unravel in front of your eyes. In the midst of the student battles with the police, the whole country erupted in sympathy in a general strike with a mass of factory occupations—the so-called May 1968 events when de Gaulle left Paris and could only achieve political stability by agreeing to large wage increases for the unions.

It was against this background that the first public meeting of an Ad Hoc Committee was convened in London to launch what we termed our "autumn offensive." The immediate reaction of the British press was to go haywire with a slew of scare-mongering stories about the VSC—an aftermath, also, of the demonstration on March 17th. The media openly speculating that what had happened in France might also explode on the streets of London. It was obvious that with this police-inspired press coverage, the authorities were employing their age-old tactics in a not too original manner, fomenting public hysteria to try and frighten people away.

Today, after over forty years of hiding the truth, many of their dirty tricks have seen the light of day in the British media, primarily thanks to the work of journalists such as Solomon Hughes of *The Guardian* and Paul Mason on television, who have shown that the security forces' tactics back-fired in a classic case of unintended consequences. By planting rumours virtually every day over several months, expanded upon by a pliant media about possible "bombs" and "violence" in the streets, the British state only succeeded in giving us the publicity millions of pounds couldn't buy; all of Britain knew a massive action against the war was being planned and every activist anywhere in the country wanted to be in London alongside us.

Several hundred people showed up for the early planning meetings of the Ad Hoc Committee at Caxton Hall in Red Lion Square—a packed hall with standing room only—including representatives of the various political groups and anti-war committees from around the country. My memory of it is that it all came off without a hitch, but I am probably wrong about that. I find it hard to imagine any such meeting taking place in London without some kind of discord. The VSC was the largest organization present and had taken the lead in organizing the event. We proposed another mass action to take place in the autumn.

Given the existing mood in Britain regarding the war and from what was happening across the English Channel, we stated from the platform that there was no reason why we could not organize over one hundred thousand, if not more, for a mass protest action. There hadn't been a mobilization like that in London in a very long time. When we dared to propose it, there were a few gasps of surprise at the audacity of it all. After a few moments of silence, an eruption of applause and cries of approval spread through the hall, as everyone began to realize we were all on the edge of something big. The far left was not accustomed to thinking on such a grand scale.

Over the next few months we scheduled a series of meetings—every two weeks at least—of the Ad Hoc Committee in the north of England to set the date and discuss the slogans for the action in London. Again, we looked to the anti-war movement in the U.S. for guidance here, and we agreed that our date would be determined by whenever they set their next major action. These meetings of the Ad Hoc Committee were essential to help us plan our work but quite often we encountered difficulties when the security apparatus of the state went into overdrive with their "dirty tricks" to try and prevent them from even happening. Several times the halls we had booked for the meetings, for example, were mysteriously cancelled by someone pretending to speak on behalf of the Committee. When we couldn't find another venue, we sometimes had to hold our meetings out in the open air. I remember a few critical times we were forced to sit out in the cold of the Yorkshire moors, more than fifty of us sitting in a large circle on the grass gathered around a large depression in the ground, conducting our business.

One effect of the State's "dirty tricks" campaign against us was to help induce a more serious sense of discipline in our ranks; everyone present understood very well that we couldn't afford the luxury of lengthy, long-winded debates around secondary issues. I can still remember these meetings as if it was yesterday, sharply focused on the business at hand. When it came to the discussion before the vote, everyone kept their comments to a minimum. Agreement on the slogans, "End British Complicity in the War!" and "Get the American Troops Out Now!" came easily.

Most of the time someone from the VSC chaired these gatherings. Discussions would usually be around our proposals; we were the only ones there, as far as I could see, who had a worked out plan of action and most of the participants looked to the VSC for guidance. This unanimity broke down, however, when we turned to discussing the proposed route of the forthcoming protest march and whether or not its final destination should be outside the American Embassy in Grosvenor Square. The VSC had proposed a change from previous demonstrations—when we had mobilized outside the U.S. Embassy—to instead assemble on the Embankment and proceed past Trafalgar Square to Hyde Park for a rally and speeches.

We argued as hard as we could that we had to be guided by tactics that would most effectively help the Vietnamese; no matter what, we could not lose sight of the objective of organizing as much public pressure as possible to get the troops out of Vietnam. This required an action in which the maximum number of people could participate, where people would feel secure and even bring their families along to it. Our aim, we argued, was not to be in conflict with the police or to riot for its own sake—perhaps getting people injured or maybe killed—but to bring about the largest political protest action that was possible.

At those meetings, with all of us sitting on the grass in the cold breezes, two counterposed, distinct lines developed in the debate. First, the International Socialists, who were by then an important force in the Ad Hoc Committee and were led by Chris Harman, as I have mentioned, argued that the demonstration should have as its main objective the encircling of the head offices of the Bank of England, in London, in a "symbolic" action of some kind to highlight how British capitalism was benefitting from the war, as a way of introducing "class politics" into the campaign. I don't remember all the ins and outs of their position at the time, but I do remember being struck by how much they were being motivated more than anything else by their seeming need to maintain a unique position for themselves with the purpose of remaining as distinct as possible from the VSC and the IMG.

It was an expression, I thought, of a crude and insular kind of "workerism," prevalent in the British Trotkskyist left in those days, that saw the colonial struggles in terms of "only the British working class coming to power can solve the problem." The I.S. was the IMG's main critic in the Ad Hoc Committee, advancing this kind of primitive "workerism" as a solution to virtually every new problem, whether it was the rise of the colonial revolution or the question of feminism. ". . . I.S. must direct the political orientation of the demo in the direction of the British struggle," its leadership had advised the membership earlier in the year.[2] "We have to differentiate ourselves from vicarious 3rd worldists, etc., by emphasizing the need for participation in, and development of, mass struggles *here*, outside the student intellectual milieu," Chris Harman had written in a circular to their membership in preparation for the VSC's March 17th, 1967 action.[3]

We disagreed. To introduce other issues in the hope of giving the movement a "working class" perspective, and putting the issue of socialism on the agenda of the Ad Hoc Committee, would have caused it to shatter. We would have only been introducing more differences into the movement rather than keeping it unified. Opposition to the war, we argued, was the highest form of class consciousness there could be and it was the responsibility of every socialist to oppose the war. This was something all those concerned with international justice had a duty to carry out, a just end in itself and not a diversion from "the real class struggle," as some of them believed; rather, it was in reality a higher form of the class struggle. Some, including the Maoists—a few of whom were showing up at the meetings—thought the new movement could somehow be magically converted into some kind of revolutionary party, but we always cautioned against such expectations and stressed the limitations of what a protest action at that particular time could achieve, no matter how large. We had built the movement on a single-issue basis around the idea of getting the Americans out of Vietnam immediately.

It was not a bitter or too factional discussion with I.S. My recollection is that it was carried out in the fairly civilized and comradely manner of people who wanted to make the project a success. We in the IMG stressed that while British imperialism could be considered "an enemy," the main enemy of the Vietnamese was the United States. So to now begin to say we should switch the campaign to making "British capitalism" the enemy would have been a misguided attempt to give some kind of "working class" content to the mobilization. It would go against the Ad Hoc Committee's "united front" character and would not be understood by the many activists who were not affiliated to any organization. Moreover, we said, if the Committee were to agree to it, the proposal for surrounding the Bank of England was tactically a recipe for disaster and would play right into the hands of all those whose only purpose was to riot and to fight the police for its own sake. The consequence, we argued, was that the Ad Hoc Committee would surely lose control of the whole affair.

It was clear that I.S. hadn't thought through the logic of their position, as far as we could see. I wasn't even certain that they had even discussed their line that much in their own ranks because, as I've mentioned already, they tended to operate much more loosely then than now and gave every appearance in those days of being somewhat disorganized. As for the IMG, we were like a rock in our aim to have a massive—which was far from certain—and peaceful demonstration.

A large majority, including the CP and YCL people, the left Labour Party activists, and even the Maoists, blocked with us to vote down the I.S. adventure. But, for their part, the Maoists and their supporters disagreed with our proposal for a demonstration that would terminate in Hyde Park. They argued we should go to the American embassy as we had on March 17th, but they didn't win much support for that position. The I.S., to their credit, eventually blocked with us in voting the Maoist's position down and quietly dropped their idea of surrounding the Bank of England.

Today, the I.S. would probably have a different memory of those debates, at least if David Widgery, in his book *The Left in Britain* is to be believed.[4]

I found Widgery's book lacking objectivity, with a highly partisan, "I.S.-centric" version of what went on in those years. Shamelessly exaggerating the I.S.'s role, Widgery says virtually nothing about the debates I have described above. Ken Coates reviewed the book in the 1978 *Socialist Register*, calling it less than useless, unreliable and sloppy on the facts, and "lamentably devoid of systemic thought."

After the Ad Hoc Committee arrived at its position, it issued an appeal to all the participating organizations to organize immediately to get as many people as possible out on the day of the action. The main organizing centre for the coming demonstration became the VSC headquarters, because the Committee did not have its own offices. Between demonstrations, the VSC would usually be very quiet, without much money in its bank account. But as soon as a future action was announced, it would jump into action and sufficient money would come in from our activists throughout the country to pay the bills. Posters—again designed by Jim Clough—and a lot of the printed material were prepared by the VSC. The office was bursting at the seams with throngs of activists coming and going. Sometimes when Jess, Pat and I would go over to 100 Commercial Road for consultation with our VSC team, we would have to step over people just to get into the office. In those hectic days, activists—many of them from out of town or even from out of the country—were sprawled out all over the floor working on preparations for the protest.

The American Embassy, Grosvenor Square, March 17th, 1968.

Chapter 16

IMG Divided On Anti-War Movement

*I*N THAT PERIOD OF STORMY PROTESTS, THE IMG SAW ITS MEMBERSHIP increase very rapidly, with most of the new recruits coming from the London area, many of them not having had much experience with any of the other far left organizations that populated the political landscape of Britain. Our people in Glasgow, led by Tony Southall, were also doing very well, but Nottingham was still suffering from the crisis caused by Ken's expulsion. Nevertheless, we could see that we had the potential to emerge as a pole of attraction for many newly radicalizing activists in the country. As I recollect it, by then we had doubled in size, with over fifty people in the London IMG, in a branch that met once a week. Jess Jess MacKenzie worked full-time for a few pounds a week, co-ordinating its activities.

Of course it's impossible to build a political group—even in the most radical times—without running into a few difficulties. This was to be expected. People often join a socialist organiztion with the best of intentions, I have learned, but if they bring along too much political baggage, it can sometimes be quite difficult to assimilate them, especially when the organization is very small and doesn't have much of a history. We already had had indications from a few new recruits that there was some unhappiness about our single mindedness concerning the Vietnam issue. This shouldn't have been surprising because we were continually subjected to sectarian attacks from other so-called "Trotskyist' groups on the issue. In my opinion, this was, in its own way, a reflection of the backwardness of British workers regarding colonial issues generally, or, as Pierre Frank frequently reminded me, an expression of Britain having built an empire on the backs of the colonial people. The ideology of the ruling class is but the ideology of the working class, he would say.

During the preparations for the October 27th action, Valerie and Keith Veness had expressed some uneasiness that we were not "concentrating enough" on trade union work and they said they felt the activity of the branch on Vietnam was, as I remember him putting it, "a diversion from the real class struggle." When I first met Valerie and Keith I had figured them to be natural working class leaders who would be a plus for the organization. They had come to us from the YCL, and prior to that had been in Healy's Young Socialists. They were a solid working class couple who I had hoped would help contribute to the group, so I made a special effort to overcome their objections to reassure them that we had the same appreciation of the working class as they had. Determined to raise the political understanding of the branch as a whole, we discussed their concerns over several meetings, trying to get them to see that a small organization such as ours had to recruit as quickly as possible those militants whose ideas were closest to its views, who it so happened were the many activists who were now working alongside us on the Vietnam issue.

Around the same time, Al Richardson, who had also been in Healy's organization and who had been president of the National Association of Labour Student Organizations (NALSO), became a member. We had won him over when our people in NALSO—which had been affiliated to the Labour Party—had successfully resisted Healy's efforts to capture it. Richardson, from the get-go, seemed obsessively fascinated with the history of the factional struggles of the various Trotskyist groups in Britain. He was a bit of an archivist, also, avidly collecting their old documents and publications. He generally kept quiet at branch meetings, not revealing his own views in our discussions with Keith and Valerie. I found that a bit odd because I had heard from Pat that over a pint in the pub after a meeting he had voiced some criticism of us for concentrating so much on Vietnam.

Differences about our Vietnam work broke out as we were preparing for the London branch's annual conference that year, 1968, where we were to elect a new executive and set out priority tasks for the next year. Keep in mind that the branch had only been in existence for just over a year. Jess MacKenzie, the branch organizer, was surprised when in the course of the discussions on the Executive Committee around her proposals for our anti-war work—recommending the branch reaffirm as its priority the building of the coming demonstration—opposition began to be voiced from some quarters. What she was proposing was no change in line, so she took it for granted everyone would agree with her. After all, she thought, she was only applying a line adopted at the group's national conference, a line that was also the International's. Keith Veness, who with our encouragement had by then become a leader in the branch— and on the platform at several of our public meetings—took the lead in challenging her, arguing that the group should now totally change its focus. He argued that our concentration on the anti-war movement had been wrong all along and that we should now withdraw from the VSC and from the preparations for the coming demonstration, concentrating instead on working in the trade unions. I was in Brussels as this was happening. Jess, Pat and the rest of the IMG leaders in London struggled to make sense of why Veness and those around him would want to turn their backs on this amazing breakthrough.

The upshot was that Veness won a majority for his point of view on the executive and, as a result, his majority position was presented to the London branch's second annual conference. Jess presented a minority report. In the branch conference, Richardson, in a very vocal way, backed Veness and a new grouping emerged winning a narrow majority for its position and taking full control of the London organization. The only compromise they permitted was to allow those of us who were currently engaged in preparing for the coming October demonstration to continue with that work. They insisted, however, that as a group the IMG should now only play a marginal role. In the elections for the new executive, Jess was summarily dumped. This ended her position as branch organizer.

During the conference, when those of us who supported the national group's position saw what was happening, we quickly caucused and agreed that it was important that I stand for election to the incoming Executive Board of the branch, so that at least the national organization would have a strengthened representation on it in the coming few months. It was difficult to do, but we felt that as leaders of the group we had to pay the necessary price for our focus on the tasks of building the mass action, and, in the interests of developing an internal democratic culture in the IMG, we also had to accept our losses as part of the process of building a viable organization.

We counseled above all else against factionalizing the discussion; we wanted to avoid a split because the politics of the dispute were very unclear. We also felt it would be a good opportunity to build the group on a stronger and more cohesive political foundation. To me, it seemed the Richardson-Veness grouping had not fully thought through their positions and neither were they homogenous in their outlook. As far as I was concerned, Richardson was a dead-end factionalist; Keith was still carrying some of the political baggage of Healy's sectarian positions on the war, but I felt he could overcome this with time.

The begrudging concessions they made to us thankfully at least allowed us to continue with our work in the VSC. Every day the London and national press were full of information and commentaries about what was happening regarding the coming mobilization along with the obvious scare stories, tending to confirm that we were on the right track. To give up this work would have been totally wrong, and would have been seen by many activists as cowardly in the face of the propaganda offensive by the ruling powers against us. It would have been irresponsible to follow the logic of Richardson and Veness' line and pull out of this activity in which our group until then had been playing a leading role. If they had pushed their position that we withdraw from that work, it would of course have led to a split in the group. Fortunately, after a few discussions, we got the majority of the branch members to agree with us and the Venesses and Richardson walked away. I've seen it written that Richardson claimed we expelled him. This is simply not correct. He was just unable to function in an organization where he was in a minority.

Barry Sheppard was of great assistance in helping us work our way through these problems. Barry, like us, understood the sectarian essence of the opposition—if not the misguidedness of the Veness and Richardson positions—but he always urged patience and trying to win time so that we could let the discussion educate our new membership and possibly persuade Veness and Richardson of our views. Barry had recently replaced Ray Sparrow in Europe as the SWP's representative and was travelling back and forth to London, bringing himself up to speed on our activities. He and Caroline Lund, his companion, were living in Brussels.

I had known Barry and Caroline since my days in New York when the YSA was being founded. A student at Massachusetts Institute of Technology when he joined the SWP, Barry became part of the new leadership team along with Peter Camejo in the YSA after Robertson and Wohlforth had been expelled from the SWP. The editor of *The Militant*, he had emerged as one of the SWP's main leaders alongside Jack Barnes and Mary-Alice Waters.

I wasn't too surprised when I learned that Ray had to return to San Francisco. He had begun to develop health problems during the previous year, suffering occasional dizzy spells for which his doctor in Brussels had been unable to diagnose a cause. In addition, he told me, he was beginning to run low on money and he needed to attend to his house in San Francisco which he had rented out. He needed to get a job quickly, he told me, to start paying off some of the debts he also had accumulated since coming to Europe.

His return to the U.S. was a big loss for us. Jess and I were sorry to see him leave; we had developed a very warm and close relationship with him. I wondered what was going to happen with the differences which were beginning to surface in the Secretariat on China and what seemed to be new differences regarding Latin America. Barry did not have the same authority as Ray with Ernest, Pierre and Livio, but even for Ray it had been a bit of struggle to be fully included in their team. I had the feeling Ernest and company were not happy with the change and did not make much effort to integrate Barry, leaving him isolated in Brussels much of the time. I remember Barry saying they did not open many doors for him so that he could get to know the emerging youth leadership in Paris. From my conversation with Ernest and Pierre before Barry had arrived, I had the feeling they felt the change signified a downgrading by the SWP of the assignment.

They were wrong, of course. What they seemed not to appreciate was that a generational change had taken place in the SWP, with a new team at the helm. This was something that Farrell Dobbs, Joe Hansen and the SWP Political Committee had been consciously working to accomplish for several years. In addition, to a certain extent, the new team, of which Barry was a key part, had also been protected in the past from some of the harsh realities of the International's weaknesses and functioning. Mary-Alice Waters, on one of her early trips to Brussels, expressed shock to me at the state of the organization—it was obvious she had been ill prepared for what she had seen. Also complicating the changeover was the blossoming of the two major political debates in the International.

Barry and I worked closely together, as much as we could, but we were not able to overcome his isolation in Brussels. I was simply too far removed, and did not have the capacity to change the situation for him to make his life more politically bearable. In any case, Jess and I were planning to head back to Toronto within a few months.

Chapter 17

October 27th, 1968

A S WE NEARED OCTOBER 27TH, THE NUMBER OF HYSTERICAL ARTICLES in the national press about the coming mobilization multiplied enormously, with many carrying provocative speculation about possible violence on that day. The hostile campaign that had been kicked off after the March 17th protest had become so intense, we began to think that the VSC faced being banned and many of us might even be jailed, so we began preparing for this possibility so that we could continue to lead the protests.[1] As a precaution, we set up an elementary alternate leadership structure with separate channels of communication should some of us be taken out of circulation. We weren't sure what was going to happen.

What was freaking out the ruling class was that the coming protest promised to be unlike any other seen in London in a long time. Previous mass activities before the Vietnam protests, such as the CND's anti-nuclear marches had been led by a collection of pacifists, Labour Party MPs, trade union leaders and assorted preachers. Our action was being organized by a radical new leadership with no connections to the establishment, an assortment of revolutionaries of different persuasions, mainly Marxists who totally rejected Wilson's policy on the war. The police and the Labour government had obviously become alarmed by the Paris events, thinking perhaps the "contagion" might spread to Britain, and who knows, might even lead to trade-union unrest. We wouldn't have minded this happening, but we did not think it was likely—not in our wildest dreams. A steady and increasingly intense campaign to try and demonize the demonstrators in the eyes of the public was orchestrated by state security forces in collaboration with the press and TV. Reports that many financial institutions in central London had temporarily moved their management operations out of the city because of a fear of rioting were all over the press and television. This became a major problem for us and it took us a while to work out a defensive strategy in response.

The way forward became clear, however, when our old friend and ally, the intellectually prestigious Ralph Miliband, a major authority on the British state, raised his voice in a loud and very emphatic way to defend us. We were elated when he told the press that whenever people gathered to protest they were only exercising their long established right to pressure the government, and that this should be a normal activity in a democratic society. The fact of the police presence itself, he said, presupposed there was something illegal about these activities. It would be much better for all if the police stayed away altogether, he suggested.

Miliband's riposte to the demonization campaign got great coverage and provided us the moral high ground we needed against the authorities—always a good place to be, we figured. We organized our supporters to immediately come in behind Miliband. We began a propaganda offensive, explaining that the main cause of violence on the previous demonstrations had been the activities of the police, something that had been reported in the press. Tariq Ali played an important role in getting this message across. He had access to the media and was always sought after by reporters and TV stations for a comment. Very comfortable and confident in front of the cameras—a very important attribute—he argued the Miliband proposal articulately, and with good effect. On the day of the demonstration, while many of the police may have been present in plain clothes, those in uniform stayed away—on the back streets, out of sight. We were as surprised as anyone that our campaign had worked so well.

In the mass protest movement that was enveloping us—each day involving more and more people—the forces over whom we had direct influence were indeed pathetically small. The most active and influential group was the VSC, of course, which despite having grown fast was still a relatively small organization of around a couple of thousand, if that, consisting of very loosely connected members in groups spread around the country. It was more of a "network" than anything else. Even with its wide support among young people, especially in the universities, compared to the Labour Party or the unions—with their millions of members, for example—it was miniscule. Measured on this scale, even the Ad Hoc committee, of which we were a constituent part, was tiny. This could be seen very dramatically in the days before the demonstration.

It was a hectic time for us in London, with hundreds of people arriving every day from France, Germany and other parts of Europe to participate in the demonstration. Tariq Ali, when he had been in Germany speaking at a mass student anti-war rally organized by Rudi Dutschke, had urged everyone to come to London for the occasion. We held many meetings, sometimes of several hundreds of people to report and discuss the Ad Hoc committee's plans. On the evening before the actual event, however, less than a hundred activists turned out for a stewards' meeting that had on its agenda the finalizing of its preparations for the following day. Although we had had a very good exchange of views at the meeting—I don't remember much disagreement—most of us were somewhat dismayed that so few people had turned up. We wondered whether we would have sufficient experienced cadre on the Embankment the next morning to help us get things moving. David Widgery, in his book, says that we asked I.S. to take over the stewarding, but he also got this wrong. They had fewer supporters at the meeting than we had.

The next day, we were still uncertain about what would happen. The previous evening we had received reports that the police were stopping buses loaded with protestors on the main roads into London and turning them back, warning people not to come into the city. The police were using the pretext that it was "dangerous," the reports said, which was clearly illegal on their part of the police. It was too late, however, for us to do anything about it. We also learned that many of the businesses on the route of the march were barricading their doors and windows as if anticipating a riot and that they might be stormed. After the stewards' meeting on the evening before the demonstration, Jess and I drove on our way home to South

London through the West End to see for ourselves. The scene was distinctly eerie, with only a few people on the streets where one would normally see many in Central London at that time of evening. All the banks and commercial buildings had plywood nailed over the windows of their main floors and small gangs of police were busy in the middle of the roads, supervising the welding shut of all manhole covers. It was as if the city was preparing for war. This, it turns out, wasn't such a stretch of the imagination, because, as it was later revealed, the Home Secretary James Callaghan was in fact in discussions with the Cabinet about mobilizing the military to deal with us. We awoke on the day of the demonstration truly not knowing what to expect. The Ad Hoc Committee had worked night and day building it. We had even widely distributed a "briefing" sheet with a headline, "Street Power", advising participants about how to behave to avoid trouble[2] and stating that: "WE WANT NO ARRESTS", but whether anyone would listen to us and how the day would turn out was anyone's guess. Television, radio and the papers were full of news about the impending mobilization. The VSC had rented a van for the day to carry our portable megaphones and literature to the demonstration. The plan we had worked out the previous evening called for a few of us to lead the demonstration from the Embankment past Ten Downing Street to deliver a letter to Wilson, and then on to Hyde Park—a total distance of about four miles, concluding with speeches from a portable platform that we would erect there.

It was still early, a few hours before the scheduled start time of 2:00pm, yet thousands could be seen in the distance heading for the assembly point, a mass of humanity flowing over the bridges of the Thames, banners bobbing in the breeze. The streets were packed; it was like a huge celebratory festival, the protestors in an ebullient mood giving no sense of fear, despite the police- inspired hysteria of the previous months. It was like a gigantic sporting event, with TV cameras everywhere and with reporters providing colour commentary about what was taking place.

It was a grey, overcast day, but with no rain—ideal for a march! But it turned out Pat Jordan, Pat Martin, Geoff Coggan, Jess and I had a more immediate problem: much to our embarrassment, our rented van couldn't move through the crowds on the way to the starting point. We couldn't reach the start, because the streets were so packed with people on their way to the demonstration, but nor could we turn back. A large mass of people had already assembled and the scheduled start time was fast approaching. So near, yet so far, I remember thinking. Finally a couple of us jumped out and explained to the protestors our need to get to the head of the protest as soon as possible. Good naturedly, they quickly cleared a path and walked us forward.

When we arrived at the location on the Embankment where the demonstration was scheduled to begin it was packed with protestors. The crowd swarmed towards us as soon as they set eyes on us. "Are you the leaders?" they called out. Most of them were strangers to me, but I recognized a few faces from our meetings over the summer and we quickly introduced ourselves. Their help was spontaneous. They wanted to get going right away. I was impressed how business-like and disciplined they were. We later realized that many of them were trade union activists and young people, and some not so young, who were around the Communist Party. They were waiting for our instructions. We quickly headed off.

One of our main concerns was about what would happen with the Maoists once we got to Trafalgar Square. It was an issue we had discussed on the VSC executive at some length. We knew they would attempt to hijack the demonstration and divert it to the American Embassy. We agreed that Tariq, me and a few stewards, along with a handful of VSC activists, would fall back as the march proceeded and situate ourselves immediately behind the main Maoist contingent. Our position was not to exclude the Maoists, but we were certainly not going to let them sucker us into a confrontation with the police, at least not without a struggle from us. It did not matter to them that in the previous weeks we had been on a public propaganda offensive against the police and the government saying that we wanted a peaceful demonstration and that the police should stay away.

We told everyone around us as we marched along that if the Maoists wanted to go to the Embassy to fight the police, that was their business and not the policy of the Ad Hoc Committee. When we got to the point where they were obviously planning to make their move, a couple of thousand marchers broke away under their leadership to head for Grosvenor Square, but we as a group moved forward and stopped the demonstration right in its tracks in the middle of the street. Tariq, who as I've mentioned had tremendous moral authority with the activists, was very effective in persuading people not to follow them. The rest of us fanned out and told everyone to stop, and we let the Maoists, anarchists and other assorted ultra-leftists go where they wished. As the Maoists and their followers ran up the street away from us, they looked back and saw that very few people were going with them, so they quickly ran back to try to cajole the demonstrators who were patiently standing there behind us to follow them, all the while hurling insults at us, especially at Tariq. We waited a few minutes until they finally headed off for their fight with the police and then we continued on our way. The next time we stopped the demonstration was at Ten Downing Street so we could deliver our letter to Wilson. There wasn't much in the letter—a few words scratched out on a sheet of paper—so we dropped it off and marched along.

In Hyde Park, we had rigged up a speaker's platform and a few of us from the Ad Hoc Committee gathered around it as we waited for the mass of demonstrators to assemble. The crowd stretched back towards the edge of the park as far as the eye could see, and yet the protestors were still streaming in. Unfortunately the portable platform we had rigged up was a flimsy arrangement, a portable, rickety contraption, and as we huddled on it to speak, it began to sway dangerously in the breeze. We were extremely lucky not to have tumbled onto the ground. Even the sound system was inadequate for the occasion. People could barely see us, never mind hear us. Tariq, Pat and a few of us addressed the assembled mass but later when I was making my own assessment of the day, I felt it had been probably the least effective part of our activities. This part of our plan had been poorly prepared because we had just been too overwhelmed by the task of preparing the action as a whole to give that much thought to what we would do once the people got to Hyde Park. Most of the speeches were ad-libbed, denouncing the Labour Government and American imperialism and the campaign of the police against us. They were very short and not that especially memorable. Fortunately, however, the demonstration that day and its impact was much greater than any speech could have been.

Long after the speeches were over, the banners could still be seen in the distance as the various contingents slowly made their way into the park. Three hours later the demonstrators were still coming in and from the aerial shots on television we saw later, all of us estimated there were many more than the 100,000 we had originally called for. The estimation of attendance numbers also highlighted another of our failings in preparing for the day; we had neglected to set up a team of counters specifically for that task.

When it comes to protest demonstrations, the one thing you can be almost certain of is that the police can't count. And that day was no different. Most of the police estimates that appeared in the press we considered too low by at least fifty percent. A few estimates in the press said there was 100,000—the number we had been aiming for. Few police were to be seen during the march, but we warned people that there were plenty around in plain clothes. We had reports that there were uniformed police in the back streets away from the demonstration, but our campaign to keep them away from the demonstration had been hugely successful.

In the weeks immediately following October 27, protest activity around Vietnam noticeably subsided. In our post-mortem of the day's events, all of us in the VSC and IMG and our allies were unanimous and elated that the day had been a huge success: our aim had been to give people an opportunity through extra-parliamentary action to register their opposition to the war and they had responded in a massive way. Of course, our hope was to try to pressure the Labour Government into changing its policies; whether we were successful in this is difficult to say and probably can only be answered by historians who have access to the record of Cabinet discussions and other sources from that time. I certainly suspect that we helped keep the distance between Washington and London much greater than either of them would have liked; at the minimum, the success of our movement tended to re-enforce the position of not sending British troops into the conflict. According to the London press it didn't have much of an effect on Wilson. This shouldn't have surprised us. Those in power, as a matter of policy, like to pretend that those who oppose them have little or no impact on their decisions. But what they couldn't hide was that Wilson's policy of support for the Americans was causing the Labour Party considerable damage in the working class and that the movement in the country against the war was indeed massive.

The movement against the Vietnam War also showed that the Labour Party's role in British society as the prime vehicle for social protest was beginning to fray at the edges. When relatively small, far left organizations—who openly proclaim their hopes for socialist revolution—can gain a mass audience and can provide crucial leadership on important issues such as Vietnam, we felt it could possibly open the door to the appearance on the political stage of a mass-based genuine socialist party.

But some of the activists who had worked hard at building the October 27th protest had some of the usual feelings of anti-climax we've learned to expect after such events. They clearly had hopes and expectations that could not be realized; they were expecting far too much from this single action, something we had pointed out frequently at the many meetings during the course of the summer in preparing for the protest. The great majority of the participants, however, had more modest aims—to show their opposition to the war in the hope that Wilson would break from the Americans and pressure them to withdraw from Vietnam. Scheduling another mass action in the short term, we figured, was not in the cards. When we talked to our allies, we realized we would have to wait to see what happened internationally before we could make such a move. We had noted that while the Japanese had organized a demonstration of 500,000 that weekend in Tokyo, the demonstrations in the U.S. had been much smaller, a result of the divisions in the movement over perspectives. The VSC, however, continued with its campaign directed at the Labour

Party constituencies and unions to raise money for the purchase of medical supplies to be sent to Vietnam. Many thousands of pounds were raised as a result of this activity, a very concrete form of solidarity.

The IMG came out of the "autumn offensive" in very good shape indeed. During the course of the summer we had more than doubled our membership and had managed to push aside the messy business of the expulsion of Ken Coates and the departure of the small grouping around the Venesses and Richardson.

Our public forums—usually sponsored under the names of the IMG, *The Week* or the F.I. and which took place approximately every month—had been very successful. Ernest Mandel spoke in April 1968 in Caxton Hall to a couple of hundred people, the first event in many years organized for a leader of the International and in the name of the International. A few of the left groups showed up to express their criticisms of Ernest—he patiently answered every one—including those of Peter Taaffe and his comrades of the Grant group, but in the main the audience was made up of some of the new youth forces who in the radical upsurge were being attracted to socialism. In the forums sponsored by *The Week*, David Horowitz was featured talking about his new book on economics, and Sheila Rowbotham, Barbara Wilson and Robin Blackburn spoke on the feminist struggle that was beginning to come on the scene. And despite the expulsion of Ken Coates, we had kept up our participation, albeit reduced, in the campaign for workers' control. Ken Coates and Tony Topham had organized several conferences in the Midlands, large gatherings of union stewards and activists with sometimes several hundred in attendance, for which we continued to mobilize, sometimes over Ken's bitter opposition. In all, it was an intoxicating time for us with high feelings of optimism and success for the future of the IMG.

TOP *March 17, Grosvenor Square*

BOTTOM *Pat Jordan in the VSC headquarters on April 18th, 1968.*
  Photo: United Press International (UPI).

Chapter 18

The International Socialists' Tony Cliff
Proposes Unity

D URING OUR ACTIVITIES IN THE SUMMER OF 1968, WE WERE ALWAYS in close contact with various members of the I. S., continuing our relationship established during the building of the Vietnam protests. Of all the groups involved in opposing the war, and despite our differences, they were the closest to us politically. In the spring we had met with their leaders for an exchange of views in preparation for a forthcoming VSC conference in May, and to get their agreement on a common slate for the National Council[1] of the VSC. Relations were such that often, when I.S. scheduled buses to take their people to the various conferences in the labour movement that seemed to take place about every month in those days, we would ride along with them on the same buses. In the course of these trips, there would be some good natured bantering back and forth between us but, overall our relations were pretty good, to the point where they felt free to put out a leaflet with Pat's and my name as speakers at their May Day activity that year, even without notifying us. We happily spoke anyway.

By then we had ceased publishing *The Week*, and had come out with new journal, *The International*, and we had grown sufficiently to set up "readers groups" in West Middlesex, South London and North London.[2] By the end of the summer we had organized a successful "cadre school" with over 100 people in attendance. It was one of the largest ever.

The IMG had grown quickly but, from what we could see, I.S. was growing at a much more rapid pace and had demonstrably increased its influence on the campuses. Whereas we still only had a handful of members active there. As I've mentioned earlier, we had disagreed with them on their approach to the anti-war movement and had criticized what we thought was their general inability to come to grips with the issue of the colonial revolution, but I'm sure when they made their own balance sheet that summer, they realized that we at some point might become serious competitors of theirs. For our part, we were always studying them and assessing them too, and saw them as having the potential to evolve into a serious force on the left.

The real issue for us was whether we could be in a common organization with them. We often discussed informally the upside and downside of such a possibility. In light of how I.S. operates today, having committed themselves to becoming a "Leninist" party, and showing great skill in building an anti-war movement that got two million on the streets against the invasion of Iraq—along the lines of the IMG at the time of Vietnam—it might seem strange, but one of our criticisms of them then was their "formlessness" as an organization. Amongst ourselves, for example, we used to characterize them as "a swamp," because they did not appear to have an elected leadership and it was always difficult to often know where they stood on a particular issue.

As far as we could see, I.S. didn't even function on the basis of political resolutions, but rather on the basis of the "opinions" of this or that leader as expressed in a particular article in their journal. Often they would have different motivations from each other about why they would support a particular position. We, of course, disagreed with them about the Labour Party; we still had an orientation to it. They had come to the conclusion that the possibility for effective socialist activity there had come to an end.

While we disagreed with their analysis of Cuba, China and Eastern Europe and the USSR—which we thought they had arrived at by inventing a unique kind of political economy that described the economies of those countries as a form of capitalism, not requiring any special solidarity from socialists—in the IMG we did not hold that their analysis of Cuba etc., or their position on the Labour Party, need necessarily stand in the way of our two groups functioning in a common organization. While we saw it as essential to work out an agreement with them to defend those countries against imperialism, the priority, we felt, should be our positions about domestic political issues.

Discussion about our future relations with I. S., however, moved sharply up our agenda when one June day, in 1968, Tony Cliff walked through the doors of Pioneer Book-service. It was very common for ordinary shoppers from the street to drop in to browse our bookshelves, and at first I didn't recognize him even though I had seen him and heard him speak several times. He was of slim build, somewhat intense in his manner and spoke with an accent, a mixture of Israeli and South African. I had never met him personally and, when I finally clued in to who he was, I remember thinking to myself that this was not a casual visit. He slowly wandered around looking at the books, amiable and unpretentious as he always was. He and I talked for a few minutes about Healy as he looked at the bookshelves, and I remember him saying that he thought the American SWP over the years had been ignorant and too tolerant of Healy's rotten organizational practices, putting up with him for far too long. His "told you so" manner was a little off-putting, but discussing Healy was not the reason he had dropped into the office.

Pat's in Nottingham, I told him, but he didn't even pause for a second at this. He was very direct with me, wanting to know why our group would not join his. The idea was not entirely new to me, as I've mentioned. We had been thinking about this more seriously since Sean Matgamna's small group—whom we had kept out of the IMG because we thought it would be too much of a headache to assimilate—had joined the I.S in a form of "entry" tactic in which he and his group initiated a long factional struggle until they were finally thrown out.

My reaction to Cliff's question was positive. I told him that the IMG's National Committee had, only a few weeks earlier, adopted a "Unification" document that envisioned "the establishment of a liaison committee which will be open to all tendencies on the left who accept as a minimum,", a five point programme "which will initiate a public discussion on the whole question of regroupment and the building of a new socialist organization."

I'm sure he was already aware of this resolution; these things have a way of getting around. It's probably what had precipitated the visit in the first place.

I promised him I would mention his visit to Pat when he returned. As soon as Pat came in the next day, I mentioned Cliff's proposal. Pat told me that he wasn't surprised. He had heard that I.S. had been talking about this over the previous few months and were going through some changes—"virtually opening the door for everyone on the left to join them," which incidentally is how the Sean Matgamna group had got in. Pat was very surprised they were moving so fast with us. It was clear we were at the top of their list.

Soon Pat got a call from Cliff saying he and Duncan Hallas, the other main leader of I.S. alongside Cliff, wished to come over to talk to us "about our future relations." It turned out that, despite our group having adopted a position for "regroupment" just a few weeks earlier, I was more positive than Pat about this development. Pat let me know that he thought we simply had too much "on our plate at the moment" to deal with this invitation, but that we should meet with Cliff and Hallas in any case to see what they had in mind. His general demeanour, however, suggested to me he was not happy with the idea.

When Pat and I met with the two I.S. leaders, it was a very friendly conversation. I remember it lasted about an hour. I don't recall the details of their initial proposals. Everything was verbal, but they moved on from our "unification" proposals to tell us they did not see any reason why the IMG could not come into their organization immediately. They hoped that the discussions about the modalities of this could begin as soon as possible. They were anxious, they told us, to bring about this unity within the next few months. It was their haste about the issue that made me hesitate a little.

I was more direct than Pat, and I began to pose hypothetical questions about the practicalities of joining them. "Would we have to give up any of our political positions?" I asked. They answered no, because they thought, they said, the differences were not that major. Would we be able to exist as an organized minority in their group and would we be able to maintain our present relations with the Fourth International? Again, they said yes. I was amazed by their generosity. They were obviously very keen to get us into their organization as soon as possible, a factor I thought would give us a certain amount of leverage in the formal discussions about unity and when it came down to committing our agreement to paper.

After the meeting with Cliff and Hallas, Pat and I talked it over at some length over several days. I tried very hard to get him to see that this could be a very important opportunity for the IMG and that it might put us in close touch with a new radical audience for our ideas and take the left generally to a new stage in its growth. I had no hesitation in thinking we would be able to hold our own in any discussions that might arise in a common organization in the future, but Pat could not see it that way. He said that our group was still in an early stage of its development and was trying to assimilate the new members it had recently recruited and so was not yet ready to confront such a quick turn. It's clear that his idea of "regroupment" was that it would be a long process—and only with people he liked.

Looking back on it, I think all he was seeing was that this would be some kind of factional "entry," like Sean Matgamna's, that would end up consuming a lot of our energy in the process. As we talked about it, I backed off pushing the matter. For one thing, I could see it would not have been very responsible of me, or fair, to have pushed him and the leaders of the group into this new orientation, when I wouldn't be around to see things through and participate. By that time Jess and I had informed the leaders of the IMG and the United Secretariat that we would be ending our assignment in Britain and returning to Canada immediately after the next Congress, the Ninth, the following year.

So Pat and I more or less agreed to disagree when we reported the Cliff and Hallas proposition to the IMG Political Committee, and Pat told Cliff the IMG did not wish to proceed. There may have been a few bromides about wanting to work together wherever we could, but the bottom line was to rebuff the I.S. initiative. A few months later, the IMG received an invitation, in any case, to send a delegation to the I.S.' annual conference in October. Bob Purdy, Mike Martin and I attended. I can't remember what went on there, but not long after that Pat terminated any possibility of getting together with I.S., or even continuing the unity discussions with them. By October 1968 he had the N.C. adopt a resolution stating, "the N.C. in order to clear any confusion resolves that because of big political difference on politics and organizational concepts, fusion is not now and has never been on the order of the day and the proposition put to us was that of our membership of I.S. as a tendency."[4] It was really a ridiculous posture. "Big political differences"! We hadn't even had a discussion with I.S. about them and how else could we be in I.S. but as a "tendency"? Of course, when Cliff and Hallas realized that the discussions about unity were off the table, they also hardened their position, to save face I imagine, as a consequence of Pat's refusal. When I reported the matter to the Secretariat in Brussels, it tended to sympathize with my view. Knowing, however, that Jess and I would be returning to Canada after the next World Congress, they also thought it wouldn't be practical to proceed, especially since Pat had such a hard line against it.

Chapter 19

The Ninth World Congress and the "guerrilla line"

T HE INTERNATIONAL EXECUTIVE COMMITTEE (IEC) IS THE GOVERNING
body of the F.I. between Congresses. In the months leading up to
the Ninth Congress (Third since Reunification, as we in North America
liked to stress), to be held in Rimini on the Adriatic coast in northern
Italy. I learned that the Secretariat would be proposing to a forthcoming
IEC meeting that the "entry tactic" be officially dumped, somewhat unceremoniously, I remember thinking, and without the matter going before
the Congress. It would not be on the agenda and neither would there be
a pre-Congress discussion about the change. In place since 1951, the
tactic had had an impact on virtually every part of the International,
especially in Europe and Canada but also in Argentina, where our group
had "entered" the Peronist movement.

In those years it was common for the Congresses to lay down the line
for the various sections, including sometimes even their tactics. I was
puzzled that, for ending the "entry tactic," there would be no organized
discussion or general balance sheet of its application, especially because
I was keenly conscious that over its life there had been a lot of controversy
surrounding it.

In the IMG the "entry tactic" had certainly been at the heart of the
dispute with Ken Coates who was still embracing, as far as I was concerned,
a tactic of "deep entry" in his work in the Labour Party. For the Canadians,
our assessment was that overall the "entry tactic" had served our movement

quite well. Today, over forty years later, however, I have a different view of the problems associated with it. I now believe there may be other means to achieve its ends. Our experience at the time was that if applied in the correct way, and suitably modified—such as keeping the "public" face of the organization front and centre in our activities, a challenge in reality to the "entry sui generis" or "deep entry" that Michel Pablo had initiated—in the last analysis it had been a means by which our Canadian group had grown since the split in 1953.

Part of the problem with Pablo's variant of the tactic was that it tended to postpone to some distant future the task of building existing Fourth International organizations, or even postpone the creation of new ones. Early on, the Canadians had recognized the pressures our "entered" members would be under in the CCF to dilute their revolutionary politics and begin to behave like "left social democrats." We were, however, mindful that if we had not taken up some kind of orientation to a mass based, mainly working class political formation, especially at a time of serious anti-communism, we would have been at risk of becoming sectarian, especially if we remained a small isolated grouping. Not that the "entry tactic" would necessarily inoculate us against such problems.

By 1963, in preparation for the Seventh World Congress, which was to set the stage for reunification, the International Secretariat had begun to challenge Pablo on the issue of "entrism." He was leading a minority tendency at the time. "(We) have set ourselves against a simple formula of universal applicability, independent of the state of the workers movement and our strength in each country . . . The notion of entrism *sui generis* everywhere, appears in addition extremely vague to us . . ." wrote Pierre Frank, putting forward the majority point of view.[1] Pierre's evaluation of the tactic had been part of the agreement between the Europeans and the North Americans for the reunification in 1963.

As I remember it, the Canadian Section's opinion was that while it might have been correct to dump "entrism sui generis"—or what we preferred to call the "deep entry" tactic—we thought the question at least merited a place on the 1969 Congress agenda. Not that we wanted to vote on history, but so that we could at least learn something from the experience and that this would be the best way to bring the matter to a satisfactory conclusion. Ross Dowson, in anticipation of this had let me know that the LSA was in the process of preparing a written contribution for such a discussion, through which they hoped to provide a summary of our experiences in the CCF and the NDP. We had anticipated that this would become a part—hopefully, a successful one—of an overall balance sheet. But that was not going to happen at the coming Congress and there was nothing I could do about it. Ross, after the Congress, wrote an evaluation of the Canadian experience with entrism, but it's my impression it became forgotten in the overall tendency struggle about guerrilla warfare that would quickly develop in the International (but more about that later).

To my surprise, the American SWP went along with the Europeans in putting the discussion of "entrism" to one side. When I expressed my annoyance to Ray Sparrow over this, he said that while he felt some sympathy with what I was saying, he was of the opinion it would be too difficult to arrive at a common understanding and that it risked opening up old wounds that might not be easily healed. If we proceeded the way I was suggesting, he told me, nothing would ever be settled in the organization. The matter was not about whom in the past may have been right or wrong about a particular tactic, but to deal with today's issues. I didn't buy it. I couldn't see why the discussion could not have been calm and reasoned.

It all depended on the balance sheet, and that may have been the problem. I knew the Americans for a very long time had deep reservations about this question after seeing how it had been applied around the world during Pablo's time. They were convinced the tactic had opened the door to several sections devaluing their own independent activities, possibly leading them into dissolving themselves into the mass organizations or giving up on revolutionary politics altogether, a danger of what was termed, "liquidationsm." Of course I got nowhere when I raised my objection in the IEC or with Ernest Mandel and Pierre Frank directly. The discussion on "entrism" would not make it onto the 1969 Congress agenda and the issue became somewhat academic. But as it turned out, the tactic was far from dead in the thinking of these comrades and would reappear—like Lazarus rising from the dead—in a United Secretariat resolution, submitted to the next Congress in 1973.

In the pre-Congress discussion in 1969, the main differences that had developed were over three major issues: how to characterize the new youth radicalization that was sweeping the world, what the Europeans were calling "the new youth vanguard"; the characterization of the Cultural Revolution in China; and the perspective for prolonged rural guerrilla warfare in Latin America. Everyone seemed to be in broad agreement about the then current international political and economic conjuncture. In an analysis consistent with a line we had been working under since the 1965 Congress, postulated in a document entitled, "The Dynamics of World Revolution," Ernest Mandel had prepared the main draft theses for the 1969 Congress to be placed before the delegates. In the "New Rise of the World Revolution", he managed to squeeze into a unified perspective that caught the spirit of the times—but which from today's vantage point would appear too grandiose and far too optimistic. He dealt with the increasing anti-imperialism, the appearance of "a new youth vanguard," the rise of class consciousness in the main capitalist countries and the growing and new crises of Stalinism, as seen in the Cultural Revolution and Czechoslovakia, where the Russians had crushed a working class anti-Stalinist revolt.

In respect to the Cultural Revolution, the SWP and the LSA, along with the F.I. Chinese grouping in Hong Kong, took strong exception to the notion that there had been " . . . very extensive outflanking of the Maoist leadership by the masses of the Red Guards . . ." In general, however, we saw the draft as being very much within the framework of earlier documents and statements going back to the International's founding in 1936, and through all of its Congresses. These analyzed international events in terms of a "world revolution" that had begun in 1917 with the Russian Revolution, and which saw the main obstacle to its success being ". . . the crises of leadership of the world proletariat" that the Fourth International had been organized to overcome. On that score, there was no disagreement.

The gathering in Rimini turned out to be one of the largest ever. I was on the Mandates Commission and my notes tell me that there were ninety-five people in attendance from thirty countries, twenty of them observers, and forty-four delegates representing seventeen sections. The IMG had eight people there, about twice what International Group had had at the previous one, a reflection of the new forces we had won to us in the intervening period. Tariq Ali, Pat Jordan and Bob Purdie were our official delegates. Also present, I remember, probably as an alternate, was Peter Gowan, a recent recruit to the IMG. Jess MacKenzie was there, as were Alan and Connie Harris. We were officially asking that the IMG's status of "sympathizing" section be upgraded to "official" section. This was granted unanimously, although Ernest Mandel had lobbied hard to have Ken Coates and his circle of supporters recognized as a "sympathizing group," arguing that in effect there had been split in the British organization. Neither Ken Coates nor any of his people were in attendance.

Representation from Europe was much higher than in previous years with an exceptionally large number from France, which had nine delegates and where the section in the previous year had increased its membership several times over. Along with its older leaders such as Pierre Frank and Michel Lequenne, the delegation included Daniel Bensaid, the Krivine brothers, of whom Alain is the best known. Pierre Rousset and Henry Weber were also there. Jess and I had a special relationship with all these comrades, having gotten to know many of them personally because they had often stayed at our apartment in Streatham when they were in London for meetings and during the Vietnam protests. The Italians, the Swiss and the Germans had larger than usual delegations and there were half-a-dozen leaders of the SWP there as observers, including Joe Hansen, Mary-Alice Waters, Jack Barnes, Barry Sheppard, Caroline Lund—who presented a report on the world youth radicalization—and Tony Thomas, a young black leader from the YSA. Ross Dowson, Art Young and Penny Simpson were there from Canada, but I especially remember a large representation from Latin America, many from Bolivia, Mexico and Peru, but with the bulk of them, more than fifteen, coming from Argentina where the section had split the year before into the Partido Revolucionario Trabajo (PRT—La Verdad) led by Nahuel Moreno and the PRT—Combatiente led by Roberto Santucho.

Santucho, thirty-three years old and one of PRT's central leaders had had a close relationship with the JCR, having fought alongside it on the barricades in the May 1968 Paris events. Relations between the two Argentinean groups were almost non-existent. Six months before the Congress, Santucho's group had submitted a request to the International Control Commission that the La Verdad group be expelled and would go on, a couple of years later, to characterize it as "an opponent grouping that is betraying the class-struggle politics defined by our national and international organization."[2]

The bulk of the discussion at the Congress revolved around China and Latin America, with the dispute following the fault lines of the pre-unification years. The disagreement about China had sharpened early in 1966 after the SWP had been assigned a task by the Secretariat to draft a resolution on the Sino-Soviet conflict. It was substantially changed after the Europeans received it. "The most significant change involves the characterization of the Mao leadership," wrote Joe Hansen to Ernest Mandel. "In the draft resolution, the Mao leadership was held to come under the general category of Stalinism although with peculiarities of its own due to the influence of the Chinese Revolution. The direction of the changes introduced into the then draft resolution was to substitute for this the characterization of the Mao leadership as left centrist . . . To characterize the Mao leadership as of a 'generally centrist character leaning towards the left' goes counter to the position taken on this question long ago by the Trotskyist movement and which appears to us to remain valid. In any case there is strong opposition in the SWP to changing the characterization of the Mao leadership."[3] Whether Maoism was "right" or "left" of other Stalinist bureaucracies was not a new question for the Europeans. This had been an issue before the "reunification" in the dispute with Pablo prior to his breakaway, when Ernest, Livio and Pierre had strongly contested his position that Maoism was to the "right" of the Soviet bureaucracy.

By the time we got to Rimini, however, the differences on China had deepened even more. The main document viewed the "cultural revolution" as part of the broad tendency of mass opposition to Stalinism, similar to what was seen in Czechoslovakia the previous year when a mass uprising led to the Soviet military intervention. "But the phenomena like, the very extensive outflanking of the Maoist leadership by masses of Red Guards in the final phase of the 'cultural revolution' in China," it stated, "must also be put in this category."[4] The SWP, the Swiss, the Canadians, along with our grouping in Hong Kong, many of whom were veterans of the movement and exiles from Stalinism in China, such as Peng Shu-Tse, took strong exception to the belief that there had been "very extensive outflanking of the Maoist leadership." They saw the "cultural revolution" and the Red Guard phenomena as primarily a destructive force doing immense damage to the Revolution and viewed it as having been unleashed by a faction led by Mao to maintain his dominance over rival wings of the bureaucracy. The years following the "cultural revolution" would tend to confirm this pessimistic outlook. According to many experts today, the resulting economic and social chaos set China's economic development back for many decades, and prepared the ground for China's eventual turn towards capitalism to cope with the economic crisis caused by that bureaucratic struggle.

By far the most important debate at the Congress, however, was about Latin America where we had had several well established sections, especially in Argentina, Bolivia, Mexico, and Peru. A resolution from the International leadership proposed a new "tactical turn" that was destined to seriously impact all of them, some to the point of destruction and loss of life. It was probably the main reason why the SWP had avoided the "entry tactic" discussion that I had been so keen to pursue. There were bigger issues at stake, and it turned out the SWP had been correct because all the evidence suggested that the Cubans were moving towards setting up a new revolutionary international formation which would pose new questions for us, including providing a tremendous opening. First and foremost, if such a formation were to come into existence, it would be essential to have a correct orientation to it, rather than let it swallow us up.

Those were stirring times. Revolution was in the air. And, with the growing youth radicalization seen in France in May 1968, many in the Fourth International and virtually all of its European leaders described this as an emerging new "international youth vanguard," who might be able to lead such a revolution. And after Che Guevara's call at the Tricontinental Conference in Havana in January 1966 for "two, three, many Vietnams" and the subsequent setting up the following year by the Cubans of the Organization of Latin American Solidarity (OLAS), whose conference many Fourth International leaders had attended, all eyes were fixed on Latin American. Guevara's attempt to establish a guerrilla base in Bolivia, his idea of guerrilla war for a prolonged period, had become very attractive to this new "youth vanguard." Many in the International hoped the guerrilla struggle would lead to a socialist "breakthrough" in Latin America. Although there was a growing audience everywhere for our ideas in those years, we were nevertheless still a tiny organization, and sometimes in our dreaming we would speculate amongst ourselves about the possibility that somehow or somewhere a Fourth International grouping could become a mass organization. Our hopes were to help establish a "workers' state" in one or more countries, or even in a portion of an existing capitalist state's territory, to show that socialism could really be built with a democratic economy, free of bureaucratic deformations under workers' control and that would become a showpiece to be emulated by workers everywhere. But like I said, it was a dream.

Many in the Fourth International hoped that Che in Bolivia could have made such an opening, making that dream a reality. And from what we know now, many of our sections in Latin American were already moving in that direction. We, the North Americans, were not so sure. When we learned that Che had opened up a guerrilla front, we were very skeptical. Many of us feared the worst and thought it might be an adventure. In his writings and through his various proxies such as Regis Debray, he had argued fervently that the seizure of power in Cuba by the 26th of July Movement represented a new model for bringing about social change. Through armed struggle and collective action, he believed that small groups of dedicated activists could galvanize revolutionary change, even in the face of severe state repression. This was at variance with our ideas of the urban working class and peasant masses seizing power by means of a mass revolutionary party, which required us to devote our efforts to building such organizations mainly in the urban centres. We weren't about to write off that option so easily. As far as we were concerned, this was the whole premise of the founding of our movement, as laid out in our "Transitional Programme." Frankly, we didn't believe that Che could succeed.

In its early stages, the discussion about Latin America was open and non-factional and there was a reasonable and collegial exchange of views. In the run up to the Rimini Congress, however, I noticed that the lines had begun to harden, especially as we learned what was happening in countries such as Argentina. Over 1967 and 1968 we began to receive news about a crisis brewing there over the issue of guerrilla warfare in the PRT. Up until 1968, the Party had been led by Nahuel Moreno, an intellectual and probably then the country's best known Trotskyist. The PRT was known as a hard, class struggle, combat kind of organization. Its members had a reputation for "iron discipline" in applying the Party's positions. With a history of involvement in working class struggles in factories, Moreno's group had had an orientation to the Peronist movement, which had—and still has—a major influence in the unions. They were one of our sections who employed the "entry tactic." To maintain his hold on power and head off a possible coup by elements of the ruling class, Juan Peron, who had initiated a limited programme for Argentina to achieve a measure of independence from imperialism, had changed the labour laws to favour the unions, and his supporters had helped to organize some of the poorest workers and peasants in the country.

Livio Maitan had toured Latin America several times and had attended the PRT Congress where a division had occurred between Moreno and

Santucho over the issue of armed struggle, with Moreno heading up what would become known as the PRT (La Verdad) grouping and Santucho the PRT (Combatiente)—both groupings being known by the names of their respective journals. Livio had reported to us at that time that the "Guevarist" line had massive popular support in the student movement in many Latin America countries. This was causing a crisis in many of the Moscow influenced CPs, and was also having a profound effect on our sections. I knew very little about Argentina and had only seen a few copies of the section's paper, *Palabra Obrera,* which from time to time arrived in our Toronto headquarters. But I remember Livio being very critical of the Moreno group, claiming its "entry" into the Peronist movement had caused it to lag behind the growing radicalization.

Prior to the reunification of the International in 1963, the Moreno grouping had been part of the International Committee, which probably affected Livio's attitude. Livio did not conceal his sympathies for the Santucho group but what was truly incredible—the truth of which we would only discover later—is that he did not reveal to us that the PRT (Combatiente) was more "Castroist" than Trotskyist, having supported the Kremlin's crushing of Czechoslovakia in 1968 and considering itself to be in the same camp as the Albanian, Chinese, North Korean and North Vietnamese Communist Parties.

We only learned of these crucial details after one of the *La Verdad* delegates brought the PRT(C)'s main programmatic statement to the Congress and turned it over to the SWP.[5] Worse, we learned that Livio was already aware of this document and hadn't said anything about it to us. This left a sour taste in our mouths. When we raised it with him, he claimed that it only represented the views of its three authors, and was not the line of the organization. This turned out to be far from the case, as we will see. Naturally, after all this, I was suspicious that Livio had had such a close relationship with the Santucho group that he may have begun to lose his objectivity and may even have had a hand in the split there.

Up until the Ninth Congress, I'm sure none of us from North America would have imagined that the line of rural guerrilla war "for a prolonged period" would become the general line of march for all of our organizations in Latin America and that it would become a strategy for the seizure of power. Up until then there had been no disagreement between the Europeans and the North Americans regarding the *tactic* of guerrilla warfare. As I've mentioned, it had been part of the agreement to overcome the division in 1963. Our common perception—or so we thought—was that its specific application had to be determined by the political conditions and relationship of class forces in a particular country, to be decided on by the section of that country. The central weakness of the resolution that was now before the delegates was that it made the tactic of guerrilla warfare "for a prolonged period" a general line for the whole continent, thereby converting it into an overarching strategy.

The Latin American resolution minced few words about what it was proposing. Reading it again today after these many years, it appears to me even more egregiously wrong, both in its content and methodology. I'm sure most members of the Fourth International today would agree with me. Keep in mind that the membership of our various sections, including in Argentina and Bolivia, were in the hundreds, and definitely not the thousands. There weren't many qualifiers in the document and the meaning was very specific: "The only realistic perspective for Latin America is that of armed struggle which may last for long years . . . Even in the case of countries where large mobilizations and class conflicts in the cities may occur first, civil war will take manifold forms of armed struggle, in which the principal axis for a whole period will be rural guerrilla warfare . . ."

In the manner of a general staff issuing orders to its troops, it naively offered specific and somewhat obvious advice: "Take advantage of every opportunity not only to increase the number of rural guerrilla nucleus (sic) but also to promote forms of armed struggle especially adapted to certain zones (for example the mining zone in Bolivia) and to undertake actions in the big cities aimed at striking the nerve centres (key point in the economy and transport, etc.) and at punishing the hangmen of the regime as well as achieving propagandistic and psychological success.

(The experience of the European resistance to Nazism would be helpful in this regard.)" I use the word "naïve" here because it seems obvious to me that most of these questions would have been dealt with in the course of the struggle, should a section have decided to take this route, and would be determined by political objectives.

And as if foretelling Santucho's eventual tragic evolution—it's as if he had a hand in writing the draft, it so neatly summarized his views—the resolution goes on to say, "A variant that merits particular study is that of very large countries where armed struggle could result in the occupation of whole regions geographically and socially favourable to this, for a prolonged period without bringing on the disintegration of the central power. In such cases, the conception of mobile columns would not necessarily be contradictory to that liberated zone."[6]

The issue of guerrilla warfare kept poking its head up in discussions of other resolutions before the delegates, such as the theses motivated by Ernest about the overall international political conjuncture. The following account comes from my notes taken at the time. I am sharing it to give the reader a flavour of the discussion. It was a passionate debate, about life and death issues—not abstractly, but on the ground. Except for Moreno of Argentina, the majority of the Latin Americans in the room, including Hugo Gonzalez Moscoso of Bolivia, supported the guerrilla line.

"We expect a lot from this Congress in helping us overcome a lot of difficulties," Moscoso told the delegates. "Our country is a jail, from which it is dangerous to leave," he said. "We expect answers and no theorizing—that's over," he said. "We want answers on how to act . . . We've understood the change. The revolutionary movement must become an army. We've heard the criticism that we are substituting ourselves for the mass movement, but the mass movement can only continue through armed struggle—it's a conclusion we've not arbitrarily come to, but we've arrived at it on the basis of our experience . . . The dictatorship made it impossible for the miners to continue as legal organizations and now they exist as underground trade unions, we've organized the national armed people's command. After hearing from some of the comrades here, should we tell these masses that they should stop because it is not the 'Marxist' way? For us, the way to build the revolutionary organization is to unite with those who are fighting, such as the Castroists. I agree with the theses and the report."

Livio Maitan made a spirited intervention arguing for the proposed new line, projecting a period of increasing military repression continuing in Latin America, and arguing that one of the main contradictions in confronting that area of the world was that there was "a ripening of a revolutionary situation, but a weak subjective factor", something that would have lasting importance. "It is not a contradiction in my head," he said, "it's a reality." Our organizations are weak, he went on, but in the "primitive accumulation of cadres" there is a danger of adventurism, and "some comrades speak generally against the line of guerrilla warfare, but they make the same mistake as Debray." The Fourth International is the fundamental link in the chain, he said. In the case of Argentina, he asked, should our group remain a propaganda group or an instrument for power? "What we do need and what we are forging is a combat-international that will fight and which tries to be the real vanguard in the taking of power."

"For that we need a strategy, for that we need to be an International of the masses," he said. "The problem is how do we build a revolutionary party? The spontaneists say we don't need one, but we can't win by arguments alone, but by showing the real necessity for one. We must wrench the leadership of the mass movement out of the hands of the revisionists and the spontaneists . . . Certain comrades believe that first you go and get the people and then you lead the struggle. Imperialism has transformed many of these countries into police states; our parties should prepare for this eventuality from the start. Falsely there is an attempt here to place the issue of guerrilla warfare in counter-position to the question of building the party when in reality the relationship is dialectical . . . there is a danger if we continue to be mainly concerned with propaganda . . . we must be a factor in each country."

A comrade known as "Cyrano" presented the Latin American report. "The dynamic of the revolution in Latin America is non-debatable here," he said. "We have seen the catastrophic defeat of the peaceful road. Permanent revolution is now understood by the masses . . . part of the attraction is Cuba. Many regimes are in crises because of mass mobilizations. Before the period we are now in, only the Trotskyists held a revolutionary outlook. Those with a 'nationalist' orientation have been bypassed by new forces. A regroupment of these forces can be carried out under the armed struggle . . . We don't propose a "Debrayist" notion—the document states this. We refuse to counter-pose the struggle of the masses in the urban centres to that of the guerrillas. We say that the urban struggle, the rural struggle and the guerrilla struggle are determined by each other . . ."

Cyrano took up the question of Che Guevara's defeat in Bolivia. It's similar to what happened to him in Guatemala, he said, he was linked to forces that were not clear about what they wanted or were opposed to taking power. In Bolivia, Che's first connection was with the CP, Cyrano said. "[Mario] Monje, the leader of the Bolivian CP, first gave the appearance of backing him [Che], for his own purposes, but when Che broke with him, the CP sabotaged any efforts to help him, cut off supplies to him and prevented his guerrilla group from recruiting new forces. For their part, the Maoist CP, Cyrano said, "expelled anyone from their ranks who were positive about him. One of our F.I. groups was prevented from intervening. In the correspondence between Che and Fidel that appeared in *Granma* there is a clear reference to our discussions. Some of the left waited, except for us who expressed ourselves openly on the matter."

"Our party is the only one," Cyrano went on, "who does not have the responsibility for his death. We organized a nucleus as early as 1963, but because we were unclear about what we were doing and had material weaknesses, by the time of Che's intervention we were still at that stage. We were still in the mountains looking for a camp. We were the first victims of the repression that led to our members being thrown into con- centration camps where, incidentally, we made initial contact with his supporters. Che's diary confirms our conviction that it could have been different. We had people who spoke the same language as the people in the area. The BCP prevented it. After Che's death, his intermediaries were desperate for our help . . ."

Many of the North Americans took to the podium, but I remember especially Joe Hansen, who was the main spokesperson for the opposition to the new line, trying his hardest to persuade the delegates to reject it. While agreeing with many of the resolution's main points, he stated that the differences are not over principles nor were they sharp. "I'm not opposed to guerrilla warfare per se," he said, "but if it's a tactic, it is wrong to prescribe it for a narrow area or for a long time," he argued, stressing that "it was wrong for the international leadership to lay down tactics for individual sections. This tends to substitution for a national section. If a national section is incapable of working out its own tactics, it's impossible for it to ever take power." For the International leadership to lay down tactics for a Section, he told the delegates, prevents comrades from working them out on their own. "It's wrong to have dogmas in the tactical field," he said, "we need comrades who are steeped in their own countries' experience otherwise it can lead to disaster." If we regard guerrilla warfare as a strategy, we have a different problem, he went on, and it becomes a primary orientation and takes the place of the need to build combat parties.

Joe also dealt with the Cubans' view of the question. It's understandable from their own experience with the Stalinists, he argued, that they would think the way they do. While we consider the Cubans allies, we have important differences with them, he continued. They have not settled accounts with the CP and even though they have cleared the way for constructing combat parties, they have yet to undertake that task. In addition, while they have come to a correct understanding about the nature of CPs, it has come late and in relation to the Soviet Union, they have traded politics for material aid, he said.

Joe took up the experience of Che's catastrophic adventure in Bolivia. Even though we must be sensitive in how we deal with it, he said, we must be really clear and draw a balance sheet of what took place there. Che's technical skill was clearly evident, but it's obvious he took too many risks and that he had made bad political errors, thinking that there was a mechanical relationship between the general situation and the detonation of the armed struggle. Timing was crucial, Joe explained, and Che's main difficulty was that he did not have a political party to help him. Che's method was "sectarian" and derived from "general dogmas," and, furthermore, he depended upon a treacherous ally, the Bolivian CP. His political preparations were clearly very inadequate; he should have had a showdown with the Bolivian CP first to clear the decks before initiating his campaign.

Joe went on, highlighting the lessons of the Cuban Revolution itself, and contrasting it with Che's mission in Bolivia. Che's armed group in Bolivia was made up of about twenty-five fighters, most of whom were Spanish-speaking and foreign to Bolivia, and whom we have since learned had enormous language difficulties and were unable even to communicate with the locals who only spoke the indigenous language, Quecha. The 26th of July Movement in Cuba, although a relatively small force starting off with less than a hundred in the mountains, had broad support in Cuba's urban centres, to the degree it had the capacity to organize general strikes. It also had access to large financial resources with millions of dollars in its bank account, Joe said, right up to the moment it marched into Havana.

In addition, he warned, we shouldn't ignore the fact that American imperialism had been taken by surprise by what had happened in Cuba in 1959 and was now alert and well prepared to prevent a similar experience from being repeated elsewhere, especially in Latin America, its own backyard. Therefore any new guerrilla operation would face the full might of its military power. Joe also suggested that the Cuban government might be changing its policy on the issue and might be less than enthusiastic after the failures of the previous ten years in which it had been obliquely involved, which probably included Masetti's guerrilla front in Argentina and Che's in Bolivia. Moreover, Joe argued, contrary to what the resolution was advising, our sections should look to further integrate themselves into the working class and its organizations such as the unions, which were bound to undergo a radicalization as they came under greater economic and social pressures.

Mexico and Santo Domingo (where there had been mass uprisings in the year before) had shown, Joe said, that the radicalization was beginning to be seen in several urban centres where we had active groups, challenging the view that we were faced with a strengthening of military regimes. Other speakers in the discussion were Peng Shu-Tse, Jeanette from the LCR, Ernest Mandel, Kolpe from India, Hugo Moreno, Tabata, Bala Tampoe and Valentine from Argentina. Most of them spoke in favour of the resolution.

In the course of the discussion, I began to feel that an exaggerated perception of our organizational capacity had begun to creep into the thinking of some of those who were promoting the new turn. After the practical experiences of being on the United Secretariat over the previous four years, I was keenly aware of the F.I.'s weak organizational state and its financial limitations. Even preparing for that Congress, with only a couple of people on staff for the work, had been an enormous task and many of the documents had not yet been translated nor distributed to many of the sections, especially those that had very limited resources to reproduce the materials. The reality was that we were a tiny international organization, so I took the floor to inform the delegates about some of the difficulties we had faced trying to find the money to pay for our most minimal expenses, and that in this respect we had gone from one crisis to the next.

But I don't think anyone was listening. We seemed to be talking past each other. One side was talking about how to organize a revolution and the other about how to fashion an instrument to lead such a revolution. It was like a dialogue of the deaf, at times, and it was clear that the new youth leadership, especially in France, was almost totally sympathetic to Ernest and Livio's views. Sometimes it was difficult to determine who was influencing whom, as the JCR comrades seemed to me to be moving around lining up delegates to support their views, allowing an element of factionalism to enter the off-the-floor conversations. The British delegation, most of whom, prior to the Congress, had been critical of the resolution, finally gave it their support, although Bob Purdie and Pat Jordan took exception to a comment by Livio that the "Fourth International will be built in Bolivia" and voted for the resolution with a qualification about that issue.

I could understand Tariq Ali's support for the guerrilla line. He was new to the organization and politically inexperienced, and very much influenced by the ultra-left mood of the times. I was very surprised, however, that Pat Jordan had switched his position, because during our discussions in London, he had been, like me, very critical of the Latin American resolution. A disquieting feature of the debate was that it began to show that the unity in the International, patiently built up over the previous six years, was starting to come apart at the seams. Disagreement tended to break along the old pre-unification lines, with most of the Europeans and Latin Americans supporting the resolution, and most of the Americans and Canadians, along with a few others, including the Moreno delegates, opposed. As I recall, the vote breakdown was approximately sixty percent for, forty against. The Congress ended with a resounding appeal to the sections to raise as much money as possible to send to the Bolivians and Santucho's group to support the new line—all to thunderous applause.

The Congress recognized the PRT (Combatiente) in Argentina as the official section and Moreno's organization as a "sympathizing" group," on the basis that Santucho's organization had the most members. On the Mandates' Commission, I was part of the discussion about that issue. Because I was ignorant of the PRT(C)'s true politics, I went along with the "most members" argument, which was clearly wrong. The wool had been pulled over my eyes. It's easy to see now that the correct and "non-factional approach" would have been to designate both groups as "sympathizing" and let their political life decide the issue. But then that would have meant paying closer attention to their political line, something that some comrades in the leadership seemed unprepared to do. The adoption of the guerilla warfare resolution on Latin America was a mistake the International would correct within a few years, but only after a terrible cost in resources and blood.

Jess and I left Italy for Toronto immediately after the gathering. Personal issues had been pressing in on us and we were anxious to get back to

Canada to pay off the personal debts we had accumulated by then. These had grown over the previous year and we could see no easy way to settle them from London. So with a measure of sadness we had said our goodbyes, but there was also a feeling of satisfaction in knowing we were leaving Britain with a viable grouping in place. It had been an incredible time to be there, in the midst of a sweeping radicalization, especially among young people. We had been an important part of the IMG's leadership and had formed close personal bonds with many of its members. I had worked closely with some amazing comrades—especially in Brussells where people such as Ernest, Pierre and Ray, had been in the International since Trotsky's time. Recognizing I was not necessarily their equal in experience or intellectually, they nevertheless, made a special effort to integrate me into their team. It had been a truly memorable experience for Jess and me, including being at the Congress and one that we would not easily forget.

Roberto Santucho, main leader of the PRT-ERP, assassinated by the military, July 19, 1976. His wife, Liliana, was murdered the same year. (From "200 Anos de Historia de Argentina," 2010)

Fuerzas Armadas Revolucionarias (FAR), El Ejicito Revolucionario del Pueblo (ERP), and Monteneros prisoners attempt a mass escape in 1972 from Rawson prison, in the Patagonian desert. Only six, their leaders, among them Roberto Santucho, got to the hi-jacked airliner, shown above at Trelew airport. Nineteen guerrillas did not reach the plane, including his wife Anna Maria, the mother of his children. Surrendering after receiving "guarantees" they would be returned to Rawson, sixteen were murdered in cold blood by the military. Only three survived to tell the truth about what had happened. (From "200 Anos de Historia de Argentina," 2010)

Chapter 20

Argentina:
Roberto Santucho and the PRT-ERP

O NE OF THE DIFFICULTIES WE FACED IN THOSE YEARS WAS OBTAINING reliable information about events taking place in Argentina, and because of the factional explosion in the PRT—and the growing tensions in the United Secretariat—we began to distrust much of the information coming our way. In addition, except for Joe Hansen and a few other North Americans, none of us at the time spoke or read Spanish. After Santucho finally broke from the Fourth International, the fate of his organization tended to recede from our memories. I've read many of the documents of the tendency struggle in the International in those years, but it's only today, after all that time, that I feel I have some idea of the sorry fate of the PRT(C) and its armed wing, the Ejercito Revolucionario Partido (ERP), especially after reading Daniel Gutman's recent history and account of what happened to it in those years.[1]

Gutman's work is based on an intensive study of the conflict. He consulted the military archives and interviewed many survivors of the struggle, including a few of those in the police and Argentinean army. What follows is mainly derived from his book. His work is an important contribution to the PRT(C)'s history, which I think is largely unknown to the English speaking world. It deserves wider circulation, especially among those who are trying to bring about social change today.

The PRT was the product of a fusion five years earlier, in 1964, of a Fourth International grouping named *Palabra Obrero* (PO), which means

Workers' Word, led by Hugo Moreno, and the much smaller group Frente Revolucionario Indoamericanista Popular (FRIP), a radical, pro-indigenous, nationalist grouping, of which Roberto Santucho was a main leader. Both organizations had been active in the Peronist-led union, La Federacion Obrero Tucaman de la Industria Azcuceros (FOTIA), the Federation of Sugar Workers of Tucaman. Tucaman, Argentina's smallest and most densely populated state, in the northeast, was the main centre of its sugar production and known for having some of the worst poverty levels in the country, where many workers lived in semi-feudal conditions. The PO, with its reputation for having an "iron will" and inculcating a highly developed sense of discipline in its members, had earlier adopted a "proletarian orientation" and had been paying special attention to the sugar workers' union with the aim of winning the workers away from Peronism.

FRIP was also active in trying to recruit in the area. A student leader at the National University of Tucaman, where he had studied accountancy, Santucho had had a long association with Tucaman, even persuading his student union at one point to adopt a policy of building solidarity with the sugar workers and to spend time coming to an understanding of the terrible conditions of their lives. Upon graduation early in 1961, newly married, he and his wife travelled throughout North America, ending up in Cuba where he was in the square on April 2nd when Fidel Castro delivered his historic and defiant speech declaring Cuba would take the revolutionary road to socialism. The rest of that year Santucho travelled all over Cuba before returning to Tucaman where he joined the FRIP. He soon got a job as an accountant in the San José sugar mill, where the FRIP and the PO jointly controlled the plant's union local.

This was during a very radical period in the province's history marked by an upsurge in sugar-worker militancy when the mills were often occupied by the workers because of non-payment of wages. The workers developed the practice of holding management hostage until their demands were met. That's when Santucho reaffirmed his long-held belief that "the rural working class with its vanguard, the sugar workers, is the detonator of the Argentine Revolution." The San José sugar mill was where most of the future leaders of the ERP were employed and received their Marxist education, and it's where Santucho first met the three PO leaders, Angel "Vasco" Bengochea, Leandro Fote and Hugo Santilli. Bengochea, a lawyer by training, had joined the Trotskyists in 1946 and had spent seven months in prison in 1957 because of his activities against the Argentinean regime. He and Santilli, a medical doctor, had abandoned their professional careers to go into industry, in line with PO's "proletarianization" policy of sending its members into the factories.

Bengochea would give the PO its first taste of armed struggle, an experience that ended in a terrible tragedy. He had travelled to Cuba to undertake political-military training. There he met and came under the influence of Che Guevara, who was looking for recruits for a guerrilla operation in Argentina, consistent with his views of continental revolution in Latin America. In his discussions with Che, Bengochea is reported to have initially resisted Che's idea of a revolutionary "foci" in Argentina, insisting that because of the developed character of the working class in his country, probably the most "Europeanized" in Latin America, a mobilization in the cities would first be required to overthrow the regime. Finally Bengochea relented, agreeing to organize, when he returned to Argentina, a guerrilla front in Tucaman with the proviso that the PO would not be required to abandon what it had built up over the years in the working class in the cities.

On his return to Argentina in June, 1963, Bengochea, probably because of the impracticalities of his small group maintaining the dual orientations he had discussed with Che, dropped the idea about work in the mass organizations of the working class in the urban centres and took upon himself the task of building an armed grouping and establishing a guerrilla base in the mountains. This sparked a crisis in the PO, with Moreno—who had rejected Che's "foci" theory—winning a majority to defeat Bengochea's line. Santucho had also opposed Bengochea at that time, telling him that the launch of a guerrilla struggle was premature and that without the backing of the organization's leaders, it would be doomed to failure. He also criticized Fote and Santilli for abandoning the sugar mill workers at a critical moment in their struggles and agreed with Moreno that the FRIP and the PO should proceed with forming a common organization. That fusion took place within a year, leading to the creation of the Partido Revolucionario Trabajadores (PRT).

Bengochea left the PO, then he—along with Fote, Santilli and a handful of their supporters, plus a few individuals from a Peronist resistance group—set about organizing Las Fuerzas Armada de la Revolucion Nacional (FARN). As its name implied, this was an armed struggle formation. They soon initiated a series of bank robberies to buy arms and to establish a guerrilla base in the mountains of Tucaman. It all came to a terrible end when a bomb Bengochea and a few of his people were working on in an apartment in Buenos Aires went off, killing him, Hugo Santillo and three other militants from his group.

The attempt by Bengochea was only one of several in those years to establish a guerrilla base in or near Tucaman. In late 1959, a faction of the Peronist movement, supported by the Peronist Youth, sent a grouping of its militants into the mountains for several months training to be guerrillas, but they never managed to carry out any armed actions and eventually almost starved to death before surrendering to the police. Che Guevara, from Cuba in 1963-64—most likely with the surreptitious support of the Cuban government, and at the same time as he was arranging to supply weapons to Bengochea—had also initiated a rural guerrilla campaign in Argentina, the Ejercito Guerrillero del Pueblo (EGP), in the jungles on a mountain range close to Salta, near the Bolivian border. Under the command of his old friend from Argentina, Jorge Ricardo Masetti, a journalist and founder of Cuba's *Prensa Latina*, Che's Argentinean initiative turned into a terrible disaster with many of the guerrillas losing their lives. Some fell off the steep cliffs as they tried to escape from the police; others starved to death or were killed after their campaign was infiltrated by the security forces. Many of the survivors ended up in prison.[2] A similar attempt had been made by the Monteneros, a well-known nationalist grouping with a history of carrying out armed actions in the cities. It also ended in failure, and in 1968 a relatively unknown grouping from Buenos Aires, the Fuerzas Armadas Peronistas (FAP) tried to do the same thing in the south of Tucaman with the aim of taking over a police station to spark an insurrection. But that collapsed after only two weeks, and fourteen people were imprisoned, since the location of their base had been reported to the police by local peasants. .[3]

In 1968, the PRT(C), not dissuaded by these failures, and with about fifty delegates present at a clandestine location for their historic Fifth Congress—with Livio Maitan in attendance—took the momentous decision to try to succeed where others had failed, and proceeded to prepare for an armed struggle against the state. The PRT(C), although one of the largest and most experienced of our sections in Latin America, is estimated to have had a membership of less than 1000 at the time.[4] Santucho, whose main disagreement with Bengochea about the question of guerrilla warfare had been about the timing of his initiative, had, in the years since Bengochea's death, worked hard at learning as much as he could about the lives and conditions of the sugar workers in Tucaman. He had been thinking about the practicalities of establishing a guerrilla base in the province for several years. He had been strongly critical of Che's efforts to set up a small base near Salta because it had become totally isolated right from the beginning and had very few connections to the rural population. Santucho had also criticized Che's attempts at guerrilla war in Bolivia because Che, he said, had proceeded without the support of the left. Nahuel (Hugo) Moreno had also considered the practicalities of guerrilla warfare in Argentina. A few years earlier, inspired by the Cubans and the OLAS conference, he had investigated such a possibility in Tucaman, but rejected the idea because of the lack of support for it among the sugar workers themselves and the difficulties of establishing a base there.

Santucho, on the other hand, believed that in Argentina the link between the "popular" classes and Peronism—the main political force opposing the military dictatorship in those years—had been broken, and he argued that the economic effects of imperialism on Argentina, which was a highly urbanized country, had caused industry to develop in the cities at the expense of rural regions, such as Tucaman, and as a result this had allowed the trade union bureaucracy to concentrate and maintain its control over the working class in the urban centres. This had led to the super-exploitation of the rural working class and its low level of unionization, Santucho believed, and would provide the space for a revolutionary party to assume the task of leading the workers of Argentina in a struggle for power.

A majority of the PRT at the Fifth Congress backed Santucho, leaving Moreno heading up a minority who argued for the Party to maintain its concentration in the factories of Buenos Aires, Cordoba and Rosario, and to look for resistance to grow there against the regime, concentrating on taking advantage of the political opening that could provide it with a mass base. In the resulting bitter division, Santucho would end up denouncing the Moreno grouping as "traitors" when they publicly criticized his actions in carrying out bank robberies and kidnappings to finance his operations.

Shortly after the Fifth Congress, Santucho and twelve others from his organization went to Cuba for two months of training in rural guerrilla warfare. Their first armed action took place early the following year. On January 7th, 1969, a commando team led by Santucho raided a bank near Buenos Aires, successfully getting away with $200,000. This became public knowledge not long after when a few members of his commando team were arrested, jailed, and admitted to membership in the PRT. The bank robbery probably explains why so many of them were able to get to the Ninth Congress in Rimini so easily. Celebrated by the delegates there—especially the youthful new leadership of the French section—they were given a boisterous welcome, with the majority seeing them as heroes of an immediate unfolding of a revolution in Argentina.

From what we know today about the events in Argentina in those years, and especially after reading Daniel Gutman's book, the debate at Rimini must have appeared somewhat academic to the PRT(C) delegates as they sat there listening. I don't remember if Santucho was a delegate, but certainly several of his top people were there. The main leader of their delegation, significantly, turned out to be Daniel Pereyra. He had joined the PRT(C) not long after arriving in Argentina from his five year imprisonment in Peru in 1962. With a handful of people from the International's section, and against the advice of Hugo Moreno, he had set up an armed struggle group, the "Tupac Maru," which carried out one the largest bank robberies in Peru's history, ostensibly to help Hugo Blanco, the section's leader. At the time Blanco was leading a mass peasant movement in the Cuzco region, defending themselves against the regime. Pereyra and his comrades were quickly apprehended by the police and most of the money was recovered, but Blanco rejected Pereyra's adventurism, and considered him to have been misguided.[5] That Pereyra would show up in the PRT(C) delegation was indicative, and surely an omen of things to come.

In reality, in the months before the Ninth Congress, Santucho was already well advanced in his preparations to launch a guerrilla struggle and the Latin American resolution looks now as nothing more than giving him a seal of approval for what he was already doing. By the end of 1968, the PRT(C) had set up its first camps in the mountains of Tucaman and had begun to steal and manufacture weapons for armed actions against the State.

But things did not go very well for them in the beginning. Within a few months of the World Congress, the PRT(C) suffered a terrible setback when one of its militants was arrested by the police. Under torture, he revealed the group's plans for guerrilla activity, including many names of its members, leading to forty being arrested, including Santucho, who was sent, along with his wife, Anna Maria Villarreal, to Rawson Prison in the Patagonian wilderness. It was a catastrophe of the first order and it revealed a certain lack of experience on the organization's part regarding security measures that should have taken into account the possibility of a member falling into the hands of the police. The few leaders who had escaped the clutches of the police, angry with what had taken place, ordered the guerrilla project terminated and annulled the original decision that had unleashed it.

Santucho, for his part, was not to be deterred. By the summer of 1972, he had made an incredible and daring escape from Rawson, during which his wife and the mother of his four children was murdered by the police. Amazingly, he then succeeded in highjacking a plane to Cuba. The decision of the PRT(C) to halt the armed struggle was reversed, and those who had supported stopping it were pushed out of the party as Santucho began to organize the Ejercito Revolucionario del Pueblo (ERP). Membership in the new formation was open to all those—not exclusively socialists—who wished to struggle against imperialism. All party members automatically became members of the ERP, but not vice-versa.

By that point, the unity of the Fourth International—carefully nurtured by both sides since the re-unification in 1963—had become severely strained, especially as a result of what was happening not only in Argentina but in Bolivia where the POR, the official section, had suffered a split. The two sides there were led, respectively, by Hugo Gonzalez Moscoso and Guillermo Lora, both long time leaders of the POR. Lora—a supporter of Gerry Healy's SLL in Britain—led the POR Masas wing, which was critical of the guerrilla line, and Gonzalez led the pro-guerrilla wing. The Combate side of the split in Bolivia had the full support of the United Secretariat, as expressed through its spokesperson, Livio Maitan, who encouraged POR-Combate's participation in the Guevarist Ejercito Liberacion Nacional (ELN) which was attempting to re-establish a "foci" in the mountains. This ended in a major disaster in July 1970, when the ELN suffered a horrible defeat. Most of its approximately seventy-five fighters—among them many members of the Gonzalez Moscoso grouping—were massacred by the Bolivian army.[6]

Even though there had been attempts in the Fourth International not to let the differences on the guerrilla question spread to other issues—for example in 1971 the United Secretariat had adopted an unanimous resolution on Chile—by 1972 the majority who had backed the guerrilla line adopted at Rimini had formed themselves into the International Marxist Tendency (IMT). The minority, comprised mainly of the Americans, the Canadians, the Swiss, the Chinese, Hugo Blanco's grouping in Peru, the Moreno grouping *(La Verdad)* in Argentina, the Venezuelans and the Australians, had formed themselves into the Leninist Trotskyist Faction

(LTF). The lines would dramatically harden between the two tendencies by April of that year when the SWP, in *The Militant,* and the LSA in Canada in its *Labour Challenge* publicly criticized the action of the PRT-ERP as ill-advised and politically wrong when, during its occupation of a Fiat plant, it murdered the executive of Fiat, Robert Sylvestre.

Jumping to the defense of the PRT-ERP's armed actions as "an unquestionable gain for the Trotskyist and revolutionary movement," the United Secretariat condemned the LTF. It is absolutely lamentable, Ernest Mandel wrote in a letter to his co-thinkers in Argentina, "that this lesson has not been learned by a minority of the International and that a Trotskyist organization has publicly dissociated themselves from PRT-ERP actions . . ."[7] Ernest's letter was written against a political background in Argentina in which, a couple of years before, a democratic "opening" had appeared when a coalition of political parties had initiated a campaign for a return to constitutional rule and large working class mobilizations had taken place against the military. By March 1971, rioting had broken out in Cordoba; within a few months, political instability ensued, with a military coup unseating the dictator, Juan Carlos Ongania. The ban against Peron would be lifted, introducing a period of political liberalization in the country.

By then, it was clear things were not going well between the IMT and its supporters in Argentina. Approving the armed occupation of Fiat—and presumably the killing of Sylvestre—in the same letter referred to above, Ernest supported them as going in the direction of "a link-up between the guerrillas and the mass struggle," but warned that "there has been errors of estimate in judging the level attained by the armed struggle . . . the enemy has to a large degree perfected his technique of repression, making a qualitative leap in this regard." The possibilities of a link-up, he complained, "have not been exploited adequately and the actions during the last year have marked a regression from the standpoint of political content."

What Ernest seemed to be ignoring—something that we had pointed out to him in the discussion—was that when a small organization takes the road of launching an armed struggle, it of necessity is forced to reduce its links with the masses. It simply doesn't have the numbers to sustain those kinds of connections, and, even just out of security concerns, maintaining those links becomes extremely difficult. Significantly, Ernest's letter points to the possibility of a "democratic opening" taking place and cautions, "It will be necessary, above all else, to combat any tendency to interpret the period of partial 'democratization' ahead, if our hypothesis proves correct, as implying a perspective of 'democratization' for an entire stage . . ."

Not long after Ernest's letter of October 31, 1972, Santucho was in Brussels sitting in front of him in personal conversation. He was on his way back to Argentina by way of Paris after a heroic and incredible escape from Rawson prison camp a few months earlier. In attendance at the meeting were Daniel Bensaid and Hubert Krivine, who say that over many hours the three of them attempted to talk him out of his idea of building a guerrilla base.[8] But by this time relations had deteriorated so badly between the IMT and the LTF that the latter was not even informed of the Brussels' discussions, nor that Santucho had even been there.

Within a couple of months, however, the IMT would begin to take its distance from Santucho, with Ernest Mandel stating on January 5th, 1973 that "the United Secretariat had made a serious mistake in not opening a frank discussion with the comrades of the Argentine section much earlier . . ." Ernest characterized the PRT(C) as being made up of "a combination of Trotskyism and populist semi-castroist currents," that there was a "problem of assimilation" and said ". . . it is necessary to conduct an extensive discussion with the Argentine section in a fraternal and frank way . . ."[9] By the following year Santucho had departed the Fourth International.

According to Daniel Gutman, by 1973 the PRT-ERP had become the most active armed grouping in the country with over thirty of its people dead and hundreds in jail. This at a time when Argentina had begun to undergo significant political change, including an upsurge in trade union led strikes and an election in March—that the PRT-ERP denounced as an "electoral farce"—that saw the military forced out of government. Juan Peron, who had been in exile in Spain, was trying to return to Argentina, but the military had banned him from standing in the election. His movement, however, won a sweeping victory, electing Hector Campora to the Presidency and ushering in an unexpected liberalization with the release of large numbers of political prisoners, many of them PRT-ERP militants or supporters. Campora lifted the ban on political parties. He was only in office forty-nine days, before standing aside to allow Peron to take control with a sweeping 62% of the popular vote. And with its return to legality, the PRT-ERP saw its popularity rise, as could be seen in the rapid increase in its press circulation: the PRT's journal, *El Combatiente* jumped to 45,000 and the ERP's *Estrella Roja* to 138,000.

Despite these obvious changed political circumstances, however, there was little moderation in its armed struggle policy. It was as if nothing had changed politically. Much to the chagrin of many of its supporters and allies alike, and other opponents of the regime such as the Montoneros, it announced it would continue "to militarily combat the imperialist business and counter-revolutionary Armed Forces." In case anyone missed the point, it carried out an attack on an army base in an attempt to obtain weapons, killing an army lieutenant in the process.

Within a short time they were declared illegal again by the new government and the PRT-ERP continued along with its preparations to build a guerrilla base in Tucaman. For this, money and military training were indispensable. For the former, they began a very successful campaign of hostage taking: in December they kidnapped Victor Samuelson, the head of Esso in Argentina, obtaining a staggering ransom of more than fourteen million dollars. For help with training, later that month they sent Louis Mattini, a metal worker, Central Committee member and one of their top people, on a mission to try and solve this problem in Cuba.

Mattini told Gutman that he had spent more than a month in Cuba cooling his heels at an official government residence waiting to talk to someone in the government about PRT-ERP plans for establishing a guerrilla base, when late one evening Fidel Castro in person—accompanied by a leader of the CCP—suddenly walked in the door unannounced and began a discussion with him that lasted most of the night. A few hours into the discussion, Mattini told Castro that they had people exploring the mountains of Tucaman, surveying suitable areas to establish bases, and that they had the first contingent of forty fighters, armed, ready and waiting in the cities. But Mattini could not have been very pleased with Fidel's reply. Fidel told him that with Peron's recent election as President, he did not think it was such a good time to launch a guerrilla struggle, reminding him that after Campora's election, Cuba had renewed its diplomatic relations with Argentina, a move Castro said he hoped would lead to a division among those Latin American countries that were supporting the U.S. blockade.

"Cuba has a very clear international policy," Castro told him. "We are not able to train armed groups where governments maintain good relations with us. The opening with Argentina is a fissure in the blockade and important, not only for Cuba, but for all revolutionaries." Mattini, however, assured Castro that they were not about to launch an armed struggle immediately against Peron, but that it would be against those who would replace Peron after his death; the PRT-ERP were anticipating a military coup in which Peron would be assassinated. Pressing on with his attempt to obtain assistance, Mattini specifically asked Castro if it would be possible that General Arnaldo Ochoa be assigned to supervise their training, once the PRT-people arrived in Cuba. Ochoa had been to Argentina many times and had a close relationship with PRT-ERP. (Ochoa would later be executed in Cuba for using his position to smuggle drugs into the country.) But Castro, ignoring the request regarding Ochoa, stressed that suitable political conditions were decisive for success in a guerrilla campaign and that they didn't exist since there was a democratic government—and, with Peron, a popular one at that—in place. Unfortunately the PRT did not listen to Castro's advice.

With the failure of Mattini's mission to Cuba, Santucho was forced to slow down the move into the mountains. He made a decision that the PRT-ERP would now rely on its own resources to train its guerrillas and acquire arms. In January 1974, they attacked a military base, the head of which was killed along with his wife and child and two soldiers. Peron used this incident as a pretext to shift further to the right and to purge his opponents on the left from the legislature, while at the same time removing several provincial governors from their positions, accusing them of being sympathetic to the rebels. He even changed the penal code to deliver harsh penalties against anyone found guilty of providing assistance to the rebels. As on the occasion of the election of Campora, many on the left—and a few liberals—were once again critical of the PRT-ERP, telling them their actions had only helped to nourish the Peronist right. For the first time, extreme right-wing paramilitary groupings, such as the "Triple A," made their appearance on the scene, targeting for intimidation or killing judges whom they saw as being too lenient in their sentencing where rebels were involved, as well as targeting lawyers who may have defended PRT-ERP members, and anyone else they suspected of sympathy for the rebels.

By March 1974, the PRT-ERP had infiltrated between forty to fifty of its militants (a few women would come later)—mostly workers and students from the major cities all over Argentina—into the mountains of Tucaman, setting up their first guerrilla operation, named the Mountain Company Ramon Rosa Jimenez. The PRT-ERP leadership was convinced that the rural and mountainous areas of Tucaman, unlike the cities, presented them with a possibility of eventually assembling a large army permitting them to launch a guerrilla war lasting many years, as had happened in China's and in Vietnam's revolutions. In this way, they believed their revolutionary forces would gradually contest the ruling classes for defined areas of Argentine territory where they would be able to establish their own democratic institutions, finally going over to a situation of "dual power" in the country and the overthrowing of the regime. This, in fact, was the perspective that had been adumbrated in the Ninth World Congress' Latin American resolution. It would also allow them, they thought, to train other revolutionaries from Latin America, part of a perspective for a continental revolution, making the Andes—in the words of Fidel Castro—"the Escambray of the Latin American Revolution" and creating an alternative to Cuba in the provision of training for other Latin American revolutionaries

The overwhelming majority of the PRT-ERP members in the campaign in Tucaman came from the cities, although there were a few local rural people in it who had been won over in previous years. Their main function was to help out with logistics, for example purchasing of supplies and providing of intelligence about the security forces. In reality few, if any, of the local people participated in the training and armed actions, very unlike in Cuba where the 26th of July Movement, when it reached the Escambray mountains, had an opposite problem, that of attracting *too many* from the rural population in the areas where they operated and before they were prepared to engage Batista's army in armed struggle.

Furthermore, these were far from propitious times to launch such an operation in Tucaman. By then the province was in a severe economic depression, due to a collapse of sugar prices on the world market and lack of government help for the industry. Even in its best years, the PRT had only five locals under its influence, out of a total of fifty-five locals of the sugar workers union, the overwhelming majority of which were under the control of the Peronists. By the time Santucho's forces had made their move into the mountains, they had even less support. Only four sugar mills remained in operation in the entire province of Tucaman, together employing a total of approximately 2,000 workers, permanent and temporary. The militant wave of a few years earlier and the high level of class consciousness among the sugar workers—that had deeply impressed Santucho so much in previous years—had by then collapsed and hundreds of thousands of workers had fled the province in a desperate search for work, mainly exiting those areas of the province where there had been high unionization.

Another difficulty they had to try and overcome was that only a few of their members had any training for the military campaign that lay ahead. At most only four of them, including Santucho, had been to Cuba for a couple of months for that purpose, and clearly the leaders knew this to be insufficient. Santucho—apparently proficient in handling weapons and known as an above average marksman with a rifle—undertook the instruction himself and they began to practice with their weapons in areas where there had been a tradition of local people hunting game.

They had hoped they would remain undetected by the authorities until they had completed training, but in April 1974, a campesino reported to the police that he had noticed a camp not far away. When two intelligence agents in disguise went into the mountains, following up on the information from the campesino, they accidently ran into the armed group. They were questioned by Santucho. The agents excuse for being in that area was that they were looking for "a lost cow." Although Santucho was suspicious of them, he permitted them to leave in any case, with a warning that they not tell anyone what they had seen. When the high command of the security forces placed this latest information alongside other intelligence in their possession, their response, surprisingly, was not to proceed into the mountains to pursue the Company, but to immediately and secretly flood 500 federal security people into the province. This was the advance party of a much larger force of several thousand that would begin a massive pacification programme in which they re-arrested all those political activists recently released from prison and began to separate the guerrillas from the local population by interrupting their food supply and setting up ambushes and killing or arresting anyone they suspected of providing support to the Company.

Isolated in his mountain redoubt, and puzzled by the military's apparent unwillingness to pursue him, the plan of "waiting for a greater deterioration in the political situation"—as had been advised by the Cubans—was cast aside. Without consulting the Central Committee of the PRT-ERP, Santucho's forces began leaving the mountains to carry out a series of "armed propaganda actions." Typical, and one of many, was an action taken on May 29th,1974, when more than fifty of his fighters seized the village of Acheral, occupying it for most of the day, setting up road blocks, surrounding the local train station and mounting a heavy machine gun on a nearby roof.

After talking to a few of the assembled local people about their oppression, and distributing leaflets and pamphlets, and painting graffiti on nearby walls, the guerrillas left as quickly as they had arrived. In the following weeks they distributed food and clothes to a few other villages, bought with the money from the Esso kidnapping. In Villa Carmel, they attacked a truck transporting sugar and distributed 400 bags of it to the local population. After each action, they would return to their base in the mountains to continue their grueling training regime.

Just maintaining themselves became very onerous. Continually on the move over rough terrain and sometimes dense jungle, training over long distances with marches many miles long, attempting to familiarize themselves with the area, not staying in any one place for too long nor lighting fires—they did all this while perpetually hungry and eating cold food. Many lost much of their body mass and a few, unable to endure the hardship, ran away. Some told Gutman that after a few months they lost so much weight they had begun to look like skeletons.

In August 1974, orders came from the Party's Central Committee to cease all action and rest up for a while—and to eat well. The instructions were to restore their energy and get ready for a major action that was scheduled to take place fairly soon. A decision had been made to attack a military regiment of almost 1,000 soldiers stationed 200 kilometres away in Catamarca, the Province's capital. At the same time, in a separate operation, they also planned to raid a munitions factory in Villa Maria, near Cordoba, the second largest city in Argentina. Although two of the guerrillas lost their lives, on balance the Villa Maria action was considered a success by the Company, with over a hundred rifles seized, along with fourteen heavy machine guns. (These weapons would be discovered not long after by the police at a farm where they had been hidden.) Regretfully, though, the action in Catamarca ended up in a catastrophic disaster— before the guerrillas had even reached their target.

In the early hours of a Sunday morning in the darkness, approximately fifty armed fighters, mostly youth, waited for several hours in a rented bus on a side road for the signal to approach the base. The group was spotted by two local cyclists who reported them to the police. Six cops quickly showed up and called out to the occupants to identify themselves.

The police began firing at the bus, immediately immobilizing it and forcing the guerrillas to flee by any means. In a desperate scramble, they smashed the bus' windows to escape. Two of the militants were killed. In the darkness and in a confused panic, the surviving ill-trained rebels scattered in all directions, escaping singly or in small groups not knowing where to go, into the strange, surrounding countryside which lacked trees and covering vegetation. A few were able to hijack automobiles to return to their base, but there were no survivors among the remaining thirty fighters. The police were ruthless. The fighters were hunted down and murdered, often while in police custody.

To avenge their deaths, the ERP retaliated with a vigourous campaign of reprisals, with the aim of killing as many military officers as possible through targeted assassinations. A wave of violence swept Argentina's major cities, with the Montoneros joining in. Many extreme right-wing paramilitary groupings, with close links to the security forces, also carried out assassinations for their own ends. They hunted down and killed anyone they suspected of having any sympathy with the PRT-ERP. Many liberal lawyers and judges were murdered, and the army began to publicly press its case to be allowed to take over the campaign in Tucaman. This demand was granted by Isabel Peron, who had become President after the sudden death of her husband, Juan. Their "Operation Independence" was then launched, leading to one of the bloodiest periods in Argentina's history. The objective was not for the army to go into the mountains, but to take over and deepen and broaden the practices begun by the police in isolating the villages from any possible contact with the armed militants—this was accomplished by occupying the villages and implementing a system of terror. Many "suspected" supporters were tortured and murdered.

With the army's direct involvement, Santucho had expected that it would soon ascend the mountains to where it could be defeated in an arena favourable to his forces. But the army had learned a thing or two from other guerrilla struggles around the world—including Cuba's—and was now applying more sophisticated tactics, as had been pointed out in the discussion in the Ninth World Congress, consistent with its policy of keeping the PRT-ERP quarantined. At night, army units would wait patiently in the dark, sometimes all night, in order to ambush anyone who appeared to be searching for supplies. Over the first three months of "Operation Independence," the army claimed 350 guerrillas had either been killed or jailed—probably an exaggeration—but no doubt including the many innocent rural people who had fallen into their clutches. Only four soldiers had died, according to the government, mainly as a result of accidents.

Believing the military leadership feared defeat and lacked the courage to ascend the mountains to meet his forces, Santucho finally made the fateful decision to go down in search of the army in an attempt to defeat them in direct confrontation. With substantial financial resources at his disposal, built up from kidnappings and bank robberies, he issued a call for many more PRT-ERP members to leave the cities and their jobs in the plants to assemble at his base in Tucaman. Grossly underestimating his enemy, he committed a fatal error that would determine the tragic outcome of the struggle. If they will not come to us, we'll go to them, he is reported to have said, and at first it looked like events might be going his way. Not long after, the army suffered many casualties when they accidentally ran into a PRT-ERP armed grouping as it was on its way to attack a military base. Although the guerrillas were forced to flee into nearby canefields to escape, they left twenty-eight soldiers dead from that encounter. By the middle of September, though, over twenty militants had lost their lives in such actions, most of which took place outside Tucaman and in the cities.

Five bombs exploded around Buenos Aires alone, with seven PRT-ERP fighters killed in one incident when a truck they were sitting in exploded. By then the army was on a determined offensive against the guerrillas, expanding its operations into the mountains, including the setting up of a base unknown to the PRT-ERP on a mountain top overlooking the zone the guerrillas controlled so as to observe them. At the same time, the military utilized relatively small squads of specially trained soldiers, much as the PRT-ERP had done, to track them down systematically in a grid pattern, patrolling and laying ambushes in the area.

On December 23, 1975, the PRT-ERP suffered a devastating defeat, paving the way for its ultimate physical elimination. Over seventy of its fighters were massacred in an attack on a military base at Monte Chingalo. Security agents had apparently infiltrated the rebels, helping the army obtain advance notice of their plans. The army was lying in wait. With this debacle, the PRT-ERP in the mountains was reduced to a relatively small handful, and the army moved in quickly to eliminate what remained, tracking down and killing anyone they encountered. A few managed to flee, among them Roberto Santucho, who along with his new companion, Liliano Delfino, were killed in a gunfight with the military in Buenos Aires in early July 1976. The last remaining leader of the campaign in the mountains, Leonel MacDonald, was murdered later that same year. By then the Central Committee of the PRT-ERP had dissolved its armed struggle campaign. In 1979 a few survivors of this failed military struggle made their way to Nicaragua to help the Sandinistas as they got near to taking power, and it was they who killed the hated ex-Nicaraguan dictator Anastasio 'Tachito' Somoza in Paraguay where he had fled by way of Miami.

As the PRT-ERP was being crushed, the army removed Isabel Peron's government from office, installing in her place General Jorge Rafael Videla, who had been in charge of the Tucaman campaign. Videla then began a war of extermination and assassination against anyone who was critical of his rule, ushering in one of the most politically repressive and violent, fascist-like periods in Argentina's history, if not in the entire history of the Americas. Over fifty thousand Argentineans were murdered or "disappeared" in a "Dirty War" against the population that lasted until just after Thatcher's 1982 war in the Malvinas.

The PRT-ERP armed struggle campaign, at its core an ultra-left adventure, was a terrible tragedy for the working class of Argentina. It ended up costing the lives of some of its best sons and daughters, among them its most experienced, smartest and most devoted fighters—a generation of young people who had given their all to bring about a new society. As a result of the wrong policies of the organization to which they had committed themselves, many either lost their lives or spent long years in prison.

It was not a proud moment for the Fourth International, which unfortunately bore some responsibility for what took place. The line of the 1969 Latin American resolution, despite all its problems, still had the support of the IMT and with a few modifications it was reaffirmed at the Tenth World Congress in 1974. The internal struggle between the IMT and the LTF lasted until 1977, with outright splits and expulsions taking place in many of the sections. But by 1976, the majority, to their credit, had begun to reevaluate the guerrilla experience and changed their positions. By 1979, agreement was arrived at in the International to nullify all decisions regarding the guerrilla war strategy, including those adopted in 1969 and 1974.

As Brian Grogan, a leader of the IMG in Britain, wrote in his introduction to the 1979 edition of Pierre Frank's history of the Fourth International[10], the adoption of a "strategy of armed struggle" had been "a serious mistake . . ." Nonetheless, from what I can see there still seems to be a residual ambiguity in the International about the balance sheet of the Argentinean experience. Grogan, in an account that barely mentions the PRT-ERP, claims that it had been a casualty of the factional situation after the Rimini Congress: "In some cases—that of the PRT/ERP in Argentina, for example—the consequence was that the process of homogenization simply did not occur and forces that had been won were subsequently lost."[11] That's a far too mild and anodyne way of stating the problem. The sad reality was that the International's leadership at the time was on the same track as Santucho. From his point of view, he was already "assimilated" and was loyally carrying out the tactics set out in the Latin American resolution. The ultra-left mood had gone deep. Even in Europe, it was so much the zeitgeist of the time that the leaders of the International were compelled to issue a statement stating that the guerrilla line *did not apply* to the advanced capitalist countries. What surprised me most about Pierre Frank's otherwise excellent short study is how much it takes its distance from the Argentineans—whose delegates were the toast of the Ninth Congress—and how minimally he deals with their virtual physical elimination by the Argentine military, relegating it to a brief footnote: "The only serious setback for the Fourth International at this time took place in Argentina. Here the vast majority of the officially recognized section, the PRT (*El Combatiente*), which was not of Trotskyist origin, laid more and more stress on the guerrilla activities of its military wing, the ERP, until it finally withdrew from the Fourth International under Cuban influence."[12] Aside from the comment about it not being "of Trotskyist origin," the notion about "Cuban influence" should now be questioned. As I've shown earlier, the Cubans, at every critical stage, had opposed the PRT-ERP's armed struggle trajectory, and it is hard to see why they would have pressured it into leaving the F.I., if indeed they had any purchase on it at all.

The human toll taken by the political errors of the Fourth International, particularly in Latin America during this period, should be documented and learned from. That is why I have gone to some extent to recount this history in Argentina, and why I strongly recommend Sangre En El Monte, Daniel Gutman's comprehensive history of this terrible experience.

PRT-ERP prepare for attack, 1975 (from "200 Anos de Historia de Argentina," 2010)

TOP *Massacre at Trelew—some of those who were murdered by the military*

BOTTOM *PRT-ERP militants at Tucaman*
  (Both photos from "200 Anos de Historia de Argentina," 2010)

Epilogue

Reflections on Post 60s Life and Politics

H ERE I CONCLUDE THE STORY OF MY EXPERIENCES OF SOCIALIST
activity in the fifties and the sixties. I don't propose to comment
much about the LSA in the years following, except to briefly outline my
own situation. A few months after I returned to Toronto from London,
I withdrew from my leadership position in the LSA, all the while remaining
a member of the organization until the early nineteen-eighties. What
follows is my account of how this came about.

In the few years since Jess and I had been in London, the LSA, although
still small, had more than tripled in size. I especially remember at my
first branch meeting being very pleasantly surprised to see so many
new—at least to me—youthful faces at our Cumberland Street headquarters
in Toronto. Over sixty people would often fill the hall for weekly membership
meetings. The branch was a hive of activity, at the forefront of many
activities in the city. A new youthful leadership had emerged around
Ross, something he had put a lot of effort into developing during his life.

There were good grounds for optimism. Our participation in the anti-
war movement was going strong under the leadership of Joe Young and
we were in a heated debate with the police about a modest proposal to
allow a forthcoming demonstration to fully occupy the street. Like many
other places in North America, we were also in the midst of a struggle
with a grouping of ultra-lefts who wanted the anti-war actions to be
mainly about fighting the police. Women's liberation had emerged as a
major issue for the first time and our female comrades were engaged in
setting up the Toronto Women's Caucus, a mainly "consciousness" raising

group comprised of many women from outside the LSA, focussing on women's social issues and beginning to agitate to legalize abortion. The women published a new journal, *The Velvet Fist*.

The Toronto branch would soon outgrow itself. With a membership of one hundred and fifteen, it divided into "East" and "West" units, each meeting on a different evening of the week at the central headquarters. North of the city, a small branch had been set up in Richmond Hill under the leadership of Bea and George Bryant. All of the Toronto organization was under the administration of a "city-wide" Executive Committee. With sixteen people on staff—if the YS was included—it was the largest the Trotskyist movement had ever been in Canada. Ross Dowson, who was probably more responsible than anyone for this success, had finally realized a long-time dream of having a print shop established in a rented building to produce the organization's publications. It was run by Harry Stone, who had been with me on one of our cross country tours before I had left for Britain.[1]

When I had gone to London in 1965, by my estimate the LSA had about eighty members across the country. By 1969 that had expanded to three hundred, or maybe more. In addition to branches in Toronto and Vancouver, the national leadership was engaged in establishing new ones in Edmonton, Winnipeg, Hamilton and Ottawa, plus a branch in Fredericton, New Brunswick.[2] In Montreal, the Ligue Socialiste Ouvrière (LSO), with Michel Mill, Penny Simpson and Art Young leading it, was publishing *La Lutte Ouvrière*, a French language monthly.

The politics of the country—at a macro level—had also undergone important changes, with a significant rise in the class struggle that could be seen in the spread of strike activity. But the central political challenge to the Canadian state in those years was the drive of the Quebecois for national independence—which we supported—posing the possibility of Quebec's separation from English Canada and the setting up of a new and independent sovereign state. A tiny ultra-left grouping, the Le Front de Liberation du Quebec (F.L.Q), formed in the early Sixties, was still in the news because of carrying out bank hold-ups and planting bombs in especially targeted mail-boxes. The Trudeau Liberal Government would soon use that as a pretext to impose martial law under the War Measures Act, throwing hundreds of activists in jail, including our comrades Penny Simpson and Art Young, and putting a heavy damper on a rising class struggle in the province.

The NDP was also having problems in confronting internal turmoil as a result of the emergence of a left-Canadian nationalist radical opposition in its midst, the "Waffle," led by Cy Gonick, James Laxer and Mel Watkins. By the time I had returned, the Waffle was sponsoring a series of rallies of its supporters across the country in preparation for the Party's October 1969 Convention. The LSA, even though it had initially been taken by surprise by the Waffle phenomenon, was giving the new movement "critical" support, while questioning its Canadian nationalist orientation. The Waffle itself would, within a short time, evolve its own left wing, led by a grouping of young intellectuals, including Varda Burstyn, Jackie Larkin, Steve Penner, Judy Rebick, Wally Seccombe and Brett Smiley, who had come under the influence of the Fourth International, mainly by way of the IMT. According to my comrades in Toronto, this had made it difficult to win them directly to the LSA because of criticisms they had been hearing from this source and because of our "orientation" to the NDP. Many amongst this loose formation would eventually split from the Waffle and form the Revolutionary Communist Tendency, and after a protracted—and sometimes painful discussion, fuse with the LSA.

All in all it was a promising period for the ideas of revolutionary socialism and it helped to explain why our group was growing so fast. And what of my fate? Not long after I got back to Toronto, I met with Ross, anxious to find out what role the Political Committee had in mind for me now that my assignment to Britain had come to an end. At the Congress in Rimini, he and I had had a couple of disagreements about the China and Latin American discussions. He hadn't been too pleased that, on the final vote, I had abstained on the China resolution, seeming to think I should have somehow consulted with him beforehand. But for me it was no big deal. I didn't consider myself part of a "tendency"—certainly none had been declared—because we were still in the early stages of the discussion and the lines as far as I was concerned had not yet hardened. My view was that we needed more discussion about the character of the Chinese CP and to what degree was it "Stalinist," especially in light of what seemed to be its left criticisms of Moscow. And although the differences about the new rural guerrilla war line were sharp, I was firmly convinced that many in the world movement had yet to even read the documents—many had not even been translated—and that the discussion out of necessity would continue for some time into the future, until the issue ran its course. The discussion would not be helped, I had felt, by either deliberately or accidentally hardening the lines. As we all knew from experience this would only have served to prevent the various points of view, especially ours, from getting a proper airing.

While Ross did not speak from the floor in the debates at the Congress, I noticed that in conversations and amongst those who had supported the counter-position to the majority resolution, he always appeared to be hell-bent on heating things up, with his sharp comments and negative characterizations of the other side. Long before organized tendencies had even been declared, he seemed to be getting into a factional mode that I thought would be less than helpful. When at one point I cautioned him about some of his outbursts, he retorted that I had obviously been in Europe too long and that I was "soft" on the Europeans. Wait until we get him back to Toronto, I overheard him tell an American delegate, we'll straighten him out!

In reality, though, the main disagreement between him and me was that he hadn't been very pleased with my decision to return to Canada. "As you know we were very anxious that Ernie should have stayed on in England," he would later write to Ernest Mandel. "I went to England several days in advance of the WC in hopes of influencing him that way. However, much to my surprise, when I arrived I found that matter had been decided beyond all reconsideration. He had already shipped off his personal effects by boat."[3]

I remember at the time it had been a bit of a puzzle to me as to why he had been so upset, because Alan and Connie Harris had arrived in London from Canada to replace Jess and me—to run Pioneer Books Service and do whatever else was required to help the Section, something that the United Secretariat had already agreed to. It was as if Jess and I hadn't received "official" permission—whatever that might mean—to return to Canada. Apparently up until then the news that we were returning had not quite registered with Ross, even though I had notified him of that well in advance—at least a year earlier—so that if the LSA was going to continue with the assignment, it could plan for a replacement. That was my understanding of why Alan and Connie were in London. And it was certainly their understanding as well, because they had not been too happy about leaving Canada.

When Ross got to London he kept insisting to me that if I remained there, he "thought" there would be enough money to help finance me. He wouldn't be more specific than that. After my experiences of how he had dealt with such matters in the past, I simply no longer took him at his word about what he "thought," and his appeals about "letting the side down" no longer carried much weight either. If I did not return, Ruth Tate would be left more or less on her own to carry the financial burden of raising our son, Michael; this fact, astonishingly had never even entered Ross' calculations. But I was not about to be dissuaded from returning to Toronto. My mind was fully made up. By then, Jess and I had to borrow money from the book service to make ends meet.

We wanted to return to Canada in a hurry so that we could each find jobs and pay off our personal debts, part of which was the money that I had borrowed from Richard Fidler, to help with Michael's support. In addition, we were both very tired to the point of burnout, another point to which Ross seemed somewhat oblivious. As far as I was concerned, we had worked very hard since we had gotten to London, and I felt we needed a little bit of time to recharge our batteries. Like many who work full-time in the revolutionary movement, we had just about depleted all of our resources and had even neglected our health in the bargain. A small detail, for example: neither of us had seen a dentist since leaving Canada. I'm sure part of Ross' motivation in trying to persuade me to change my plans was that he was anticipating that the political differences expressed in the World Congress would deepen— he wasn't wrong about that—and he was on a kind of mission to strengthen in London those forces who were partial to the North Americans' views in the developing debate about armed struggle in Latin America.

By the time I got back to Toronto, however, I thought I had put those small disagreements with Ross behind me. This is not to say it had not affected my evaluation of him as a leader. By then I had begun to see in a new and less benign light his unreliability in regards to financial matters and his seeming indifference to my personal concerns about why I had to return to Canada. I was getting a new insight into his personality and a new appreciation of his bull-headedness in manipulating others to fit in with his plans. Nevertheless, I had no serious political differences with him—or the rest of the Political Committee—and was totally committed to building the LSA. As a member of the National Committee and the PC—a position I retained the whole time I was in Britain—I still considered myself to be one of the leaders of the organization. I was certainly one of the more experienced members, and I was fully expecting when I returned to continue being part of its leadership.

When I met with Ross, I again repeated my financial concerns, but I told him I was prepared to take on whatever the PC had in mind for me. But I was startled when he very quickly replied—without me having raised it in the first place—that there were absolutely no resources to put me on staff. But he thought it possible, he told me, that I might head up one of the defence committees the LSA was involved in, and that I would be able to use that position to raise sufficient funds for my support. This was a not too subtle brush-off by him, as far as I was concerned. Having been away from Toronto for many years and not knowing the lay of the land, it would have meant a very uncertain economic future for me indeed. But I understood very clearly the underlying message: things had changed for some reason or other and I was on my own; he no longer considered me to be part of the "team."

I must admit, however, that I didn't protest too much. I found it a kind of relief in the end because it meant that I would be able to concentrate on finding a job. I told him I would let him know later whether I would take up his proposal. I immediately understood what was implied and couldn't help but feel a sense of betrayal. It's not that I was necessarily looking forward to working full time again for the organization, but Ross' reaction to me, alongside the strange guardedness I had begun to detect in the attitude towards me of a few leading comrades whom I had known for a long time before going to London, alerted me to the fact that something else might be going on with him and that my status in the organization was not the same as when I had left. Many months later, in a December 16, 1969 letter to Ernest Mandel, obviously in response to questions from him about me, Ross would say, "we offered to take him on staff, however he said that he did not want that and sought postponement of any serious leadership commitment for 6 months."[4] Ernest, of course, was in no position to know it, but what Ross wrote was at variance with the facts.

Not long after that conversation, I got into a new dispute with Ross about the LSA's plans to enter the forthcoming 1969 Toronto municipal elections. It was during a preliminary discussion on the PC, and it did nothing to improve my relations with him because he took the matter so personally. In the initial discussions about the election, it seemed to me that there was an automatic assumption on everyone's part that we would again have Ross head up our ticket for Mayor, as he had done many times before. When I raised a question about this, it was as if I had kicked over a hornet's nest, because Ross took my remarks to be some kind of personal attack. My point had been that Ross, who had been our candidate for Mayor in virtually every municipal election since the Second World War, could easily be dismissed out of hand by the media as being but one of those kinds of "perennial" crank, odd-ball candidates, of whom there were usually several in each election. Perhaps we should run someone else, I had ventured.

I got no support from other PC members and didn't put a motion on the table to change candidates, but Ross rejected the idea out of hand, so we moved on to other business. Every so often in the ensuing weeks after that discussion, I noticed, whenever I happened to be in the headquarters, he would regale me and others with reports of this or that person who had dropped by the bookstore to tell him how much they had appreciated his running for Mayor in the past and were asking him if he was running again. But the idea of an alternative to him had by then begun to take hold in the organization. In the October municipal elections of that year, the LSA ran John Riddell for Mayor, and very soon, in an unrelated change, Richard Fidler became editor of the *Workers Vanguard*, which not long after that became *Labour Challenge*.

That's when I resigned from the Political Committee. I'd had enough by then. I had been around long enough to know when most of the discussion about the business at hand has already taken place—somewhere else and without me—and that the meetings have become a kind of formality. That's what was happening on the LSA-PC, with absolutely no justification, politically or otherwise, as far as I was concerned. I had no disagreements with the political positions of the LSA, on Canada or internationally, but Ross, in his own none too subtle way, was quarantining me. The last straw for me was when a vote of my abstention that I had specifically asked to be recorded—on a resolution on China from the International Secretariat—was deliberately expunged from the record of the meeting. When I eventually saw the minutes of the meeting and noticed its absence, I protested vociferously, of course, but as the other PC members just sat there impassively listening to him, Ross tried to justify his action by saying that the "abstention" would not be "understood" in Europe or in New York. Then, adding insult to injury, the meeting voted to accept the minutes "as read" over my objections.

That was enough for me and I declared I was quitting the Political Committee forthwith, a body I had been a member of since the fifties. And when the annual branch conference rolled around not long after that, I dared to test the leadership's attitude towards me again by standing against the "official slate" for the Executive Committee of the branch, that is, the slate which the "outgoing" Committee was proposing. I was defeated, of course, after Ross and the Toronto branch leadership in secret meetings caucused against me to ensure that their "slate" would be elected, by surreptitiously putting the word out that I should be kept off. It was a pathetic manoeuvre by him and those who headed up the branch, but a sort of test for me because Ross was letting me know who was boss.

Even my partner, Jess MacKenzie, became a victim of this kind of petty factionalism around this time. When the Toronto branch was looking for someone to take over the operation of our bookstore on Cumberland Street, Jess, obviously one of the more politically experienced people, had thought it was something she would like to do. She was certainly well qualified for the position. Aside from her political work in London, she had run our Pioneer Book Service very effectively and efficiently. And, before going to London, she had been National Treasurer of the Young Socialists, and had worked in the business office of a major telephone company. She seemed to have the qualifications and in good faith had told the branch organizer she was prepared to take it on. Incredibly, she was turned down flat because she "lacked experience"! Someone with a lot less experience was given the position. The rejection of Jess was a loss for the organization, and shameful, especially in the way it had taken place.

Jess and I still remained active in the Toronto branch, helping out where we could. Having been away from Canada for a while, getting a regular job hadn't been easy but within a couple of weeks I was working at my trade again, on shift work in a crummy little steam plant in Toronto's north end, mainly in order to acquire some kind of job history so that I could find a better position somewhere else. Most importantly, Jess and I had begun to pay off our debts. And within a few months I had managed to land a job in the largest meat-packing plant in the country, Canada Packers in Toronto's west end. It was so big it stretched over several city blocks, a plant that slaughtered over three thousand head of cattle and five thousand pigs each day and where its approximately three thousand workers were in the Packinghouse Workers Union. The plant's union Local was under the control of a few left social democrats in the NDP, but had a reputation for militancy. The bulk of the workforce was immigrant, non-English speaking, I remember, with many from Macedonia—a result of the personnel office being headed up by a Macedonian, I later found out. It was a good place to work with one of the largest Locals in the city and it gave me a chance to get back into union activity.

I had been in the union, the UPWA, before then, in a flour mill for a short period in the fifties, and strangely enough it was as if time itself had been frozen since then, because a goodly number of the militants I had known earlier were still active in the union. After a few meetings we became reacquainted. Within a few months I had become the union steward for the department that ran the plant's giant refrigeration system where most of the engineers worked. One of the first challenges I confronted was a raid by the International Union of Operating Engineers, a craft union that was trying to carve the Engineers out of our bargaining unit. I was able to help the Local's leadership turn this around and eventually the raid failed, and this increased my stature among the Local's activists. Although I didn't realize it at the time, the meat packing industry in Toronto was on the verge of a massive restructuring that would see most packing plants re-located out of the city to western Canada where the cattle were raised and wages were substantially lower.

In reality, I didn't really mind being active in the union and no longer on staff for our group. That's when I began to think that because I would be working at my trade the rest of my life, I should look into the possibility of upgrading my technical qualifications, if only just to make it easier for me to find a job, should the need arise. I proceeded to do this taking evening courses while on shift-work. Upgrading work skills was not an unusual practice in our group when I had first joined it; we operated on the assumption that eventually the bulk of our membership would be based in industry and we always advised our members to try and improve their skills and bump into better paying jobs. This policy would be forgotten by the end of the decade when we and our American co-thinkers, in anticipation of a "deep crisis" in the economy and a rise of class consciousness in the working class, began our disastrous "turn to industry."

During this first couple of years, unavoidably my contact with the International in Europe was severely reduced, even though I was still a member of the International Control Commission that had been elected at the World Congress. Gisela Mandel, Ernest's wife, and Ray Sparrow were its other members. This Commission, in those days, was elected at World Congresses and was supposed to be made up of experienced comrades of mature judgment, capable of looking in an impartial way into such issues as accusations and charges of a moral and ethical nature, especially against leaders of the movement. While I was on it, it was called upon a couple of times—with the agreement of both International tendencies—to go to Britain. The first time was to deal with allegations that the leadership of the Section was "oppressing" the minority; the second time was to investigate a moral question involving the alleged actions of one Section's leader against another. In the first case, the factionalism in Britain had gotten so bad I remember that at one point, accusations had been aired about an incident involving a photograph of the American SWP's Joe Hansen that, disgracefully, had been used as a dart-board at a gathering of the group's members in a pub. I undertook the trip at a terrible time in Britain. It was during a power workers' strike and frequently power blackouts just about shut down everything. It was very cold—even in our hotels—as Gisela, Ray and I travelled the country interviewing people about what had gone on in the Section. We all ended up with heavy colds. In that instance, we found the Section's majority had behaved badly towards its minority and we issued a long report to that effect.[5]

Regarding the "moral" question, it turned out to be a very sad occasion for me becoming something of a cautionary tale. The Commission was called upon to look into charges that Pat Jordan, who by then was heading up a minority tendency in the IMG, had been guilty of outrageous and irresponsible personal conduct towards the Section's then leader, John Ross, who also was a member of the United Secretariat. Ross had raised the very grave accusation against Pat in the Secretariat that Pat had instigated a personal and reprehensible attack on him which, aside from everything else, had also endangered his personal security and the security of his family.

John Ross had reported to the Secretariat that one evening at his home he had received a series of very strange phone calls asking his wife for sexual favours. Apparently these kinds of obnoxious calls had continued for a period of time until finally Ross managed to engage one of the callers in conversation; eventually the person revealed to John that he had seen his phone number on the wall of a public toilet at Liverpool Street railway station with a message offering free sex. When Ross and other leaders of the group hurried over to investigate, they saw the offensive graffiti scrawled on the wall, in what they concluded was Pat Jordan's handwriting. They photographed it, of course. When confronted with the accusation and the photographs, Pat vehemently denied he had anything to do with the matter, saying the handwriting was not his. When Gisela, Ray and I saw the photos and compared them to Pat's handwriting, all of us were convinced that the writing was certainly Pat's. Of course, I had seen Pat's writing many times before then and had no difficulty whatsoever in making my mind up, even though I thought it to be totally out of character of the mild mannered person I had known a few years earlier. It's unbelievable where factionalism can lead, I thought to myself. I felt terrible, thinking that probably Pat had been out drinking one evening and had gotten carried away by his hostility to Ross. I'm pretty certain our report was unanimous and that we recommended sanctions be taken against him, including his removal from his positions in the leadership bodies of the organization.

Looking back at the matter these many years later, I recall how all of us on the Commission, when we saw the photographs, were a hundred percent certain that it was Pat's writing. We were all familiar with his very distinctive handwriting. What's amazing is that, for some reason, we never even met with Pat personally, nor did we discuss the possibility that the whole thing might have been a provocation arranged by the British security forces against the group. Looking back on it now, that was the least we owed someone who had given their all to the movement, who had helped bring it into existence and had led it for so many years. So much for our thoroughness and bringing some justice to the situation!

Hindsight can of course be twenty-twenty, but Barry Sheppard raised that possibility with me when we talked about the Pat Jordan case recently. We should never let our guard down or underestimate the sophistication and ability of the security forces to disrupt the socialist movement, he said. The SWP's victorious legal suit against the FBI provided ample evidence of this. They have a vast array of "black bag tricks" at their disposal for such purposes; they certainly had the capacity and the capability of faking Pat Jordan's writing in a very convincing way on a lavatory wall, enough to fool even those of us who had been at one time his closest comrades. There'll always remain a doubt in my mind about the matter. John Ross and his supporters would later go on to "enter" the Labour Party and break from the International; Ross became a political advisor and assistant to Ken Livingstone. When Livingstone was elected Mayor of London, John became the city's head of transportation.

While I was still a supporter of the LTF internationally and was critical of the way things were going with the Fourth International in Europe , I had developed a few reservations about the LSA in Toronto, aside from how I had been treated. I was beginning to feel that we were perhaps making mistakes in how we were going about things. For example, I objected to the notion that somehow the LSA was now "a revolutionary party", a term that seemed to be used more and more to define ourselves, rather than a more modest characterization such as "propaganda group". My criterion for a "revolutionary party" was the standard Marxist one: it had to be a mass organization and have some important connections to the working class. I felt that we were trying to leap over the hard fact, a form of self-delusion really, that we were still a small group with a membership of only a few hundred people. At one point, Ross Dowson wasn't very pleased with me when I expressed these views during a talk I gave to a branch meeting, telling me that the fact the LSA had "a revolutionary programme and a history" meant that we were indeed such a party, or at least the "embryo" of such a thing.[6] To which I retorted that only history would decide if that was the case.

In addition, I had begun to develop reservations about the large resources the organization was then putting into its physical and organizational infrastructure. By then we had a professional staff for an organization many times our size—Ross' concept of building the "skeleton" of a revolutionary party to which the masses would later provide the flesh—and a couple of large rented headquarters. These included a large Victorian home in the centre of the city for the Young Socialists, and another that we were in the process of moving into, a small building of several stories on Queen Street near Spadina avenue—with lots of space for offices on the upper floors and a large sized meeting hall on the ground floor, all behind a bookstore. We ended up pouring many thousands of dollars into that project, renovating the building, constructing a bookstore and offices and re-enforcing its floors so that we could move our print shop there, which Ross insisted upon over everyone's objections, including comrades such as George Bryant who was in charge of the renovations. Ross' rationale was that a time might come when commercial printers would no longer print our paper because of a prohibition or pressure from the security forces.

But think about it for a minute. If there was to be such a crisis where the state for some reason or other would be clamping down on the left, would the authorities observe the niceties of allowing us to print our paper, even in our own printshop? No matter the rationale, as far as I was concerned, we seemed hell-bent on creating a mini-version of the American SWP. This included the purchase of land on the banks of the Salmon River, near Belleville, Ontario—what became known as Camp Poundmaker—and the construction of buildings for lecture space and sleeping facilities, where educational activity took place every summer and where many of our members spent their summer vacations. Coming back from Britain, I was unaware of the logic of why this was taking place, but it all seemed to be happening at a frenetic pace. It was difficult to discuss the issue without seeming to be challenging Ross' authority as he drove the project onward. I learned later that many others had similar reservations about how he was carrying on, and that this may even have played a part in their thinking a few years later when they changed the leadership of the organization.

Not long after all this, Ross began to develop important differences with the rest of the leadership of the LSA about Canadian nationalism. If Quebec could be seen as having the status of an internal colony in Canada, he came to believe the "same could be said of Canada as a whole" in relation to the United States.[7] And with the growing mood of anti-Americanism in the country, primarily a by-product of the Vietnam War, he had begun to advocate a new policy for the organization—"to meet the challenge of the anti-imperialist sentiment developing in an anti-Canadian capitalist direction"—in which he saw the "new Canadian nationalism" as being "unique in the world" and "essentially progressive." Such a policy, if it had been adopted, would have certainly been a major departure for us. Our traditional position had been to regard the ideology of Canadian nationalism as reactionary and to see the Canadian ruling class as "junior partners" of the American ruling class. In light of the rise of neo-liberalism, and from what we know today, I would amend that position to delete the "junior" part.

Ross, at that time, also took exception to the modification of our orientation towards the NDP, saying that "criticisms of the NDP leadership's policies have been unrealistic and exaggerated." His positions received very little traction in the organization, however, and by February 1974, he and his eighteen supporters—the "Labour Party Tendency"—had walked out.[8] There was no justification for the split, as I told him at the time, when he and I met to talk it over. "My people are walking away and I'm trying to save the cadre," was his excuse, but as far as I was concerned, his split was totally unprincipled and it was sad to see him throw away his hard won legacy so readily. There was no reason the discussion could not have continued, but being in a minority had obviously become intolerable for him. He proceeded to set up the "Socialist League" that later became the "Forward Group," and which for a while published a journal. Ross would be cut down by a debilitating stroke in 1988, from which he never recovered, dying in 2002. More than anyone else during some of the Fourth International's most difficult times in Canada, he had—sometimes almost single-handedly, and out of the sheer force of his will—been responsible for its survival and continuity. He touched all of our lives.

As for me, I remained with the organization until the end of the decade. It's not my intention to provide a detailed history of its evolution here, but it closely paralleled the trajectory of the SWP in those years, which is very well documented by Barry Sheppard in his memoir.[9] I would only add that an important element in its decline had to be due to the severe weakening of the hard earned political authority of the International in the thinking of the American and Canadian leaders, a sad byproduct of the long and acrimonious debate that had lasted for almost a decade. In essence, we never recovered from that crisis. I saw a sign of that a few years before the SWP broke from the International. I was talking to Mary-Alice Waters about what was happening in Europe, and she seemed to be indifferent about its difficulties, a striking departure from the time of Joe Hansen and Ray Sparrow. The influence of the International as a corrective factor in the SWP's thinking, that necessary dispassionate and comradely examination of its policies from the outside that in its better days had been the International's strength—part of the reason for having an International in the first place—had become so severely degraded as to be almost non-existent.

That was only one factor in its decline, and maybe not the most important. My last major activity with the group was in helping to implement the "turn to industry," a policy that had been largely inspired by the SWP and which we had adopted on the false assumption that the North American economy was entering a deep crisis and that we would now be confronted with a period of ascending class struggles. The evidence the SWP pointed to for this "turn" was the rise of opposition slates in many of the major unions, such as the Sadlowski campaign in the Steelworkers and major rank and file opposition caucuses in the Teamsters. The idea behind the "turn" was to get ourselves into a position to participate in the "coming class battles," as we liked to say then, or, in the words of the SWP's Jack Barnes, when the workers would storm out of the factories with their red flags flying. But our analysis of the economic conjuncture proved to be sadly wrong and, as far as I'm concerned, the beginning of our political difficulties. Instead, the North American economy entered one of the longest periods of growth in its history that would eventually see the fall of the Soviet Union and the expansion of capitalism into China and Eastern Europe, something we North Americans were woefully late in recognizing.

Regarding the "turn to industry," I would like to say that I was critical of it and foresaw the problems we would confront. But, unfortunately, that would not be true. While I was a little uncomfortable with the do-or-die approach of how the line was being applied—I would have preferred, I remember, a more pragmatic approach to increasing our forces in industry—I must confess that I was fully and even enthusiastically behind the line. I worked hard to get our people prepared for implementing it, many of whom, especially our women comrades, had only ever worked in offices. I can't remember how many of our members we pulled off the campuses, but many were persuaded to abandon their careers as teachers and professionals—in one case a veterinarian, for example—and get jobs in factories.

It wasn't only the rank and file of the organization who applied the new line. A few main leaders of the organization, intellectuals who had worked on staff, also went into the factories—in order to set an example. One thing about the LSA: once it had decided on something, it blasted ahead to implement it in a very vigourous way. For example, twice a week in the evenings during the initial phase, I helped organize gatherings of those who were considering "making the turn." I would help them practice such basic procedures as putting together an employment resume, and show them how to use small tools and such elementary things as how to fasten a bit into a hand-drill. These lessons were so that they would have at least a minimum of familiarity with tools when they showed up for their first day on the job.

It was difficult for us, at first, to carry out the turn, but soon we began to have success, at least in getting jobs. For example, early on we managed to establish a sizable fraction of over thirty people in Douglas Aircraft, a plant organized by the UAW and one of the largest industrial employers in the city. But that didn't last very long, because, to my increasing annoyance, most of our newly minted aircraft workers were soon pulled out of the plant and assigned to go into the garment industry, primarily because the SWP in New York was doing that. Whatever the rationale for what the Americans were doing, it made utterly no sense in Toronto, as far as I was concerned. Most of the garment factories in the city were unorganized at the time with their workforces made up of non-English speaking, recent immigrants, mainly Vietnamese, and almost no union activity there. As anyone with a grain of sense understands, newly arrived immigrants, although often cruelly exploited, in the main do not provide the best fodder for militant activity. In fact, there had been very little history in those years of these garment workers struggling to improve their conditions. The new LSA line, however, evolved to the position, as if we were a mass party, that we had to be "where the most oppressed are," instead of where there was a possibility of some militant trade union activity and the likelihood of recruitment, a serious issue for a small propaganda group such as ours.

In addition, I soon found out that the leadership of the group—at least those who were faithfully following the SWP line—was also advising our people to stay clear of such elementary trade union activity as standing for a shop steward's position, for example, or running for office on the Local's executive. They even had a policy against our members improving their own job situation and perhaps increasing their pay by bumping into more skilled positions, something most ordinary workers do when they get a job in a plant. The LSA now considered getting a trade to be "joining the most privileged layers" in the plant. It was a kind of madness. It ran against the grain of everything we had ever done in the unions before. The new line meant we were not prepared to participate in the unions as they were, but to wait for some kind of ideal situation to arise—

sometime in the future—when there would be a rise in class consciousness that would help us overthrow the existing union bureaucracy.

Although I did not see it at the time, I'm now convinced it was a line that helped lead to the destruction of the organization. It couldn't be maintained because we were setting our members impossible tasks. As a consequence, many good people simply walked away from us. And when those comrades in industry complained to the group's leadership about the problems with the line, they were told that *they* were the problem. Not long after that the organization changed its name to the Communist League (CL) and ceased publishing a Canadian journal, using *The Militant* instead, thus becoming a virtual extension into Canada of the American SWP. The CL began to disparage everyone else on the left outside the organization as "petit-bourgeois."

On the anti-war front, furthermore, contrary to our policy at the time of the Vietnam era, when the Iraq invasion was underway the CL became notorious on the left for its non-participation in the anti-war movement and even its hostility to it, characterizing the massive demonstrations in Britain and Canada against the Iraq War as being mainly "patriotic" and "anti-American." Severely reduced by loss of members, the CL was finally forced to close down its main branches in Toronto and Vancouver; today it only exists in Montreal where it runs a bookshop, really a distribution point for the SWP's Pathfinder Books, but I'll leave it to someone else to provide more details about how this came about.

As for me, I remained active with my union in various leadership positions. And at the end of the nineties I had the privilege of being part of a very successful, united front campaign against the privatization of Ontario's electricity system. It turned out to be one of the few successes of the labour movement in those years, delivering a crippling blow to the province's neo-liberal Tory government. Jess and I to this day consider ourselves to be revolutionary socialists. We continue to participate wherever we can in promoting fundamental change in our society.

Isaac and Tamara Deutscher, Isaac Deutscher Archives, IISH, Amsterdam

Appendix 1

Transcript of Speeches, Isaac Deutscher
Memorial Meeting, Mahatma Gandhi Hall,
September 22, 1967, London

Chair Ralph Miliband
Speakers Daniel Singer, David Horowitz, Perry Anderson,
Marcel Liebman, K.S. Karol and Lawrence Daly.

RALPH MILIBAND
Ladies and gentlemen, we are meeting tonight to pay tribute to Isaac
Deutscher, the man and his work, but I should like to say at once, that
we do not propose to turn this meeting simply into a meeting of lamentation.
Of course, all of us in this hall and many people, many people outside,
deeply mourn in a bitter and personal way, the tragic and premature
death of one who was an inspiration and example to so many. But I think
I may say that Isaac Deutscher himself would not have wished this simply
to be a meeting of lamentation and eulogy alone, if at all.

What we must try and do, what we propose to do, is in paying tribute
to him and his work, we vote to set the meaning and content of that
work, and the contribution it has made to that cause which to him was
dearer than any other, the strengthening, the resuscitation almost, of an
international socialist movement, and it is this spirit that I hope we may
see in this meeting. Before calling upon those on the platform to address
you, I should like to read two messages which I have received, one from

Bertrand Russell, a message written at the time of Isaac Deutscher's death for the *Bulletin of the Bertrand Russell Foundation*, and which he has asked should be read at this memorial meeting. It goes as follows:

"The respect which I have felt for Isaac Deutscher, originated in an appreciation of his scholarship. It was enriched greatly by my acquaintance with the man. As an historian he was outstanding. His works on the Russian Revolution are a monumental achievement. He was able to show the glory of that Revolution whilst never entering into the conspiracy of concealment of its defects which many western socialists considered necessary. His independence was always repellant to orthodoxy. Isaac Deutscher allowed himself to be used by no one. His acute criticisms of the Communist powers could not be exploited in the propaganda of the Cold War, for he embodied profoundly humane convictions which disturbed the complacency of the West by uncovering the barbarities so inexorably linked to its affluence. I associated with him every value which inspired the International War Crimes Tribunal. It is fitting that he was the first to accept membership of the tribunal. The death of Isaac Deutscher is a severe blow to all who are interested in finding the truth in international politics. His scholarship was careful and impeccable. At the same time, his opinions were those of a man whose feelings are right and just. The combination is rare. Still rarer was the determination to act upon those beliefs unhesitatingly. He, in whom those qualities were combined, will not easily be replaced."

And the other message is from Professor E.H. Carr, who writes:

"I am afraid I shall be away at the time of the memorial meeting, otherwise I should very much have liked to be there. I have known Isaac very well for more than twenty years. It is not the kind of occasion on which one would talk about personal relations, but I would like to say a few words about him in his capacity as a historian of the USSR, for he was a great deal more than a biographer of some of its leading figures. I do not know any writer on the subject, who seems to me to have thrown so much light on it, and I have constantly learned from his writings as well as from his criticisms, published and unpublished, of my own. And there is no one with whose views on the subject I have found myself so closely in agreement. It is a terrible loss that his career should have been cut short and that we shall not have his crowning biography of Lenin. This is an irreparable loss, particularly in a field where well informed and balanced judgment is so rare."

All the people on this platform knew Isaac Deutscher, some of them extremely closely for many years. He was their mentor and friend. The first person I should like to call upon to address you is Daniel Singer, the London correspondent, the Paris correspondent of *The Economist*, who stood in relation to him in a manner as close as that as a member of the family.

DANIEL SINGER
Because I had the great privilege of knowing Isaac Deutscher all my conscious life, I have been asked to tell you something about the man behind the brilliant writer, the great historian, the socialist thinker and fighter. I must confess that at first I was rather worried. Personal grief is something one hides or expresses in a small circle of friends, and then I remembered a passage in his biography in which he refers to Trotsky as essentially a political man, obviously the whole monumental Trilogy shows that Trotsky was a man of blood and flesh. Similarly all those who knew Isaac Deutscher can tell you how humane and warm-hearted he was. Besides, born when he was and where he was, he did not storm the Winter Palace, or lead the Red Army, and yet his other life, too, was shaped essentially by his political convictions. This is what I shall now try to show how quite apart from his writings and his exceptional gifts, I think Deutscher's life too has a meaning and a message, here and everywhere for people of mine, and younger and future, generations. True, he was born sixty years ago near Krakow, in a peculiar community that is no longer, the Jewish community of Eastern Europe, wiped out by Hitler. Oppressed and respectful of learning, that community provided more than its share of children for the revolutionary struggle. It provided Rosa Luxemburg and a good proportion of the Bolshevik leadership. But we should not idealize this east European Jewry. It had its class and social

differences, its religious fanaticism and superstitions. Only this can explain why a man like Isaac's father, a cultured well-to-do printer, an admirer of Heine and LaSalle, allowed his son to betray the Talmud. How Isaac's religious career ended at the age of thirteen, most of you probably know, but the story is worth telling again, because it shows in the child the spirit of the man. To check his growing doubts about the existence of God, he picked the night of a Jewish holiday to bravely swallow his ham sandwich and his beers. Young Isaac was already defying the Gods. He was going to be a great poet, mystical to start with, then a Futurist; he showed such promise in his teens that quickly he became the star of tomorrow, but already he felt crowded by his environment. He then travelled to the capital. It was in Moscow, in my very home, that the young poet came in contact with Marxist socialists. The young man was rightfully changed. Only recently he described how impatient he then was to change the world. Brought up amid collapsing empires and crowded societies and with problems and social upheavals within primitive capitalist societies, where socially, amid changing worlds, he was not going to cultivate a garden, accepting passively the world and its doom. He was going to fight with others to change it. The rebel became a revolutionary.

Isaac Deutscher joined the Communist Party. There he found an outlet for his talents and energy in both illegal and semi-legal fashion, carrying out propaganda in the army, lecturing and preparing pamphlets, the young man was rapidly climbing the party ladder. But already then, socialism was, for him, inseparable from respect for man and that, all but true, the Stalinist disease was spreading beyond Russia's frontiers, a violent campaign was being waged against Trotsky. The issues at stake were important ones, including an assessment of the rise of Nazism, the young Deutscher was not content with just looking at the indictment— he read avidly both sides of the case. In 1932, he was expelled from the Party and became one of the leaders of the Trotskyist opposition. There followed several years of difficult propaganda, but also of learning. Tipping, shaken by his expulsion, Deutscher read from the sources of classical Marxism to test his convictions. It was then that he studied Das

Kapital so thoroughly and emerged from the discovery with thinking
that he now dominated much vaster horizons.

Incidentally, in recent years he was puzzled by his British critics. I am
thinking particularly of many clowns performing on television and in the
Sunday papers. They were wondering how such an intelligent man could
cling to such an old-fashioned doctrine. Deutscher was puzzled because
he could not understand how men born after Copernicus could still harbor
a belief in an astronomy in terms of Ptolemy. Marxism was not for Deutscher
a new term for abstract disputation and youthful quotations. It was very
much a challenging and critical method. Nor was it a fatalistic doctrine.
It was, for the oppressed, an instrument of the struggle for the transformation
of the world and of man. "Stalin" was not his first work. Deutscher, who
was publishing pamphlets and a short-lived magazine, also wrote his first
major work then, a history of Poland, but as the police were knocking at
the door of our flat where Isaac was then living, his manuscript had to
be burnt in the kitchen. The police were shutting down his network and
Hitler's army was closing in. Deutscher, the internationalist, felt the need
for a larger stage. In 1939, he came to this country. War soon broke out.
He felt terribly lonely in this strange town. It was only a year or so later
that he was to meet Tamara. Tamara, who until the very end was going
to be his companion, his critic and his collaborator; Tamara was going to
help him in the hours of tension and solitude.

Meanwhile, the Polish government in exile sent this subversive corporal
Deutscher to a distant disciplinary camp in Scotland. He was to have been
moved from there, thanks to his pen. The future master of English prose
was still struggling with the language, but his analytical power was sufficient
to impress the editor of *The Economist*. His journalistic performance in
The Economist, in *The Observer* but also in *The Tribune,* was public
knowledge. One day I hope somebody will write about this wartime revolutionary on Fleet Street. What I want to mention here is that Deutscher
remained true to himself. One illustration will be enough. He told me
that during the war his only difficulties from *The Observer* were connected
with his criticisms of the Soviet Union. Because of the struggle of the

Russian people, he was not going to forget those in the concentration camps, quite the contrary. A few years later during the Cold War and after, the very same people were calling Deutscher an apologist for Russia.

From journalism he turned to writing books. The choice of biography was, in a sense, accidental. What mattered was to reach a fairly wide public with his message about Russia. It mattered to him as a socialist to give a balanced view of the first workers' state. It was important to remind people that the nationalization of the means of production was a necessary but not a sufficient condition for establishing socialism. It was important to treat the Soviet Union as a species of its own in post capitalist society since this was the only way in which Marxist tools of analysis could be applied to its performance. It was vital in the Machiavellian days of the Cold War that somebody should write about the caricature of the workers' paradise or land of slaves. How important it was, we got some idea in the period of disillusionment following Khrushchev's superficial indictment. Others will tell you how Deutscher, the historian, accomplished this indispensable task. I just want to mention two points. They both show about...
[1] the first, once again, is the respect for truth in all its complexity. It would have been easy to describe Stalin as just as the gravedigger of the revolution. For a man of Deutscher's background, it required much greater effort to describe him in Marxist terms as the product of primitive socialist accumulation. Similarly, Trotsky had Deutscher's full sympathy and admiration, but he did not write about him like a socialist realist or about Stalin as a Catholic would write about a pope. He showed his greatness and his tragedy in the gap between theory and practice and his hero's super-human effort to close that gap. The second point, the books show is Deutscher's basic optimism. Look once again at the monumental trilogy with its beautiful balanced sentences, reflecting a balanced analysis. In its subtle construction, the final chapter, "Victory in Defeat," echoes the earlier "Defeat in Victory." True, like his hero, Deutscher would have stood on the side of the wretched, even if their struggle had been hopeless. But he did not think that it was hopeless. Oh, he had no magic formula, neither magic short cuts, nor a secret timetable. His faith rested on his belief in

man who ultimately would choose socialism rather than madness and suicide. He kept this deep conviction throughout a terrible period, a terrible interlude, he kept it in years of despair when revolutionaries were in Stalin's concentration camps, in years of contempt when Nazi order raged over Europe, in years of disenchantment, when the West seemed to have entirely forgotten its socialist heritage, it could be then said of him what he wrote of Trotsky, "Never has any man lived who so closely communioned with the suffering and the strivings of oppressed humanity and in such utter loneliness." But he lived long enough to see brighter lights on the horizon and to hear his message echoing around the world.

I am convinced that Deutscher's fight, like his work, had universal meaning; that what was so exceptional in his life, beyond his extraordinary talent and character. True, he turned to socialism, not because of the consciousness of his class interests, yet this can be said about every intellectual joining the socialist movement. True, he was born in a Jewish community that has vanished, but Jews after all have just given us proof that they are in no way immune to nationalism than anybody else. At the same time Deutscher was confirming, in an interview that his internationalism was inseparable from his socialism. Genuinely anything nationalist was alien to him.

There is no dividing line between his Polish or his English values. There is continuity between the young man impatient to change the world and a member of the Russell Tribunal or the author of "The Unfinished Revolution". This is why his example is of value for us too. On this occasion where, painfully, we are aware a man is mortal but this no reason for losing faith. For us, for whom there is no God, no Caesar, no personal solution, Deutscher has shown the only way with dignity by struggling, whatever the odds, to change the world by fighting for the socialist transformation of mankind.

Isaac Deutscher is no longer with us. What this must mean for Tamara, his companion, I can guess judging by the emptiness I feel myself. He was so young. Age is not just a question of years. If by youth, we mean the refusal to submit, to surrender, to yield, then Deutscher was the youngest of us all. And he had so many plans, so many projects, some still to accomplish. But what we must remember is what he had achieved in his lifetime. He was fond of saying that Russians one day would be his most voracious readers and certainly that day will come when through his books they will discover their past history, a knowledge without which they cannot properly build their future. But already now, elsewhere, his analysis of Soviet society helps socialist to consolidate their faith. Cuban revolutionaries, unorthodox Italian Communists, American fighters against the war in Vietnam and Japanese students, the New Left throughout the world, find encouragement and inspiration in his work. His life, like his work is an example. There is no socialist man because as yet there is no socialist society. When one will emerge, it will be too rational to erect tombs in its "Red Square". Men who have helped mankind to reach this socialist future will be celebrated in history books and in the memory of future generations. I cannot pay a greater tribute to Isaac Deutscher than to claim, seemingly born in the wrong time and in the wrong place, he will figure prominently next to Trotsky in such a revolutionary culture.

(Applause)

RALPH MILIBAND

The next speaker upon whom I would like to call is David Horowitz, who perhaps exemplifies as well as anybody can, the close link which came to be established in the last years of his life, between Isaac Deutscher and that new rising generation of intellectuals and socialists, in whom we place so much confidence—David Horowitz.

DAVID HOROWITZ

At this painful time when the memory of the man himself is so vivid in our minds, those of us who knew Isaac Deutscher have duty to bear witness to the life and to the work.

In him, the tragedy of human death, the irrevocable loss of a being, utterly unique and irreplaceable is magnified to such dimension that it is understood by tens of thousands, who knew him only through his books. How much more then, is it to us, to whom he was a teacher and a friend. Tonight, however, I should like to speak about him in personal terms only as they reflect upon the public life, upon his place and role in the revolutionary movement in which he will be seen by future generations to have been a most vital figure, for with Deutscher, the revolutionary deed was the word.

What I remember most about Isaac Deutscher was the sense I always had in his presence of listening to a voice from a wholly different and incredibly cultured world. His conversation was rich with the reminiscences of names of places which I did not know. And even when familiar, they were spoken of within a framework which is fascinatingly remote. I felt with Deutscher as though through him I was in contact with the living past and touching deep down into the well-springs of European culture, of revolutionary culture and the still vibrant outlook of the classical Bolshevik era. I believe that when Deutscher listened to me, and to others of my generation, he also had the experience of communicating across an immense chasm of culture and historical time and that while we searched his phrases and sentences for roots, he peered into ours, seeking response. Exactly what response he sought, can only be guessed. But I remember the light which flooded his face when he returned from his trip to Berkeley and Washington, and the thrill with which he spoke of the great Vietnam protests to which he had been invited by the American New Left. It was this New Left to which Deutscher looked and I know that much of the precious time that he lavished all too prodigally on me and others like me, was a token of the faith and hope that he placed in our generation. Nor was it an accident that the terrible isolation from the left that Deutscher experienced during most of the post-war years was broken finally only by this new generation.

Deutscher, the biographer of Stalin and Trotsky, left no autobiographical statement. In fragments of his work, which like all art, contain a large element of introspection, we can see reflected essential features of his own life and can begin to understand his relations to the old revolutionary left and the new. Ten years ago, Deutscher gave a lecture under the title, "The Message of the Non-Jewish Jew", in which he discussed six Jewish heretics, including Spinoza, Marx, Rosa Luxemburg and Trotsky. As Deutscher often used a literary image to bind up complex theoretical themes of his larger works, so he began this lecture with a symbolic story. While still a child, he had come across a scene in the Midrush from Rabbi Meir, the great pillar of Mosaic orthodoxy, who took lessons in theology from a heretic, bearing the nickname Akher, "The Stranger."

Once on a Sabbath, Rabbi Meir had gone out on a ship with his teacher and had listened so intently to the words of wisdom falling from heretical lips that he failed to notice that they had reached a ritual boundary which Jews are not allowed to cross on the Sabbath. At this point, the great heretic indicated to his pupil, the Rabbi, that they had reached the boundary, whereupon the Rabbi went back to the Jewish community while the heretic rode on beyond the boundaries of Jewry. The young Deutscher was deeply impressed by the figure of Akher and the enigma which the story posed to an orthodox viewpoint. Why, the boy wondered, did Rabbi Meir take his lessons from the heretic? Who was he? He appeared to be in Jewry, and yet out of it. He showed a curious respect for his people's orthodoxy when he sent him back to the Jews on the holy Sabbath, yet he himself, disregarding canon and ritual, rode beyond the boundaries. What made him transcend Judaism? These were the questions that agitated the young Deutscher.

In retrospect, it is hardly surprising that the biographer of the heretic, Trotsky, should, in the middle fifties, more than a third of a century later, still be compelled by the hebetic tale. Indeed, how well the figure of Akher fits Deutscher himself. For was not Deutscher also the heretic of Communism? The heretic, who in the post-Stalin decade became a teacher, mainly to rank and file Communists, but also, to not a few rabbis of Communism as well, to those of us such as a former Communist miner, after Deutscher's death , to those who were groping in the fifties for an explanation of the brutally irrational distortion which had cramped the life of the socialist movement, the almost lone voice of Deutscher came as a blinding revelation. And was not Deutscher the heretic stranger who appeared to be in Communism and yet not in it, to be of Communism and yet not of it. Who like Akher, showed a curious respect for his people's orthodoxy and a care lest they wandered beyond the boundaries of Marxism and of communism and become lost.

Was it not Deutscher, who alone among European socialists, was invited by the American New Left, to whom his Marxism itself was heretical, to address them at their great anti-war teach-ins and was it not Deutscher who proclaimed at Berkeley to this New Left, the urgency of giving back the class struggle its old dignity and of restoring meaning once again to the idea of communism? Listen again to the voice of Deutscher's communist pupil. For many of us, he was a regenerator of hope. In him we found the link between humanism and socialism which allowed us to rediscover Marx himself in our own history. Indeed, was not the very essence of Deutscher's work, the transcendence of Communism in a Hegelian sense, of preserving the best, the real achievements of the old, even while surpassing and annulling it towards the new. In the figure of Akher, Deutscher had come to recognize not only a Jewish tradition, but also a prototype of those revolutionaries of modern thought, from Spinoza to Marx, who found Jewry too narrow, too archaic and too constricting and looked for ideals and fulfillment beyond it. Such an ideal, Marx, Trotsky, Rosa Luxemburg and Deutscher himself, found in the struggle for an international socialist society!

In 1926 Deutscher joined the Polish Communist Party and entered the revolutionary ranks. Then, as the Russian Revolution, isolated by the failure of the revolutions in the West, began to succumb to the despotism and backwardness of the Russian environment, Deutscher joined the Trotskyist opposition which was fighting a losing battle within the Revolution to arrest its departure from Marxist and socialist norms. In 1932, he was expelled from the Party for spreading panic about Nazism, and during the next years, he continued his opposition, exposing the mass terror in Russia and the Purge Trials in which the old Bolshevik leadership perished.

In 1938 however, when convinced that the Third International was morally dead, Trotsky launched its successor. Deutscher demurred. The creation of every one of the earlier Internationals, argued Deutscher, constituted a definite threat to bourgeois rule. This would not be the case with the Fourth International, because no significant section of the working class would respond to its manifesto and it would become a mere collection of sects. It was necessary to wait. It was at this point that Deutscher's lonely sojourn began, a sojourn that made possible his unique contribution to the world revolutionary movement and its future regeneration. For having belonged to those who Stalin had truly defeated, Deutscher set about to systematically examine why Stalin had succeeded and why the historic development had taken the course that it did.

In the end, Deutscher came to see Stalinism differently from Trotsky. He saw it not as a usurpation of Bolshevik power, but as a distorted evolution of a current within Bolshevism itself, brought out by its isolation and the autocratic backwardness of its environment. He saw in Stalinism, not aThermidorian bureaucracy arresting the revolutionary development, but a bureaucratized revolution carrying through that development with the barbarous means and primitive outlook of its native surroundings. For this, Deutscher was made a heretic and an outcast on the left. Then, by the Stalinists for maintaining his Marxist ideas and outlook against the debasement of the Revolution, denounced by the Trotskyists for recognizing that the brutally realized achievements of the Stalinist bureaucracy were revolutionary, Deutscher remained totally isolated throughout the first decade of the Cold War. Then the historic development took a new turn and it was these very traits for which he had been damned, that now made him a teacher and inspiration to the generation of nineteen fifty-six and to those of us who grew to political maturity afterwards. For us too, the Stalinist development of Soviet Russia had historic substance and validity. The forced march from the age of the wooden farrow to the era of the Sputnik and the atom bomb, may not have been a socialist march in the classical Marxist sense, but it certainly represented a tremendous leap towards liberation in terms of about two-thirds of the world's population that was still sunk in the mire and misery of under-development and backwardness. Deutscher, above all, recognized the ethical significance of this ascent and the revolutionary, if frugal and wasteful role of Stalinism in presiding over it. At the same time, he possessed that critical attitude towards Stalinism, that Marxist criticism of its deeds and claims which he owed to Trotsky and the Left Opposition and which was absolutely crucial for us and so vital to any regeneration of the revolutionary left in the West. To this regeneration which he above all else struggled for, and to which he dedicated his genius, Deutscher made still another essential contribution and it's best indicated perhaps by a passage that Deutscher wrote in *Tribune* in February 1945, at a time when the Stalinist terror had almost a decade to run. He wrote:

"Just as it is possible for a strong appearance of capitalism to stick to its democratic form and to oppose capitalism in totalitarian form, so it is also possible and necessary for socialist to fight for socialist democracy and against the totalitarian distortion of socialism. However, the difference between capitalism and socialism is that capitalism historically gravitates towards fascism, whilst socialism gravitates towards freedom. The defender of the democratic form of capitalism is in a sense, revolting against the inner logic of the social system he defends. The defender of socialist freedom and against the quasi-socialist totalitarianism is in the long run in harmony with the trend of history and must eventually steer away from the totalitarian backwater into the open skies of a free society."

It was Deutscher, who by analyzing the roots of Stalinist despotism with the tools of Marxism and by prophetically indicating the direction which the stark development was pointing, restored to my generation that confidence in Marxist theory and that revolutionary optimism without which there can be no revolutionary action, for this alone, we and the revolutionary generations to come, will pay him homage.

(Applause)

RALPH MILIBAND

Deutscher received a book, a history of the Russian revolution, which Marcel Liebman has just published in Belgium and in France. Before calling upon Mr. Liebman to speak, I think I might perhaps say there is a typical side to Isaac Deutscher's interest in that book. For when Marcel, a friend for some years of Isaac Deutscher, sent him the manuscript of the book, Deutscher didn't merely acknowledge the receipt of the book or send it back with some comments, but as so often with other people's writings, particularly with people whose minds he respected, he went through it, took time, argued, sent back criticisms and comment as well as felicitations and eulogy because he typifies that. I have great pleasure in calling upon Mr. Liebman to address you.

MARCEL LIEBMAN

Ladies and gentlemen, I could, of course, approve every word after Bertrand Russell's message and all his remarks on the significance of Isaac Deutscher for history and for socialism. I'm afraid I view my contribution to this meeting, in a rather dry way to which I try to stick. Before trying to assess Deutscher's significance as a historian, I just want to say this, that for young, less young, intellectual Marxists, intellectual workers, he meant, of course, a shining example but much more than a shining example, he brought us, in very barren and difficult surroundings, in a sort of intellectual and political desert, he brought to all of us, a sense of dignity which we lacked, for many reasons which are well known. Being so, what I have tried to do is to outline briefly what was Isaac Deutscher's original contribution to the history, but more than to the history of the Russian Revolution but also to the interpretation of revolutionaries and of Soviet Russian society and its evolution.

It goes without saying, that there are two categories of historians who had absolutely nothing in common with Isaac Deutscher and in comparison with these historians, he absolutely, in a very sharp way, disassociated himself. There were, first of all, the conservative historians and observers of Soviet Russia, who seemed to have been unable to digest October and the aftermath of October, and who still consider the October revolution, not as a social phenomenon which ought to be described and analyzed, but as a social disaster, and because of that, who do not succeed in analyzing, but only succeed in exposing and denouncing. And in a very, as a sort of paradox, side by side, with that school of historians and observers, there is another set, another category of historians, or pseudo-historians, the friends, or the pseudo-friends of the Russian Revolution who have come to eventually to found , what has had been rightly called, the Stalinist School of Falsification. It goes without saying that Deutscher had nothing in common with either category of those historians. What did I think more interesting, is to compare Deutscher's approach and interpretation of the Russian Revolution and the Soviet Russian evolution, to compare his approach of this huge and complex problem to the approach of Marxist, socialists, left-wing critics, some Marxist socialists and left wing critics of Soviet Russia, because in this field, its originality and its depth and insight is very well exemplified and illustrated.

I would say, very briefly, that the differences, sometimes the disagreements and divergences between Isaac Deutscher and those Marxists and socialist critics of Soviet Russia, can be summarized in three different points: First of all, the nature of Soviet Russia under Lenin's leadership, secondly the fight in Russia for Lenin's heritage, and thirdly, the nature of Stalin's Russia, and above all, the nature of Soviet society as a whole. The first point is interpretation, and even a description of Russia under Lenin. It is for socialists, admirers and friends of the Russian Revolution, a too easily admitted idea that there existed a very sharp contrast between, on the first side, Russia under Lenin, which was presented a sort of nostalgia, was not alien to this representation which was represented as a perfect example of popular, of democratic, of popular and proletarian democracy. A sharp contrast between that regime, and on the other side, Stalin, Russia under Stalin from 1922 or 1924 onwards.

The sharp contrast has been very clearly expressed in a fairly recent resolution which has been voted by a Congress of the Fourth International, a resolution saying , and I quote, "Stalin destroyed the proletarian democracy prevailing in the years of Lenin and Trotsky." The whole picture and I would rather use the word "fresco", to give the impression, to give the idea of the dimension of Deutscher's description of the Russian Revolution. The whole picture, accurate, precise, I would say scientific picture which Deutscher gave of Russia under Lenin runs counter to this simplification which was not of course exempt, deprived of any truth which was exactly a very great simplification.

What Deutscher showed with such authority and accuracy was that the conditions which prevailed in Russia, not in 1924 or not later, but already in 1920 and 1921, the conditions which prevailed in Russia at that time, left very little room for the democratic ideals of men like Lenin and like Trotsky. That after the civil war, with its terrible human and material damages, with the effect that the Russian working class was, to quote the very words of Isaac Deutscher, "atomized" by the economic disaster of the civil war, in a context where one could almost say that not only the vanguard of the working class, but the very working class itself had diminished and had been dispersed by the effects of the civil war and such surrounding a Soviet democracy of the kind which had been created by October, such a Soviet democracy had become impossible. In other words, that it is too simple, much too simple to speak of Lenin's democracy and to oppose Lenin's democracy to Stalin's chilling suppression of that democracy.

A second point on which Deutscher disassociated himself from very simplified interpretations of the Russian history in the twenties, was about the fight for Lenin's heritage. Here, it is too often accepted, or it was too often accepted, that the main cause of Trotsky's defeat and the main cause for Stalin's crimes was the sheer savagery, the sheer weakness of Stalin, the sheer brutality of his method, and only the terror which he used so abundantly against his enemies. Of course, this is part of the truth, but only part of the truth, what Deutscher showed was that the tactical errors, the tactical mistakes which Trotsky made in the Twenties were also of great importance and of which one can give, I think, two small, two important examples. First, the fact that Trotsky didn't use the weapon he had in his hand, namely the political weapon he had in hand, namely Lenin's testament, Lenin's anti-Stalin testament, and secondly, the refusal of Trotsky to draw an alliance with the right Communists, the right-wing of the Communist Party, Bukharin and his friends.

Deutscher goes even so far as to say that because of these mistakes, Trotsky committed, and I quote his words, "committed political suicide." But even those mistakes are of secondary importance, the type of mistakes of secondary importance as compared to the main issue, the main cause which according to Deutscher, explains Stalin's triumph in the Twenties and Thirties, and this main cause is the state, economics, social, political conditions of which I said a word a minute ago. In an isolated state like Russia, like Soviet Russia, in a country so badly prepared for the huge task of socialist education, in a country where so many of the conditions were the conditions of a very backward society and given that isolation which of course Stalin was not quite irresponsible. Given these conditions, the ideals of proletarian democracy inside the Party and inside Soviet society, these ideals which were an important part in the programme of the Left Opposition, these ideals were bound to be defeated.

It goes without saying that Deutscher never gave up his deep and so justified admiration for a man like Trotsky. Nobody better than Deutscher understood and explained the disquiet, the greatness, the political, moral and intellectual greatness of a man like Trotsky. But when this has been said, it remains and here one must pay one eulogy more to Deutscher's objectivity, to his extraordinary power to control his own feelings and to appear as the historian, a rational and …historian* (*Tape is inaudible here). When this is said, one must stress the words which have been used by Deutscher to describe Trotsky's fight in the years of the Twenties when Deutscher said that Trotsky was a fighter against his time. Being a fighter against his time, his defeat wasn't only the result of Stalin's real, of course, wickedness. It was not only the result of Trotsky's real mistakes, but mainly, the result of the conditions prevailing in Russia and in Europe in the Twenties.

And the third point which I want to make very briefly, the third difference and even disagreement, which occurred between Deutscher's account of Russia's evolution and some Marxist socialists, serious critics of Russia, of Soviet Russia, is the whole interpretation Deutscher gave of the nature of Stalinism and the whole interpretation he gave on very broad and general terms, of the nature of Soviet Russia, ran counter— to clichés—counter to very easy formulas, and even slogans and admitted ideas. And here too Deutscher, who was such an admirer of Trotsky, didn't fail and didn't hesitate to criticize Trotsky on a point where Trotsky's ideas seemed to Deutscher, rather weak. I quote Deutscher , what he said when he wrote the following sentences: "When Trotsky wrote that the film of revolution was running backwards under the influence of Stalin, he meant that it was moving toward a planned economy, industrial expansion and mass education." And indeed, despite all bureaucratic distortions and debasement, Trotsky himself recognized to be the essential prerequisites for socialism. In other words, that the picture of Stalinism as being a regime which was killing democracy, which was the very negation of Soviet, of socialist values and of Soviet and socialist political and social structures, that this picture is true, but was only a part of the truth. And that side by side with these mistakes and defaults and crimes, the world economic achievements of a society which had abolished capitalism and of which the leading bureaucracy refused to restore capitalism. And here again it was a very balanced view, so objective a view, it gave rise to discussion, sometimes to criticism of which one example was given by the American Trotskyist, J.P. Cannon, when he said that "Deutscher was a Bernstein of Trotskyism."

Whatever one may think of the whole picture and the whole interpretation Deutscher gave on the evolution and on the future of Russia, and to have some good faith that this picture and this interpretation was in some way optimistic. Even in those aspects, in those parts of Deutscher's work where discussion is possible, it remains a fact, a fact which has all the strength, the might of an undisputable fact, that among all the historians, among all the observers, friendly, less friendly, hostile, critical, among all the observers of Soviet Russia, that only there is one who is outstanding for the coherence, the depth of his vision of the whole history of Soviet Russia, and that man is obviously Isaac Deutscher.

I want to conclude by quoting the final words of Engels, in his introduction to Marx's, class war, "The Civil War in France", Engels wrote, and I quote, "The Social- Democratic philistine has once more been filled with wholesome terror at the words, Dictatorship of the Proletariat. Well and good gentlemen, you want to know what this dictatorship looks like? Look at the Paris Commune. That was the Dictatorship of the Proletariat." Often you will use the very same words Engels used and fail. The philistine has been filled with wholesome contempt at the words of scientific socialism. Well and good, ladies and gentlemen, do you want to know what the scientific socialism looks like, do you want to know what Marxism looks like, look at Isaac Deutscher's work—that was scientific socialism, that was living Marxism.

(Applause)

RALPH MILIBAND

I should now like to call upon Perry Anderson, the editor of *New Left Review*, the magazine with which Isaac Deutscher had established friendly, if often critical relations.

PERRY ANDERSON

Other speakers tonight have stressed that Isaac Deutscher was a historian, a Marxist and a revolutionary. I would like to say a few words about the connections between these three dimensions of him as a man. In particular, I would like to say something about the form of his writings, that is, their style and the content of them, that is, their themes. Deutscher's writings on Soviet history and society are very much more than a mere local chronicle of what happened in Russia from 1900 to the present day. Their sweep, their depth and their brilliance won him an audience throughout the world. But in the thirty years of his life and work in England, it is significant that he was never given any place in a university until at the end of his life he was invited to give the Trevelyan Lectures in Cambridge as a visitor.

There was no accident in this. Deutscher's work was profoundly threatening to capitalist society and to its ideological institutions. He was hated and feared as a Marxist by the mediocre academicians who dominated these institutions. They did everything to ensure that he was never allowed to teach a younger generation personally and directly, even, on one occasion, vetoing in desperation his nomination to a University Chair when it had already been offered to him. The result of this long and relentless ostracism was that Deutscher had to earn much of his living as a journalist in London, as Marx did before him. That journalism produced essays of great and permanent importance, as it did with Marx. But those who saw him obliged to devote so much of his time to it, were aware that it was at a cost to his historical work itself. His biography of Lenin might now, perhaps, have been written if he had not had these constant financial pressures on him. This was the daily price he paid for his Marxism in this country.

It was not just the fact of his Marxism which made him so feared by bourgeois historians, of course, it was its quality. Deutscher himself once wrote that he had, and I quote here, "a heightened sensitivity to the style of all reason on social and political problems." He goes on, "I thought that I could recognize the quality of any socialist or communist statement, by its language and form." Now, this dictum certainly applies to his own work. His prose, as all of you will know, was superb in English. But this was not just a literary gift—and this is the point I want to insist on—it expressed very deeply Deutscher's relationship to Marxism as a philosophy. Nothing is more striking in his work than its complete freedom from the technical language of Marxism—what is usually called its "jargon". This freedom, was in fact, the measure, not of Deutscher's immense patience of Marxism as a philosophy, but of his effortless control of it. His Marxism was classical in an age of allegories, that is to say, it was so natural to him that he could speak it and use it without resorting to any specialized or technical idiom.

Jargon is only the index of the difficulty which a Marxist has in overcoming his normal inherited habits of thought and speech. It is like the arbitrary, clumsy constructions of someone who has known but not truly mastered a foreign language. Deutscher, on the contrary, moved within Marxism so freely and spontaneously that he made it appear often as simply identical with intelligent argument. C. Wright Mills once described Deutscher's historical work to me as a gigantic insinuation, an insinuation of what? Of the truth and actuality of Marxism, of course. It was an insinuation, of course, because he never stated the axioms of Marxism systematically and explicitly. Deutscher's work was his own proof of it in practice. Deutscher's classical clarity was thus unique amongst the great Marxist intellectuals of the West. Virtually all the other great Marxists of recent decades, Gramsci, Lucacs, Sartre, Althusser or Marcuse, have expressed themselves in a difficult and complex vocabulary, often very removed from ordinary language. I do not think this is a criticism of them. They produced the Marxism they could, which is our Marxism, in the insurmountable historical conditions in which they found themselves.

Deutscher, who came from the border lands of the October Revolution, was heir to a different tradition. It gave him an ease with Marxism that allowed him to write massive historical works which yet won world-wide non-sectarian audiences. These works were themselves something of a contrast to much of western Marxism. They were not a philosophical discourse on method such as has preoccupied so many contemporary Marxists, from Lukacs to Sartre and Althusser. They were about the central, substantive problems of 20th century socialism, the destiny of the revolution.

Deutscher's writings on Russia—which were apparently particular and specific works of history—were actually also universal elements of any Marxist theory. For no socialist or revolutionary politics today is possible, without a preliminary judgment on the major experimental laboratory which the century has so far provided to verify or modify Marxists' ideas of socialism. In Deutscher's writings, history becomes politics and politics becomes revolutionary theory. There was no accident in this.

Deutscher, for those who knew him personally was, as a man, above all a revolutionary. It was his revolutionary passion which determined the distinctive focus and themes of his work, once circumstances had separated him from the possibility of active political practice. Deutscher, exiled from Poland, rejoined the Revolution by writing the epic of it, an epic which is also, in a sense, the theory of it. Deutscher, whom circumstances isolated from political struggle so relentlessly after the thirties, succeeded in being more immediately and truly political to the end, than any other major Marxist writer of his generation. He was a model of a revolutionary thinker in the Bolshevik tradition. In contemporary Britain, nothing was more unfamiliar or more exemplary.

(Applause)

RALPH MILIBAND
I should now like to call on K.S. Karol, also an old friend of Isaac Deutscher, and a fellow journalist.

K.S. KAROL
Ladies and gentlemen, allow me to begin this tribute to Isaac Deutscher with a few souvenirs from a country which was the object of his passion and study, namely from the Soviet Union. I was born in Poland, from the same background or comparable background as Isaac Deutscher, but from one generation later. And as it happened, by the vicissitude of war, at the age of fifteen, I was confronted with the Soviet reality in practice. I happened to be a Soviet citizen because Poland didn't exist anymore, and had to share for several years, for seven years, the life of the generation of Russians, similar to myself. There is usually an image that Stalin's Russia and the Russia of that period, was one vast jail. I wouldn't deny that there were jails in Russia, and I was myself for a time in one of them, but the image is not true. In Stalin's Russia, people could and were allowed to discuss and to speak, particularly in privacy and particularly young people like my friends, with whom I was in the army and subsequently in the university. But what we were discussing was mostly about the present, without knowing too much what had happened in the past, after the Revolution, but with some feelings that those were dangerous things, that a lot of people had suffered from them, that it is better to look only to the future without caring too much about the past and about discussing

too much about ideas.

There is Stalin, of course. There was a version of Marxism which was in the official manuals. This was, these things were admitted as a kind of obvious truth and were applied mostly to the world outside, because after all, Lenin writing concerned three-quarters, if not four-fifths of his work, was on Tsarist Russia and society, pre-revolutionary, on how to make a revolution in that kind of a country. And this Marxism was, I would say, something which was completely without influence, but was not considered a possible instrument to discuss the present or the future. The present and the future were connected to Stalin, because for us, for this generation of Russians after all, it was Stalin who had led us during the war, and even if we knew that probably the man was sometimes rather dangerous, there was also a conviction where Stalin had led the victory, therefore it was better to follow this man. And particularly, I must say during the years, nineteen forty-four, forty five, the years of victory, there was a kind of liberalization in Russia.

One could speak much more freely, and there was a period of great hope towards the future, hopes that was connected with the prospect of the imminent victory, but nobody had any real idea about what this better future would really be, and how it would happen. We were expecting something, hoping, but I repeat, without much discussion, neither of ideas nor of the past history. Those closed chapters were supposed to be closed forever and considered to be rather irrelevant. As it happened, you know, that in the years immediately after the victory, already in forty-five, happened which we did not expect. Our comrades were coming from prison camps, and instead of being with us, were taken into other kinds of camps which were called "checking" camps. There began immediately again, a new waves of difficulties. And the contrast between the official rhetoric and daily life was becoming more and more unbearable. Well, nobody could explain what it was and how it was, and it was at that time that I left Russia, in 1946 and two or three years later, I came to Paris, with, again, those feelings, that after all it was the country which suffered more than any other for the victory during the war. It was a country in which I was brought up, and I didn't want to be against it, and at the same time, it was a country whose shortcomings I knew too well from my experience and I was unable to deny them or to defend them. And with these divided feelings, with this divided mind, when I started to contemplate a career as a journalist, I had the occasion to read firstly, Isaac Deutscher's book on Stalin, and subsequently to meet him.

It will be an exaggeration and I don't think any tribute needs exaggeration, to say that this one book explained everything to me about my experience, but it is certainly true that his book and his hypotheses for the future, which Isaac Deutscher wrote about, was really a revelation for me, something that, tremendously, put into a real perspective what I knew from the facts from any given passage of my life in Russia. And it also gave me an example, that it is possible to be a critic of Soviet Russia, a critic of this form of socialism without becoming an isolated enemy of Russia or even an ally of Russian or Soviet Russian enemies. Therefore, I owe a great debt to Isaac Deutscher for, as a personal example, and for what he was and brought to me, but I must add that the experience later showed to me that not only Isaac Deutscher was right in his analysis of the evolution of Russia, of post-revolutionary Russia, but his knowledge of this analysis is fundamental to this particular generation, to this generation of Russians and of the whole people in Eastern Europe.

Because, I maintain, I have many friends, both in Russia and in Poland and I saw, and I can confirm, that it is not possible to close a chapter of a history and to say it didn't exist by just bringing a kind of cynical mentality of something which is incompatible with socialism, and with a society which nevertheless is a society in transition to socialism. I had the feeling some of them were coming with a great enthusiasm after the 20th Congress, and coming later after Khrushchev's removal from power, but none of them could maintain for a long time this enthusiasm because they didn't dare and they couldn't digest the past. As a result, they are a phenomenon of a politicization which is at the root of the difficulties in Russia and which sooner or later will be overcome because I don't think that this country can really develop with this non-political or a-political generation. But the second revelation to me was that I was very recently in Cuba where I met a new generation of Communists who were, because perhaps of the distance and of age, who made the revolution themselves without Stalin and without knowing very much about the past dramas of the workers' movement in Europe. But once in power, once trying to build socialist Cuba they discovered, very soon, that they needed ideas and they needed historical knowledge and nothing is more impressive today in Cuba than to see precisely this generation of men, discussing with passion what were the polemics between Preobrazhensky and Bukharin, the things which happened in Russia years ago, not because it is of an academic interest, but because they know that if the revolution is to be taken from the place where Lenin left it and not from today's reforms as they don't accept the view that it is impossible to change man and it is impossible to free him from the money civilization, from all forms of alienation.

They don't accept the view that if political incentives don't work, they don't accept the view that after the revolution the new generation is becoming less revolutionary. They believe that they should be more, and in order to get analysis of their problems, they are studying precisely the same discussions that were taking place inside Russia after the Revolution and the same problems that were to be solved and they believe, I hope, rightly that what has happened in Russia is not necessarily a historical phenomenon but a local, particular deviation. And I think and I saw that of course, the works of Isaac Deutscher are of unique contribution because there are not many like they are, of course, original, but can't get today, and today many people are reading in texts of Russian or other economists who are participating in the discussion in Russia. But to have the whole picture of what has happened in Russia after the Revolution, what has happened with one generation, why this particular form of deviation has appeared in Russia, they need this broad Marxist analysis, they need to know the society in order not to make such mistakes, the same way as the young Russians, they need to know their history and their society in order to overcome this. And I think that after my trip to Cuba, and after seeing how Cubans are passionately interested in those problems and what is their attitude towards the work of Isaac Deutscher, that the day will come and perhaps sooner than we believe that indeed the same will happen in Russia and everywhere in the socialist world and that day will be the greatest reward for Isaac Deutscher because he devoted his life precisely for just this future.

(Applause)

RALPH MILIBAND
Our last speaker is Lawrence Daly, General Secretary of the Scottish Mineworkers Union. Isaac was, in many ways, not involved in the British labour movement in a direct sense, but he had a boundless belief in its potentiality, and it is fitting that we should have one of its best representatives to speak to us tonight, Lawrence Daly.

LAWRENCE DALY
Comrade Chairman and comrades, when Isaac Deutscher was serving his period of compulsory labour in the Polish Army's disciplinary camp in Scotland during the war, I, unknown to him of course, and he to me, was serving my period of compulsory labour, under British war-time regulations, only a few miles away in a Scottish coal-mine and I only emerged from that coalmine about three years ago. But for many years before that, my mind had been acting as a very imperfect vehicle for the conveyance of some of the ideas of Deutscher in as much as I understood them, to at least a number of my comrades who worked in that coal mine. And I have heard Deutscher's books, and Deutscher's works and writings, discussed by admittedly very small numbers of coal-miners on the surface of the mine and deep in the bowels of the earth and this was an experience which was not unique in our village and in my own coal-mine. It has been repeated in other parts of the British coal-fields. And I have no doubt the same can be said in almost every major industry in Britain, in shipyards, in factories and so on. The numbers of places in which such discussions have taken place and the numbers of people,

above all the numbers of active trade-unionists who have been involved in these discussions, is alas, still far too few. But I think that increasingly through the educational activities of the trade-union movement, though sometimes it is not intentional, through trade-union students learning from Workers Education Association lecturers, tutors in extra-mural classes and so on and sometimes from other activists within the movement, directly associated with political groups and parties that many thousands more are becoming, or coming to understand that here is or was a historian and political analyst who could enable them to understand many of the problems which puzzled them, particularly in relation to the Communist world, especially from the late forties onwards.

I did not have the privilege of knowing Isaac Deutscher in those years, indeed I met him but briefly for the first time this year in the city of Stockholm, for only a four days and throughout that time our private conversations together could not have lasted for any more than two or three hours. And that was mainly confined to our journey together back over to London at the end of the Tribunal's first session. But as I had a conversation on the plane coming over with a very lively and congenial companion, I could hardly have believed that it was credible that we would be gathered here, paying tribute to his memory in such a few months. There was no apparent physical sign of his impending collapse nor could it have occurred to me that I would be honoured by being requested to pay tribute to him from this platform. But although my association was a very, very, brief one, my intellectual association, if you like, although it was always one-way traffic, had extended over a considerable number of years and he had indeed been influencing my thinking for a long time before 1967, and the thinking of considerable number of other people in the British labour and trade-union movement. Many of the activists in the labour movement had not only read his historical works, but had followed from time to time his periodic political commentaries in journals like *Tribune* and so on. And indeed, in recent years his contributions to journals like the *New Left Review* and the *Socialist Register*, have I think been among the very best and most instructive of his works as a political analyst. It is perhaps an indication of the principled character of the man, perhaps also of his keen sense of smell, that from the very beginning he refused to be associated in any way with the "cultural free" in the columns of *Encounter*. I think that is a very important claim that can be made on Isaac Deutscher's behalf. His books certainly, his books on Stalin, on Trotsky, certainly enlightened thousands of active trade unionists, people who are not only trade union conscious, but politically conscious and they undoubtedly played a very important part in rescuing some thousands of people in this country, dedicated workers in the labour movement, from a kind of mummified Marxism, within whose confines they had been constricted.

For many of those activists, he rent asunder those constrictions of both Stalinism and reformism. It I think was typical of his passion for objective truth that although he was an admirer but not an idolater of Trotsky, that he himself in his book on Stalin, should have chronicled the evidence, which as Deutscher himself said, refuted Trotsky's claim that Stalin in the pre-1917 period had been a nonentity. And perhaps it was the very same passion for objective truth that led him from 1932 onwards, to have no direct association or participation in any particular political party. There will be those who will claim, and for all I know they may be right, that this was a source of weakness, but I am certainly convinced that at the very same time, it must have been a profound source of intellectual strength. Certainly, his isolation or independence never allured him into the camp of those for whom the God had failed.

He was bound; it seemed to me, to the international revolutionary movement, with all its disagreements and all its deficiencies, by powerful emotional and intellectual ties. Unlike people like Koestler, his disillusionment with Stalinism which came rather earlier than Koestler's did not lead him into making a choice, of the yogi or the Colonel Blimp as the alternative to the commissar. His historical, his recognition of the historical inevitability and of the moral justification for political agitation and revolutionary action, was very profound in spite of his knowledge of the grave distortions which disfigured the very movement which gave these actions, birth. But his profound political insight enabled him to answer well in advance, the critics, the negative critics of the revolution. I was looking today at the *Guardian* and came across a review of Yevgenia Ginzburg's memoirs by Emanuel Litvinoff and I thought it would be of interest to quote to you if you have not seen it what Litvinoff said at the beginning of his review. He said, "Only in our century would one bother to make a distinction between the miseries inflicted upon the people by Hitler, on the one hand, and by Stalin on the other. It is about time we acknowledged them to be the left and right profiles of the same evil."

Almost twenty years before, in the final chapter of his severely critical, biography of Stalin, Deutscher had answered Litvinoff by saying: "The fact cannot be ignored that the ideal inherent in Stalinism, one to which Stalin has given a grossly distorted expression, is not domination of man by man or nation by nation, or race by race, but their fundamental equality. Hitler was the leader of a sterile counter-revolution, while Stalin has been both the leader and the exploiter of a tragic self-contradictory, but creative revolution." And Deutscher's deep historical perspective has enabled him not only to answer the Litvinoffs in advance, but to guide many, like myself, who have had their difficulties and doubts at different periods. But the fact that Deutscher's works are not readily and freely available today in Prague or in Moscow, or in Peking, is an indication of how many the distortions of these revolutions still remain. And perhaps more serious and significant for us in Britain, is the fact that although his works are freely available here, he is still unknown to all too many thousands of even active people in the trade-union movement, in the hundred and one industries in Britain. And in some cases, in cases which involve some of the most active and dedicated people in our movement, he is to their minds, even though in most cases they have not read him, already anathema. They have read his critics, very briefly. And one of the tasks for us, it seems to me, that we have to perform and one of the greatest tributes that we can make to Deutscher's memory, is to do our utmost to eliminate that ignorance and that hostility.

I have no objection to any amount of dialogue with a few archbishops or even lesser ecclesiastical figures, but I think it would be more fruitful for our movement if a number of people who have, if not actually, adopted a hostile attitude to Deutscher, were to begin even now, though posthumously, a dialogue with the ideas and works of Deutscher. This is not to advocate uncritical acceptance of all of Deutscher's writings. To no person more than Deutscher would that have been abhorrent and repellent, but his scholarly objectivity, his historical perspective, his dialectical subtlety, the richness and vigour of his prose and his tremendous courage in presenting and defending his views are qualities which it seems to me, no movement requires more than ours here in Britain today.

Above all, we require, as part of our tribute to Deutscher, to revive at a new level the spirit of international solidarity which informed every single page of his writings. And this was expressed, this tremendous spirit of internationalism of Isaac's, in the work he undertook for the International War Crimes Tribunal. I recall that in the course of a single afternoon at the request of the Tribunal, he drafted an introduction to the final report of the first session, which in effect was a powerful, clarion call to the international labour movement and would have won widespread acclaim as a new international revolutionary manifesto. I perhaps should apologize for the fact that I was a member of the Tribunal who urged its complete rejection, for reasons that are not the business of this meeting, but my astonishment could be imagined when I tell you the first person to agree with my proposal, was Isaac Deutscher.

It's really a measure of the true greatness of the man that his brilliance and his genius were tempered by a very, very genuine modesty. In the short period that I knew him, I found that he could be assertive, he could be impatient, he could sometimes be very angry and of course, often he could be very, very charming. And his anger sometimes was amusing. I will never forget that when he and I arrived in Stockholm our separate ways and got to the first meeting of the Tribunal, through no fault of the Tribunal, through no fault of our own, arrived about a week late and we discovered to our deep concern that some organizational decisions had been taken with which we were not totally in agreement, and one particular decision about which we were very, very, exceptionally concerned, that I even thought ought to be reconsidered by the Tribunal. I must say, I agreed with the Chairman who said, look comrade, we spent five hours discussing that question two nights ago and we are not going to re-open the discussion. But Isaac insisted, and very angrily said, "But you must re-open the discussion!" There was he, a Polish revolutionary exile and I some kind of a queer Scottish, nationalist republican and Isaac said, "Look, I insist that you re-open the discussion because comrade Daly, and I, the English representatives are here." (Laughter) Unfortunately or otherwise, he was over-ruled, but his contribution to the day-by-day work of the Tribunal and to the mass meetings in Stockholm and Copenhagen, which were held sometime before the Tribunal on Vietnam and so on, was of inestimable value.

And it is indeed an extremely severe blow to the International War Crimes Tribunal that we have been faced with his early and untimely demise because he regarded the struggle in Vietnam as the very heart of the world-wide international struggle for the liberation of mankind from every form of exploitation. And it was remarkable that he was prepared to devote so much time to the Tribunal when he was at the same time so heavily preoccupied with so many other pressing tasks, the most important which, of course, was the endeavor to complete his "Life of Lenin", which he told me, even if he were to abandon the work of the Tribunal completely, would take him something like another two years and it is not the least of our losses that we have to mourn tonight that if the manuscript is ever finished, it will not be finished by his hands, but it is fortunate also for us that we shall still be able to glean his views on the leader of the Russian Revolution from his volumes on Stalin and Trotsky, and some of his numerous essays. And of these, I think, certainly one of the most significant, if not the most significant, was his lectures on what he so rightly called, "The Unfinished Revolution," which I read with great excitement, which it seemed to me, concentrated the very essence of Deutscher's own historical and analytic work. His entire opus is a very rich storehouse for the apprentice revolutionary.

(Applause)

[Transcribed by Jess MacKenzie and Ernest Tate.]

© John Walmsley 1968

© John Walmsley 1968

TOP *Richard Branson marching on the American Embassy, March 17th, 1968.*

BOTTOM *Police uniforms blotched with flour as a result of being pelted with flour 'bombs,' Grosvenor Square, March 17th, 1968.*

Appendix II

Secret Police Report about the VSC and the October 27th, 1968 demonstration

As result of an investigation by the British Guardian's Solomon Hughes and ITV's Paul Mason in 2008, into the London police's disruptive tactics against the anti-Vietnam War movement, especially as it prepared for a protest march for October 27, 1968, the police were forced to make public a three inch thick file of reports about their disinformation campaign against the protest, a cyncial violation of the British people's democratic rights, kept hidden for forty years. The story broke on BBC television in May of that year.[1]

As I wrote to Solomon Hughes at the time, "Some of the police statements are simply factually wrong and surprisingly ill informed, and I'm sure, they were meant to re-enforce their own political prejudices. Or maybe they were smoking some strong stuff. Every little tit-bit of information, the gossip, the stupid speculations by un-named people, who could even be other plain clothes cops, the talk about cutting GPO lines setting vehicles on fire, etc., is just silly, and meant to put the wind up their superiors, I'm sure . . . and it certainly shows the scope of the protests and the vicious role of the police, with sections of the press playing along, in trying to isolate those of us who were organizing opposition to the war."

What follows below is one of the documents in the file:

SECRET POLICE REPORT
Secret *[marked "SECRET" top and bottom of all three pages]*
Metropolitan Police Special Branch

SUBJECT: VIETNAM SOLIDARITY CAMPAIGN "AUTUMN OFFENSIVE"
Reference to papers 346/68/15 (2)
10th day of September 1968

The climate of opinion among extreme left-wing elements in this country in relation to public political protest has undergone a radical change over the last few years. The emphasis has shifted first from orderly, peaceful, cooperative meetings and processions to passive resistance and "sit downs" and now to active confrontation with the authorities to attempt to force social changes and alterations of government policy. Indeed, the more vociferous spokesmen of the left are calling fro the complete overthrow of parliamentary democracy and the substitution of various brands of "socialism" and "workers control". They claim that this can only be achieved by "action on the streets", and although few of them will admit it publicly, or in the press, that they desire a state of anarchy, it is nevertheless tacitly accepted that such a conditions is a necessary preamble to engineering a breakdown of out present system of government and achieving a revolutionary change in the society in which we live.

Between 1956 and 1963 the Campaign For Nuclear Disarmament acted as a catalyst for the discontent of the British left, and this organisation was used as a platform and a stalking horse by almost all the dissident groups. The virtual cessation of nuclear bomb-testing removed the strongest plank from the C.N.D platform, and the committee of 100 took up the banner of protest. This latter organisation became more extreme with the passage of time, and when it foundered earlier this year was almost wholly anarchistic in character.

The Vietnam War was the next issue taken up by British political extremists. Protest was sporadic at first, but in Jun 1966 a new organisation

called the Vietnam Solidarity Campaign was formed under the leadership
of Ralph SCHOENMAN, the notorious American agitator, and financed
by Bertrand RUSSELL. The Trotskyist influence was strong from the
beginning; although anarchists and pacifists were attracted by the anti-
war and anti-establishment flavour of the group they have never possessed
power within it and it remains the preserve of revolutionary factions.
A parallel organisation, the British Committee for Peace in Vietnam,
founded in 1965, is communist-controlled and moderate in tone. 1967
saw the rise of a number of Maoist groups, notably the Friends of China
led by Albert MANCHANDA, and the Maoists are active in the British
Vietnam Solidarity Front and openly advocate the use of violence. The
"Stop It" committee of expatriate Americans is also involved in the
protest activity over the Vietnam War; the members are split on the
violence issue.

The leaders of the Vietnam Solidarity Campaign belong chiefly to two
Trotskyist factions—the International Socialism and International Marxist
groups. Pat JORDAN, a veteran Trotskyist, is the power behind the scenes;
Ed GUITON, Mike MARTIN and Ernie TATE are leading officials. Others
closely involved in V.S.C. activity are XXXXXX of the Revolutionary
Socialists Student Federation and XXXXXXX of the Radical Students
Alliance. Tariq ALI is popularly supposed to be a leading light in the
V.S.C. and the student protest movement: this is not the case. His power
and influence are in inverse ratio to his acknowledged flair for personal
publicity and his natural gifts as a mob orator.

It is a matter of common knowledge that disorderly demonstrations
took place in Grosvenor Square outside the American Embassy in October
1967 and March 1968 under V.S.C. auspices, and that there were numerous
arrests and much damage to property. The pattern at both these demonstrations were remarkably similar. A meeting, followed by a march to
the American Embassy, followed by disorder in the square and adjacent
streets. In the second demonstration a number of aliens and students
from provincial universities took part. Another anti-American demonstration
in July 1968, nominally under communist auspices, was heavily infiltrated

by V.S.C supporters and again there was disorder and many arrests. At this time an announcement was made that there would be a week of activity in October 1968 under the general title of the "autumn offensive" culminating in a mass demonstration on the weekend of the 26th/27th October 1968.

In the past few months a number of revolutionary leaders have produced study papers on this demonstration, the theme is common. It is said that the anti-Vietnam war protest movement is merely part of the continuing struggle to bring about world-wide revolution and that this demonstration can only be regarded as a skirmish before the larger battle. The figure of 100,000 demonstrators began to be bandied about; there was general agreement that this number of militant demonstrators would bring about a total breakdown of law and order. To this end a number of moribund V.S.C. branches were resurrected and local activity stimulated. The existing London branches are:

Earls Court
Hampstead
Kilburn
Notting Hill Gate
Fulham
Lambeth
Walthamstow
Hornsey
Highgate and Holloway
Hackney

Additionally the following ad-hoc committees have been formed to co-ordinate local activity:

North London ad-hoc committee
North West London ad-hoc committee
North West London Action Group
Wes Middlesex Vietnam ad-hoc committee
Libertarian ad-hoc committee

The national headquarters of the Vietnam Solidarity Campaign are at 120 commercial road, E.1. The organisation occupies offices on the second-floor, and the following persons are employed full time on the premises

XXXXX
XXXXX
XXXXX

During the early planning stages of this demonstration it was apparent that the question of the use of calculated violence as a political weapon was causing division in the ranks of the V.S.C members. The Maoists felt that violence was inevitable and said so. The more cautious representatives of the International Socialism and International Marxist groups paid lip service to the vision of a peaceful demonstration. In the event the Maoists did not gain any places on the National Council or the national ad-hoc committee, and are outpaced as apostles of violence by the more volatile anarchists. All the indications are that the Maoists and anarchists will disregard any sort of instructions—from Police or march leaders—and take an independent line on the day

XXXX REDACTED PARAGRAPH XXXX

The following buildings have been suggested as alternative "targets" at one time or another

XXXX REDACTED LIST OF TARGETS XXX

XXX REDACTED FINAL PRAGRAPH XXX

Notes

Chapter One. The Fourth International in Britain

1 Chris Arthur Archives, 711/A/4-5, Warwick University.
2 On the Situation in the R.S.L." Report to the Secretariat by Alan Harris, United Secretariat Minutes, July 26th, 1965; Cont. 110 -3, R.D.Fonds, LAC.
3 "Report on England", by Alan Harris, International Executive Committee Meeting, January 1-3, 1965, Cont. 110-3, R.D.Fonds, LAC.
4 *The Week*, Volume 4, No.17, November, 1965, Chris Arthur Archives, Warwick U.
5 Hugo Blanco, to this day, still remains active in peasant and mine-workers' struggles in Peru.
6 Op. Cit. Anderson, p580.
7 Letter to Ernest Mandel from Ken Coates, April 20, 1965, Ernest Mandel Archives, IISH.
8 *The Week*, November 18, 1965, Volume 4, No. 19,Chris Arthur Archives, 711/A/3/2, Warwick U.
9 "Briefing", was a daily critique put out by the Left.
10 "Why I Should Be Reinstated", A final plea to the NEC Tribunal investigating my expulsion and the affairs of the Nottingham City Party, by Ken Coates.
11 "Militant Years: Car workers' struggles in Britain in the 60's and 70's", by Alan Thornett, Resistance Books, 2011, pp368.

Chapter Three. Ralph Schoenman and the Bertrand Russell Peace Foundation

1 *The Week*, February 17, 1965, Vol. 3, No 7, Chris Arthur Archives, 711/A/3/3, Warwick U.
2 Letter to Ernest Mandel from Ken Coates, 28th November, 1965, Ernest Mandel Archives, IISH.
3 Letter to Ken Coates, December 11, 1965, Ernest Mandel Archives, IISH.
4 LSA-PC Minutes, May 23, 1966, Toronto, Ernest Mandel Papers, File 33, IISH.
5 Summary Report of Meetings in Hanoi between President Ho Chi Minh, Prime Minister Pham Van Dong and Personal Representatives of Bertrand Russell, Mr. Ralph Schoenman and Mr. Russell Stetler.", November 1966, Isaac Deutscher Papers, File 170, IISH.

6   P.130,"Radical Son", Horowitz.

7   "Bertrand Russell: A Life", by Caroline Moore, Viking Penguin, 1993.

8   E-mail to me from Ralph Schoenman, June 16, 2012.

9   *The Week*, Volume 4, No 20, November 25, 1965, Chris Arthur Archives, 711/A/3/4 Warwick U.

10 "Empire and Revolution: A radical interpretation of contemporary history," by David Horowitz, Random House, 1969, pp.275.

11 "Student: The Political Activities Of The Berkeley Students", by David Horowitz, 1962, Ballantine.

12 "Free World Colossus", a critique of American foreign policy in the cold war, by David Horowitz, McGibbon and Kee, London, 1965.

13 "Containment and Revolution, Western Policy Towards Social Revolution: 1917 to Vietnam" Edited by David Horowitz, Anthony Blond, 1967, pp 252.

14 Letter to Horowitz from Isaac Deutscher, July 19, 1967, Deutscher Papers, IISH.

15 *Marxism and Existentialism*, a series of essays edited by George Novack, pp 344, Dell, 1966.

16 "Shakespeare: An Existential View," by David Horowitz, Tavistock, pp 132, 1965.

Chapter Four. Vietnam: *"an international war crime"*

1   p581, "The Selected Letters Bertrand Russell, the public years, 1914-1970", 2001, Routledge.

2   *The Week*, Vol.5, No8, Feb, 1966, Chris Arthur Archives, 711/A/3/3, Warwick.U.

3   "Sterling and Strings," by Peter Davies, London Review of Books, November 20th, 2008.

4   "Statement of Schoenman Biographical Details", Box 10.15, .384, #175883, Bertrand Russell Archives, (B.R.A.) McMaster University, Hamilton, Ontario, Canada.

5   "Khrushchev also decided to signal a softer line to Washington. In a long public letter to the philosopher Bertrand Russell, he said he was prepared to meet Kennedy to resolve the crisis." Op. cit., P256, "One Hell of a Gamble".

6   P264, C64.03, B.R.A., McMaster U.

7   "Letter from U.Thant", Bertrand Russell Peace Foundation brochure, Box .167, #P390050248832895, B.R.A., McMaster U.

8   *International Citizens' Tribunals*, by Arthur and Judith Apter Klinghoffer, Palgrave, 2002, 256pp

9   *History of Western Philosophy*, by Bertrand Russell, Alan and Unwin, 1946

10 *A Bibliography of Bertrand Russell*, 2, 1890-1990 by Kenneth Blackwell and Hary Ruja, p287, c65.43, B.R.A.

11 *The Week*, April 21, 1965, Vol.3, No. 16, Chris Arthur Archive, 711/A/3/3, Warwick U.

12 Op.cit., P149, Klinghoffer.

13 Hand-written note to Melba Hernandez from Ralph Schoenman, undated, but appears to have been written in May or June,1967, Box 10.2, .371, #170678, B.R.A.

14 Op-cit, p147 and p159, "Radical Son", Horowitz.

Chapter Five. The Vietnam Solidarity Campaign

1 Leaflet for the meeting, B167, No. 174947, B.R.A.
2 Text of Ralph Schoenman's speech, December 20th, 1965, Box 10.12, No. 175053, B.R.A.
3 "The New American Anti-war Movement", by Fred Halstead, *The Week*, December 2, 1965, Vol.4, No.21.
4 "Report of a Meeting in Hanoi between President Ho Chi Minh, Prime Minister Pham Van Dong and Personal Representatives of Bertrand Russell, Ralph Schoenman and Russell Stetler", Tamara Deutscher Archives, File 170, I.I.S.H.
5 "A Speech Over Hanoi Radio To Fellow Americans", by Ralph Schoenman, *The Week*, Vol. 5, No 14, April 16, 1966.
6 *The Week*, Vol.5, No.14, April 16, 1966
7 *The Week*, Vol.5, No.19, May 12, 1966
8 Op.cit. P.146, "Radical Son", Horowitz.
9 "Memorandum on the Immediate Steps for the Vietnam Solidarity Campaign," by Pat Jordan, Box 10.12, .379, #175883, B.R.A.
10 P.5, *Out Now! A Participant's Account of the American Movement against the Vietnam War*, Fred Halstead, , Monad Press, pp759, 1978.
11 Minutes of V.S.C. National Committee, June 18, 1967, Box 10.12, .379, #175093, B.R.A.
12 "Dear Mr. Schoenman", from A. Machanda, Dec.21, 1965,10.12, .319, #175142, B.R.A.
13 *The Week*, Vol.5, No.24, June 16, 1966.
14 *The Week*, Vol. 5, No 60, May 1966
15 *Vietnam Solidarity Bulletin*, June 1966, Vol.1, No.3, 10.12, #175022, B.R.A.
16 "Solidarity with Vietnam," a draft proposal for discussion by A. Machanda,10.12, #174987, B.R.A.
17 Letter to Gerry Healy, unsigned, but in Ken Coates hand-writing, in response to Healy's letter of July 8th, 1966, to Ralph Schoenman. Box 10.12, .379, 175136, B.R.A.

Chapter Six. The Russell International War Crimes Tribunal

1 Letter to Isaac Deutscher from Bertrand Russell, March 2, 1967, Isaac Deutscher Papers, File 67, I.I.S.H.
2 P. 39, *Against the Crime of Silence: Proceeding of the Russell International War Crimes Tribunal*, edited by John Duffet, B.R.P.F and O'Hare Books, 1968

3   Quintin and his wife Branca, both of whom Jess and I became friendly with in those years, would later move to the right during the break-up of Yugoslavia when they became partisans of Croatia.

4   "Private Memorandum to Professor Laurent Schwartz", from Ralph Schoenman, undated, Box 10.15, #175879, B.R.A

5   "Summary of Report of Meetings in Hanoi between President Ho Chi Minh, Premier Pham Van Dong and Personal Representatives of Bertrand Russell, Mr. Ralph Schoenman and Mr. Russell Stetler." Tamara Deutscher Papers, File 70, I.I.S.H.

6   Op.cit. P.22, "Out Now . . .", Halstead.

7   Op.cit. *Private Memorandum to Professor Laurent Schwartz" from Ralph Schoenman.

8   Letter to "Chers Amis", December 1966, Isaac Deutscher Papers, I.I.S.H.

9   Letter to Russell, marked "Private", February 14th, 1967, Isaac Deutscher Archives, File 67, I.I.S.H.

10 Letter to Deutscher, February 7, 1967, Isaac Deutscher Archive, File 67, I.I.S.H.

11 Op.cit.,"Memorandum to Professor Laurent Schwartz", from Ralph Schoenman.

12 "Bertrand Russell Speech to the First Meeting of the War Crimes Tribunal", www.vietnamese-american.org/contents.html

13 Transcript of the London Session, Box 10.15, #175777, B.R.A.

14 Transcription of minutes of the War Crimes Tribunal, Sunday, 13th., November,1966. Box 10.15, #175777, B.R.A.

15 Russell, Letter to Tribunal members, marked:"Private", May 4th, 1967, MSS.302/4/2, 1966-9, Lawrence Daly Archive, Warwick U.

16 "I hope you have seen Sartre's most important interview in *Nouvelle Observateur* on the Tribunal." Letter to Anders from Schoenman, December 3rd, 966, Box 10.1 .371, #170257, B.R.A.

17 "Dear Isaac Deutscher", from Gunther Anders, December 27, 1966. File 61, I.D. Papers, I.I.S.H.

18 Op.cit. "Private Memo to Laurent Schwartz", from Schoenman.

19 "Letter to Gunther Anders", from Chris Farley, July 31, 1967, Box 10.2, #170779, B.R.A.

20 Letter to Ralph Schoenman from Ernest Mandel, January 22, 1967, Ernest Mandel Papers, File 38, I.I.S.H.

21 Op.cit. "Private Memo to Laurent Schwartz", from Ralph Schoenman.

22 Letter to Dedijer from Schoenman, January 6, 1967, Box 10.1, .371, #170332, B.R.A.

23 Letter to Deutscher from Russell, March 2nd., 1967, Isaac Deutscher Papers, File 67, I.I.S.H.

24 Letter to Russell from Deutscher, March10, 1965, Isaac Deutscher Papers, File 67, I.I.S.H.

25 Letter to Anders from Schoenman, April 4, 1967, Box 10.2, .371, #170555, B.R.A.

26 Letter to Tribunal members from Russell, March 2nd, 1967, Deutscher Papers, No. 67, I.I.S.H.

27 *The Week*, April 20th, 1967, Volume 7, No. 16.

28 Op.cit.,"Private Memo to Laurent Schwartz" from Schoenman.

29 Letter to Ralph Schoenman from Deirdre Griswold, May 18,1966,Box 9.47, #179256, B.R.A.

30 Appeal from Y.A.W.F. to potential supporters, unsigned, undated, Box 9.47, #179255, B.R.A.

31 Letter to the Editor of the *Tribune*, May 22nd, 1967, by Ralph Schoenman", Lawrence Daly Archive, MSS.302/4/2, Warwick U.

32 Op.cit., "Private Memorandum to Laurent Schwartz", from Schoenman.

33 Letter to Vladimir Dedijer from Russell, May 14, 1967, Lawrence Daly Archive, 1966-1969, MSS.302/4/2, Warwick U.

34 Letter Russell from Deutscher, May 22, 1967, Isaac Deutscher Papers, File 67, I.I.S.H.

35 Letter Daly from Deutscher, June 24, 1967, Lawrence Daly Archive, Warwick U.

36 Letter to Schwartz from Russell, June 25th, 1967, Tamara Deutscher Papers, File 179, I.I.S.H.

37 "To: Members of the International War Crimes Tribunal", marked "Private, from Russell, May 4th, 1967, Lawrence Daly Archives, MSS.302/4/2, Warwick U

38 Letter to Schwartz from Deutscher, June 8, 1967, Deutscher Papers, I.I.S.H.

39 Letter to Dedijer from Farley, February 2, 1967, 10.12, #170404, B.R.A.

40 Letter to Russell from Schwartz, June 24th, 1967, Tamara Deutscher Papers, File 179, I.I.S.H.

41 Letter to Schwartz from Schoenman, September 25th, 1967,10.2, #170794, B.R.A.

42 Letter to Deutscher from Russell, May 24th, 1967, Deutscher Papers, File 65, I.I.S.H.

43 "The Historical Background of the United States Aggression in Vietnam since World War Two", prepared by Gabriel Kolko for the Stockholm session of the I.W.C.T., C70.07, .385, #163791, B.R.A.

44 Letter to Eichii Yamanishi from Deutscher,July 9,1967, #68, Deutscher Papers, I.I.S.H.

45 Letter to Schwartz from Russell, June 27th, 1967, B.R.A.

46 Letter to Schwartz from Russell, June 25th, 1967, Tamara Deutscher Papers, File 179, I.I.S.H.

47 Letter to Russell from Schwartz, June 25th, 1967, Tamara Deutscher Papers, File 179, I.I.S.H.

48 To the Editor of the Tribune, by Ralph Schoenman, May 22, 1967, Lawrence Daly Archives, Warwick U.

49 Russell to Dedijer, May 14th, 1967,Lawrence Daly Archives, Warwick U.

50 Russell to Deutscher from, May 24th, 1967, Deutscher Papers, File 65, I.I.S.H.

51 Deutscher to Daly, June 24th, 1967, Lawrence Daly Papers, MSS.302/4/2, Warwick U.

52 Deutscher to Russell, May 27th,1967, B.R.A., Box 10.2, #170722.

53 Deutscher to Sartre, May 22, 1967, Isaac Deutscher Papers, File 65, I.I.S.H.

54 Russell to Anders, June 16th 1967, Box 10.2, #170740, B.R.A.

55 Deutscher to Schwartz, June 8th, 1967, File 67, Deutscher Papers, I.I.S.H.

56 Deutscher to Russell, June 8th, 1967, Tamara Deutscher Papers, File 67, I.I.S.H.

57 Russell to Daly, July 27, 1967, MSS.302/4/2, Warwick U.

58 "Declaration by Jean-Paul Sartre and Supporters", Deutscher Papers, File 68, I.I.S.H.

59 "Communique from the Secretariat, I.W.C.T.", Deutscher Papers, File 68, I.I.S.H.

60 "Statement of the Tribunal", signed by Sartre, Dedijer and Schwartz, Box 10.2, #170721, B.R.A.

61 Russell Stetler to Schwartz, August 11, 1967, Box 10.2, .371, #170784, B.R.A.

62 Stetler to Mandel, January 25th, 1968, Ernest Mandel Papers, File 38, I.I.S.H.

63 "Breakdown of Confidence in the Tribunal, Members Absent, The Situation Almost Chaotic", by Gosta Julin, *Dagen Nyheter*, November 23, 1967, Daly Archives, MSS.302/4/2, Warwick U.

64 Schoenman to Mandel, August 28, 1968, Mandel Papers, File 44, I.I.S.H.

65 Schoenman to Mandel, Mandel Papers, December 4th, 1968, File 44, I.I.S.H.

Chapter Seven. Isaac Deutscher

1 Deutscher to Montauk, June 18, 1966, Deutscher Papers, File 63, I.I.S.H

2 Deutscher to Miliband, December 18, 1965, I.D. Papers, File 59, I.I.S.H.

3 See appendix 1, "Transcript of Speeches, Isaac Deutscher Memorial Meeting, Mahatma Gandhi Hall, September 22, 1967, London"

4 "Chers Amis" from Isaac Deutscher, December 6th, 1966, File 61, I.D. Papers, I.I.S.H.

5 *The Prophet Armed, The Prophet Unarmed and The Prophet Outcast*, Oxford University Press.

6 Letter to the Editor of *The Jewish Chronicle*, October 30th, 1965, Isaac Deutscher Papers, File 58, I.I.S.H.

7 "The enclosed review of Pautovsky's book was written by Tamara, not by myself. I dipped into the book . . ." "Dear Pat (the *Economist*), November 5, 1965, I.D. Papers, File 58, I.I.S.H.

8 *The Unfinished Revolution: Russia 1917-1967*, by Isaac Deutscher, Oxford University Press, 1967.

9 P81, *Isaiah Berlin*, by Michael Ignatieff, Penguin, 1998.

10 *The Non-Jewish Jew and Other Essays*, 1954, by Isaac Deutscher, Oxford University Press.

11 Draft of a letter (undated) originally destined for Sir Isaiah Berlin, a copy of which was forwarded to Dr. Leo van Rossum, of I.I.S.H., by Tamara Deutscher, February 12, 1981. Tamara Deutscher Papers, File 73, I.I.S.H.

12 "Dear Isaac and Tamara" from Helen Klass, September 29, 1965, "Dear Helen" from Tamara Deutscher, October 8, 1965, #58, Isaac Deutscher Papers , I.I.S.H.

13 "Dear Mrs. Deutscher" from Sir Isaiah Berlin, April 22, 1969, File 73, Tamara Deutscher Papers, I.I.S.H.

14 Op.cit., p329, *Isaiah Berlin*, by Michael Ignatieff.

15 "Dear Mr. Hekkenberg" from I.D., File 58, I.D.Papers, I.I.S.H.

16 To Gerry Healy from Tamara Deutscher, September 15, 1967, File 70, Tamara Deutscher Papers, I.I.S.H

17 "Dear Isaac" from Joe Hansen, December 31, 1963, File 50, I.D.Paper, I.I.S.H.

18 *Stalin: A Political Biography*, by Isaac Deutscher, Oxford University Press, pp 684, 1949.

19 *Russia—What Next?*, by Isaac Deutscher, Oxford University Press,1953

20 "Trotsky or Deutscher", *Fourth International*, Winter, 1954.

21 Op.cit., p215, *Russia—What Next?*

22 Op.cit., p208, *Russia—What Next?*

23 *The Age of Permanent Revolution: A Trotsky Anthology*, Dell Publishing, 1964.

24 Op.cit.,p108, "The Unfinished Revolution".

25 p 347, *Fidel and Che: A Revolutionary Friendship*, by Simon Reid-Henry. Walker and Company, 2009.

Chapter Eight. *"We shall not hesitate to deal appropriately . . ."*

1 Published by the SWP, June, 1966.

2 *Letter from Bertrand Russell, November 29, 1966, Box 9.31, #1573946, B.R.A.

3 Report on "the Tate incident, by E.Tate, in *Education for Socialist Bulletin*, entitled, "Healy's Big Lie: The Slander Campaign against Joseph Hansen, George Novack, and the Fourth International", published by the SWP, 1976.

4 *The Militant*, November 28, 1966.

Chapter Nine. The Russell Foundation Expands

1 *Rush to Judgment,* by Mark Lane, Hold, Rinehart and Winston, 1966.

2 Vol.6, No. 20, December 3rd, 1966

Chapter Ten. The Fourth International in London

1 "The Global Gamble—America's Faustian Bid for World Domination", Peter Gowan, Verso, 2002

Chapter Twelve. The Death of Che Guevara

1   "The Underlying Differences in Method", by Joes Hansen, July, 1973, International Internal Discussion Bulletin, Volume 10, No.12

2   *Late Capitalism* by Ernest Mandel, Verso Classics, 23, 1998.

3   *Ernest Mandel: A Rebel's Dream Deferred,* by Jan Willem Stutje. Translated by Christopher Beck and Peter Drucker, Verso, 2009, 392pp.

4   Op.cit., P.168, Pierre Frank, 1979.

Chapter Thirteen. Crises in the Russell Foundation

1   *Revolution in the Revolution,* by Regis DeBray, Penguin Books, 1967.

2   Op.cit., p745, Anderson.

3   Op.cit, p 675,Anderson.

4   Russell to Daly, October 1, 1967, MSS.302/4/2, 5B, Daly Archives, Warwick U.

5   Transcript of a radio interview with Ralph Schoenman in New York, Box 10.15, #175831,B.R.A.

6   "Truth as a Casualty", Ralph Schoenman, 2008, archives.econ.utah.edu/ archives/marxism/2008w04/msg00001.html

7   Memorandum on the Basic Organizational Problems in the Foundation", by Geoff Coggan, October 18th, 1967, MSS.149/1/2/3, Chris Arthur Archives, Warwick U.

8   "An Outline of the Financial Situation of the Foundation", by David Horowitz, (undated), MSS.149/1/2/3, Chris Arthur Archives, Warwick U

9   Op.cit.,Geoff Coggan's " Memorandum".

10   Memorandum to the Control Commission" by R.Sole (Geoff Coggan), undated, Chris Arthur Archives, MSS.149/1/2/3, Warwick U.

11   Memo for the Directors' Meeting, by Geoff Coggan, October 12, 1967, Chris Arthur Archives, MSS.149/1/2/3, Warwick.U.

12   "Memorandum on the Basic Organizational Problems in the Foundation", by Geoff Coggan, October 18, 1967, Chris Arthur Archives, MSS.149/1/2/3, Warwick U.

13   Letter to the Directors from Ken Coates, October 12, 1967,Chris Arthur Archives, MSS.149/1/2/3, Warwick U.

14   "Comrade Kork (Ken Coates) and the Theory of Creative People", by Peter Peterson (Pat Jordan), undated, Chris Arthur Archives, MSS.149/1/2/3, Warwick U

15   "Memo on Financial Crises", by Ken Coates, October 11, 1967, Chris Arthur Archives, MSS.149/1/2/3, Warwick U.

16   "Memorandum On Finance and Organization: October 16, 1967",by Chris Farley, Chris Arthur Archives, MSS.149/1/2/3, Warwick U.

17   "Memorandum to the Control Commission", by R. Sole (Geoff Coggan). Chris Arthur Archives, MSS.149/1/2/3, Warwick U

18 "Where is Comrade Kork (Ken Coates) going?" by Peter Peterson (Pat Jordan), Chris Arthur Archives, MSS.149/1/2/3, Warwick U.

19 "Comrade Kork (Coates) and the theory of 'Creative People'", by Peter Peterson (Pat Jordan). Chris Arthur Archives, MSS.149/1/2/3, Warwick U.

20 "Memo On Future Of Foundation", by Pat Jordan and Geoff Coggan, October 17, 1967 Chris Arthur Archives, MSS.149/1/2/3, Warwick U

21 "Our Financial Position: Do We Panic Or Think Clearly" by Pat Jordan, (undated) Chris Arthur Archives, MSS.149/1/2/3, Warwick U.

22 Op.cit. Horowitz.

23 Letter to Tony Topham from Pat Jordan, hand dated, possibly October 13, 1967. MSS.149/1/2/3, Chris Arthur Archives, Warwick U

24 Letter to Pat Jordan, October 19, 1967, MSS.149/1/2/3, Chris Arthur Archives, Warwick U.

25 "Memorandum Concerning a Letter addressed to me by J.P. (Pat Jordan)", by T.A. (Tony Topham) October 22, 1967, MSS.149/1/2/3, Chris Arthur Archives, Warwick U.

26 *The Sun,* June 24, 1968.

27 "Private Memorandum Concerning Ralph Schoenman", by Bertrand Russell, from pages 640-651, "The Life of Bertrand Russell", by Ronald W. Clark, 1975, Knopf, New York.

28 Press release from the F.F.S.J., December 10, 1969, Tamara Deutscher Papers, File 75, I.I.S.H.

29 Letter to Pat Jordan from Bertrand Russell, February 21,1967, Box 9.29, .315, # 153735, B.R.A.

30 *The Autobiography of Bertrand Russell: The Final Years,* Bantam,1970.

31 *The Selected Letters of Bertrand Russell, The Public Years, 1914-1970,* Edited by Nicholas Griffin, Routledge, 2002.

32 Op.it. "Private Memorandum Concerning Ralph Schoenman", by Bertrand Russell.

33 *Daily Telegraph,* September 11, 1970

34 Letter to Tamara Deutscher", December 18, 1969, Tamara Deutscher Papers, File 75, I.I.S.H.

35 "Ralph Schoenman—A Word of Explanation," by Ken Coates and Chris Farley, June, 1970, cited in Klinghoffer, p161.

Chapter Fourteen. Tariq Ali and The Battle of Grosvenor Square

1 *Redemption,* by Tariq Ali, 1990, Chatto and Windus, London

Chapter Fifteen. An "autumn offensive"

1 "An Open Letter to All Those Who Are Actively Concerned About the Continued Escalation Of the American Aggression in Vietnam", V.S.C. statement, undated, Box 10.12, #174984, B.R.A.

2 International Socialists, Working Committee Minutes, March 23, 1968. Chris Arthur Archives, MSS/1S2/1/1/3, Warwick U.

3 Chris Harman circular to I.S. members regarding the March 17th demonstration,1968. Chris Arthur Archives, MSS/1S2/1/1/3, Warwick U.

4 *The Left in Britain,* 1956-1968, by David Widgery, Penguin Books, 1976, 549 pages.

Chapter Seventeen. October 27, 1968

1 Undated minutes of the IMG Political Committee, possibly late March, 1968, Chris Arthur Archives, Warwick U.

2 "WE STICK TOGETHER-Our physical solidarity demonstrates our political solidarity with each other and with our Vietnamese comrades. We link arms; we stay in the streets; we draw stragglers back into the demonstration. This is the only way to defend ourselves from any possible interference." . . . "WE WANT NO ARRESTS—Whatever happens, the situation can never be met by individual, adventurist actions. Responsible, collective action can only be that taken by the mass of the demonstrators as a physical whole. We minimize the chance of arrests when we make it impossible for any individual to single himself out for the police, and impossible for the police to single out any individual. Self-destined martyrs please note that the Committee has no lawyers and no money to get some with!" Mss. 21/3369/29. Warwick U.

Chapter Eighteen. The International Socialists' Tony Cliff Proposes Unity

1 I.M.G. Political Committee Minutes, April 27, 1968, Chris Arthur Archives, Warwick U.

2 Op Cit, "Minutes of the Political Committee, April 27th 1968."

3 Minutes of the IMG National Committee, May 11-12, 1968, CAA, Warwick U.

4 Minutes of the IMG National Committee, October 1968, File 51-52, CAA, Warwick U.

Chapter Nineteen. The Ninth World Congress and the guerrilla line

1 "For the Seventh World Congress and Reunification", by Pierre Frank, April, 1963, Internal Bulletin, No. 37, of the International Secretariat of the Fourth International, International Institute for Research and Education, (IIRE), Amsterdam.

2 "Concerning the La Verdad Group," Letter to the Executive Committee of the International, August 20th, 1971, from the PRT(C), International Information Bulletin, No.2 1972, June 1972, LAC.

3 Letter to Ernest Mandel from Joe Hansen, April 11, 1966, Ernest Mandel Archives, IISH.

4 P.690, "Report on the New Rise of the World Revolution," by E.Germain (Ernest Mandel), *Intercontinental Press,* July 14, 1969, Vol. 7, No.26.

5 "El Unico Camino Hasta el Poder Obrero y el Socialismo", ("The Only Road to Workers Power and Socialism", *International Information Bulletin* No. 4, October 1972.

6 Ninth World Congress Resolution on Latin America, p720, *Intercontinental Press*, Volume 7, No.26, July 14, 1969.

Chapter Twenty. Argentina: Robert Santucho and the PRT-ERP

1 *Sangre En El Monte, la increible aventura del ERP en los cerros tucamanos*, Sudamericana, 2010, pp 256.

2 Op. Cit. p 559, *Che Guevara, a revolutionary life*, by Jon Lee Anderson

3 Op.cit. *Sangre en el Monte*, Gutman.

4 "Por las sendas argentinas . . .", El PRT-ERP *La guerilla marxista*, by Pablo Pozzi, Febrero, 2001, Eudeba, Universidad de Buenos Aires.

5 Op. cit. p 9, Hansen, "The Underlying Differences . . ."

6 p200, *Bolivia's Radical Tradition: Permanent Revolution in the Andes*, by S. Sandor John, University of Arizona Press, 2011, pp 318.

7 Letter to the PRT(Combatiente), from Ernest Mandel, October 31, 1972. *International Discussion Bulletin*, Vol 10, No7, Marxist Internet Archive.

8 p189, *Ernest Mandel, A Rebel's Dream Deferred*, by Jan Willem Stutje, Verso, 2009.

9 "In Defense of Leninism: In Defense of the Fourth International," by Ernest Germain, *International Internal Discussion Bulletin*, Volume 10, 4, April 1973.

10 *The Fourth International:The Long March of the Trotskyists* by Pierre Frank, Resistance Books, 1979.

11 Op.cit. p12, *The Long March* . . .

12 Op.cit, p118, *The Long March* . . .

Epilogue.

1 "Report of Functioning of Metro Local", May 29th, 1972, RD Fonds, R10995, Volume 45-1, LAC.

2 *Workers Vanguard*, Volume 1, No19, October 5, 1970.

3 Letter to Ernest Mandel from Ross Dowson, December 16, 69, Box: MG 28, 1V 11, Container 107-24, LAC.

4 Letter to Ernest Mandel, December 16, 1969, Box MG 28, 1V 11, Container 107-24, RD Fonds, LAC.

5 Report of the Fact Finding Commission, March 12 1972, RD Fonds, R10995, Container 10, File 12, LAC.

6 Ross Dowson notes about the talk, quoting me as stating, "We are not a party." R10995, Volume 45-1, R.D.Fonds, L.A.C.

7 Notes by Ross Dowson regarding an article, "Mounting Struggles in Quebec", in the July-August 1973, *International Socialist Review*, R10995, Volume 45-1, LAC.

8 "Statement of the walk-out group," February 19, 1974, LSA/LSO, *Internal Information Bulletin*, Vol 2, No6, May 1974, R10995, Volume 45-4, LAC.

9 *The Party: The Socialist Workers Party 1960-1988*, by Barry Sheppard, Volume Two, 2012, 350pp, Resistance Books, London.

Appendix *I.*

1 Tape is inaudible for a few seconds at this point.

Appendix *II.*

1 http://news.bbc.co.uk/1/hi/programmes/newsnight/7424867.stm

Index of Names

Resistance Books

FORTHCOMING TITLES

May 2014

We the Indians: The indigenous peoples of Peru and the struggle for land, by Hugo Blanco with foreword by Edward Galeano and introduction by Iain Bruce. Published in association with Merlin Press and the IIRE.

This book paints a graphic picture of the essential and central battle for the land in vivid first-hand accounts with historical contextualisation. Blanco's own understated role shines through.

RECENTLY PUBLISHED

Green Capitalism: why it can't work, by Daniel Tanuro, November 2013 Published in association with Merlin Press and the IIRE.

Daniel Tanuro refutes the major proposals currently being advanced to resolve the climate crisis. He argues that these fail to challenge the drive for profit and the dynamic of capital accumulation such as eco-taxes, commodification of natural resources, and carbon trading. Daniel Tanuro rigorously attempts to demonstrate the impossibility of a socially sustainable transition towards "green capitalism".

Dangerous Liaisons—the marriages and divorces of Marxism and Feminism, Cinzia Arruzza, March 2013, £7. Published in association with Merlin Press and the IIRE.

An accessible introduction to the relationship between the workers' movement and the women's movement. The first part is historical, the second theoretical. Historical examples range from the mid-19th century to the 1970s and include events, debates and key personalities from China, Russia, the USA, France, Italy, Spain and Britain. It shows time and again the controversial and often difficult relationship between feminism and Marxism. The theoretical questions discussed include the origins of women's oppression, domestic labour, dual systems theory, performativity and differentialism.

China's Rise—strength and fragility, Au Loong Yu, November 2012, £12. Published in association with Merlin Press and the IIRE.

Au Loong Yu offers a profound analysis of the rise of China in the manner it should be done: through placing front and centre a meticulous examination of its capitalist ruling class and of the variegated ways in which it appropriates a surplus. By starting from the multiple forms of property through which the country's dominant bureaucratic state capitalists sustain themselves, Au is able at one and the same time to lay bare the roots of the Chinese economic miracle and the foundations of its durable authoritarian political order, to expose the politico-economic contradictions that are likely to limit growth and bring crisis to the system, and to illuminate the sources of the fierce class struggles that continue to wrack town and country and threaten, over time, to open the way to political alternatives. Truly a tour de force.

—*Robert Brenner, Professor of history and director of the Center for Social Theory and Comparative History at UCLA, editor of the socialist journal* Against the Current, *and editorial committee member of* New Left Review.

STILL AVAILABLE

Capitalism—Crises and Alternatives, Michel Husson, Andy Kilmister, Susan Pashkoff, Sean Thompson, Özlem Onaran , Eric Toussaint, et al., Özlem Onaran and Fred Leplat eds., February 2012, £7. (Resistance Books and IIRE pub.)

Ireland's Credit Crunch, Kearing, Morrison & Corrigan, October 2010, £5. (Resistance Books pub.)

Militant years—car workers' struggles in Britain in the 60s and 70s, Alan Thornett, February 2011, £12. (Resistance Books pub.)

New Parties of the Left—Experiences from Europe, Daniel Bensaïd, Alain Krivine, Alda Sousa, Alan Thornett et al., May 2011, £7. (Resistance Books and IIRE pub.)

Women's Liberation & Socialist Revolution: Documents of the Fourth International, Penelope Duggan ed., October 2010, £6. (Resistance Books and IIRE pub.)

The Global Fight for Climate Justice—Anti-capitalist responses to global warming and environmental destruction, Ian Angus ed., June 2009, £8. (Resistance Books pub.)

Strategies of Resistance & 'Who Are the Trotskyists', Daniel Bensaïd, November 2009, £6. (Resistance Books and IIRE pub.)

Revolution and Counter-revolution in Europe from 1918 to 1968, Pierre Frank, May 2011, £7. (Resistance Books and IIRE pub.)

The Long March of the Trotskyists: Contributions to the history of the International, Pierre Frank, Daniel Bensaïd, Ernest Mandel, October 2010, £5. (Resistance Books and IIRE pub.)

Building Unity Against Fascism: Classic Marxist Writings, Leon Trotsky, Daniel Guérin, Ted Grant et al., October 2010, £4. (Resistance Books and IIRE pub.)

Socialists and the Capitalist Recession (with Ernest Mandel's 'Basic Theories of Karl Marx'), Raphie De Santos, Michel Husson, Claudio Katz et al., March 2009, £5. (Resistance Books and IIRE pub.)

Respect: Documents of the crisis, Fred Leplat ed., 2008, £3. (Resistance Books pub.)

Take the Power to Change the World, Phil Hearse ed., June 2007, £5. (Resistance Books and IIRE pub.)

The Party: The Socialist Workers Party 1960-1988. Volume 2: Interregnum, decline and collapse, 1973-1988, Barry Sheppard, November 2012, £10. (Resistance Books pub.)

Foundations of Christianity: a study in Christian origins, Karl Kautsky, £12. (Resistance Books pub.)

The Permanent Revolution & Results and Prospects, Leon Trotsky, £9. (Resistance Books pub.)

My Life Under White Supremacy and in Exile, Leonard Nikani, February 2009, £8. (Resistance Books pub.)

Cuba at Sea, Ron Ridenour, May 2008, £7. (Resistance Books pub.)

Ecosocialism or Barbarism (new expanded edition), Jane Kelly ed., February 2008, £5. (Resistance Books pub.)

Cuba: Beyond the Crossroads, Ron Ridenour, April 2007, £4. (Resistance Books pub.)

Middle East: war, imperialism, and ecology—sixty years of resistance, Roland Rance & Terry Conway eds. and Gilbert Achcar (contributor) et al., March 2007, £6. (Resistance Books pub.)

It's never too late to love or rebel, Celia Hart, August 2006, £5. (Resistance Books pub.)

October Readings: The development of the concept of Permanent Revolution, D. R. O'Connor Lysaght ed., October 2010, £4. (Resistance Books pub.)

Living Internationalism: the IIRE's history, Murray Smith and Joost Kircz eds., January 2011, £4. (Resistance Books and IIRE pub.)

Books can be purchased through the website at **www.resistancebooks.org,** or by writing to **Resistance Books, PO Box 62732, London, SW2 9GQ.** Cheques to be made payable to "Resistance" and £2 p&p is to be added for each book.

Resistance Books

contact@socialistresistance.org
PO Box 62732, London, SW2 9GQ; Phone: 020 7346 8889

About Resistance Books

Resistance Books is the publishing arm of Socialist Resistance, a revolutionary Marxist organisation which is the British section of the Fourth International. Resistance Books also publishes books jointly with Merlin Press and the International Institute for Research and Education in Amsterdam.

Further information about Resistance Books, including a full list of titles currently available and how to purchase them, can be obtained at **www.resistancebooks.org**, or by writing to **Resistance Books, PO Box 62732, London, SW2 9GQ.**

Socialist Resistance is an organisation active in the trade union movement and in campaigns against austerity and in defence of the welfare state. We oppose imperialist interventions, and help organise solidarity with Palestine. We are eco-socialist—we argue that much of what is produced under capitalism is socially useless and either redundant or directly harmful. We have been long-standing supporters of women's liberation and the struggles of lesbians, gay people, bisexuals and transgender people.

Socialist Resistance is the bi-monthly magazine of the organisation, which can be read online at www.socialistresistance.org. Socialist Resistance can be contacted by email at **contact@socialistresistance.org**. *International Viewpoint* is the English language online magazine of the Fourth International which can be read online at **www.internationalviewpoint.org.**

The International Institute for Research and Education (IIRE) was opened in 1982 in Amsterdam. The IIRE is now also located in Manila and Islamabad. Its main activity has been the organisation of courses in the service of progressive forces around the world. The seminars and study groups deal with all subjects related to the emancipation of the world's oppressed and exploited. The IIRE publishes Notebooks for Study and Research to focus on themes of contemporary debate, or historical and theoretical importance. For a full list visit http://bit. ly/IIRENSR or subscribe online at: http://bit. ly/NSRsub. To order, email iire@iire.org or write to International Institute for Research and Education, Lombokstraat 40, Amsterdam, NL-1094.

Resistance Books

contact@socialistresistance.org
PO Box 62732, London, SW2 9GQ; Phone: 020 7346 8889